PSYCHOANALYTIC TERMS AND CONCEPTS

PSYCHOANALYTIC TERMS AND CONCEPTS

EDITED BY
BURNESS E. MOORE, M.D.
AND BERNARD D. FINE, M.D.

THE AMERICAN PSYCHOANALYTIC
ASSOCIATION AND
YALE UNIVERSITY PRESS
NEW HAVEN AND LONDON

Published with assistance from the foundation established in memory of Calvin Chapin of the Class of 1788, Yale College.

Designed by Nancy Ovedovitz and set in Times Roman type by The Composing Room of Michigan, Inc. Printed in the United States of America by Vail-Ballou Press, Binghamton, New York.

Library of Congress Cataloging-in-Publication Data

Psychoanalytic terms and concepts / edited by Burness E. Moore and Bernard D. Fine.
p. cm.
Includes bibliographical references.
ISBN 0-300-04577-8 (Yale University Press : alk. paper). — ISBN 0-300-04701-0 (Yale University Press : pbk. alk. paper)
1. Psychoanalysis—Dictionaries. I. Moore, Burness E. II. Fine, Bernard D. III. American Psychoanalytic Association.
RC501.4P79 1990
616.89'17'03—dc20 89-36223
CIP

The paper in this book meets the guidelines for permanence and durability of the Committee on Production Guidelines for Book Longevity of the Council on Library Resources.

10 9 8 7 6 5 4 3

CONTENTS

PREFACE

With the explosion of psychoanalytic findings and propositions in the United States after the Second World War, professionals, scholars, and the sophisticated public faced the need to understand the terms and idioms of this science. At that time a great deal of the essential literature was in German, much of it by Sigmund Freud, and the English translations available were uneven and limited. The terms used, many of them adaptations from everyday language or the vocabularies of other sciences, conveyed meanings influenced by their origins, which led to ambiguity in their new context. Understanding and usage of psychoanalytic terms were dependent on historical, thematic, or linguistic considerations, and interpretations often differed. The evolving character of psychoanalysis was another source of ambiguity and confusion.

To help alleviate this confusion, in 1967 the *Glossary of Psychoanalytic Terms and Concepts* was prepared and published under the aegis of the American Psychoanalytic Association. A revised edition was published in 1968.

This third edition of the glossary has been greatly revised and expanded. New terms and concepts have been added, and many previous definitions have been clarified and updated. References have been provided at the end of most of the short essays. The earlier editions were already more than glossaries, and this book strains that designation to the breaking point. It might be considered a compendium or mini-encyclopedia, but it does not easily fit either rubric. For that reason its title is simply *Psychoanalytic Terms and Concepts*.

The principal purpose of this volume is to

define and explain terms, but we have also attempted to situate each term within the framework of psychoanalytic theory by commenting on its historical development, when relevant, and on its relationship to other terms and concepts. Although this book is based primarily on Freudian theory, the definitions are not based exclusively on Freud's work (except in those cases where there have been no additions to his early contributions).[1]

This book includes a heterogeneous group of topics related to psychoanalysis. Among those included are major organizing concepts and their subsidiary terms; various psychic phenomena; complex, overdetermined mental processes, behavioral manifestations, and activities; symptoms and nosological entities; principles of mental functioning; and analytic treatment. A few topics not customarily thought of as analytic (for example, boredom, dependency, normality) have been included because they have been the subject of intensive psychoanalytic study. Furthermore, we have included terms from the work of Carl Jung; Melanie Klein and her followers; Wilfred R. Bion, W. Ronald D. Fairbairn, and D. W. Winnicott of the British object relations school; and the self psychology school founded by Heinz Kohut.

In this vast field no one reference work is likely to be sufficient. For primarily psychiatric nomenclature the reader is referred to the *Glossary of the American Psychiatric Association* or to psychiatric dictionaries.

Definitions are always somewhat arbitrary. Theoretical conceptualization is difficult in any science. A certain degree of abstraction is necessary, but it must encompass the clinical; generalizations are essential, yet room must be left for exceptions; alternate hypotheses are advanced, often using the same terminology but in a different sense; and concepts evolve. In this context, we believe a lexicon that is more than a collection of brief definitions serves a useful purpose.

1. For a critical commentary on the origins and historical development of theoretical ideas and their designation in Freud's writings, see J. Laplanche and J.-B. Pontalis, *The Language of Psycho-Analysis* (London: Hogarth Press, 1973).

ACKNOWLEDGMENTS

A multitude of people deserve credit for making this book possible. Its preparation has been a special project of the American Psychoanalytic Association, and the editors are grateful to the Executive Committee and members of the association for their whole-hearted support. We are particularly indebted to the seventy-four members who contributed to the two previous editions for setting a standard and a style that we have continued to follow. For this expanded third edition, nearly two hundred members researched their assigned subjects and submitted preliminary drafts of definitions. They often thanked the editors for the opportunity to participate in this joint effort to improve our understanding of the terminology of psychoanalysis. In turn, we wish to express our appreciation for their cooperation. Naturally, some have contributed more than others, and special credit is due those who submitted essays on several topics: Salman Akhtar, Renato Almansi, Stuart S. Asch, J. Alexis Burland, Judith F. Chused, Paul Gray, John Frosch, Steven T. Levy, Jon K. Meyer, Henri Parens, Milton Viederman, Stanley S. Weiss, and Leon Wurmser.

Except for the selection of non-Freudian terms and their definition, we have depended almost exclusively on American psychoanalysts. We are especially indebted to Andrew Samuels and his colleagues Bani Shorter and Fred Plaut for the Jungian terms; Alexander Tarnopolsky, Donald Rinsley, and John Sutherland for Fairbairn's terms; Manuel Furer, James S. Grotstein, and Ramon Ganzarain for Bion's and Klein's terms, which Hanna Segal also reviewed; Ernest Wolf, Morton Shane, and Estelle Shane for Kohut's terms; and Simon Grolnick, Christopher Bollas, and F. Robert Rodman for Winnicott's terms. The editors, of course, accept final responsibility for the selections made and the wording of the definitions throughout the book.

Members of our Editorial Board have spent hours at each meeting of the American Psychoanalytic Association for several years discussing the format of this book, selecting terms, suggesting contributors, and assessing the adequacy of contributions. In addition they have reviewed and often rewritten essays on terms within their areas of expertise. Our consultants were asked to serve in a more limited way by providing advice on editorial matters, but their participation has been virtually indistinguishable from that of the regular members of the board. As editors or former editors of important journals, they brought to this undertaking a unique fund of knowledge about psychoanalytic literature, authors, and procedure. George Klumpner volunteered helpful suggestions about indexing and cross-referencing. The terms defined in this volume came primarily from a list compiled by the Committee on Indexing under the chairmanship, successively, of Mark Kanzer, Bernard D. Fine, and George Klumpner. We are also grateful to Mark Kanzer for his assistance with the first edition and for serving on the Editorial Board when this revision was beginning. The help of the Editorial Board has been invaluable and our work together has been rewarding both scientifically and personally.

Beyond these many direct contributors there are others to whom we would like to express our gratitude for rendering some special service at one time or another. Eugene Kone of New Haven—public relations consultant for many professional organizations, including the American Psychoanalytic Association at one time—first advanced the idea of a glossary as a useful public information instrument. Ellen Gilbert, David Ross, and Jeannette Taylor, librarians of the A. A. Brill Library of the New York Psychoanalytic Institute, gave valuable assistance in providing references. The administrative details were capably handled by the Central Office of the American Psychoanalytic Association, for which we warmly thank Helen Fischer, the administrative director, and her staff. The patience and care with which our project secretary, Elizabeth Scholl, typed and retyped messy manuscripts are worthy of appreciation. During the project we have had two guiding beacons, Gladys Topkis, senior editor at Yale University Press, and Lottie M. Newman. We want Mrs. Topkis to know how much we appreciate her persuasion, encouragement, and forbearance, as well as the patience of Yale University Press about missed deadlines. The many psychoanalytic authors who have worked with Mrs. Newman appreciate, as we do, her discriminating judgment about what is appropriate, proper, and to the point in editorial matters. Her tactfulness in conveying that judgment has been a lesson in diplomacy, useful to any editor dealing with diverse authors.

BURNESS E. MOORE
BERNARD D. FINE

THE CONTRIBUTORS

David W. Abse
Salman Akhtar
David W. Allen
George H. Allison
Renato J. Almansi
Sol Altschul
Morton J. Aronson
Stuart S. Asch
Jose Barchilon
Francis D. Baudry
Jerome S. Beigler
Sidney J. Blatt
Peter Blos
Harold P. Blum
Lawrence D. Blum
Dale Boesky
Christopher Bollas
Paul A. Bradlow
Ira Brenner
Alexander Broden
Sylvia Brody
Peter J. Buckley
Dan H. Buie, Jr.
J. Alexis Burland
Pietro Castelnuovo-Tedesco
Judith F. Chused
Virginia L. Clower
Stanley J. Coen
Calvin A. Colarusso
Allan Compton
Barbara G. Deutsch
Paul A. Dewald
Robert Dickes
Theodore L. Dorpat
T. Wayne Downey
Jan Drucker
Jerome Ennis

Aaron H. Esman
Bernard D. Fine
Paul J. Fink
Lionel Finkelstein
Stephen K. Firestein
Newell Fischer
Alvin Frank
Elio J. Frattaroli
David A. Freedman
David F. Freeman
Richard C. Friedman
John Frosch
Thomas Fulmer
Manuel Furer
Erna Furman
Sidney S. Furst
Erik Gann
Ramon C. Ganzarain
Helen K. Gediman
Raymond H. Gehl
Jules Glenn
Eugene L. Goldberg
Leo Goldberger
Warren H. Goodman
Gene Gordon
Paul Gray
Sheila Hafner Gray
Robert S. Grayson
Simon A. Grolnick
George E. Gross
Stanley Grossman
James S. Grotstein
Eugene Halpert
Marjorie Harley
Irving B. Harrison
Arlene N. Heyman
Leon Hoffman
Charles C. Hogan
Alex E. Holder
Mardi J. Horowitz
Winslow R. Hunt
Francis A. J. Ianni
Lawrence B. Inderbitzen
Richard A. Isay
Theodore J. Jacobs
Daniel S. Jaffe
William D. Jeffrey
Allan Jong
Milton E. Jucovy
John S. Kafka
Henry Kaminer
Alex H. Kaplan
Laila Karme
Louis Kaywin
Edward H. Knight
Selma Kramer
Anton O. Kris
Henry Krystal
Eric Lager
Harvey G. Lapides
Louis A. Leaff
Stanley A. Leavy
Robert J. Leider
Eva P. Lester
Steven T. Levy
Joseph D. Lichtenberg
Joseph E. Lifschutz
Nathaniel J. London
Jeffrey Lustman
Houston MacIntosh
Margaret S. Mahler
Irwin M. Marcus
Norman M. Margolis
John B. McDevitt
Edith R. McNutt
Bernard C. Meyer
Jon K. Meyer
David Milrod
Ira L. Mintz
Arnold H. Modell
Burness E. Moore
James L. Morris
Alfredo Namnum
John M. Nardo
Edward Nersessian
Peter B. Neubauer
Teruko S. Neuwalder
E. Scott Nininger
Jack Novick
Henry Nunberg
Wendy Olesker
Stanley L. Olinick

Jerome D. Oremland
Shelley Orgel
Darius G. Ornston, Jr.
Daniel S. Papernik
Henri Parens
Morris L. Peltz
Ethel S. Person
Andrew Peto
Arnold Z. Pfeffer
George H. Pollock
Sydney E. Pulver
Owen Renik
Donald B. Rinsley
David Z. Ritvo
Ana-Maria Rizzuto
Michael Robbins
F. Robert Rodman
Herman Roiphe
Allan D. Rosenblatt
John M. Ross
Nathaniel Ross
Arnold Rothstein
Ralph E. Roughton
David M. Sachs
Leo Sadow
Andrew Samuels
Charles A. Sarnoff
Herbert J. Schlesinger
Nathan Schlessinger
Howard H. Schlossman
Nathan P. Segel
S. Warren Seides
Estelle Shane
Morton Shane
Theodore Shapiro
Susan P. Sherkow
Moisy Shopper
Lorraine D. Siggins
Melvin Singer
Joseph H. Smith
Charles W. Socarides
Jack L. Solomon
Rebecca Z. Solomon
Stephen M. Sonnenberg
Vann Spruiell
Melvin Stanger
John Sutherland
Alexander Tarnopolsky
Phyllis Tyson
Robert L. Tyson
Milton Viederman
Sara A. Vogel
Vamik D. Volkan
Allan J. Waltzman
Edward M. Weinshel
Stanley S. Weiss
Howard K. Welsh
E. Burton White, Jr.
Roy M. Whitman
George H. Wiedeman
C. Philip Wilson
Ernest S. Wolf
Edwin C. Wood
Leon Wurmser
Herbert M. Wyman
Hugo J. Zee

EDITORIAL NOTE

This book follows the usual format of a lexicon with topics arranged alphabetically. Whenever possible, a central concept has been made the subject of an essay in which that concept and all subsidiary terms are defined and their interrelationships discussed. If the subsidiary terms contain the name of the major concept, they are not listed separately but are defined within the essay about the central concept. (For example, *object choice* and *object relations* are discussed in the essay defining the term *object*). Other secondary terms are listed in alphabetical order in the main text and the reader is referred to the topic under which they are defined. All terms defined under other subjects are printed in italics to facilitate the search for them.

The terminology of each psychoanalytic school is presented in a section devoted to that school, but the terms defined there also appear alphabetically in the main text, referring the reader to the appropriate section.

We have attempted to make the definition of each topic self-sufficient, but no brief discussion can meet the needs of the serious student; therefore cross-references to related terms in this volume as well as references to other works on the subject are given at the end of each essay. The cross-references put the term in a broader context, lead the reader to more detailed definitions of some subordinate terms, point out closely related terms, or mention subjects that add to the definition at hand. References to publications at the end of each essay refer to the original source for the term, to articles reviewing the subject, or to papers that contribute a special viewpoint. Though limited in number, these references enable the reader to expand readily his or her knowledge of the terms in this volume.

Most topics were assigned to more than one contributor. The editors and members of the Editorial Board worked together on the preliminary drafts submitted to unify the conceptualization of each term. We felt that this plan, which worked well in the original glossary, would best ensure uniformity of style, length, and quality. Thus the essays are not signed or initialed because they are composites.

ABBREVIATIONS

We have adopted the following abbreviations for books and journals frequently referred to:

IJP — *International Journal of Psycho-analysis*

JAPA — *Journal of the American Psychoanalytic Association*

SE — *Standard Edition of the Complete Psychological Works of Sigmund Freud,* ed. James Strachey (London: Hogarth Press and the Institute of Psycho-Analysis, 1953–74.)

PSOC — *Psychoanalytic Study of the Child* (New Haven: Yale University Press)

PQ — *Psychoanalytic Quarterly*

WAF — *The Writings of Anna Freud,* ed. Anna Freud (New York: International Universities Press, 1966–74).

PMC — *Psychoanalysis: The Major Concepts,* ed. Burness E. Moore and Bernard D. Fine (New Haven: Yale University Press)

THE PROBLEM OF DEFINITION IN PSYCHOANALYSIS

Burness E. Moore

Every professional field has a special vocabulary to describe and categorize its observations, hypothesize about the interrelatedness of phenomena, and conceptualize explanatory propositions. These languages tend to develop slowly and somewhat haphazardly, by accretion. Systematization can be tackled only later, when a sufficient body of observations has accumulated and organizing and integrating commonalities have become apparent. In the meantime, some terms will have acquired a variety of meanings while other groups of words will all mean essentially the same thing. From time to time, therefore, professionals must take stock of the vocabularies they use and attempt to distinguish among the various meanings terms have acquired.

Psychoanalysis is no exception to this process; it is not surprising, therefore, that new compilations of psychoanalytic terms have appeared repeatedly through the past half century. While Freud did not systematically define terms himself, he gave willing assistance to Richard F. Sterba, whose preparation of a *Handwörterbuch der Psychoanalyse* (1936–37) was unfortunately interrupted by World War II. Ernest Jones attempted to develop an "international vocabulary" that would be free of any idiosyncratic connations (Ornston, 1985b, 1988). Freud "stepped around" Jones's selections and avoided most of his international vocabulary, but the meetings of Jones's Glossary Committee greatly influenced James Strachey's choices in translating. Since then a number of compilations have appeared, each with a slightly different conception (Fodor and Gaynor, 1950; English and English, 1958;

Moore and Fine, 1967; Laplanche and Pontalis, 1967; Rycroft, 1968; Eidelberg, 1968; Nagera, 1969–71; Wolman, 1977). Some of the reference works, such as *The Language of Psychoanalysis* by Laplanche and Pontalis, include not only definitions but also historical commentaries complete with references and quotations. These successive attempts to define psychoanalytic theory reflect dissatisfaction with existing approaches as well as the need to take account of advances in theory.

Freud often modified his theoretical conclusions on the basis of further observations (for example, he modified the seduction theory, revised the dual instinct and anxiety theories, and utilized successive models of the mind). Usually he did not seek to clarify new theory in relation to old, and he was little concerned with the systematization of theory. Some of his immediate followers, however, were very much occupied with this "cleaning-up" chore, in particular Heinz Hartmann, Ernst Kris, Rudolph M. Loewenstein, Otto Fenichel, David Rapaport, Merton M. Gill, Eric Erikson, and Edith Jacobson. The place of psychoanalysis in science (Hook, 1959), the formation of psychoanalytic theory (Waelder, 1962; Basch, 1973), and models of the mind (Abrams, 1971; Gedo and Goldberg, 1973) have been of continuing interest to psychoanalysts.

For the most part, theoreticians have been concerned with the explanatory usefulness of psychoanalytic constructs and their epistemological conformity. We cannot completely ignore such issues, but they are not our immediate concern. In the preparation of glossaries or compendia, the primary objective is what Basch has called "expression" (1973, p. 47), and Langer "the presentation of an idea, usually by the proper and apt use of words" (1962, p. 78). The historical development of the idea, although relevant, cannot be fully elaborated. The standardization of terms is essential for teaching, research, and the development of theory; and it is impossible to compare data without a common frame of reference, a common language that colleagues now and in the future use to convey specific meaning by means of symbols that have the same referents. Lexicons and glossaries facilitate the transmittal of knowledge to beginners by condensing the meanings concepts have acquired over a long time, by integrating later meanings with earlier ones, and by helping to clarify the current status of particular terms and concepts.

It would be unfair to the reader, however, to extol the value of such reference works without also pointing out some of the difficulties in defining psychoanalytic terms, difficulties that may affect the intended clarification of meaning. These include the problem of translation, since Freud and many of his early followers wrote in German; the selection of terms and determination of the space to be given each, which should reflect their relative importance; the choice of contributors and reviewers; and the modification of outmoded theory. Finally, as Kubie (1972) commented, there are fallacies in language itself, and we must avoid misusing it lest we entrench ambiguous and fallacious concepts by giving them authority.

Sigmund Freud made the initial observations, conceptualized the mental processes, and, intentionally or not, devised a terminology for his new depth psychology. Despite the advances in psychoanalysis reflected in the current literature, it is still an important objective for the English lexicologist to capture the meanings of terms originally expressed in idiosyncratic German. The difficulties of this task are increased by the distortions introduced by Freud's various translators, whose efforts were hampered by the structural difficulties of translation itself and by the unique differences between English and German, especially with regard to scientific nomenclature.

The Sapir-Whorf principle of linguistic relativity holds that the structure of language influences the way a person understands reality and behaves with respect to it (Carroll, 1956). In the introduction to his *Critical Dictionary of Psychoanalysis,* Rycroft points out that "something significant happens to the idea or a theory when it is translated into another language" (1968, p. xii). Through examples, Rycroft shows that difficulties are caused not only by single words but also by linguistic structure and habits of thought, which vary with the culture, the times, and the language.

Beyond these structural differences between languages are the difficulties arising from idiosyncratic usage—and the translator's inadvertent shifting of that meaning. That Freud received the Goethe Prize for literature attests to his felicitous use of words to present his ideas, but his unique style has not emerged unscathed from the minefields of translation. Freud adapted his terminology from the psychological, psychopathological, and neurophysiological sciences of his time, and he often relied on common words. Using a variety of linguistic techniques to convey the complex and indefinable workings of unconscious mental processes, "he would evoke a common experience, a familiar image or a biological analogy, . . . gradually add complications, and refine better questions from his first comparisons . . . [using words] to create a resonance among some rather diffuse feelings [between patient, analyst, and readers] and to set the stage for his arresting metaphors" (Ornston, 1982, pp. 412–15). "By constantly shifting his language, he enriched and clarified his accounts of what he called descriptive coordinates and organizing abstractions" (p. 410). Freud's conceptual inconsistency, expressed in poetic wordplay—puns, irony, and personification of mechanisms, authorities, and apparatuses—lent an ambiguity and flexibility to his writings that enabled him to say several different things at the same time. Thus, Freud communicated his concepts via consummate use of vivid and emotionally compelling language, evoking in the reader a feeling for the problem at hand. He did not adhere to precise definitions of technical terms.

A burgeoning literature in many languages addresses Freud's own sources and style and the changes introduced by his translators and interpreters. Without attempting to review the findings, which are still controversial, I shall summarize a few of the many problems now recognized.*

Freud's method of investigation was fluid and he conceived of the unconscious in a rich variety of ways, which enable the reader to keep several images in mind at the same time. Strachey and other English translators consistently replaced Freud's affect-laden, everyday German words with abstractions derived from Greek or Latin and changed Freud's dynamic, active constructions into static, passive ones. Strachey also ignored Freud's description of his own ideas as ways of thinking about the unconscious and mental processes. Strachey reduced Freud's descriptions to a vernacular replete with implications of space, structure, and forces generating energy. Freud often used the same word in various ways and used different words to describe similar ideas. Strachey reversed this tendency in an attempt to be systematic. Thus, Strachey's translations sound more mechanical and structured than does Freud's German prose, and the translations are artificially scientific. Though Strachey indicated his awareness of the difficulties of translation in his General Preface to the *Standard Edition,* he seems nevertheless to have accepted his own reading of Freud's psychology as the only proper one, to have believed that he was providing the "correct rendering of Freud's meaning," and to have believed that

*I am greatly indebted to Dr. Darius Ornston for a personal memorandum summarizing his various studies and writings on the influence of Strachey's translation of Freud.

his translation was free of his own opinions about theory (Strachey, 1966, p. xix; Ornston, 1985b, p. 394).

Here we must take note of a related hazard in regard to our efforts. We are defining concepts which for the most part were originally thought out in German by Freud, then filtered through Strachey, and further altered by the work of several generations of scholars in a variety of languages. The concepts have mutated; they are no longer Freud's original ideas. We also must keep in mind the fact that definitions are the condensed interpretations of many people—analogous to still further translations. The result may compound the fallacies of Strachey's translation of Freud, but it nevertheless reflects the present status of psychoanalysis. Since Aristotle it has been accepted that a definition should state the essence of a concept. Interpretation and condensation simplify terms, thereby aiding comprehension. But simplification may also delimit terms too strictly or too loosely. Hence, though nonessentials should be eliminated, definitions of psychoanalytic concepts frequently benefit from some additional explanation. In this book we have tried to find the optimal balance, which means that many of our definitions go beyond glossary length to become short essays.

In giving expression to the ideas of Freud and other psychoanalysts, we must keep in mind that, as Schafer stresses, "To designate is also to create and to enforce. . . . To the extent that we link or equate such names as, for example, femininity and passivity, we exert a profound and lasting formative influence on what it is said to be like to be feminine or passive" (1974, p. 478). The process of selecting terms and concepts and determining how much space to give to each involves a similar risk of perpetuating the fallacies of theorizing. Devoting a lengthy essay to a relatively unimportant subject, for example, gives it exaggerated significance. Furthermore, our "authoritative" restatements of Freud's theories will affect learning if they substantiate outmoded thinking. Thus, while it may be argued that historical imperatives require the presentation of Freud's ideas in their original form, some correction of outdated theory is equally necessary if we are not to contribute to misperceptions of the current status of psychoanalysis. The definitions and commentaries in Laplanche and Pontalis's *Language of Psychoanalysis* (1973), for example, are invaluable to scholars in that they precisely chart the psychoanalytic port from which various international movements have embarked; unfortunately some of the conceptual vessels are of World War I vintage and may sink under scrutiny.

But who is to decide what to select and what to correct? Jean Bergeret (1985) called for the establishment of a Psychoanalytical Scientific Council open to contributions from all countries to create the minimum conditions necessary for scientific debate. However, previous attempts at international consensus on definitions were not encouraging. We chose instead, whenever possible, to select one or more authors who had reviewed a subject or demonstrated exemplary clarity of understanding or elucidation. Many of these authors' contributions were referred to other scholars for evaluation, synthesis, revision, and rewriting—inevitably involving more translation and interpretation, with all the limitations already discussed.

A common language in psychoanalysis would be helpful. Instead, we find "increasing psychoanalytic diversity . . . a pluralism of theoretical perspectives, of linguistic and thought conventions, of distinctive regional, cultural, and language emphases" (Wallerstein, 1988, p. 5). Divergent groups are held together by adherence to Freud's central concepts—recognition of the unconscious, repression, resistance, and transference. To take full advantage of our commonalities in advancing analysis, we need to understand one another's general theories better. Therefore we have included in this volume terms derived from schools that are not strictly Freudian, chosen on the basis of the relative frequency of their appearance in the world psychoanalytic literature. In each case the terms were reviewed by persons thoroughly familiar with the literature of the school.

Soon after the appearance of the first edition of this work, Kubie observed that glossaries tend to give definitions that confuse "quantitative metaphors with quantitative measures, description with explanation, metaphor with hypotheses, [and] the adjectival value of a word with its nominative implications." He deplored "the fallacy of treating the part as the whole, the post hoc fallacy of confusing sequence with causal relationships, and the teleological fallacy of confusing sequence with purpose" (1972). Given the ubiquity of these phenomena and Freud's own effective use of metaphor in presenting his ideas, Kubie's statement led us to consider to what extent the presentation of theory might be invalidated by such tendencies, which involve not only science but the fundamentals of language itself. According to Rapoport, "The process of transmitting accumulated knowledge, which Korzybski called time-binding, is accomplished by the use of symbols" (1955, p. 63). Until recently, when chimpanzees upset our cherished illusion, it was thought that the use of symbols was a crucial and unique characteristic of the human race. In contrast to a signal, which is nothing more than a stimulus to which a response has been conditioned, a symbol evokes response only in relation to other symbols. In different contexts the same symbol can elicit different responses; it cannot be defined outside of a context. Combined in definite sequences, symbols constitute language, a "symbolic universe" which helps human beings perceive, understand, communicate, and shape their environment and which is, in turn, shaped by that environment.

The terms, concepts, hypotheses, theories, and laws that are the basic tools of theory building in any science are merely symbols manipulated in accordance with the rules of grammar and logic. Whether a definition is meaningful is a semantic question, determined by the relations between terms and their referents, unrelated to either grammar or logic. Terms are defined operationally according to observable effects sufficiently invariable to warrant application of the term to each occurrence of the effect. Definitions are compromise agreements, which should never be confused with facts.

Kubie (1975) advocated the use of adjectives, instead of nouns, in describing mental phenomena—nouns, he believed, lead to anthropomorphic thinking and to the reification of abstraction. He preferred to speak of "unconscious processing" instead of "the unconscious." Schafer (1976) regards all mental phenomena as actions, to be described by verbs and adverbs. Such attempts at clarification do not prevent confusing the literal-minded; they also risk introducing other problems. In discussing abstract concepts, we use words and expressions in a different sense from that which otherwise belongs to them. Metaphor, simile, metonymy, synedoche, and irony are employed to give life, style, or emphasis to an idea. When a simile or metaphor captures the essence of an idea, it appears in definitions. Studies by Rubinstein (1972) and Wurmser (1977) defend the use of metaphor in explicating theory.

Metaphors, which depend on the abstraction of similar attributes from otherwise dissimilar objects and events, are always ambiguous in a very specific sense, whereas synonyms are not. Nevertheless, a metaphorically transformed word usually elicits its own literal meaning as well, providing double meaning with a minimum of expression, abstracting and classifying through condensation. New meanings are thus given to words seemingly unrelated to the original ones. In this way, metaphors may compensate for deficiencies of language and aid in its development. By compelling one to look for similarities, they may bring out an attribute with greater poignancy. A single metaphor is capable of conveying a meaning beyond that of any literal combination of words—thus augmenting the resources of our language. It may also hint of significance, in part creating and in part disclosing inner meaning. Hence it may convey an individuality of emotion not possible with literal language.

Kubie (1975) objects that metaphors are never more than approximate; at best they are only analogies which are partially true and partially false. Metaphors depend on projections from inner subjective experience. In addition, he claims, they are all too frequently misapplied and misused and lead to failure to recognize the difference between metaphor and theory. Though a metaphor may serve an approximate descriptive purpose, even that description often misleads, since it may be accepted as an explanation. Other theorists point out that we cannot think of abstractions without metaphorical models. Wurmser (1977) argues for the use of metaphor in theory presentation, and Wallerstein (1988) concludes that all theory is metaphor.

Language may interfere with proper understanding, but we have to use what is available. Analytic language would be dull indeed if it were confined to adjectival designations, as Kubie advocates, or to verbs, as Schafer proposes, or to similes. Although a metaphor may be transformed into a simile by the introduction of the word *as* or *like,* its cognitive and affective impact is thereby diminished. And while newer computer models may more accurately represent the functioning of the brain, older muscular or hydraulic analogies and mythological parables ring truer in terms of experience and emotion. They are related in symbolic imagery to primary process phenomena, and their use may help in the integration of psychic processes. These are significant considerations in human communication, important factors in holding attention and facilitating comprehension. While we should try to avoid linguistic pitfalls in psychoanalytic discourse, "It is questionable whether the revision of terminology will reduce our problems, and continuing demands to delete vocabularies of discourse in order to solve scientific or social problems may function as a lamppost does for the alcoholic: as a crutch, rather than as a means of illumination" (Begelman, 1971, p. 47). Instead of advocating reductionism, we must cultivate a semantic awareness, so that we can distinguish between symbol and referent, between inference and observation, between a valid conclusion and a statement of fact—in short, we must remain aware of the distortions that verbalization necessarily introduces into our perceptions. Such an awareness is most needed in the area of scientific investigation, the transmittal of its findings, the transmutation of those findings into theory, and the communication of theory to others.

References

Abrams, S. (1971). The psychoanalytic unconsciouses. In *The Unconscious Today,* ed. M. Kanzer. New York: Int. Univ. Press.

Basch, M. F. (1973). Psychoanalysis and theory formation. *Ann. Psychoanal.* 1:39–52.

Begelman, D. A. (1971). Misnaming, metaphors, the medical model and some muddles. *Psychiatry,* 34:38–58.

Bergeret, J. (1985). Reflections on the scientific responsibilities of the International Psychoanalytical Association. Memorandum distributed at 34th IPA Congress, Hamburg.

Carroll, G. (1956). *Language, Thought and Reality.* Cambridge & London: M.I.T. Press & John Wiley.

Eidelberg, L. (1968). *Encyclopedia of Psychoanalysis.* New York: The Free Press; London: Collier-Macmillan.

English, H. B. & English, A. C. (1958). *A Comprehensive Dictionary of Psychological and Psychoanalytical Terms.* New York: David McKay.

Fodor, N. & Gaynor, F. (1950). *Freud: Dictionary of Psychoanalysis.* New York: Philosophical Library.

Gedo, J. & Goldberg, A. (1973). *Models of the Mind.* Chicago & London: Univ. of Chicago Press.

Harrison, S. J. (1970). Is psychoanalysis "our science?" *JAPA,* 18:125–149.
Hook, S. (1959). *Psychoanalysis, Scientific Method and Philosophy.* New York: Grove Press.
Kubie, L. S. (1972). Personal communication.
——— (1975). The language tools of psychoanalysis. *Int. Rev. Psychoanal.,* 2:11–24.
Langer, S. K. (1962). Problems and techniques of psychoanalytic validation and progress. In *Psychoanalysis as Science,* ed. E. Pumpian-Mindlin. Stanford: Stanford Univ. Press.
Laplanche, J. & Pontalis, J.-B. (1967). *Vocabulaire de la Psychoanalyse.* Paris: Presses Universitaires de France.
——— (1973). *The Language of Psychoanalysis.* London: Hogarth Press.
Moore, B. E. & Fine, B. D., eds. (1967). *A Glossary of Psychoanalytic Terms and Concepts.* New York: Amer. Psychoanal. Assn.
Nagera, H., ed. (1969–71). *Basic Psychoanalytic Concepts.* New York: Int. Univ. Press.
Ornston, D. G. (1982). Strachey's influence. *IJP,* 63:409–426.
——— (1985a). Freud's conception is different from Strachey's. *JAPA,* 33:379–412.
——— (1985b). The invention of "cathexis" and Strachey's strategy. *Int. Rev. Psychoanal.,* 12:391–399.
——— (1988). How standard is the "Standard Edition?" In *Freud in Exile,* ed. E. Timms & N. Segal. New Haven: Yale Univ. Press.
Rapoport, A. (1955). The role of symbols in human behavior. *Psychiatric Research Reports,* vol. 2, ed. J. S. Gottlieb et al. Washington: Amer. Psychiat. Assn.
Rubinstein, B. B. (1972). On metaphor and related phenomena. In *Psychoanalysis and Contemporary Science,* ed. A. R. Holt & E. Peterfreund., New York: Int. Univ. Press, vol. 1, pp. 70–108.
Rycroft, C. (1968). *A Critical Dictionary of Psychoanalysis.* New York: Basic Books.
Schafer, R. (1974). Problems in Freud's psychology of women. *JAPA,* 22:459–485.
——— (1976). *A New Language for Psychoanalysis.* New Haven: Yale Univ. Press.
Sterba, R. F. (1936–37). *Handworterbuch der Psychoanalyse.* Vienna: Int. Psychoanal. Verlag.
Strachey, J. (1966). General preface. *SE,* 1:xiii–xxii.
Waelder, R. (1962). Book review of *Psychoanalysis, Scientific Method and Philosophy,* ed. S. Hook. *JAPA,* 10:617–637.
Wallerstein, R. S. (1988). One psychoanalysis or many? *IJP,* 69:5–21.
Wolman, B. B. ed. (1977). *The International Encyclopedia of Psychiatry, Psychology, Psychoanalysis, and Neurology.* New York: Aesculapius.
Wurmser, L. (1977). A defense of the use of metaphor in analytic theory formation. *PQ,* 46:466–498.

PSYCHOANALYTIC TERMS AND CONCEPTS

■ ABREACTION

The discharge through speech of the affect associated with the memory of a trauma. Freud originally thought that abreaction, brought about by hypnotic suggestion or by the therapist's urging the patient to remember, was the mechanism for the cure of hysterical symptoms in the cathartic method. As he moved from the techniques of suggestion to psychoanalysis, Freud came to believe that the most important element of psychoanalytic therapy was the patient's working through of resistances to free association. The goal of achieving abreaction, of bringing "a particular moment or problem into focus," "receded into the background" (Freud, 1914). Today it is widely believed that abreaction is not specifically sought in psychoanalysis; however, it can have an ameliorative effect and may therefore be a therapeutic aim in the treatment of certain conditions, particularly acute traumatic neuroses.

See AFFECTS.

References

Bibring, E. (1954). Psychoanalysis and the dynamic psychotherapies. *JAPA,* 2:745–770.
Freud, S. (1893–95). Studies on hysteria. *SE,* 2.
——— (1914). Remembering, repeating, and working-through. *SE,* 12:146–156.

■ ABSTINENCE

A technical principle which holds that the avoidance of transference gratification increases frustration; fosters regression; facilitates the emergence, recognition, and understanding of the transference neurosis; and promotes working through and structural change.

Abstinence is considered by many to be an aspect of *neutrality,* but it is a separate technical principle specifically related to the frustration of transference wishes.

Freud introduced the rule of abstinence in a discussion of transference resistance and analytic neutrality: "The treatment must be carried out in abstinence. By this I do not mean physical abstinence alone, nor yet the deprivation of everything that the patient desires, for perhaps no sick patient could tolerate this. Instead, I shall state it as a fundamental principle that the patient's need and longing should be allowed to persist in her, in order that they may serve as forces impelling her to do work and to make changes" (1915, p. 165).

Several factors have led to disagreement regarding the scope of analytic abstinence: (1) ambiguity in Freud's technical recommendations and in descriptions of his actual clinical practice; (2) disagreement about whether abstinence requires that the analyst avoid gratification of transference wishes only or of all wishes; (3) the issue of what is therapeutic in analysis. While many analysts consider interpretation and insight to be the sole therapeutic agents in psychoanalytic treatment, others consider aspects of the object or self–object relationship with the analyst to be essential to the therapeutic process.

See NEUTRALITY.

References

Freud, S. (1915). Observations in transference-love. *SE*, 12:157–171.

——— (1919). Lines of advance in psycho-analytic therapy. *SE*, 17:157–168.

Poland, W. S. (1984). On the analyst's neutrality. *JAPA*, 32:283–299.

Wolf, E. S. (1976). Ambience and abstinence. *Annu. Psychoanal.*, 4:101–115.

■ ACCEPTED OBJECT

See FAIRBAIRN'S THEORY.

■ ACTING OUT

□ Acting In

The expression through action, rather than in words, of a memory, an attitude, or a conflict by a person in psychoanalysis or another form of treatment that is based on verbalization. In its narrowest definition, *acting out* occurs in, or in reaction to, the psychoanalytic situation, and the analysand is not aware that he or she is avoiding something. For example, one might act in a defiant way toward the analyst without remembering similar feelings and attitudes toward parental authority. This type of behavior is sometimes called "acting out in the transference." Feelings about the analyst may also be projected onto persons in the analysand's everyday life; in this case acting out occurs outside the treatment setting. The term *acting in* was originally introduced to describe reenactments in the form of body movements or postures on the couch, but is now commonly used to emphasize "acting out" that occurs in the analytic situation as opposed to outside.

The important distinction, however, is not whether the behavior occurs in or out of the analyst's office but the fact that something is reproduced in action—that is, "acted out"—rather than remembered and verbalized. When acting out, a patient repeats an act without becoming aware of the meaning of the act; in that sense he or she is resisting the analytic process. On the other hand, there are times, especially in dealing with derivatives of very early or very traumatic events, when verbalization is impossible. Then some form of acting out may be the only way the experience can be introduced into the analysis. In these cases the same mechanism that may otherwise be seen as undesirable resistance offers the only possible avenue of communication, through reliving.

Other confusions about the term have arisen through the years. Freud conceptualized transference itself as acting out: analysands repeated with the analyst rather than remembering. However, many analysts now think of acting out in opposition to transference—the patient avoids the transference by acting it out outside the office. Another imprecise, but common, use of the term results when the definition is broadened to include the behavior of people who externalize their conflicts in actions without any connection to a treatment process. Thus, the general behavior of impulsive characters, the symptomatic acts of neurotic persons, the deviant actions of delinquents, and the misbehavior of normal adolescents have all been called *acting out*. These kinds of behavior are somewhat similar to the acting out that arises in the analytic situation in that impulses are discharged into action rather than through fantasies and into words; but they are different in that they are derivatives of the pathology rather than a response to the treatment process.

The disadvantage of this broadening of the definition is that the term comes to mean little more than "bad behavior," whereas the narrower definition, as linked to the treatment process, reveals a complex, subtle, clinically useful concept. For example, not all acting out involves action: silence in the sessions or refusal to act in a situation that calls for action may be acting out. And the same behavior may at times be acting out and at other times not. For example, a patient may enter treatment with a habitual pattern of behavior (therefore not acting out) that more or less disappears in the course of analysis. If the behavior later begins to recur at times of heightened transference intensity or increased resistance, we would call it acting out. Thus, acting out is defined not by what the behavior is or by where it occurs but by the function it serves both intrapsychically and in the analytic process.

See ACTION; IMPULSE DISORDERS; SYMPTOMATIC ACT; TRANSFERENCE.

References

Boesky, D. (1982). Acting out. IJP, 63:39–55.
Erard, R. (1983). New wine in old skins. *Int. Rev. Psychoanal.*, 10:63–73.
Freud, S. (1914). Remembering, repeating, and working-through. *SE*, 12:145–156.
Rangell, L. (1968). A point of view on acting out. *IJP*, 49:195–201.
Roughton, R. Acting out. *PMC*. Forthcoming.

■ ACTION

In a broad sense all motivated behavior. *Action* implies intentionality, purpose, and meaning, though the intention need not be conscious, meaning may be only latent, and the action need not be observable; nor need it involve motor activity. Reflexes, other physiological phenomena, and events that impinge on the individual from the outside are not actions in the psychological sense. While *act* and *action* are often used interchangeably, the former connotes something done or effected, whereas the latter implies a process that involves more than one step, is continuous, or is capable of repetition. A sequence is involved that begins with a psychic impulse which is modified by various psychic functions and eventually either carried out or inhibited.

Thinking, fantasizing, and speaking, as well as inhibition of an impulse or refusal to act, are all considered motivated behavior, hence they are actions, in the inclusive definition given above. But there is considerable inconsistency in psychoanalytic thinking about the matter. Usually action is thought of as involving motor expression, that is, activity involving the somatic musculature and directed toward the self, external objects, or the inanimate environment. Analysands are asked to forgo such action and to free-associate while lying on the couch, thereby implying that feeling and speaking are not actions. Nevertheless, it is commonly recognized that silence and sometimes speech may constitute acting out just as much as certain destructive, complex behavior carried on outside the treatment setting.

There is no coherent psychoanalytic theory of action as such. The literature on action has arisen from clinical problems more than from systematic conceptualization—psychoanalysts have been more concerned with acting out than with action. Failure to distinguish between the two concepts has contributed to the broadening, and weakening, of the concept of acting out. Schafer (1976) worked within a comprehensive definition of action in his attempt to reformulate psychoanalysis as the study of human action, but rigorous application of his "action language" has not been widely accepted.

Clinical psychoanalytic discourse seems to need a dichotomy, however defined, that places the core elements of the psychoanalytic process (feeling, thinking, remembering, fantasizing, free-associating, and communicating through speech) in opposition to other components of action, many but not all of which will involve motor expression. Analysts think of action primarily as something opposing the psychoanalytic process, for example, when psychopathology takes the form of disruptive, maladaptive, or inappropriate behavior. There are, however, many action components or subsets of action that relate to psychoanalysis.

Adaptive action is the result of the resolution and integration of needs, defenses, and external reality in a satisfactory compromise that leads to relative inner harmony and effective mastery. It does not imply absence of conflict; rather, it refers to effective ego functioning that integrates drive derivatives and superego influences at an optimal level of influence. In psychoanalytic treatment, working through and integrating insights can lead to change only if reinforced by corresponding action.

Neurotic action is a broad category of pathological behavior, arising in a variety of psychopathological entities where the action component is a prominent expression of neurotic conflict. Compulsive rituals and self-defeating patterns of behavior are examples. Ego functioning is less effective in individuals suffering from neurosis and tends to be dominated by drive derivatives and rigid defenses. The neurotic action may symbolize unconscious conflict or may repeat early traumas.

Impulsive action differs from neurotic action in that the action is usually neither symbolic nor specific; instead, it is the result of a general disorder of impulse control involving intolerance for frustration and delay.

Acting out is narrowly defined as arising in response to a transference-mediated treatment situation.

Freud conceptualized thinking as experimental action carried out with small amounts of energy. Later referred to as *trial action,* the thinking process allows an individual to utilize perception, memory, and judgment to predict the likely outcome of a course of action without actually carrying it out.

In discussing *rational* and *irrational action*, Hartmann (1947) emphasized that adaptive behavior results when all psychic tendencies are subordinated to the organizing function of the ego.

Action is the natural mode of expression for children and the means of communicating with them in therapy. Piaget, Mahler, and others have demonstrated the role of motor behavior in development and identity formation. Adolescents use action to help regulate tension, and some borderline patients use action as a defense against loss of identity. Action, in the form of body movements and postures, may also serve as a means of communication. Rangell (1981) has written extensively on the relation of insight and action in leading to mastery and change.

Action has been defined here in terms of behavior, and the two terms do have similar meanings. For a discussion of the differences, *see* BEHAVIOR. *Also see* ACTING OUT; IMPULSE DISORDERS; SYMPTOM; SYMPTOMATIC ACT.

References

Hartmann, H. (1947). On rational and irrational action. In *Essays on Ego Psychology*. New York: Int. Univ. Press, 1964, pp. 37–68.

Panel (1970). Action, acting out, and the symptomatic act. N. Atkins, reporter. *JAPA*, 18:631–643.

Rangell, L. (1981). From insight to change. *JAPA*, 29:119–141.

Roughton, R. Action and acting out. *PMC*. Forthcoming.

Schafer, R. (1976). *A New Language for Psychoanalysis*. New Haven: Yale Univ. Press.

■ ACTIVE / PASSIVE

In ordinary discourse, attributes of behavior indicating the degree of physical action involved in achieving an objective. The terms are used in this sense in psychoanalysis as well. They are also employed to indicate the degree of mental activity, but more commonly they are applied to the aim of the instinctual drives. The aim is active when a person seeks an object on which to satisfy sexual or aggressive wishes or needs. It is passive when one wishes to have another gratify instinctual wishes on oneself—to be the object of loving or aggressive attention. This description of the instinctual aim holds true regardless of the mental or physical effort exerted to achieve the active or passive instinctual aim. An individual whose aim is passive may have to exert considerable effort to seduce or provoke another into discharging instinctual drive derivatives toward him or her. In that sense he or she is being active. Both activity and passivity belong to a continuum from normal to abnormal and both express wishes ranging from a desire for reciprocal active response to a pathological desire to be acted upon sadistically. This reciprocity is particularly evident in sadomasochistic and exhibitionistic/voyeuristic interactions. Active aims and acts that facilitate mastery, reality testing, and learning—which are adaptive—should be distinguished from aggressive aims and acts, which are destructive.

The term *passive* may also be used to describe an inactive body state that nevertheless allows for active mentation. Very young infants, in spite of apparent passivity, are highly active mentally, as they process sensory perceptions and lay down memories. Both activity and passivity are integral to the maturing of functions governed by the ego. In the course of normal development the child increasingly performs functions actively which earlier were performed for him or her by adults, and a gradual change from passivity to activity is evident in locomotion, feeding, the development of language, and the control of impulses. By actively repeating in dreams, memory, fantasy, thought, affect, and action what has been experienced passively before (whether pleasantly or unpleasantly), the ego attempts to achieve mastery over internal and external stimuli—attempts to produce and control cause and effect. The polarity refers, therefore, not only to instinctual tendencies but also to ego traits constituting a major aspect of defense and character structure. Degrees of passive experience during infancy may have significant effects on the nascent body image and on the subsequent development of higher or lower thresholds for the exercise of active strivings in the preoedipal and oedipal phases, and therefore on character formation.

Although activity has often been equated with masculinity and passivity with femininity in the past, this association is considered imprecise and misleading. The forms of expression of such traits and their objectives may simply be different in the two sexes. The physical activity often seen as desirable in boys may be impelled by an unconscious wish to receive passive libidinal or aggressive gratifications. Conspicuous passivity, often mistaken as a sign of impulse control, may stem from a defensive denial of sadistic or masochistic fantasies or impulses. To understand the clinical meaning of observed activity and passivity, one must know the subject's unconscious aims in relation to current id and superego demands and conflicts.

These terms have also been used to describe the structural concepts—id, ego, and superego—which are conceived of as active or passive at various times and in relation to each other. For example, the ego is thought to take an active role in relation to the id when it maintains control over the discharge of the id's instinctual drives. If overwhelmed by an instinctual upsurge, on the other hand, the ego passively experiences the discharge. Such usage has been criticized as reification.

See AGGRESSION; MASCULINITY/FEMININITY; SADOMASOCHISM.

References

Brody, S. (1964). *Passivity*. New York: Int. Univ. Press.

Fenichel, O. (1945). *The Psychoanalytic Theory of Neurosis*. New York: Norton.

Freud, A. (1965). *Normality and Pathology in Childhood*. New York: Int. Univ. Press.

Freud, S. (1915). Instincts and their vicissitudes. *SE*, 14:117–140.

■ ACTUAL NEUROSIS

Freud used this term to denote certain neurotic symptoms that were to be distinguished from the psychoneuroses (hysteria, phobia, and obsessional neurosis) on three grounds: (1) the cause for actual neuroses was to be found in individuals' contemporary sexual life (the German *aktual* means "present-day") while that for psychoneuroses was related to events in early childhood; (2) the etiology of the actual neuroses was somatic while that of the psychoneuroses was psychical; the symptoms of actual neuroses were physiological reactions to current faulty sexual practices and did not require the psychodynamic mechanisms underlying the symptom formation of the psychoneuroses; and (3) actual neuroses were not amenable to psychoanalytic treatment.

In 1894, Freud differentiated the two conditions designated as actual neuroses, *neurasthenia proper* and *anxiety neurosis,* from Beard's concept of neurasthenia. With neurasthenia proper, which he attributed to excessive masturbation, Freud associated the symptoms of fatigue, headache, intestinal disturbances including constipation, tingling sensations (paresthesias), and sexual weakness. The clinical picture he described for anxiety neurosis included irritability, restlessness, states of anxious expectation, anxiety attacks, phobias, dizziness, tremor, sweating, breathing disturbances, nausea, rapid or irregular heart action, diarrhea, and sleep disorders. In patients with anxiety neurosis, sexual practices interfering with the frequency, rhythm, or quality of discharge appropriate to the individual were thought to disturb the integration of psychical and somatic functions in the sexual act. Deflection of somatic sexual excitation from the psychic sphere presumably dammed up libido and transformed it into anxiety with visceral, motor, and autonomic manifestations. Thus, the concept of actual neurosis was associated with Freud's first, toxicologic theory of anxiety, which provided a physiological as opposed to a primarily psychological basis for symptoms.

Although Freud never completely relinquished the concept of actual neurosis, it is now disappearing from analytic nosology because, however important current factors may be as precipitating causes, the analyst can almost always detect the symbolic expression of older conflicts in the symptoms. When libidinal needs are not being met because of a defensive conflict, however, certain nonspecific symptoms may result; that is, a sort of secondary actual neurosis may accompany psychoneuroses. Indeed, modern clinical evidence suggests that lack of sexual gratification may cause irritability, tension, unexplained fatigue, and so on. Finally, it should be noted that while Freud spoke of only unmet contemporary sexual needs as underlying these symptoms, symptoms may also result from defensively suppressed aggression.

See NEUROSIS; PSYCHONEUROSIS.

References

Fink, P. J. (1970). Correlations between 'actual' neurosis and the work of Masters and Johnson. *PQ*, 39:38–51.

Laplanche, J. & Pontalis, M. J.-B. (1973). *The Language of Psychoanalysis*. New York: Norton, pp. 10–12.

Masters, W. H. & Johnson, V. E. (1966). *Human Sexual Response*. Boston: Little, Brown.

Nunberg, H. (1956). *Principles of Psychoanalysis*. New York: Int. Univ. Press.

■ ADAPTATION

The capacity to cope appropriately and advantageously with the environment. While adaptation requires reasonable conformity to the reality of the external world, it frequently involves activity directed at changing or more adequately controlling the environment. The term encompasses both the state of "fitting together" (*adaptedness*) that exists between the individual and his or her environment and the psychological processes leading to that state. These processes are called *alloplastic* when the individual alters the environment to meet inner needs and wishes; they are *autoplastic* when inner or psychic modifications are made in response to perceptions of the outside world.

Psychoanalytic developmental theory is essentially the observation, study, and understanding of the process of ontogenetic adaptation. Successful or progressive adaptation is recognized as one criterion of healthy ego functioning indicative of a harmonious relationship among ego, id, superego, and the external world. Character formation involves internalizing a stable protective environment and increasing one's adaptive capacity and ability to modify the external environment.

The concept of adaptation was first explicitly elaborated in psychoanalysis by Hartmann (1939). "Adaptation may come about by changes which the individual effects in his environment . . . as well as by appropriate changes in his psychophysiological system. Here Freud's concepts of alloplastic and autoplastic change are apposite" (p. 26). Hartmann also described a third form of adaptation, the selection of a new environment that combines aspects of alloplastic and autoplastic change. He commented, "We call a man well-adapted if his productivity, his ability to enjoy life, and his mental equilibrium are undisturbed" (p. 23). For psychoanalysis, the most important aspect of the environment is the psychosocial/interpersonal, involving the significant persons in the individual's life.

Another principle of adaptation elucidated by Hartmann is *change of function*. To evaluate the adaptive significance of a specific behavior, the analyst must differentiate between the current function of that behavior and its developmental origins—a behavior's functions often change during adaptation, so that a behavior eventually serves a purpose different from its original one. By remaining aware of change of function we can avoid the so-called *genetic fallacy*, the facile assumption that present-day behavior is directly derived from that of the past.

Adaptation is a central concept linking psychoanalysis and psychology to biology. Adaptation, which has active and passive components, should be clearly differentiated from adjustment, which is an essentially passive autoplastic phenomenon.

See CHANGE OF FUNCTION; CHARACTER; GENETIC FALLACY.

References

Hartmann, H. (1939). *Ego Psychology and the Problem of Adaptation*. New York: Int. Univ. Press, 1958.

——— (1964). *Essays in Ego Psychology*. New York: Int. Univ. Press, 1964.

Michaels, R. & Yaeger, R. K. Adaptation. *PMC*. Forthcoming.

Waelder, R. (1930). The principle of multiple function. *PQ*, 5:45–62, 1936.

Weinshel, E. (1971). The ego in health and normality. *JAPA*, 18:682–735.

■ ADAPTIVE VIEWPOINT

See METAPSYCHOLOGY.

■ ADOLESCENCE

The period of life during which psychic reorganization is required to accommodate the maturational changes accompanying and following puberty. Adolescence thus denotes the process of adaptation to pubescence and sexual maturation. Blos (1962) has defined it as the terminal stage of the fourth phase of psychosexual development, the genital stage, thereby placing the psychological developmental processes after puberty in the continuum begun in early infancy and resumed after interruption during the latency period. During early adolescence, endogenous as well as exogenous conditions affect the ego, temporarily weakening it in its attempts to deal with the surge of intense instinctual drives. Accompanying these changes are elaborate fantasies in connection with direct masturbation; these activities cause conflict and anxiety, in part related to the realistic possibility of heterosexual intercourse and pregnancy. Genital sexual impulses become intensified and those related to other erotogenic zones are subordinated to genital primacy, although derivatives of component instincts remain evident.

The individual regresses to earlier modes of relating to objects, and needs for dependency, fears, and conflicts prevalent during previous phases of development revive. Gender identity is reworked and consolidated. A second individuation process, comparable to the preoedipal separation-individuation phase, is necessary so that the individual can find substitutes for primary objects; in this process the adolescent revises representations of the parents and becomes capable of making selective identifications. The loosening of infantile object ties produces feelings of loneliness and isolation that may disrupt the process. To accommodate to new identifications, the individual must alter some of his or her ideals and moral codes; the superego is disorganized and reorganized, resulting in the ego's gaining relative power over the superego. This shift makes it possible for the individual to achieve a measure of drive gratification, thus maintaining psychic equilibrium.

Typical defense mechanisms that support ego functioning during adolescence include displacement onto extrafamilial, nonincestuous sources of gratification and models for ego-ideal and superego standards; reversal of affect (dependency wishes turn into revolt, respect and admiration into contempt and derision); hostility turned against the self; and withdrawal of object investment to the self, resulting in grandiose fantasies and hypochondriacal concerns. Specific adolescent defenses include asceticism, intellectualization (A. Freud, 1936), prolonged adolescence, and uniformism (Blos, 1954). Advances in abstract thinking are often accompanied by preoccupation with formulating opinions, ideas, and ideals regarding ethical, political, and social problems, which are pursued with fervor; intellectual horizons are widened, and intellectual and artistic creativity may blossom. These psychological changes help the individual to forge a unique sense of personal identity.

Due to the resourcefulness of the ego at the termination of latency and the chronological variability of physical maturation, many adolescent disturbances are transient and not subject to analysis. Pathological characteristics of the various stages of adolescence and the technical problems they present are discussed under Adolescent analysis.

See ADAPTATION; ADOLESCENT ANALYSIS (and references); COMPONENT INSTINCTS; DEFENSE; EGO; GENITALITY; OBJECT; PSYCHOSEXUAL DEVELOPMENT; REGRESSION.

■ ADOLESCENT ANALYSIS

A psychoanalytic treatment that initiates and promotes the adolescent process which has failed in taking its normal course. Its goal is to effect adolescent-specific psychic restructuring. States of structural dissolution as well as consolidation are dealt with by constructing conflict, counteracting infantilization, and resolving conflict surrounding the various phases of adolescence. The adolescent's personality adaptation to puberty is transacted largely in culturally and socially defined terms. Analysis operates within this context.

The general character of adolescent analysis is determined by the fact that a relatively weak ego is confronted during puberty by intensified drives. Therefore treatment combines ego support with analysis of the defenses mentioned above (see Adolescence). The analyst must discriminate between the normative and pathological features of adolescent regression and analyze their acting-out component (a defense against passivity), especially in the transference. Transference brings drive and object fixations into the analysis; these serve as vehicles to promote the individuation process of adolescence. Periodically, the adolescent needs to experience the analyst as a "real object," useful for remodeling the superego and forming the adult ego ideal.

Pathological residues of the dyadic (preoedipal) stage are significant determinants in adolescent neurosis or developmental disturbance; thus these earlier determinants must be addressed in the analysis along with triadic (oedipal) interpretations. This view modifies the classic recapitulation theory of adolescence in that it claims that dyadic polarities and triadic conflicts are not only recapitulated but are brought to a definitive resolution at adolescence (Blos, 1979). Until late adolescence dyadic isogender attachment needs do not reach a resolution—that is, protoadolescent bisexuality is renounced late. Homosexual anxieties and propensities, omnipresent in adolescent analysis, are analyzed as residues of dyadic isogender fixations and their oedipal sequelae. Adolescent analysis is permeated by the developmental task of the deidealization of self and object. This process leads to the surrender and transformation of infantile narcissism and enhances the capacity for reality testing. It also introduces into adolescent analysis the work of mourning (signaled by depressive moods) as a precondition for advancement to adulthood.

The characteristics of the various stages of adolescence, together with external circumstances, determine the nature of the analytic approach. During *preadolescence* (approximately ages eleven to thirteen), enhanced hormonal stimulation (principally adrenal) greatly increases the influence of the drives. Separation from parental objects is paralleled by the formation of peer groups, which involves changes in superego functioning. Minor physical changes generate anxiety and regressive defenses; anal levels of self–object organization and the return of negativism are common; the malleability and reasonableness characteristic of latency-age children wane. In treatment verbal communication is limited, but more mature play activity with the analyst helps maintain a working relationship. Peer group conflict and developing intellectual inhibitions help overcome resistance to treatment. On the other hand, the young adolescent experiences the analysis itself as a narcissistic injury. Through interpretation and empathic acceptance, the analyst assists him or her to resolve conflict over early object relations. The resulting decrease in anxiety reduces the patient's inhibitions, facilitating social and intellectual functioning. This progress, however, often leads to the adolescent's devaluation of the analyst along with the parents and the end of analysis.

Early adolescence (approximately thirteen to seventeen years) is marked by rapid increase in growth and an outpouring of sexual hormones; physiological and sexual maturity is usually achieved by the end of this stage. The body image is seriously disrupted, leading to ego distortions with many and varied somatic anxieties. Superego support for ego functions and the control of drives has been weakened by the earlier decathexis of parental forms and values. Preoccupation with masturbation helps reestablish a sense of self, while rebellion and defiance serve to discharge instinctual drive energy and enhance identity formation within the separation from parents. Autonomous ego functions (time sense, causal thinking, and so on) diminish because of instinctualization. Social withdrawal, scholastic inhibition, depression, and affect storms (particularly shame and rage) can be severe. Classic analysis is difficult with young adolescents because they externalize conflict, act out, tend toward paranoia, and search for magical solutions. Scholastic and family demands, often experienced as crises, also limit the time for analytic work. Though the patient may verbalize a great deal, free-association is limited by the attitude crisis. The analyst should maintain an objective friendliness while temporarily functioning as an auxiliary ego, especially with respect to reality testing and causal thinking. The anaclitic aspects of the transference assist greatly in sustaining analysis.

During *middle adolescence* (approximately ages seventeen to nineteen years) physical change is less extreme, ego mastery of the body image improves, and a firmer self-representation and sense of identity begin to appear. Shallow cathexis of oedipally tinged compromise objects leads to intense but often temporary sexual interaction. The drives are bound and organized by integrative and adaptive ego functions leading to sublimation and career and object involvement within a more mature character structure. Acting out diminishes and impulse control improves, permitting analysis to progress with forms and techniques typical of an adult setting except for the analyst's occasional support as an auxiliary ego.

In *late adolescence* (approximately nineteen to twenty-two years), the psychic apparatus is relatively stable. Goals and object relations have narrowed to approximate the individual's capabilities. A firm sense of self and identity helps him or her find fulfillment in the external reality of the career and object choice developed within subjective reality. The symptom picture and criteria for analyzability are essentially the same as for the adult, and analytic technique requires little variation.

See ADOLESCENCE; ANALYSIS.

References

Blos, P. (1954). Prolonged adolescence. *Amer. J. Orthopsychiat.*, 24:733–742.
——— (1962). *On Adolescence*. New York: Free Press.
——— (1979). Modifications in the traditional psychoanalytic theory of adolescent development. *Adolescent Psychiat.*, 8:8–24.
Esman, A. H. (1975). *The Psychology of Adolescence*. New York: Int. Univ. Press.
Freud, A. (1958). Adolescence. *WAF*, 5:136–166.
Harley, M. (1974). *Analyst and Adolescent at Work*. New York: Quadrangle.
Tyson, P. & Tyson, R. L. The psychoanalytic theory of development. *PMC*. Forthcoming.

■ AFFECTIVE DISORDERS

A group of diagnostic entities in which exaggerated affective reactions are the primary manifestations. Depression, elation, or an alteration of the two characterize the clinical states included in this grouping. Except for the inclusion in affective disorders of those conditions in which elation is the predominant affect (mania, hypomania, and the manic phase of manic-depressive disorders), the category would be virtually synonymous with depressive disorders. Syndromes in which the affect of anxiety is outstanding are discussed separately, but anxiety is ubiquitous in mental illness and overtly present to varying degrees in the entities mentioned here.

The third edition of *The Diagnostic and Statistical Manual* of the American Psychiatric Association (*DSM-III*) lists under "Major Affective Disorders" those conditions of psychotic proportion such as *mania, depression,* and *bipolar disorder* (in which manic and depressive episodes alternate). Under "Other Specific Affective Disorders" it includes *cyclothymic disorder,* in which alternating manic and depressive phases are of less than psychotic severity; and *dysthymic disorder* (or *depressive neurosis*), in which relatively persistent depression is not of sufficient severity and duration to meet the criteria for a major depressive episode. In addition, *DSM-III* describes *atypical bipolar disorders* and *atypical depressions* as well as *adjustment disorder* with depressed mood. There is evidence that bipolar disorders have a genetic basis resulting in a specific biochemical abnormality. Some people apparently also have a genetic vulnerability to depression, but psychological factors are probably a significant precipitant for the disorder of major depression and an important element in its perpetuation.

In the psychoanalytic literature there is a preference for retaining terminology, developed over the years, that is based on certain common psychodynamic constellations in these disorders corresponding to what is described in this book under the headings Depression, Elation, and Mania. *Mania, depression, manic-depressive syndrome,* and *involutional depression* are the psychoanalytic terms for the psychotic disorders corresponding to the major affective disorders of DSM-III, although the same affective symptoms may appear in conjunction with schizophrenia, borderline, and neurotic disorders. The psychoanalytic category *depressive neuroses* includes the DSM-III cyclothymic and dysthymic disorders and reactive depression. (This last occurs as an acute but limited reaction to situations that constitute a particular threat to the individual.) In some persons depression and its accompanying characteristics are chronic, that is, they are a part of the characterological picture rather than symptoms. These conditions are described in greater detail separately.

See ANACLITIC DEPRESSION; ANXIETY DISORDER; DEPRESSION; DEPRESSIVE NEUROSES; ELATION; HYPOMANIA; INVOLUTIONAL DEPRESSION; MANIA; MANIC-DEPRESSIVE SYNDROME.

References

American Psychiatric Association. (1987). *Diagnostic and Statistical Manual of Mental Disorders,* 3d ed., revised. Washington, D.C.

■ AFFECTS

Complex psychophysiological states that include a subjective experience as well as cognitive and physiological components. Various distinctions have been drawn between *feelings, emotions,* and *affects. Feelings* refer to the central, subjectively experienced state (which may be blocked from consciousness); *emotions,* to the outwardly observable manifestations of feelings; and *affects,* to all the related phenomena, some of which are unconscious. The terms are often used interchangeably, however, to refer to a range from primitive to complex, cognitively differentiated psychic states. A relatively stable and long-lasting affective state, evoked and perpetuated by the continuing influence of unconscious fantasy, is called a *mood.*

In current usage, then, *affects* refer to three levels of conceptualization: (1) clinical manifestations such as the reported feeling state, especially in relation to the pleasure–unpleasure continuum; (2) neurobiological concomitants including hormonal, secretory, vegetative, and/or somatic phenomena; and (3) a metapsychological concept which has been related to psychic energy, instinctual drives and their discharge, signal affects without drive discharge, the ego and its structure, structural conflict, object relations, self psychology, and a superordinate organizing system.

The subjective feeling component of affects always has a pleasurable or unpleasurable quality (except for feelings involving detachment and isolation); affective states thus almost always have motivational qualities. The cognitive components of affects involve ideas and fantasies linked to the affective state during the course of its development. While specific for each individual, these ideas and fantasies are organized around themes related to the motivational quality of the affective state. Anxiety, for example, is activated by the perception of danger, and the cognition accompanying it is organized around that theme, although its specific content depends on the experiences and fantasies of the individual in situations of perceived danger from infancy on.

The physiological component of affect is mediated through both the autonomic nervous system (blushing, sweating, crying, increased peristalsis, rapid pulse are all possible physiological responses) and the voluntary nervous system (changes in posture, facial expressions, tone of voice). The factors determining the strength and composition of the physiological component of a specific affective state are not clear.

Developmentally, affects arise from fixed, genetically endowed, physiological response patterns. It has been claimed that nine such patterns (surprise, interest, joy, distress, anger, fear, shame, contempt, and disgust) are universal, prominent, and readily identifiable during the first year of life, although this claim is controversial. The initial biological response quickly becomes linked to encoded memory traces, so that familiar perceptual patterns mobilize the appropriate affective response in anticipation of what the infant has come to expect by association. Since these associations frequently involve libidinal and aggressive objects and are experienced as related to the self, affects are usually intimately linked to object representations, self representations, and fantasies related to drive states. The last linkage led Freud to state that affects are drive derivatives, but they are now considered ego structures that may or may not be drive-related or involved in conflict.

Affects have an important adaptive function in alerting and preparing the individual for appropriate response to his or her external and internal environment, and for communicating his or her internal state to others and evoking responses from caretakers and other important individuals. Perceptions related to immediate stimuli and their intrapsychic representations (evaluated, integrated, and responded to along the lines of past experience) determine the nature of a feeling state. The evaluation of such perceptions takes place simultaneously along many vectors, depending on whether the stimulus arouses feelings of danger, trauma, safety, pleasure, well-being, self-esteem, instinct gratification, mastery, function pleasure, guilt, shame, or a combination of these. Derivatives of affects may elicit painful feelings and associations or may signal danger; they may be dealt with by a variety of defensive maneuvers.

The lack of an adequate, comprehensive theory of affects has led to competing psychoanalytic positions on affect theory: for example, theorists dispute the existence of unconscious affect or preoedipal guilt, the significance of direct observations of development, and whether certain affects (depression, for example) are diagnostic categories or configurations of symptoms. There is also controversy as to whether given affects derive from one period more than another; and disagreement exists as to which developmental periods (for example, oedipal or preoedipal) give rise to specific affective illnesses or symptom clusters.

References

Basch, M. F. (1976). The concept of affect. *JAPA,* 24:759–777.

Brenner, C. (1974). On the nature and development of affects. *PQ,* 43:532–556.

Emde, R. N. (1980). Toward a psychoanalytic theory of affect: I & II. In *The Course of Life,* ed. S. I. Greenspan & G. H. Pollock. Washington: NIMH, pp. 63–111.

Leaff, L. A. (1971). Affect versus feeling. *JAPA,* 19:780–786.

Panel (1974). Toward a theory of affects. P. Castelneuvo-Tedesco, reporter. *JAPA,* 22: 612–625.

Panel (1980). New directions in affect theory. E. P. Lester, reporter. *JAPA,* 30:197–211.

Rangell, L. Affects. *PMC.* Forthcoming.

Sandler, J. & Sandler, A.-M. (1978). On the development of object relationships and affects. *IJP,* 59:285–296.

■ AGENCY

See STRUCTURE.

■ AGGRESSION

□ Aggressive Drive

The manifest strivings, either physical or verbal, to subjugate or to prevail over others. The expression of aggression may be direct, as in an overt attack of war or the controlled competition of sports; it may be indirect and disguised, as in jokes or the overprotectiveness of resentful parents; it may be expressed passively, as in procrastination that obstructs another person's aims; or it may be turned against the self, as in self-defeating character traits or some instances of suicide. Although the term is most often used to imply hostile, destructive intent, it is sometimes broadened to include acts that seem to originate from initiative, ambition, or the just demand for rights. Such acts are sometimes designated *assertion* in order to indicate that they do not seem to arise from hostile motives.

Some psychoanalytic theorists describe all these various forms of action as the overt behavioral manifestations of an *aggressive drive,* as modified by the functions of the ego. Debate continues as to whether the aggressive drive is innately and primarily hostile and destructive toward the object at which it is directed, with those seemingly nonhostile instances (assertion) being the result of the neutralizing functions of the ego; or whether the aggressive drive is initially a function of nonhostile active striving in the service of mastery and adaptation, only taking on hostile and destructive qualities in response to frustration and conflict. Freud's later conceptualization of aggression as the manifestation of an innate self-destructive death instinct has not been widely accepted by psychoanalysts. Kleinian theory, however, does attribute a dominant and primarily destructive quality to the aggressive drive and sees it as the major source of conflict and personality development.

The aggressive drive and libido are thought of as the two primary instinctual drives. It is not clear, however, whether aggression and libido are separate forms of drive energy at birth, becoming fused in the course of development, or whether they are initially indistinguishable and only later evolve into separate entities. The aggressive drive does seem to undergo vicissitudes of development, taking on characteristic forms under the influence of the oral, anal, and phallic subphases. According to some theorists, this progressive development involves the increasing fusion of libidinal and aggressive impulses, thereby limiting the destructive manifestations of aggression and endowing the ego with neutralized energy for many of its functional capacities, both normal and pathological. At the same time, the ego appropriates and masters the aggression of the id in the service of increasingly differentiated levels of adaptation. In addition, the fate of the aggressive component of the oedipus complex intimately influences the structuralization of the superego.

Thus, aggression plays a significant role in personality development, as well as in one source of intrapsychic conflict and its resolution. Aggressive drives may be used defensively against libidinal conflicts, just as they may be defended against by libidinal wishes and fantasies. While the aggressive drives and the adaptive or defensive functions of the ego are often in conflict, there are both normal and pathological formations in which the ego functions permit the aggressive drive to be expressed harmoniously and free of conflict. Manifestations of the aggressive drive range in intensity from nonhostile, self-assertive, and self-preservative mastery, through irritation, anger, and resentment, to the extremes of fury and murderous violent rage. These drive manifestations also fall along the spectrum from conscious to unconscious awareness and may stimulate the use of various defenses and adaptive mechanisms.

See CONFLICT; ID; INSTINCTUAL DRIVE; LIBIDO THEORY.

References

Freud, A. (1971). Comments on aggression. *IJP*, 53:163–172.

Hartmann, H., Kris, E. & Loewenstein, R. M. (1949). Notes on the theory of aggression. *PSOC*, 3/4.9–36.

Heimann, P. & Valenstein, A. F. (1972). The psychoanalytical concept of aggression. *IJP*, 53:31–36.

Parens, H. (1979). *The Development of Aggression in Early Childhood*. New York: Jason Aronson.

Solnit, A. J. & Ritvo, S. Instinct theory. *PMC*. Forthcoming.

Stone, L. (1971). Reflections on the psychoanalytic concept of aggression. *PQ*, 40:195–244.

■ AGGRESSIVE ENERGY

See PSYCHIC ENERGY.

■ ALEXITHYMIA

A cognitive style and affective disturbance commonly found in patients suffering from psychosomatic, addictive, or post-traumatic conditions. The alexithymic state is characterized by poorly differentiated and poorly verbalized affects that do not serve the signal function adequately (do not communicate effectively). Psychosomatic patients, for instance, often ignore psychic and somatic danger signals, presenting a stoical appearance, sometimes with a stiff posture and wooden facies. Addictive patients particularly fear the somatic components of affects and try to block them, especially by chemical means. Post-traumatic patients are often unable to experience pleasure (a condition known as *anhedonia*).

Individuals suffering from alexithymia think in an operative way and may appear to be superadjusted to reality. In psychotherapy, however, a cognitive disturbance becomes apparent as the patient tends to recount trivial, chronologically ordered actions, reactions, and events of daily life with monotonous detail. In general, these individuals lack imagination, intuition, empathy, and drive-fulfillment fantasy, especially in relation to objects. Instead, they seem oriented toward things and even treat themselves as robots. These problems seriously limit their responsiveness to psychoanalytic psychotherapy; psychosomatic illness or substance abuse is frequently exacerbated should these individuals enter psychotherapy.

The term was introduced by Sifneos in 1967 and further clarified and elaborated by Nemiah and Sifneos in 1970. In the large body of literature that treats the concept, some authors attribute the manifestations to primary neuroanatomical deficits, while others point to various psychological problems, primary and secondary. McDougall and others see the phenomena from a psychoanalytic point of view as a group of developmental defenses closely allied with denial and splitting. A similar group of defenses, described in 1963 by Marty and his coworkers in France, was named *la pensée opératoire*.

See ANHEDONIA; DEFENSE; DENIAL; SPLITTING.

References

Krystal, H. (1982). Alexithymia and the effectiveness of psychoanalytic treatment. *Int. J. Psychoanal. Psychother.*, 9:353–388.

Marty, P. & de M'Uzan, M. (1963). La pensée opératoire. *Rev. Psychanalitique*, 27 suppl.:345–356.

McDougall, J. (1984). The "dis-affected" patient. *PQ,* 53:386–409.
Nemiah, J. C. & Sifneos, P. E. (1970). Affect and fantasy in patients with psychosomatic disorders. In *Modern Trends in Psychosomatic Medicine,* ed. O. W. Hill. London: Butterworths, vol. 2, pp. 26–34.
Sifneos, P. E. (1975). Problems of psychotherapy of patients with alexithymic characteristics and physical disease. *Psychother. & Psychosom.,* 26:65–70.
Taylor, G. J. (1977). Alexithymia and countertransference. *Psychother. & Psychosom.,* 28:141–147.

■ ALLOPLASTIC ADAPTATION

See ADAPTATION.

■ ALPHA ELEMENTS

See BION'S THEORY.

■ ALPHA FUNCTION

See BION'S THEORY.

■ ALTERED EGO STATES

Conditions resulting from a defensive regressive distortion of certain ego functions and a breakdown of the integrative capacity of the ego. Some disturbance of ego functions is to be expected whenever significant conflicts exist and defenses are called into action; it may be observed in virtually all psychopathological conditions, neurotic, borderline, or psychotic. In the literature, however, the term *altered ego state* refers to a condition in which perceptions—relating to the self or parts of the self, objects, and the surroundings—are episodically distorted in a consistent fashion, leading to feelings of unreality. The occasions are transient, lasting from a few minutes to several days, but they may recur throughout life. Any of the senses may be affected; space, time, consciousness, identity, and the sense of reality are often involved. Vision may be foggy; images may appear larger or smaller, lights dimmer or brighter; bodily sensations may vary from tingling to numbness or deadness; touch and taste may be modified. The individual may feel that parts of the body are detached or the mind may seem separated from the body, accompanied by a sense of estrangement from the self or the environment. The affected person tends to be aware of and observing the apparent changes in himself or the outside world. The manifestations may be protean; some are so common as to have their own specific designation, though these are not nosological entities: examples are micropsia, the Isakower phenomenon, the déjà vu phenomenon, depersonalization, and derealization. Closely related conditions affecting consciousness and identity, such as dissociative trance states, hypnotic states, confusional states, fugues, stupors, and multiple personalities, differ from the preceding examples in that they involve less awareness of the split in the ego.

The distortion in ego functions in these conditions occurs in the service of defending the ego, often through the medium of fantasy, against perceptions or ideas that might be dangerous on a conscious or, more likely, an unconscious level. The phenomena represent a defensive regression to earlier libidinal and ego modes. The ego splits into an intact, observing portion and an experiencing one. The altered ego phenomena may appear in both normal and pathological contexts and do not seem to be related to conflicts emanating from a particular phase of psychosexual development. They occur in everyday life at times of crisis and in psychoanalytic treatment when instinctual impulses unacceptable to the ego ideal come close to the surface.

See CONFLICT; CONSCIOUS; DEFENSE; DÉJÀ VU; DEPERSONALIZATION; DEREALIZATION; EGO FUNCTION.

References

Arlow, J. A. (1966). Depersonalization and derealization. In *Psychoanalysis: A General Psychology,* ed. R. M. Loewenstein, L. M. Newman, M. Schur & A. J. Solnit. New York: Int. Univ. Press, pp. 456–478.
Dickes, R. (1965). The defensive function of an altered state of consciousness. *JAPA,* 13:356–403.
Fenichel, O. (1945). *The Psychoanalytic Theory of Neurosis.* New York: Norton.
Stamm, J. L. (1962). Altered ego states allied to depersonalization. *JAPA,* 10:762–783.

■ ALTERED STATES OF CONSCIOUSNESS

See CONSCIOUS.

■ ALTER-EGO TRANSFERENCE

See SELF PSYCHOLOGY.

■ AMBIVALENCE

Describes the simultaneous existence of opposite feelings, attitudes, and tendencies toward another person, thing, or situation. In this most general sense, ambivalence is universal and not significant because affection is often complicated by hostility, and many hostile relations are tempered by affection. When, however, the strength of these conflicting feelings increases to the point where action seems unavoidable yet unacceptable, some defensive maneuver is undertaken which often leads directly to mental illness (for example, psychosis, obsessional neurosis). Under these circumstances, the ambivalence is repressed; that is, only one of the two sets of feelings is permitted to become conscious. Usually the hostility is repressed, but sometimes the affection. Successful detection of the repressed component and its successful demonstration to the patient usually exerts a therapeutic influence.

In discussing the active and passive trends in the sadistic-anal organization of component instincts, Freud (1905) attributed the term and concept of ambivalence to Bleuler and said that it is characterized by the fact that opposing pairs of instincts are developed to an approximately equal extent. He also employed the concept to account for the simultaneous existence of negative and positive transference (1912). Abraham (1924) used the coexistence of love and hostility as a basis for designating *preambivalent,* ambivalent, and *postambivalent* object relationships. The early oral stage was regarded as preambivalent, while a later stage, associated with biting, was considered ambivalent. Ambivalence also characterizes the anal-sadistic stage. The genital stage occurs after the infant has learned to spare the object psychically, to save it from destruction; it is termed postambivalent. Ambivalence is a predominant element in Melanie Klein's theories, leading to the idea that the ambivalently regarded object is split into "good" and "bad" objects.

See COMPONENT INSTINCTS; INSTINCTUAL DRIVE; PSYCHOSEXUAL DEVELOPMENT; TRANSFERENCE.

References

Abraham, K. (1924). A short study of the development of the libido, viewed in the light of mental disorders. In *Selected Papers.* London: Hogarth Press, 1927, pp. 418–501.

Freud, S. (1905). Three essays on the theory of sexuality. *SE,* 7:130–243.

——— (1912). The dynamics of transference. *SE,* 12:99–108.

■ AMNESIA

Loss of memory—literally, forgetfulness—which may be psychogenic or of organic origin. Following physical injury in which cerebral function is disrupted due to concussion or more severe damage, amnesia tends to be both retrograde and anterograde. Such organic factors as senility, infection, and toxins (notably alcohol) may play a role. In the alcoholic psychosis known as Korsakoff's syndrome, *paramnesia* (a disturbance of memory in which real facts and fantasies are confused) may occur, with a compensatory filling in of memory gaps called *confabulation.* Psychogenic amnesia is a defensive process that operates continuously to cope with emotionally disturbing experiences by distorting memory. Such defensive distortion or blocking of memory is now referred to as *repression,* although Freud originally used that term to refer generically to a number of defenses not then clearly differentiated. He believed that an anticathexis was necessary to keep memories out of conscious awareness.

Infantile amnesia leaves gaps in memory for the first several years of life. Though it is often thought of as "normal" forgetting attributable to the immaturity of the child's mind, infantile amnesia represents the ego's defensive effort to deal with early-life events and reactions that would otherwise be traumatic. Through the process of repression, events, ideas, and affects involved in such experiences become unconscious. Residues may remain in the form of symptoms or *screen memories*—fragments of memories (often seemingly trivial) that seem to be retained, sometimes with remarkable clarity, and serve to conceal more disturbing aspects of a situation. In a larger sense, all childhood memories are probably altered in some way by condensation, displacement backward or forward, or shift in emotional emphasis. Thus, processes that affect memory and those that determine the formation of hysterical symptoms are basically similar. One of the major goals of psychoanalytic treatment is to lift amnesias, especially those of early childhood, thus permitting the patient to reexperience consciously and to master events that were overwhelming at the time they occurred.

See CATHEXIS; DEFENSE; MEMORY; PSYCHIC ENERGY; REPRESSION; SCREEN MEMORY.

References

Freud, S. (1899). Screen memories. *SE,* 3:303–322.

——— (1901). The psychopathology of everyday life. *SE,* 6:43–52.

——— (1940). An outline of psychoanalysis. *SE,* 23:74–75.

Laughlin, H. P. (1967). *The Neuroses.* Washington: Butterworth.

■ ANACLITIC DEPRESSION

A syndrome consisting of symptoms of apprehension, sadness, weeping, withdrawal, and refusal to eat, suffered by some infants at around nine months of age. Its appearance is dependent on a good mother–child relationship for the first six months of life followed by the absence of the mother figure for at least three months. If the mother figure returns within three months, all symptoms abate. If separation continues longer, symptoms become more severe and may progress to insomnia, weight loss, retarded development, apathy, stupor, and even death.

The syndrome was first described by R. A. Spitz and K. M. Wolf (Spitz, 1946). *Anaclitic* signifies dependence on another—in this case the mother—whose loss precipitates the depression. Bowlby (1960), who also wrote of the infant's reaction to separation, modified Spitz's separation sequence to protest, despair, and detachment. Mahler (1968) explains Spitz's observations in terms of the separation-individuation phases of development. By the second half of the first year, she says, the infant has achieved a symbiotic relationship with the mother figure. Since at this point the symbiotic partner is no longer interchangeable, separation from mother produces severe symptoms.

See SEPARATION; SEPARATION-INDIVIDUATION.

References

Bowlby, J. (1960). Grief and mourning in infancy and early childhood. *PSOC*, 15:9–52.

Mahler, M. S. (1968). *On Human Symbiosis and the Vicissitudes of Individuation*. New York: Int. Univ. Press.

Spitz, R. A. (1946). Anaclitic depression. *PSOC*, 2:313–342.

■ ANACLITIC OBJECT CHOICE

See OBJECT.

■ ANAGOGIC INTERPRETATION

See INTERPRETATION.

■ ANALITY

A broad term referring to the characteristics associated with the *anal stage* of development, the period from one to three years of age. Because of the physically maturing ability to control the sphincter, the child's attention shifts from the oral zone to the *anal zone*, which provides further outlets for libidinal gratification (referred to in this instance as *anal erotism*) and for the emerging aggressive drive characterized as *anal sadism*. The *anal-sadistic stage* refers to the manifestations of both these drives not only in connection with the anal functions of expulsion and retention but also directed toward the fecal product. Thus the polarities and contrasts of erotism/sadism, expulsion/retention, and anal function/anal product form paradigms that are reflected in conflicts around ambivalence, activity/passivity, masculinity/femininity, mastery, separation, and individuation. The vicissitudes of these conflicts have far-reaching effects on intrapsychic maturation and developing object relationships.

Adaptive and maladaptive character traits, often seemingly contradictory, derive from the psychic organization that takes place during this period of psychosexual development. (The term *anal phase* refers to the psychic organization rather than the time period.) As compromise formations, these traits both express and defend against anal erotism and sadism, sometimes as sublimations. Orderliness, obstinacy, frugality, and parsimony are common features of the *anal character*, for whom anal development has retained an exaggerated significance. Heightened ambivalence, untidiness, defiance, rage, and sadomasochistic tendencies are also representative of the conflicts surrounding this period. Various aspects of obsessive-compulsive neurosis suggest anal fixation.

See OBSESSION; PSYCHOSEXUAL DEVELOPMENT.

References

Abraham, K. (1924). A short study of the development of the libido, viewed in the light of mental disorders. In *Selected Papers*. New York: Basic Books, 1953, pp. 418–501.

Freud, S. (1908). Character and anal erotism. *SE*, 9:167–175.

Heimann, P. (1962). Notes on the anal stage. *IJP*, 43:406–414.

Jones, E. (1918). Anal-erotic character traits. In *Papers on Psychoanalysis*. London: Ballière, Tindall, & Cox, 1948.

Menninger, W. (1943). Characterologic and symptomatic expressions related to the anal phase of psychosexual development. *PQ*, 12:161–193.

■ ANALYSIS
□ Analytic Process
□ Analytic Situation

In general, an abbreviated way of referring to psychoanalysis, used with respect to all of its applications. It is used here in a narrower sense to refer to a method or procedure for understanding the unconscious through the use of dreams and associations, whereby id, ego, and superego derivatives, conflict, and the resulting compromise formations may be recognized. Analysis is used as a method of investigation and as a therapeutic modality in *psychoanalysis proper,* described below, and in *analytic psychotherapy.*

Briefly described, analysis takes place in a particular setting at a consistent time and frequency (*the analytic situation*). This one-to-one relationship between analyst and analysand/patient differs from other forms of psychotherapy in that it imposes certain specific demands and frustrations. The patient is required to recline in a position such that the analyst cannot be seen, and he or she is instructed to report freely and without exception all the thoughts and feelings that pass through his or her mind (*free association*), suspending the critical and logical selection taken for granted in the usual social situation. The patient often experiences sensory and affective deprivation if, when it is appropriate, the analyst remains silent and seemingly unresponsive. This setting and procedure initiates an *analytic process* by encouraging a transient regression in the analysand, in which previously unconscious (repressed) memories, forbidden infantile wishes, and fantasies reemerge. As these become expressed in derivative fashion in dreams and in the patient's associations about past and current ideas and events, they also become focused on the person of the analyst (*transference*). This is facilitated by the analyst's relative anonymity and neutrality, and a *transference neurosis,* a "new edition" of the infantile neurosis, is formed. The effect of this transference neurosis on the analytic process enables the analyst to recognize what feelings and attitudes of the patient are residuals of past events and traumas; the analyst can then reconstruct earlier levels of development and the affects, conflicts, and compromise formations associated with them. The analyst interprets these, thus bringing them into the patient's consciousness. They are worked through and their effect modified by integration of the past with the present, nullifying to varying degrees the pathological effect of the previously unconscious conflicts. Patients cling, however, to patterns of feeling and behavior that have had some value for them, and the work of analysis is not accomplished without considerable *resistance,* to which the transference itself contributes. A *therapeutic* or *working alliance* between the patient and the analyst, based on positive trust and confidence in mutually shared goals, helps the patient to continue working in the face of his or her own strong resistance.

Through the recognition of conflict and elimination of the consequent defenses and resistances to perception and memory, which determine the unconscious quality of some behavior, the patient's total personality is enriched. Psychic energies involved in conflict are presumed to become freed and neutralized, available for the synthetic and integrating functions of the ego. The requirement that the patient remain physically inactive during the analytic hour facilitates the transfer of energy from the motor aspects of behavior to the psychic, thus improving the patient's capacity to wait, postpone gratification, and tolerate frustration in accordance with the demands of reality. This helps him or her attain an appropriate balance between work and recreation, between loving and being loved.

The analytic process described above includes three phases: (1) the establishment of the analytic situation; (2) the emergence and interpretation of the transference neurosis; and (3) the working through of conflicts, resistances, and transference in a termination phase. The technical conditions that make this process possible are described under the heading *Analytic technique.* There are aspects of all three phases which are not specific to psychoanalysis—they may be recognized in most types of individual psychotherapy. However, only in classic psychoanalysis do the setting and method deliberately encourage the type and degree of regression that results in affectively charged reemergence of unresolved childhood conflicts in the current relationship between patient and analyst. The analytic situation provides a stable frame of reference within which the patient and analyst mobilize in each other intrapsychic processes that help the patient work toward movement, insight, and change as the tensions generated within him or her are monitored and interpreted by the analyst. The interaction between patient and analyst, the analyst's modes of understanding (including empathy and countertransference), and the patient's growing awareness of his or her own unconscious mental processes (*analytic insight*) are vital factors in the process. The patient's achievement of greater insight, mastery, and maturity through the subjective experience of the transference neurosis and its interpretation in the analytic situation is considered the essence of the analytic process.

See ANALYTIC TECHNIQUE; CONFLICT; COUNTERTRANSFERENCE; DEFENSE; EMPATHY; FREE ASSOCIATION; INTERPRETATION; PSYCHOANALYSIS; REGRESSION; RESISTANCE; RECONSTRUCTION; TRANSFERENCE.

References

Arlow, J. A. (1979). The genesis of interpretation. *JAPA,* 27 (suppl.):193–206.

Freud, S. (1911–15). Papers on technique in *SE,* 12:85–171.

Kanzer, M. (1981). Freud's "analytic pact." *JAPA,* 29:69–87.
Schlesinger, N. & Robbins, F. P. (1983). *A Developmental View of the Psychoanalytic Process.* New York: Int. Univ. Press.
Stone, L. (1961). *The Psychoanalytic Situation.* New York: Int. Univ. Press.

■ ANALYTIC TECHNIQUE

A collective term embracing any or all of the procedures employed by the analyst in the appropriate induction, conduct, and termination of a psychoanalysis. It refers to a professional methodology of applying psychoanalytic theory clinically for didactic or therapeutic purposes.

Essentially, the method provides for a situation in which a systematic exploration is undertaken of the patient's automatic, unconscious solutions to conflict, based on the fact that since childhood he or she has perceived certain wishes, fantasies, emotions, and impulses as too dangerous to manage at a conscious level. The major aim of such exploration is to help the patient achieve increasingly mature conscious or preconscious solutions to his conflicts.

Typical aspects of psychoanalytic technique are: (1) daily sessions (usually four to five per week), which lend continuity to the analytic process; (2) a setting that does not gratify the patient's conflicted, warded-off strivings, which become increasingly directed toward the analyst (the *rule of abstinence*); (3) the *anonymity of the analyst* and his or her judiciously exercised objectivity or "neutrality"; (4) the patient's use of the couch such that the analyst remains out of his or her line of vision—a procedure that favors the patient's essential task, verbal free association (the central feature of the basic or fundamental rule of analysis) and the achievement of a progressively greater mutual spontaneity as the patient increasingly understands the intrapsychic obstacles to spontaneity mobilized by the conditions of the analytic situation. (5) Related to this, the assurance of absolute *confidentiality* is vital to all analytic work. (6) The tensions and interactions occurring between patient and analyst as a result of the patient's regression, the ensuing frustration of unconscious strivings, the development of transference feelings, resistance, and the analyst's interventions (as described under the heading Analysis) are also aspects of analytic technique.

Technically important for the process of change—a modification in the patient's unconscious need for defense in the form of resistance to greater inner freedom and awareness—is the analyst's consistent focus on the patient's psychological activities in the face of conflict over growing consciousness of specific emerging elements. The analyst should share such observations—usually in the form of interpretations or related interventions. Together with the patient's expanding capacity for self-observation, the analyst's interpretations are essential to bring the patient closer to awareness of unconscious repressive measures and to achievement of autonomous control over them. The response of some patients to the process (for example, *acting out*) may require *deviations from the standard* or *classical technique,* such as the *parameters* described by Eissler.

In the application of technical procedures there is a contemporary emphasis on the theoretical perspectives afforded by the structural theory. This implies recognition of the unconscious nature of the ego's defensive activities when mobilized by signal anxiety in the face of a variety of threats implicit in the analytic situation. This emphasis contrasts with familiar, also effective, technical measures that depend to a greater extent upon the influence of a positive transference. The latter gives less priority to interpretation of defenses, attempting instead to overcome resistance through more direct interpretation of warded-off (repressed) instinctual derivatives.

See ACTING OUT; ANALYSIS; ANXIETY; CONFLICT; DEFENSE; FREE ASSOCIATION; INTERPRETATION; PARAMETER; RECONSTRUCTION; REGRESSION; STRUCTURAL THEORY.

References

Freud, A. (1936). *The Ego and the Mechanisms of Defense.* New York: Int. Univ. Press. 1966.
Freud, S. (1915–17). Introductory lectures on psychoanalysis. *SE,* 15 & 16.
——— (1926). Inhibitions, symptoms, and anxiety. *SE,* 20:87–174.
Fenichel, O. (1941). *Problems of Psychoanalytic Technique.* Albany, N.Y.: Psychoanalytic Quarterly.
Greenson, R. R. (1978). *Explorations in Psychoanalysis.* New York: Int. Univ. Press.
Hendrick, I. (1958). *Facts and Theories of Psychoanalysis,* 3rd ed. New York: Knopf.
Loewenstein, R. M. (1951–72). *Practice and Precept in Psychoanalytic Technique.* New Haven: Yale Univ. Press, 1982.
Valenstein, A. F. (1979). The concept of "classical" psychoanalysis. *JAPA,* 27 (suppl.):113–136.

■ ANALYTIC THERAPY

Therapy based on psychoanalytic principles but using techniques different from those of analysis. Analytic therapy can be defined on a continuum from expressive or exploratory to supportive or repressive. It differs from analysis in its setting, technique, process, and goals. The patient does not lie on the couch, and sessions are less frequent. Free association is not used, but freedom of communication is encouraged. Patient and therapist maintain a friendly and reliable alliance, avoiding a transference neurosis. The therapist is more active—in addition to interpretation he or she freely employs suggestion, environmental manipulation, guidance, clarification, and reality testing. Analytic therapy is more focused, highlighting the real and immediate. It is usually briefer than analysis and emphasizes accessible and readily intelligible dynamisms. The aim is not character reorganization but removing symptoms and solving specific difficulties and problems.

Analysts consider analytic therapy important and valuable for many patients who cannot or should not undertake psychoanalysis.

See ANALYSIS; PSYCHOANALYSIS; PSYCHOTHERAPY.

References

Joseph, E. D. & Wallerstein, R. S. (1982). *Psychotherapy*. New York: Int. Univ. Press.
Rangell, L. (1981). Psychoanalysis and dynamic psychotherapy. *PQ.*, 50:665–693.

■ ANALYTICAL PSYCHOLOGY

Ideas and practices associated with the theories and work of Carl J. Jung (1875–1961). While working at the Burghölzli Mental Hospital in Switzerland, Jung became an enthusiastic follower of Freud after rereading *The Interpretation of Dreams* in 1903. He recognized that his previous experimental work with word association confirmed Freud's findings regarding repression, but he was skeptical about the assumption that only the sexual was repressed. Freud applauded Jung's early contributions to psychoanalysis and integrated them into his own conceptualizations. For a time he viewed Jung as his successor to lead the psychoanalytic movement after his death, but after five years of intense work together Jung's and Freud's thinking gradually diverged. By 1912 the split between them was final, and Jung went on to establish the school he called analytical psychology.

Jung's life work involved an effort to understand the nature of personality. His theory conceives of interacting energy systems that exist at birth with undifferentiated potentialities. Through contact with life these potentials are differentiated and transformed into conscious experience. *Consciousness* and the *unconscious,* according to Jung, are two dynamic, interacting realms of the personality. The conscious realm contains two structures: a central *ego,* regarded as the source of the individual's feeling of identity and continuity; and the *persona,* the individual's "public mask" or "face to the world." The persona consists of the roles, attitudes, and behavior presented to others in response to societal demands. When the persona is accentuated to the detriment of unconscious strivings, psychological stress results.

The unconscious is also divided into two aspects, the personal and the collective. The personal unconscious is more superficial, containing repressed experiences that were never more than dimly conscious or were too painful to accept in consciousness at all. The personal unconscious contains *complexes,* orderings of ideas, feelings, actions, and experiences around affectively charged nuclei. Examples are the mother complex, the oedipus complex, and the castration complex, the latter two frequently referred to in psychoanalytic literature. For Jung the personal unconscious contains not only sexual and mythic elements, but also ethical standards, a premise that Freud later recognized in his concept of the superego, which is in part unconscious.

Jung applied the concept of the *collective unconscious* more widely and insistently than did Freud. The collective unconscious, in Jung's view, is shared in a mystical way by all humankind. It contains the deeper, universal, and primal aspects of the personality, and its energies are thought capable of creating images independent of conscious experience. These are the raw material of dreams, fantasies, and other creative experiences, similar in form in all people and concerned with the central themes with which human beings have always struggled: good and evil, power, gender issues, birth and mortality. The images are clustered by Jung into prototypes or *archetypes.* The *animus* and the *anima,* for example, represent the masculine and feminine aspects of the personality.

To describe the different manifestations of personality, Jung developed a conceptual model including two basic attitudes—introversion and extroversion—and four common psychological functions—a rational pair (thinking and feeling) and a perceptual pair (sensation and intuition). This conceptual schema provided for a sixteen-category *typology* of personalities that has been popular in academic circles.

The concept of development is central to Jung's ideas, but he was little concerned with early childhood development. Instead he conceived of life as divided into two periods. The first half involves establishing one's place in the world and making the essential choices of occupation, mate, values, and interests. The second half is primarily concerned with confronting and adapting to mortality. The sequential progression of life is directed toward *individuation,* a lifelong process in which a person becomes "a psychological 'in-dividual,' that is, a separate indivisibility or 'whole'" (Jung, 1961, p. 383). Individuation involves a continual pressure to make available to consciousness the potential latent in the original structure and to relieve inherent tensions by reconciling or balancing opposites. Ideally, the outcome of individuation is a smoothly functioning, integrated individual, capable of achieving the full potential of his or her personality. Individuation, in Jung's view, is a universal human process, but cultural institutions, symbols, and nonconscious forms (such as religious systems and rituals) have been developed by humankind to deal with the psychological problems that arise during the process.

The reader will recognize that Freudian and Jungian constructs contain intermeshing meanings. The concepts of *introversion* and *extroversion,* in which libido is directed inward or outward (in the psychoanalytic terminology of that period), and the concept of complexes were originated while Jung was allied with psychoanalysis, but he expanded them later, as he did the idea of the collective unconscious. The concepts of anima and animus, persona, archetype and archetypal ideas, self and shadow, as well as Jung's later typology, were developed as part of analytical psychology, but their relationships with Freudian constructs are evident. Animus and anima, for instance, expand on Freud's observations of a universal bisexuality.

■ ANALYTICAL PSYCHOLOGY TERMS

□ Anima; Animus

Terms in analytical psychology suggesting the personification of one sex within the other. The female figure within the man Jung called the *anima* (from the Latin for soul), and the male in women, the *animus* (from the Latin for mind or intellect). While anima and animus may appear as human figures, it is more accurate to consider them as representative of archetypal patterns. For example, anima speaks of imagination, fantasy, and play; animus of focused consciousness, authority, and respect. Hence they can be understood as representing alternative modes of perception, behavior, and evaluation. It is now seen as fallacious to link such psychological traits to sex, but the fact that "contrasexual" (against one's own sex) figures appear in dreams, and so on, suggests a symbolic process: a man or woman will express symbolically that which is foreign to him or her in the form of a being with a foreign (that is, different) body. However, the very strangeness of anima and animus images gives them their psychological value as harbingers, and often guides, of psychological change.

See ANALYTICAL PSYCHOLOGY TERMS: Archetype; Imago. Refer to Binswanger, 1963; Jung, 1921–57, vol. 9, pp. 11–22; Jung, 1957; Jung, 1963, at the end of this section.

□ Archetype

An innate, inherited pattern of psychological performance, linked to instinct and, when activated, manifested in behavior and emotion. Jung's theory of the archetypes developed in three stages. In 1912 he wrote of *primordial images,* similar to cultural motifs represented everywhere throughout history; their main features were their power, depth, and autonomy. Primordial imagery provided for Jung the empirical content for his theory of the *collective unconscious.* By 1917 he was writing of *dominants,* nodal points in the psyche that attract energy and hence influence a person's functioning. He first made use of the term *archetype* in 1919 to avoid any suggestion that it was the content and not the irrepresentable, fundamental structure that was inherited.

The literature refers to the *archetype-as-such,* to be distinguished clearly from archetypal images, motifs, themes, and patterns. The archetype is psychosomatic, linking instinct and image. Jung did not regard psychology and imagery as correlates or reflections of biological drives, and his assertion that images evoke the aim of the instincts implies that images deserve a place equal to that of instincts. All imagery partakes of the archetypal to some extent. It is erroneous to effect too rigid a divide between the personal and collective unconscious, for the archetype, as a skeletal concept, requires ordinary experience to become fully fleshed out. Notes of innate structure exist in present-day psychoanalysis, notably in the Kleinian school: Isaacs (unconscious fantasy), Bion (preconception), and Money-Kyrle. Jung may also be considered a pioneer of European structuralism.

See ANALYTICAL PSYCHOLOGY TERMS: Collective Unconscious. Refer to Jacobi, 1959; Jung, 1921–57, vol. 7, pp. 99–113; and vol. 8, pp. 159–234; Samuels, 1985, at the end of this section.

□ Collective Unconscious

Like Freud, Jung used the term *unconscious* in two ways: to describe mental contents inaccessible to the ego, and to posit a psychic system with its own character, laws, and functions. But Jung did not regard the unconscious solely as a repository of repressed, usually infantile, personal experience; in addition, he saw it as a form of psychological activity altogether transcending personal experience and relating directly to the phylogenetic, instinctual bases of the human race. In his view the contents of the collective unconscious have never been in consciousness; they reflect the influence of archetypal processes. Speaking metaphorically, Jung assigns to the collective unconscious a form of "knowledge," even of thought. This may be expressed in the language of philosophy as the "final cause" of a psychological tendency or line of development—the "sake" for which it happens or is brought about. Though Jung did not say that the unconscious causes things to happen in an actual sense, a person may experience the final causes that operate in the unconscious as promoting the pattern and meaning of his or her life. This aspect of the unconscious is referred to as *teleological* (from the Greek *telos,* meaning "end" or "goal").

See ANALYTICAL PSYCHOLOGY TERMS: Archetype (including references); Imago; Self; and SYMBOL.

□ Complex

Refers to a collection of images, imagos, and ideas, clustered around a core derived from one or more archetypes and characterized by a common emotional aura. When complexes come into play (become constellated), they contribute to behavior and affect whether a person is conscious of them or not. They are useful tools in the understanding of neurotic symptoms.

At one time Jung thought the concept so important that he considered calling his school *complex psychology*. He referred to the complex as the *via regia* to the unconscious and as "the architect of dreams." Contemporary analytical psychology has revised this assessment, and the idea is now valued more for its capacity to link the personal and archetypal components of an individual's various experiences, particularly those that occurred in infancy and childhood. Jung developed the concept of complexes between 1904 and 1911 via the now-discontinued word association test. Freud valued his discovery as an empirical proof of Freud's concept of the unconscious. Though few psychoanalysts now use the term (save for referring to the oedipus and castration complexes), some argue that structural theory itself is a theory of complexes, and that ego, superego, and id are examples of complexes.

See ANALYTICAL PSYCHOLOGY TERMS: Archetype (including references); Imago.

□ Imago

Used instead of *image* to underline the fact that many images, particularly those of other people, are generated subjectively according to the internal state and dynamics of the subject. *Imago* also implies that many images (for example, those of parents) do not arise out of actual personal experiences with parents but are based on unconscious fantasies or are derived from the activities of the archetypes. An imago that has operated for some time functions like an expectation or as a filter through which certain categories of people are perceived. Hence, an imago affects feelings and behavior toward others and determines how others are perceived.

Complexes are composed of imagos. For example, the imago of the mother signifies the infant's innate tendency to organize his or her experiences of early vulnerability around positive and negative poles. The positive pole draws together such qualities as "maternal solicitude and sympathy; the magical authority of the female; the wisdom and spiritual exaltation that transcend reason; and helpful instinct or impulse; all that is benign, all that cherishes and sustains, that fosters growth and fertility." The negative pole suggests "anything secret, hidden, dark; the abyss, the world of the dead, anything that devours, seduces, and poisons, that is terrifying and inescapable like fate." (Jung, 1938, p. 82). Viewed developmentally, this refers to the splitting of the image of mother into good and bad variants. Jung pointed out that such contrasting images are widespread culturally, so that humankind as a whole does not find it odd or unbearable that the mother imago should be split. However, ideally the infant should eventually come to terms with the indivisibility of his or her mother and bring these opposite perceptions of her together.

The term *imago* is used in psychoanalysis to signify a self or object representation.

See ANALYTICAL PSYCHOLOGY TERMS: Archetype (including references); Collective Unconscious; Complex. Refer to Jung, 1921–57, vol. 9, pp. 75–110; vol. 5; Samuels, 1985, at the end of this section.

□ Individuation

As defined by Jung, emphasizes three things: (1) the goal of the process is the development of the whole personality; (2) individuation does not occur in a state of isolation but presupposes and includes collective relationships; and (3) individuation involves a degree of opposition to social norms that have no absolute validity. Jung carefully distinguishes his concept of individuation from personality integration or ego consciousness; its essence is that the self should become divested of whatever is false in the persona and should struggle free from the suggestive power of the archetypes.

Individuation may proceed in an unobtrusive manner or may be facilitated in analysis, but some of Jung's statements have contributed to the unfortunate impression that individuation is somehow only for an elite. There are some dangers inherent in the process: an intense involvement with the inner world and its fascinating images may lead to narcissistic preoccupation; and manifestations such as antisocial activity or psychotic breakdown may be considered justifiable results of an individuation process. The symbolism of individuation is often approached via an understanding of how conflicting opposites may reunite to produce a new synthesis in the personality. Jung claimed that mandalas (drawings of geometric figures with more or less regular subdivisions, divided by four or multiples thereof) express the totality of the psyche as it is apperceived and experienced in individuation. Though Jung felt that individuation proper was confined to the second half of life, contemporary analytical psychology tends to refer to individuation processes as taking place over a lifetime. Whether integration must of necessity precede individuation is an unanswered question, though obviously it is better if the ego is made strong enough, via integration, to withstand individuation phenomena when they erupt into consciousness.

See ANALYTICAL PSYCHOLOGY TERMS: Archetype; Persona; Self. Refer to Fordham, 1969; Jung, 1921–57, vol. 11, at the end of this section.

□ Persona

Derived from the Latin word for the mask worn by actors in classical times and referring to the social mask or face a person puts on to confront the world. *Persona* can be used to refer to gender identity, a stage of development (such as adolescence), or a profession. A person may consciously or unconsciously highlight one aspect of his or her personality as a persona, and over a lifetime many personae may be worn—several at any moment.

Jung conceived of persona as an archetype, meaning that it is inevitable. In any society a means of facilitating relationships and exchange is required; this function is carried out partly by the persona. The persona is not inherently pathological or false. There is, however, a risk of pathology if a person identifies too closely with his or her persona. This would imply lack of awareness of much beyond the social role (for example, lawyer, analyst, laborer), too rigid a conception of gender role, or a failure to take into account the changing requirements of life at different stages of development. In Jung's model of the structure of the psyche, persona is the mediator between the ego and the external world. The anima and animus perform the same mediating function between the ego and the internal world.

See ANALYTICAL PSYCHOLOGY TERMS: Anima, Animus (including references); Archetype (including references).

□ Self

Has been used in analytical psychology from 1916 on with certain distinct meanings: (1) the totality of the psyche; (2) the tendency of the psyche to function in an ordered and patterned manner, leading to intimations of purpose and order; (3) the psyche's tendency to produce images and symbols of something "beyond" the ego (images of God or of heroic personages fulfill this role, referring human beings to the need for and possibility of growth and development); and (4) the psychological unity of the human infant at birth. This unity gradually breaks up as life experiences accumulate, but it serves as the template or blueprint for later experiences of wholeness and integration. Sometimes the mother is referred to as "carrying" the infant's self. By this is meant something akin to the process called *mirroring* in psychoanalysis.

Refer to Jaffe, 1971; Fordham, 1976; Jung, 1921–57, vol. 9, pp. 11–22; Samuels, 1985; Stevens, 1982, at the end of this section.

□ Shadow

The negative side of the personality—the sum of all the unpleasant qualities one wants to hide; the inferior, worthless, and primitive side of human nature; one's own "dark" side. Jung emphasizes that everyone has a shadow; everything substantial casts a shadow, the ego is to shadow as light is to shade, and it is the shadow which makes us human. Jung gave Freud the credit for calling the attention of modern humanity to this aspect of ourselves.

As the shadow cannot be eradicated (this should not even be attempted), the best that can be hoped for is to come to terms with it. A stated purpose of Jungian analysis is to facilitate the patient's achieving a nonjudgmental attitude toward his or her instinctual side, in order to extract what is of worth therein. It is possible to develop a consciousness concerning those people and situations most likely to call forth the shadow side.

Refer to Jung, 1921–57, vol. 11.

□ Typology

A system developed by Jung to demonstrate and ascertain different modes of psychological functioning among people. He used basic *attitudes* toward the world and certain properties or *functions* of mental life to delineate several *psychological types*. Some individuals are more excited or energized by the internal world and others by the external world; these are *introverts* and *extraverts* respectively. Jung identified four functions of mental life: (1) *thinking*—knowing what a thing is, naming it, and linking it to other things; (2) *feeling*—a consideration of the value of something or having a viewpoint or perspective on something; (3) *sensation*—all facts available to the senses; noting that something is, but not what it is; and finally (4) *intuition*—a sense of where something is going and what the possibilities are. Jung designated persons as having a primary or *superior function* in each of these four categories when they showed the most developed and refined functioning; as having *auxiliary function* when it was only slightly less than superior; and as having *inferior function* when it was least developed, most unconscious, least accessible, and most problematic.

Using the two attitudes of introversion and extraversion and the superior and auxiliary functions, it is possible to produce a list of sixteen basic personality types. Several psychological tests based on Jung's hypotheses are used clinically and in educational and industrial applications. Some analytical psychologists welcome typology because of its "scientific" nature; others use it as a rule-of-thumb approach to provide an overall assessment of a person's functioning. Jung used his typology as a means of understanding the differences between himself and Freud (he regarded himself as introverted and Freud as extraverted), and he believed that interpersonal dysfunction can be understood in terms of the typological differences.

Refer to Jung, 1921–57, vol. 6; Samuels, 1985, at the end of this section.

References

Binswanger, H. (1963). Positive aspects of the animus. Zurich: Spring.

Fordham, M. (1969). *Children as Individuals*. London: Hodder & Stoughton.

——— (1976). *The Self and Autism*. London: Academic Press.

Jacobi, J. (1959). *Complex/Archetype/Symbol in the Work of C. G. Jung*. Princeton, N.J.: Princeton Univ. Press.

Jaffe, A. (1971). *The Myth of Meaning*. New York: Putnam.

Jung, C. G. (1921–57). *Collected Works of C. G. Jung*. Princeton, N.J.: Princeton Univ. Press.

——— (1938). Psychological aspects of the mother archetype. In *Collected Works*, vol. 9, pt. 1, pp. 75–110.

——— (1957). *Animus and Anima*. Zurich: Spring.

——— (1963). *Memories, Dreams, Reflections*. New York: Pantheon.

Samuels, A. (1985). *Jung and the Post-Jungians*. London: Routledge & Kegan Paul.

Stevens, A. (1982). *Archetype*. London: Routledge & Kegan Paul.

■ ANALYZABILITY

Refers to a complex judgment of a patient's suitability for psychoanalysis as a mode of therapy. The criteria for this judgment, because they are based on evolving concepts of theory and technique, have changed over the years and may vary from analyst to analyst. The determination of analyzability was originally based on diagnostic categories—only individuals under the age of fifty and suffering from transference neuroses (hysteria, phobia, and obsessive-compulsive disorder) were deemed acceptable. With the elaboration of ego psychology and especially of the various mechanisms of defense, the scope of analysis has tended to widen to the point where individual analysts believe there is no barrier to the application of psychoanalytic therapy in patients with severe character disorders, addictions, perversions, narcissistic disorders, borderline conditions, and even psychoses. For some of the more severe disorders, however, modifications of the classical analytic technique may be indicated.

Most analysts now base their judgment of analyzability on an evaluation of the patient's entire personality organization and life situation. This includes, among other things, the intactness and maturation of the psychic apparatus (id, ego, and superego) and its various functions and the patient's motivation for treatment. It is important that his or her suffering be of sufficient intensity to warrant this serious undertaking; and the patient's desire for treatment should not result from legal pressures or the overly strong influence of family members.

Requirements stemming from the psychoanalytic process itself include the ability to free-associate, to make the sacrifices of time and money required, to tolerate frustration, to form a therapeutic alliance that will withstand the vicissitudes of regressive transference experiences, and to tolerate anxiety and other strong affects without recourse to flight or acting out. Also crucial are the analyst's experience, his or her capacity for empathy, and his or her ability to withstand without undue reactive countertransference the frequently intense affective interpersonal experience in which he or she will be participating. This may be increasingly important as more problematic patients undergo analysis.

Some features of a patient's clinical picture, personality pattern, and life situation may suggest that he or she is not likely to benefit from analysis at present. Self–object differentiation must be sufficient to achieve a stable, workable transference. Inadequate reality testing with magical thinking or the use of such very primitive defenses as projection, denial, overidealization, or devaluation; excessive tendencies toward self-mutilation or destruction; and sadistic or criminal behavior are all contraindications for analysis. So is any physical condition that would prevent or seriously interfere with the practical application of analysis, including physical incapacities sufficient to prevent attendance at sessions or medical, surgical, or other problems requiring urgent attention. In addition, certain aspects of a prospective patient's neurosis or character may block or disrupt analysis if present in sufficient degree. Examples are strong punitive tendencies, uncontrollable impulsiveness, pathological lying, extreme anxiety, or any unrelenting resistance to being in treatment.

The number of factors to be considered, of which the foregoing constitute a partial list, has led to difference among analysts as to the best mode of evaluation. One or two unstructured sessions, multiple sessions, questions aimed at eliciting specific historical information, a period of trial analysis, or even a period of preparatory psychotherapy, especially for problem patients—all these evaluative methods are used.

Analyzability can be verified only after treatment of sufficient duration to permit the following developments: the patient should demonstrate responsiveness to the analyst's recognition and interpretation of resistances, should develop transference and usually a well-defined transference neurosis, should achieve a more satisfactory resolution of unconscious conflict, should modify the transference so that it does not interfere with the realities and necessities of life, and should establish a continuing self-analytic growth process.

References

Bachrach, H. M. & Leaff, L. A. (1978). Analyzability. *JAPA,* 26:881–920.

Kernberg, O. F. (1976). *Object Relations Theory and Clinical Psychoanalysis.* New York: Jason Aronson, pp. 139–160.

Stone, L. (1954). The widening scope of indications for psychoanalysis. *JAPA,* 2:567–594.

Tyson, R. & Sandler, J. (1971). Problems in the selection of patients for psychoanalysis. *Brit. J. Med. Psychol.,* 44:211–228.

Waldhorn, H. F. (1960). Assessment of analyzability. *PQ,* 29:478–506.

■ ANALYZING INSTRUMENT

Otto Isakower's (1963) concept of the joint participation of analysand and analyst within the analytic setting as a unique instrument or tool utilized to help bring about the analytic process.

Each participant is required to contribute to the team activity so as to produce a transient formation having an ad hoc analytic function. The analysand agrees to attend closely and persistently to his emerging thoughts, feelings, and perceptions and to express them verbally despite mixed or negative feelings about them. Submitting to these conditions follows the *basic* or *fundamental rule,* and the result is described as *free association*—that is, free from conscious control.

The analyst's participation depends on (1) listening to all the analysand's verbalizations, as well as paying attention to nonverbal communications; (2) attending to his or her own emerging thoughts, reactions, and perceptions; (3) controlling or analyzing any critical or negative reactions to the patient's associations; (4) avoiding focused attention and allowing his or her own thoughts to move freely by eliminating conscious efforts to remember. The result is called *listening with free-floating attention.*

Isakower regarded the free association of the patient and the free-floating attention of the analyst as two halves of the analyzing instrument. The aim of this joint activity is to bring about optimal ego regression in the analysand and to allow the analyst to perceive the unconscious of the analysand and to respond appropriately, consciously and unconsciously. When analysand and analyst have arrived at comparable (but not equivalent) states of partial ego regression (somewhat similar to a presleep state), various involuntary thoughts, images, and perceptions become available to each. Appropriate empathy is a significant factor in the analyst's functioning. His or her communication to the analysand of his or her own thoughts, images, or perceptions of the analytic situation is often reciprocated by the analysand, thus facilitating the emergence, understanding, and interpretation of the analysand's fantasy/memory constellation.

Use of the analyzing instrument is confined to the analytic hour. At the end of the hour, the two halves separate, to be reunited during the next hour. Isakower believed that the goal of supervision is to help the analyst candidate develop, utilize, and refine the analyzing instrument, as well as to detect and understand when and why the instrument ceases to function during a particular hour.

See ANALYSIS; WORK EGO.

References

Balter, L., Lothane, Z. & Spencer, J. H. (1980). On the analyzing instrument. *PQ*, 49:474–504.

Isakower, O. (1963). Minutes of the faculty meeting, New York Psychoanalytic Institute, Oct. 14–Nov. 20. A. Z. Pfeffer, reporter.

Malcove, L. (1975). The analytic situation. *J. Phila. Assn. Psychoanal.*, 2:1–14.

Panel (1975). The analytic situation. S. T. Shapiro, reporter. *J. Phila. Assn. Psychoanal.*, 2:15–19.

■ ANHEDONIA

Marked lack of pleasure in acts or situations that are usually pleasurable; an incapacity for happiness. The concept of pleasure must be distinguished from that of gratification, and the concept of distress from that of pain; clinically and hypnotically they have been demonstrated to be separate and separable. All these phenomena may be conscious or unconscious. There appears to be an inborn capacity for pleasure, varying from individual to individual, which can be permanently impaired by infantile or adult trauma.

Anhedonia is especially common in schizophrenic patients but also occurs in severely depressive individuals. It is often combined with traumatic alexithymia; in such instances it represents a regression in affect form.

The neurophysiology of hedonic regulation has received considerable attention in recent years with the discovery of pleasure and distress centers in the brain and numerous polypeptide neurotransmitters involved in the sensations of pleasure and distress. The hedonic aspect of emotions appears to be only secondarily and loosely connected with the experience of affect.

See AFFECT; ALEXITHYMIA; PLEASURE/UNPLEASURE PRINCIPLE.

References

Fawcett, J., Clark, D. C., Scheftner, W. H. & Hedecker, D. (1983). Differences between anhedonia and normal hedonic depressive states. *Arch. Gen. Psychiat.*, 40:1027–1030.

Krystal, H. (1981). The hedonic element in affectivity. *J. Psychoanal.*, 9:93–113.

Meehl, P. E. (1962). Hedonic capacity. *Bull. Menn. Clin.*, 39:295–307.

■ ANIMA, ANIMUS

See ANALYTICAL PSYCHOLOGY TERMS.

■ ANONYMITY

The state of being unknown. In psychoanalysis, personal facts about the analyst should remain unknown to the analysand. This is a relative matter, of course, since such facts as the analyst's name, address, general appearance, and manner, and the type of furnishings in his or her office, are inevitably known. It is part of the technique of psychoanalysis, however, to maintain and protect anonymity. The patient's speculations or fantasies about the person or family of the analyst are neither confirmed nor denied in order to preserve the analyst as a transference object onto whom the patient can project wishes and conflicts. When the patient does accidentally learn personal facts about the analyst, the patient's reactions to such knowledge and his or her embellishment of the known facts can be analyzed.

Self-revelation (the opposite of anonymity) may occasionally be unavoidable with severely pathological patients, but it usually impedes psychoanalytic progress by limiting the breadth of transference projections and their availability for interpretation.

See ABSTINENCE; NEUTRALITY.

References

Gill, M. M. (1984). Psychoanalysis and psychotherapy. *Int. Rev. Psychoanal.*, 11:161–180.

Poland, W. S. (1984). On the analyst's neutrality. *JAPA*, 32:283–300.

Shapiro, T. (1984). On neutrality. *JAPA*, 32:269–282.

■ ANOREXIA NERVOSA

An eating disorder occurring predominantly in girls and women and characterized by a relentless pursuit of thinness and absolute control over the body. Hunger is suppressed and denied and eating voluntarily restricted, while hyperactivity often increases metabolic needs. Patients with this disorder do not suffer from lack of appetite, as the term *anorexia* suggests, but from a fear of being fat; they are terrified of being overwhelmed by insatiable oral impulses. In many cases of anorexia *bulimia,* eating binges or gorging followed by vomiting and/or laxative use, alternates with dieting.

Anorexia usually begins at puberty and may persist in modified form throughout life. Other members of the family are often overconcerned with appearance and dieting. The mother is typically domineering and controlling, and the father has a minimal relationship with the daughter. Various medical and sociological factors, including the widespread cultural fear of being fat, seem to play a part in the increased incidence of cases.

The condition, which may progress to hypothalamic amenorrhea, cachexia, and even death, is a psychosomatic symptom complex that occurs in a variety of character pathologies: hysterical, obsessive-compulsive, borderline, and psychotic. It is frequently accompanied by other psychosomatic symptoms, atypical depression, acting out, and addictions. The physical metabolic-endocrine findings are the result of self-induced starvation and are readily reversible. The symptoms mask oedipal and preoedipal conflicts similar in all types of anorexic patients. However, *restrictors* (those who starve themselves) have rigid, controlling egos compared to *bulimics,* whose egos are relatively deficient in impulse control; although they try to starve themselves, they are periodically overwhelmed not only by oral impulses but by impulses of other kinds.

Anorexic patients show a wide spectrum of psychopathology and ego deviation. Ego disturbances include perceptual disorders involving distortion of the body image—denial of emaciation and longstanding fear of ugliness and fatness. Structural ego defects appear to be related to early failure in separation and individuation tasks. The anorexic pursues her strong need for autonomy and effectiveness, maladaptively by attempting excessively rigid control over the body. Anorexic patients are markedly ambivalent especially toward the mother. Feminine genital wishes are defended against by regression to primary object relations and pregenital drive discharge, leading to fears of merger and primitive identification with the omnipotent mother. The individual refuses food to attain autonomy and self-effectiveness and suppresses affect in order to feel separate. In some patients oedipal wishes and rejection of pregnancy fantasies lead to an oral-aggressive position where cannibalistic fantasies and incorporative wishes give rise to fear that they will destroy the maternal object.

The ego of the anorexic patient is split, containing areas of pseudonormal functioning and a varying capacity for transference. Psychoanalytic therapy and even psychoanalysis, utilizing parameters similar to those developed for the treatment of severe character disorders, may be indicated, but conjoint therapy of the parents is advisable in the case of adolescents.

See CHARACTER; IMPULSE DISORDER; PSYCHOSOMATIC CONDITION.

References

Sours, J. A. (1974). The anorexia nervosa syndrome. *IJP,* 55:567–576.

——— (1980). *Starving to Death in a Sea of Objects.* New York: Aronson.

Sperling, M. (1976). Anorexia nervosa. In *Psychosomatic Disorders in Childhood,* ed. O. Sperling. New York: Aronson, pp. 129–173.

Wilson, C. P., Hogan, C. & Mintz, I. (1983). *Fear of Being Fat.* New York: Aronson.

Wilson, C. P. & Mintz, I. (1982). Abstaining and bulimic anorexics. *Primary Care,* 9:459–472.

■ ANTILIBIDINAL EGO

See FAIRBAIRN'S THEORY.

■ ANXIETY

An unpleasurable affect or emotional state characterized by feelings of unpleasant anticipation—a sense of imminent danger. Its intensity and duration vary considerably. Anxiety has both physiological and psychological correlates; common physiological manifestations are acceleration of heart and breathing rates, tremor, sweating, diarrhea, and muscle tension; psychologically anxiety is experienced with apprehensive self-absorption as a feeling of being powerless when faced with an impending danger that is vague or unknown. The feeling may be accompanied or entirely replaced by the bodily sensations. Anxiety, which is related to a danger that is unconscious, should be distinguished from fear, which is a response to a consciously recognized external and realistic danger.

The concept of anxiety is of central significance in psychoanalysis, since neurotic symptoms are viewed as attempts to avoid the painful and distressing experience of anxiety. Symptoms do not cause anxiety; if anxiety coexists consciously with neurotic symptoms, it usually indicates that the symptoms have failed to bind all the anxiety.

Freud originally attributed anxiety to disturbances in sexual functioning. In his *first theory of anxiety,* he theorized that libido which had not been adequately discharged was transformed into anxiety. Various limitations and contradictions in this formulation are apparent: anxiety was seen as the cause of sexual repression, but repression itself was said to occur as a result of anxiety; if repression caused anxiety, lifting repression should relieve it but did not always do so; finally, the similarity of anxiety to fear—which did not involve accumulation of sexual tension—was puzzling.

Freud's *second theory of anxiety* (1926) approached it from the standpoint of the ego, conceiving of anxiety as a response to a threat to the individual. In *realistic anxiety* (that is, fear), the threat emanated from a known, external and significant danger, while in *neurotic anxiety* the danger was internal. Freud distinguished two types of anxiety-provoking situation. In the first, prototypically the situation of birth, anxiety results from excessive stimulation which the organism does not have the capacity to modulate (or bind). This *automatic anxiety* was considered more likely during infancy and childhood when the ego is immature and weak. The more commonly recognized situation, however, occurs after the defensive organization of the psyche has matured. Anxiety then arises in anticipation of danger, rather than as its result. This is called *signal anxiety*. In response to this signal reaction, defensive operations of the ego are set into motion. In situations of objective danger, the anxiety signal is part of an adaptive response, while in situations of psychic conflict, the signal may prompt a warding-off from consciousness (and/or action) of the emerging impulses or painful feelings. In its most refined and functionally efficient form, the anxiety signal is limited to a "thoughtlike" awareness and ability to cope with specific danger situations. In contrast, when the intensity of the anxiety experience is very much greater, it may not remain under control, leading to temporary functional disorganization of the affected person. It is then described as a *panic* or *traumatic state*. Panic is thought to be related to developmentally early states involving an extreme sense of helplessness; the response is global.

Freud described a series of typical *danger situations* that occur in a child's development. The first of these is loss of the love object, the caretaking person (usually the mother) on whom the child is entirely dependent. Later, when the value of the object begins to be perceived and object constancy has developed, the threat of losing the object's love becomes apparent. Still later, fear of bodily injury (castration) assumes a prominent influence. Finally, in the latency period, the characteristic fear is that the internalized parental representations (that is, the superego) will cease to love and will punish or abandon the child. Freud noted that while these "dangers" are phase-specific, they can exist concurrently in the adult ego. The persistence of earlier forms of anxiety in later stages of development is a reflection of neurotic fixation; the neurotic person unconsciously fears one of these earlier dangers and experiences anxiety reactions or symptoms that serve to ward off or bind the anxiety.

Freud's second theory of anxiety shifted emphasis from a basically physiological perspective to an unmistakably psychological one. By describing anxiety as related to the anticipation of danger, he provided a concept that has much broader application and greater explanatory power. The new theory also marked a shift in Freud's thinking about the ego, which he began to view as a composite of mental functions that is active, resourceful, and of great significance in the structure of the mind.

See AFFECTS; CONFLICT; EGO FUNCTION.

References
Brenner, C. (1976). *Psychoanalytic Technique and Psychic Conflict*. New York: Int. Univ. Press.
Freud, S. (1926). Inhibitions, symptoms, and anxiety. *SE,* 20:75–174.
——— (1933). New introductory lectures on psychoanalysis. *SE,* 22.1–182.
Meissner, W. W., Mack, J. E. & Semrad, E. V. (1975). Classical psychoanalysis. In *Comprehensive Textbook of Psychiatry,* ed. A. M. Freedman, H. I. Kaplan & B. J. Sadock. Baltimore: Williams & Wilkins, pp. 482–565.
Rangell, L. Affects. *PMC*. Forthcoming.

■ ANXIETY DISORDER
□ Anxiety Character
□ Anxiety Neurosis
□ Anxiety State

The current psychiatric designation for a symptomatic condition in which anxiety is a central factor, whether experienced consciously or not. Anxiety disorders do not include schizophrenia, primary affective illness, or organic brain dysfunction. Except for the exclusions, the nosological classification takes into account the psychoanalytic conception of anxiety as a signal affect, arising out of conflict over opposing forces within the mind and resulting in various compromise formations, presented in a variety of symptoms. The patient may not experience anxiety and the analyst may not observe it; in other cases anxiety is evident as a transient, recurrent, sustained, or protracted phenomenon, depending on the efficacy of the defensive maneuvers employed. Thus the *DSM-III* category "Anxiety Disorders" includes both conditions involving overt anxiety and conditions characterized by phobias and/or obsessions and compulsions in which anxiety becomes overt only when defensive efforts are thwarted. But conditions defending against anxiety by physical conversion or dissociation (hysterias) are assigned to other categories. This apparent inconsistency leads to confusion in *DSM-III;* other inconsistencies appear in what follows.

Conditions exhibiting primarily anxiety of variable intensity or duration, such as panic disorder or generalized anxiety disorder, are placed under anxiety disorders in *DSM-III* in a subcategory designated "Anxiety States (Anxiety Neurosis)." This classification ignores the history of anxiety neurosis as a syndrome. Freud first described it in 1895 as characterized by general irritability, anxious expectation accompanied by what would now be regarded as the physiological concomitants of anxiety, phobias related to physiological dangers and locomotion, and obsessional and sometimes hysterical symptoms. This "anxiety neurosis" he regarded as an "actual neurosis" (from the German *aktual,* meaning "current" or "present-day"), attributable to sexual practices that blocked adequate or appropriate discharge of sexual excitation, which then found somatic instead of psychical expression. Freud distinguished anxiety neurosis from psychoneuroses (hysteria and the obsessional neurosis), whose causes he assumed were entirely psychic and related to early childhood conflicts, though he recognized mixed forms. The idea that deflected somatic sexual excitation and dammed-up libido can be transformed into anxiety belonged to Freud's first theory of anxiety. The notion of actual neurosis is no longer accepted unreservedly, yet the clinical picture of anxiety neurosis is recognized as valid. A physiological basis for panic attacks, presumably genetic, has been demonstrated; on this basis it seems warranted to separate panic disorders and generalized anxiety conditions from hysteria, phobias, and obsessional syndromes. However, this historical background is often overlooked, and anxiety neurosis regarded simply as a form of psychoneurosis.

While *anxiety disorder, anxiety neurosis,* and *anxiety state* have been used synonymously to designate a neurotic condition whose main clinical feature is free-floating anxiety, some distinctions should be made. *Anxiety state,* a phenomenal term, should be reserved for the situation when the psychophysiological manifestations of anxiety are apparent, whether transient or extended. A person may be in a state of anxiety (in the face of external danger, for instance) without having an anxiety disorder or neurosis. Conversely, someone with an anxiety disorder (e.g., a phobia or obsessional condition) may not be overtly anxious at a given time, because he or she has taken action to defend against anxiety. Anxiety is described as *free-floating* when it has not become attached to a specific situation, as in the case of the phobic neurosis. Its presence is now viewed as an indication that the defensive function of the ego has failed to protect against a threatening unconscious fantasy.

Anxiety character is a seldom-used term applied to individuals who exhibit a regular state of low- or moderate-level chronic anxiety. The affected person is usually not aware of feeling anxious, even though he or she is engaged in continuous mental or behavioral activity intended to dissipate or control it. Such a person might also be classified by the more general designation *neurotic character,* indicating someone whose everyday behavior is predominantly influenced by unconscious conflict but who is little aware of anxiety or other neurotic symptoms.

Anxiety hysteria was introduced by Stekel in 1908 and adopted by Freud in 1909 to describe a neurotic condition involving overt anxiety states. It is markedly similar structurally to conversion hysteria, but it includes a strong tendency to phobia formation. Freud thought at the time that it represented a combination of an anxiety neurosis (that is an "actual," physical neurosis without psychical mechanisms) and hysteria, a psychoneurosis in which mental conflict is converted into bodily symptoms. Freud believed that anxiety hysteria and conversion hysteria were alike insofar as repression had succeeded in both instances in separating affects from ideas. The difference was that in anxiety hysteria the libido liberated from pathogenic ideas by repression is not converted but is set free as anxiety, which the mind attempts to bind by more or less gradually associating it with and limiting it to a particular situation that can be avoided (the process of phobia formation).

Anxiety hysteria is not a common diagnosis, but anxiety hysteria and phobia are not absolute synonyms, despite the widespread tendency to view them as such. Anxiety hysteria emphasizes the constitutive mechanism of the neurosis in question. The clinical syndrome Freud described does exist; in children it appears to be related to attempts to resolve conflicts of the phallic-oedipal phase of development, as Freud originally suggested. Outbreaks of anxiety and subsequent attempts to circumscribe it in phobias or other ways are now regarded to indicate mental conflict for which defensive operations are not yet adequate to control instinctual strivings without obvious distress. If symptoms are present in addition to the anxiety, analysts today call the syndrome by whatever name fits it descriptively, in this case *phobic neurosis*.

Post-traumatic stress disorder is also included among the anxiety disorders in the DSM-III. It is described in this volume under Traumatic neurosis.

See ACTUAL NEUROSIS; ANXIETY; CONFLICT; COMPROMISE FORMATION; PHOBIA; SYMPTOMS; TRAUMATIC NEUROSIS.

References

American Psychiatric Association (1987). *Diagnostic and Statistical Manual of Mental Disorders,* 3rd ed., revised. Washington, D.C.

Brenner, C. (1982). *The Mind in Conflict.* New York: Int. Univ. Press.

Freud, S. (1895). On the ground for detaching a particular syndrome from neurasthenia under the description "anxiety neurosis." *SE,* 3:85–117.

______ (1908). Preface to Wilhelm Stekel's *Nervous Anxiety-States and Their Treatment. SE,* 9:250–251.

______ (1909). Analysis of a phobia in a five-year-old boy. *SE,* 10:5–149.

Laplanche, J. & Pontalis, J. B. (1973). *The Language of Psychoanalysis.* New York: Norton.

Meissner, W. W., Mack, J. E. & Semrad, E. V. (1975). Classical psychoanalysis. In *Comprehensive Textbook of Psychiatry,* ed. A. M. Freedman, H. I. Kaplan & B. J. Sadock. Baltimore: Williams & Wilkens, vol. 2, pp. 482–565.

■ APATHY

Absence of emotional feeling. The apathetic person experiences neither pleasure nor displeasure; thus the apathetic state differs from boredom because it lacks the tension and irritability usually associated with the latter. Apathy is often considered the end result of severe and prolonged affective deprivation or overwhelming stress. It is the product of a defensive struggle against intolerable feelings of abandonment and, especially in wartime, threatened annihilation. Manifestly it assumes the character of detachment—a "giving up" of the object world—but analytic work frequently reveals the continuing existence of unconscious attachments that are defensively denied or disavowed.

See AFFECT; BOREDOM; OBJECT.

References

Blau, A. (1955). A unitary hypothesis of emotion. *PQ,* 24:75–103 (esp. 96–97).

Greenson, R. R. (1949). The psychology of apathy. *PQ,* 18:290–302.

■ APPLIED PSYCHOANALYSIS

Use of insights and concepts gained from clinical psychoanalysis to enlarge and deepen the understanding of various aspects of human nature, culture, and society. Most prominent have been studies in the fields of history, biography, literature, art, religion, mythology, and anthropology.

The distinction between clinical and applied psychoanalysis is not absolute since findings of clinical value have been contributed in papers focusing on applied psychoanalysis. A noteworthy example is Freud's (1911) celebrated study of paranoia based on the autobiography of Daniel Paul Schreber, an exercise in applied psychoanalysis that made a signal contribution to the understanding of certain clinical phenomena.

The application of psychoanalysis to biography and history has given rise to the terms *psychobiography* and *psychohistory,* which suggest an artificial and misleading compartmentalization in the recording of human history.

References

Freud, S. (1911). Psychoanalytic notes upon an autobiographical account of a case of paranoia. *SE,* 12:3–84.

Jones, E. (1934). Editorial preface to the *Collected Papers of Sigmund Freud,* 4. London: Hogarth Press.

Langer, W. (1958). The next assignment. *Amer. Imago,* 15:235–266.

Meyer, B. C. (1972). The contribution of psychoanalysis to biography. *Psychoanal. Contemp. Sci.,* 1:373–391.

■ ARCHAIC EGO STATES

The persistence into adult life of feelings attributable to the early stages of development of the ego. A common example is the "oceanic feeling," a description of which was provided to Freud (1930) by Romain Rolland. It is a feeling of something limitless, unbounded, an indissoluble bond between the self and the external world. Freud observed that this experience could be traced to the sense of connectedness and lack of differentiation between the young child and his or her mother, and he considered the possibility that it might contribute to religious sentiment. The experience of the "uncanny" can also be understood as an archaic ego state: Freud (1919) compared it to the return of what is old and familiar. He gives as examples coincidences that appear to confirm the belief in the omnipotence of thoughts, and belief in ghosts and "doubles." These beliefs are experienced as uncanny because they revive an early narcissistic stage of the ego that accepted animism. Some post-Freudian examples of archaic ego states include the persistence into adult life of transitional phenomena (Winnicott, 1953), certain states of creativity (Modell, 1970), the selfobject phenomena of Kohut (1971), and disturbances of the sense of time (Arlow, 1984). These states can be observed in daily life and more extensively in the transference experiences of neurotic and borderline patients.

See OCEANIC FEELING; SELF PSYCHOLOGY; WINNICOTT'S THEORY: Transitional Object, Transitional Phenomenon; Uncanny.

References
Arlow, J. A. (1984). Disturbances of the sense of time. *PQ*, 53:13–37.
Freud, S. (1919). The uncanny. *SE*, 17:217–252.
——— (1930). Civilization and its discontents. *SE*, 21:57–146.
Kohut, H. (1971). *The Analysis of the Self*. New York: Int. Univ. Press.
Modell, A. H. (1970). The transitional object and the creative act. *PQ*, 39:240–250.
Winnicott, D. W. (1953). Transitional objects and transitional phenomena. In *Collected Papers*. New York: Basic Books, 1958.

■ ARCHETYPE

See ANALYTICAL PSYCHOLOGY TERMS.

■ "AS-IF" PERSONALITY

Designates persons with severe personality disorders who create an illusion of conviction and involvement although they lack commitment to the thoughts and emotions they express. Absence of depth in emotional experience and a tendency to imitate are important features of this pattern. Originally thought to be a separate diagnostic entity occurring exclusively in women, the "as-if" personality has gradually gained a descriptive status, referring to traits or behavior that are part of a variety of disorders in men as well as in women—it can even be seen in normal adolescents. The initial description, published in 1934, drew attention to early disorders of development in object relations, identifications, and self-representations.

References
Deutsch, H. (1934). Some forms of emotional disturbance and their relationship to schizophrenia. *PQ*, 11:301–322, 1942.
Milrod, D. (1982). The wished-for self-image. *PSOC*, 37:95–120.
Panel (1966). Clinical and theoretical aspects of "as-if" characters. J. Weiss, reporter. *JAPA*, 14:569–590.
Reich, A. (1953). Narcissistic object choice in women. *JAPA*, 1:22–44.

■ ATTENTION CATHEXIS

See CATHEXIS; CONSCIOUS.

■ AUTISTIC PHASE

See SEPARATION-INDIVIDUATION.

■ AUTOEROTISM

In a broad sense, behavior through which an individual obtains sexual gratification from his or her own body. In Freud's (1905) definition the instinct's relationship to its object is the important element: "the instinct is not directed towards other people, but obtains satisfaction from the subject's own body" (p. 181). This implies the absence of a whole object (another person), but not necessarily an objectless state, since a fantasized part object (for example, a breast) is often involved. Moreover, the sexual drive may be detached from nonsexual functions that previously made the subject dependent on the object. For example, sucking becomes autoerotic when it no longer serves the function of alleviating hunger. Freud added that autoerotism is a form of infantile sexual behavior in which the activity of the different "component instincts" find both stimulation and satisfaction in the same site (an organ or erotogenic zone). Later he assumed that in narcissism the ego, as the unified image of the body, is the object of narcissistic libido. Autoerotism was then regarded as a developmental stage preceding this convergence of component instincts upon a common object. This view was based on the premise that a unity such as the ego could not exist from the start, while the autoerotic instincts are present from birth.

In 1905 Freud appeared to place the whole of infantile sexuality under the head of autoerotism, in contrast to adult sexuality, which involves an object choice. But this separation does not merely involve time; it also involves structural differentiation. "Autoerotism is not the attribute of a specific instinctual activity (oral, anal, etc.), but it is rather to be found in each such activity, both as an early phase and, in later development, as the component factor of organ-pleasure" (Laplanche and Pontalis, 1973, p. 47).

Autoerotism is now rarely used in the sense of a developmental concept; the term remains useful, however, because it can be associated with any of the instinctual activities (oral, anal, and so on) and because it refers to a characteristic found in both early and late developmental phases.

See COMPONENT INSTINCTS, INFANTILE SEXUALITY; MASTURBATION; NARCISSISM.

References

Freud, S. (1905). Three essays on the theory of sexuality. *SE,* 7:125–243.

——— (1915). Instincts and their vicissitudes. *SE,* 14:132–134.

Laplanche, J. & Pontalis, J.-B. (1973). *The Language of Psychoanalysis.* London: Hogarth Press.

■ AUTONOMY

The condition of being self-governing and independent. In the psychoanalytic framework the term refers to the relative freedom of ego functions from the influence of the drives and ensuing conflict, a concept introduced by Hartmann (1939). Several functions are relatively resistant to instinctual forces, among them perception, motility (walking, use of the hands, and so on), intention (planning, anticipation, purpose), intelligence, thinking, speech, and language. These functions are said to have *primary autonomy.* They develop relatively independent from the powerful forces of sexuality and aggressiveness, unlike such functions as object relations, defenses, and so on. But the relativity of such autonomy must be emphasized. Recent studies have shown, for instance, to what extent perceptual processes can be better understood if instinctual impulses and defensive operations are taken into account; perceived reality is not simply a mirror of a fixed external reality.

Forms of behavior that begin as defenses against instinctual drives but become free of such influences in the course of development are said to have *secondary autonomy.* An example is the individual who rebels against an authoritarian father to whom he unconsciously wishes to submit but in the course of development transforms his rebelliousness into constructive social criticism. The effective form his rebellion finally takes becomes emancipated from the passivity and reaction formation in which it was nourished.

See EGO; EGO FUNCTION.

References

Hartmann, H. (1939). *Ego Psychology and the Problem of Adaptation.* New York: Int. Univ. Press, 1958.

——— (1951). Technical implications of ego psychology. *PQ,* 20:31–43.

■ AUTOPLASTIC ADAPTATION

See ADAPTATION.

■ AVERAGE EXPECTABLE ENVIRONMENT

A concept introduced by Hartmann (1939) to refer to the condition in the "outer world" that will permit at least "average" physical and psychological development of an individual. Hartmann considered that in view of the infant's helplessness and total dependence on his or her objects, the unfolding of psychic structures requires an environmental situation that is appropriate to the needs of the individual. *Average expectable* implies a "fit" between the individual and the environment in contrast to an environment and/or a mother–child relationship that is abnormal, atypical, or unusually stressful. For the infant, the average expectable environment is first the average expectable or "good enough mother" (Winnicott, 1965). *Average* and *expectable* are relative terms. The variables for both individual and environment are infinite, but the worse the fit between the two, the more the pathology.

See ADAPTATION; DEVELOPMENT; WINNICOTT'S TERMS: Good Enough Mother.

References

Hartmann, H. (1939). *Ego Psychology and the Problem of Adaptation.* New York: Int. Univ. Press, 1958.

——— (1964). *Essays on Ego Psychology.* New York: Int. Univ. Press.

Winnicott, D. W. (1965). *The Maturational Processes and the Facilitating Environment.* New York: Int. Univ. Press.

■ AWE

A term used in two quite different senses. The first is illustrated by the figure of speech "to stand in awe of" another person. The second sense comprises incidents with a momentary overwhelming impact, typically associated with the outstanding size, beauty, or majesty of an artificial or natural wonder or of that which is perceived as supernatural. It is likely that both uses of the term have identical psychological origins. *Awe* signifying reverence tinged with fear is typified in analytic literature as *phallic awe,* which originates after the infant has gained a clear sense of his or own individuality and is momentarily overwhelmed, paradigmatically on witnessing the father's erect penis. A second signification of the word is the sense of *wonder,* traced back to early recognition, after individuation, of attributes of the mother's body, paradigmatically her breast and nipple. Moments of awe reflect marked regression with diffusion of ego boundaries. A sense of one's inclusiveness in cosmic space and time characterizes these experiences. Awe experiences in childhood and adolescence often have a profound and lasting impact and are associated with inspiration and creativity. They give rise to the feeling of humility that accompanies awareness of one's personal limitations in the face of the grandeur of nature, human achievement, and religious experience. Rituals of many kinds, including visits to shrines and scenic wonders, as well as attendance at great operatic and theatrical performances often give rise to awe, which leads to a sense of community among members of the group. Awe experiences characterized by dread, terror, or horror, with an uncanny quality, suggest the lasting impact of early infantile trauma. These feelings are abundantly illustrated in the short stories of Edgar Allan Poe.

References

Finkenstein, L. (1975). Awe and premature ejaculation. *PQ,* 44:2,232–252.

Greenacre, P. (1953). Penis awe and its relation to penis envy. In *Drives, Affects, Behavior,* ed. R. M. Loewenstein. New York: Int. Univ. Press, pp. 176–190.

——— (1956). Experiences of awe in childhood. *PSOC,* 11:9–30.

Harrison, I. B. (1975). On the maternal origins of awe. *PSOC,* 30:181–195.

■ BASIC ASSUMPTIONS

See BION'S THEORY.

■ BASIC ENDOPSYCHIC SITUATION

See FAIRBAIRN'S THEORY.

■ BASIC RULE

See FREE ASSOCIATION.

■ BEATING FANTASY

A fantasy of beating and being beaten, usually associated with sexual excitement and therefore with a variety of sadomasochistic fantasies. Such ideation may be a condition of excitement in masturbation, imagined during otherwise seemingly usual sexual intercourse, or manifestly enacted with a partner. The fantasizer may identify with either role or with both. Generally, the role of the beater is associated with unconscious wishful ideas of activity, phallic aggressivity, and masculinity. The role of the beaten exemplifies passivity and unconscious ideas of femininity.

In an important contribution to the study of perversion, "A Child Is Being Beaten," Freud (1919) described two classical patterns of such structuring. In girls the fantasy is preceded by a triumphant fantasy of a rival sibling being beaten by the father. However, the significant underlying unconscious fantasy in both sexes was understood to be derived from guilty incestuous wishes toward the father, which eventuate in conscious fantasies of a boy being beaten. In the case of girls, the oedipal picture eventuates in a thinly disguised father substitute beating the boy. In contrast, the underlying constellation in boys corresponds to that of the negative oedipus complex. Through a series of transformations, the mother or a mother figure is substituted for the father. Hence, in girls the masochistic attitude is primarily related to oedipal guilt, in boys to regressive feminine strivings.

See FANTASY; MASCULINITY/FEMININITY; OEDIPUS COMPLEX; SADOMASOCHISM.

References

Freud, S. (1919). "A child is being beaten." *SE,* 17:175–204.

——— (1924). The economic problem of masochism. *SE,* 19:157–172.

■ BEHAVIOR

Observable conduct or demeanor. A term in common use among psychoanalysts, but never specifically defined. It is closely related to *action* and at times they are used interchangeably, especially when behavior/action is being contrasted with thought or verbalization in a psychoanalytic process.

There are nuances of difference, however, which are inconsistently adhered to. At times, *behavior* seems to be a subset of *action,* with behavior defined as publicly observable phenomena, whereas action need not be. In other usages, *behavior* seems to be the whole, made up of the interplay of mental, verbal, and motor actions (Lagache, 1953).

Recognizing that there is considerable overlap between the meanings assigned to *behavior* and to *action,* they are differentiated essentially in that *behavior* is more consistently seen as observable, more complex or patterned, having duration, and likely to be repeated.

Psychoanalysts speak of *behavior disorders* and pathological behavior when observable disturbances of behavior are the prominent manifestations of pathology, whether the underlying cause is organic-physiological or psychogenic.

Behaviorism is a psychological theory which maintains that only observable events can be studied scientifically, in contrast to the psychoanalytic inferences about the inner life and the importance placed on introspection. *Behavior therapy* or *behavior modification* is a form of treatment, based on the principles of experimental psychology and learning theory, which attempts to change maladaptive behavior through techniques of conditioning. The focus is on changing observable behavior rather than on finding its underlying cause.

See ACTION.

References

Harre, R. and Lamb, R. (1983). *The Encyclopedic Dictionary of Psychology.* Cambridge: M.I.T. Press.

Lagache, D. (1953). Behavior and psychoanalytic experience. In *Drives, Affects, Behavior,* ed. R. Loewenstein. New York: Int. Univ. Press.

■ BEREAVEMENT

See GRIEF; MOURNING.

■ BETA ELEMENTS

See BION'S THEORY.

■ BION'S THEORY

Wilfred R. Bion was born in 1897 in Muttra, India, the son of a British civil servant from a family of Huguenot descent. He was educated in England from the age of eight. He started his psychoanalytic training in 1930 with John Rickman and continued later with Melanie Klein. Bion was president of the British Psychoanalytical Society from 1962 to 1965. In 1968 he moved to Los Angeles, where he practiced until his death in 1981. His main psychoanalytic contributions were in group psychology and psychotic thinking.

Bion described two behaviors present in every group, designating them the *Work Group* modality and the *Basic Assumptions* style. The Work Group defines its task, acknowledges its purpose, and promotes its members' cooperation. Bion's theory focuses on why groups often do not behave in the sensible way characteristic of the work modality. He distinguished three basic assumptions—*Dependency, Fight/Flight,* and *Pairing*—that represent different styles of group functioning, oriented not outward, toward reality, but inward, toward fantasy. These assumptions often interfere with the work task, but their energy can also be harnessed to serve the task. The Basic Assumptions represent a disowned part of the individual; they are consequently anonymous and so can function quite ruthlessly, which is why they are feared (Rioch, 1970).

Applying Kleinian analytic concepts to groups, Bion compared their situations to a regression to early stages of mental functioning in which psychosislike anxieties and primitive defenses against them—namely, projective identification and splitting—are reactivated (Ganzarain, 1980, 1988). Group regression destroys the group's capacity to symbolize and to communicate verbally. The more the group functions at the level of the Basic Assumptions, "the less it makes any rational use of verbal communication while nonverbal exchanges prevail . . . . groups would, in Freud's view, approximate to neurotic patterns of behavior, whereas in my view they would approximate to patterns of psychotic behavior" (Bion, 1961, p. 181). Bion tentatively formulated as an intermediary goal of psychoanalytic group psychotherapy to lay bare such psychotic patterns, while the "central goal [is] to work through the primitive group defenses (or Basic Assumptions) against the members' common psychotic anxieties, reactivated in the regressed transferential relationships in the group. He did not elaborate, however, a detailed account on how to reach this goal" (Ganzarain, 1988).

Bion also used Kleinian ideas to understand psychotic thinking, particularly the concepts of splitting and projective identification, which he saw as characteristic defenses of the "schizo-paranoid position." Hatred of reality, he said, can turn instinctive aggression inward, destroying the functions of perception, so that objective, external reality cannot be acknowledged accurately. Such self-destruction may also affect the ability to grasp emotional, subjective, intrapsychic reality. Hence the functions of the organs of the senses and of self-awareness become disorganized after being projected and split off in multiple minute fragments. Further, hostile attacks on linking conspire against integrative abilities, making elaboration or transformation of thought almost impossible and thereby limiting psychotic individuals to predominantly rudimentary, unintegrated, fragmentary thoughts.

Bion also studied the exchanges between analyst and patient, clarifying the way the analyst acts as a "container," intuitively understanding and transforming the patient's communications, including the latter's projected unconscious anxieties. How the analyst's mind works is explored in detail in Bion's book *Attention and Interpretation*.

□ Alpha Element

Mental data available for the concatenations of mental transformations, like intermediary ingredients of mental metabolism made suitable for mental functioning, such as in dreams, memory, emotions, and so on. Alpha elements comprise the ego's acceptance of the impact of sensory and emotional experience (that is, beta elements) as a result of alpha function.

□ Alpha Function

The process whereby the raw data of emotional experience (beta elements) are accepted by the mind and transformed into mental elements that are suitable for mental "digestion" (alpha elements), such as for feeling, thinking, dreaming, and so on. Alpha function includes much of what is meant by *primary process* but also includes some of the functions of secondary process, particularly insofar as it predicates the acceptance of the reality of the experience.

□ Beta Element

A piece of the sensory data of emotional events, either before the data have been accepted as experiences and then transformed (via alpha function) or an ingredient of preexperience which, though impacting the psyche, is denied entry and access to alpha functions and is therefore not transformed into a mental element. The beta elements are suitable only for unprocessed projective identification.

□ Container/Contained (♀ ♂)

A designation for the basis of any relationship between two or more people, whether infant and mother, man and woman, or individual and society. In the most basic model, the infant projects a part of his or her psyche, especially uncontrolled emotions, to be contained by the mother, who absorbs them, "translates" them into specific meanings, and acts upon them thoughtfully, the whole transaction resulting in a transformation of the infant's projective identifications into meaningful thought. The concept approximates Winnicott's *holding environment* and Kohut's *selfobjects*.

□ Preconception/Conception

The relationship between the anticipation of the arrival of an experience (for example, the breast) and its realization, in which case a conception has developed as a result of transformation of its preconception. Preconceptions may be either inherent (innate in the platonic sense) or acquired from previous experience.

□ Reverie

The attitude the mother adopts in order to be a suitable container for her infant's projections, which, until absorbed by the maternal container, constitute a "nameless dread." The state of reverie closely approximates Winnicott's "primary maternal preoccupation."

References

Bion, W. R. (1961). *Experiences in Groups*. London: Tavistock.

——— (1962). A theory of thinking. *IJP*, 40:306–310.

——— (1962). *Learning from Experience*. London: William Heinemann.

——— (1963). *Elements of Psycho-Analysis*. London: William Heinemann.

——— (1965). *Transformations*. London: William Heinemann.

——— (1970). *Attention and Interpretation*. London: Tavistock.

——— (1985). *All My Sins Remembered*, ed. Francesca Bion. Abingdon: Fleetwood Press.

Ganzarain, R. (1980). Psychotic-like anxieties and primitive defenses. *Issues on Ego Psychology*, 3(2):42–48.

——— (1988). A comparative study of Bion's concepts about groups. In *Object Relations Group Psychotherapy*. Madison, Ct.: Int. Univ. Press.

Grinberg, L., Sor, D. & Tabak de Bianchedi, E. (1975). *Introduction to the Work of Bion*, trans. A. Hahn. Scotland: Clunie Press.

Rioch, M. (1970). The work of W. R. Bion on groups. *Psychiatry*, 33:56–66.

■ BIPOLAR DISORDER

See AFFECTIVE DISORDERS.

■ BIPOLAR SELF

See SELF PSYCHOLOGY; THERAPEUTIC AIM.

■ BISEXUALITY

(1) A universal human mental disposition, and (2) actual sexual behavior. Through identification with both parental objects, every human being has the potential, to a greater or lesser degree, to invest libidinally in both sexes. By adulthood one component tends to be largely unconscious and a relatively exclusive hetero- or homosexual orientation has evolved. Bisexual men and women do not deal with sexual anxieties by repression, and so alternate hetero- and homosexual behavior. Although the frequency of each type of sexual contact may vary, homosexual erotism is often predominant.

Two patterns of bisexual behavior are common. In one, the individual sustains a heterosexual relationship, including marriage and children, for the reproductive and social benefits while meeting erotic needs via homosexual congress. In the other pattern the individual pursues a homosexual lifestyle, which he or she finds libidinally satisfying, but occasionally seeks a heterosexual outlet to replenish self-esteem.

In general, bisexual psychopathology may be arranged along ego strength and object relations gradients. At one end of the spectrum, bisexuality reflects problems of primitive self-demarcation; fluid gender and sexual identities give rise to what is essentially a polymorphous selection of sexual partners. At the other end of the spectrum are patients with relatively sound body images and self representations whose needs—such as exculpation of guilt, counterphobic defenses against castration anxiety, replenishment of self-esteem—require sexual union with both sexes. Bisexual behavior is therefore encountered in a variety of conditions ranging from the neurotic to borderline and psychotic.

See HETEROSEXUALITY; HOMOSEXUALITY.

References

Meyer, J. (1985). Ego-dystonic homosexuality. In *Comprehensive Textbook of Psychiatry,* 4th ed., ed. H. Kaplan & B. Sadock. Baltimore: Williams & Wilkins, pp. 1056–1065.

Stoller, R. (1972). The "bedrock" of masculinity and femininity: bisexuality. *Arch. Gen. Psychiat.,* 26:207–212.

■ BODY EGO
□ Body Image
□ Body Schema

In the beginning of his theory building Freud referred to the early stages of the ego as largely made up of a body ego. This was during the period before the structural theory (1923). At this time his use of the term *ego* varied, sometimes referring to the individual, sometimes to a psychic organization or structure, and sometimes to what would now be called the self (Hartmann, 1964). Currently the ego is regarded as one of the structures of the psychic apparatus, characterized by various functions and having important contents or substructures, among them self and object representations. In the early stages of ego development the first elements of self representation are laid down within the ego, and these first impressionistic images of the self, as opposed to the nonself, are inevitably based on the individual's body. Freud was referring to these primordial physical elements in the early stages of formation of self representation when he spoke of a *body ego.* Most of the infant's attention is focused on nursing, the search for pleasurable gratification, and the avoidance of unpleasure (hunger). Consequently the mouth (through its sucking function) becomes the earliest important nucleus of the beginning self representation, to which quickly are added the hand (touching, grasping) and the eye (looking) (Hoffer, 1949). A definite *schema* or pattern of the *body image* unfolds over time as the child and the ego develop. From a body image largely made up of mouth, hand, eye, and head, the body gradually becomes filled out, as it is influenced by the phases of libidinal development. Locomotion and the erect posture add new structure and functions, and gradually the mouth and head recede in importance physiologically and psychologically. Eventually, during the oedipal phase and later at puberty, the genital organs become more highly cathected and supplant in prominence the other aspects of the body image. The body schema therefore changes in relation to maturational and developmental forces.

The terms *body ego, image,* or *schema* artificially separate out from the total self representation one narrow aspect, namely, that dealing with the mental representation of the body and its functions. In developmental terms, the body is where self representation begins; but it gradually develops into a representation of the entire psychophysiological self with the past, the present, the drives, the ego and its functions, and eventually the superego forces included (Jacobson, 1964).

See EGO; REPRESENTATION; SELF.

References
Hartmann, H. (1964). The development of the ego concept in Freud's work. *IJP*, 37:425.
Hoffer, W. (1949). Mouth, hand, and ego integration. *PSOC*, 3/4:49–56.
Jacobson, E. (1964). *The Self and the Object World.* New York: Int. Univ. Press.

■ BORDERLINE PERSONALITY DISORDER
□ Borderline Personality Organization
□ Borderline State

Borderline states are positions or way stations in the process of decompensation from a nonpsychotic to a psychotic state, or in the process of regression from a neurotic to a psychotic level of psychic organization. The term might be used, for example, to describe a patient who no longer appears neurotic but is not yet floridly schizophrenic. In this sense it was introduced by Robert Knight in 1953.

The term *borderline personality* encompasses two different but overlapping concepts. *Borderline personality disorder* is a descriptive phenomenological concept which refers to a discrete psychiatric syndrome—a micropsychotic episode, transient, reversible, and ego-dystonic, characterized by diffuse impulsivity, chronic anger, unstable interpersonal relationships, identity disturbances, frequent feelings of boredom and emptiness, and a tendency toward self-damaging acts. *Borderline personality organization* (as defined by Kernberg, 1967), on the other hand, is a much broader concept. It refers to a character structure that shows (1) basically intact reality testing; (2) persistence of contradictory early identifications in an unsynthesized framework leading to lack of an integrated ego identity (this may show up in contradictory character traits, temporal discontinuity of the self experience, lack of authenticity, gender dysphoria, and vulnerability to the subjective experience of emptiness); (3) predominance of splitting (often buttressed by denial and various projective mechanisms) over repression as the ego's customary manner of handling ambivalence; and finally (4) a fixation on the rapprochement phase of separation-individuation with a resultant instability of the self concept, lack of object constancy, overdependence on external objects, inability to tolerate ambivalence, and a marked preoedipal influence on the oedipus complex.

The two concepts are on different levels of abstraction. The first designates a nosological syndrome, while the second has developmental and structural implications. But the two concepts definitely overlap. A borderline personality organization underlies all cases of borderline personality disorder. There are, however, other descriptive personality syndromes that also have an underlying borderline personality organization. These include narcissistic, schizoid, and antisocial character disorders as well as certain cases of substance abuse, alcoholism, and sexual perversion.

In a more descriptive framework, borderline personality organization pertains to an individual whose manifestly unstable behavior belies his or her apparently more stable underlying character structure. Individuals with this diagnosis lead somewhat chaotic lives; they find it difficult to tolerate being alone; they are impulsive, nonreflective, and self-preoccupied. They do not clearly distinguish themselves from others and use others to rid themselves of bad feelings or to gratify wishes to feel entirely good. They also allow themselves to be used by others. Repetitive frustration, rather than success, is the usual outcome, followed by rage and despair. Borderline individuals utilize projection and introjection extensively as defenses and demonstrate feelings and attitudes of hostility and rejection. Psychotic phenomena, both paranoid and delusional, are intermittently evident. These patients seem to lack integration of identity and personality; they frequently talk and act in a self-contradictory manner.

Considerable theoretical controversy exists about how best to conceptualize borderline personality organization. Disagreement centers on whether the condition is the result of conflict and defense (as in psychoneurosis), developmental arrest due to inadequate object relationships, or developmental deviation based on adaptation to pathological primary objects. Kernberg's original formulation employs the traditional model of psychoneurosis but relies heavily on the theories of Melanie Klein, especially with regard to the defenses of splitting and projective identification in conflicts involving the aggressive drive. British object relations theorists, whose ideas also derive from Klein, use the term *schizoid personality* to designate a similar personality structure. Self psychologists claim that the borderline individual lacks a cohesive self and is therefore incapable of forming even the most primitive kind of transference. Traditionally oriented analysts view patients with such conditions as polyneurotic personalities with conflicts and symptoms from multiple developmental levels, perhaps compounded by structural defects.

The diagnosis of borderline personality is easier to make in an extended therapeutic or analytic relationship than in a single interview situation. However, in most circumstances it is difficult, if not impossible, to treat borderline individuals by classical psychoanalytic technique (even with parameters) because, among other problems presented, they demand gratification and prefer action over the verbalization, reflection, and understanding that characterize psychoanalysis.

See CHARACTER; PSYCHONEUROSIS; PSYCHOSIS; SCHIZOID CHARACTER.

References

Abend, S. M., Porder, M. S. & Willick, M. S. (1983). *Borderline Patients*. New York: Int. Univ. Press.
Akhtar, S. (1984). The syndrome of identity diffusion. *Amer. J. Psychiat.*, 141:1381–1385.
Kernberg, O. F. (1967). Borderline personality organization. *JAPA*, 15:641–685.
_______ (1975). *Borderline Conditions and Pathological Narcissism*. New York: Jason Aronson.
Knight, R. (1953). Borderline states. *Bull. Menn. Clin.*, 17:1–12.
Mahler, M. S. (1979). *Selected Papers of Margaret S. Mahler*, vol. 2. New York: Jason Aronson.
Stone, M. H. (1980). *Borderline Syndromes*. New York: McGraw Hill.

■ BOREDOM

A painful affective state characterized by diffuse tension, restlessness, and feelings of dissatisfaction. It tends to occur in situations the individual experiences as monotonous and lacking in gratification or stimulation; this may reflect the actual circumstances of the situation or the personality structure and needs of the individual involved. Boredom has been interpreted as arising from a defensive struggle against unacceptable fantasies and impulses in which the ideational content of the impulse is repressed but the tension achieves affective representation. However, a developmental predisposition undoubtedly exists; children and other people with passive and "field dependent" character styles appear particularly susceptible to boredom.

See AFFECTS; APATHY.

References

Esman, A. (1979). Some reflections on boredom. *JAPA*, 27:423–439.
Fenichel, O. (1934). On the psychology of boredom. *Collected Papers*. New York: Norton, 1953, vol. 1, pp. 293–302.
Wangh, M. (1979). Some psychoanalytic observations on boredom. *IJP*, 60:515–527.

■ BOUND ENERGY

See PSYCHIC ENERGY.

■ BREAST ENVY

Discontent with one's own body and covetousness toward the female breast—either its possession, its size, or its content (milk). Both boys and girls experience breast envy, but it is more widespread and intense in boys. In either sex an early determinant may be fixation upon, or regression to, early oral wishes for the mother's breast and feelings of deprivation associated with its loss through weaning. Breast envy is further conditioned by the oedipal and castration complexes characteristic of each sex. In a girl it may express feelings of inadequacy deriving from her lack of a penis (this lack is experienced unconsciously as castration and is displaced from the genitals to the breasts), or it may reflect envy of mother's adult female attributes, which give her an advantage in the oedipal rivalry. In boys and men, it can be a male counterpart to penis envy, one of the consequences of the "small penis complex," which is also a derivative of castration anxiety.

Through the equation of the breast with the penis, breast envy can represent one aspect of the unconscious fantasy of a phallic woman, serving to deny the danger of castration suggested by observation of the female lack of a penis. Such fantasies are ubiquitous, but they are particularly prominent in the psychodynamics and pathology of the perversions. For some boys the breast may play the role of the fetish, which unconsciously represents the female penis.

Kleinian theory attaches even greater significance to the breast and breast envy in normative development and pathology.

See CASTRATION; KLEINIAN THEORY: Envy; PENIS ENVY; PERVERSION; PHALLUS.

References

Bak, R. C. (1953). Fetishism. *JAPA*, 1:285–298.
Boehm, F. (1930). The femininity-complex in men. *IJP*, 11:444–469.
Freud, S. (1927). Fetishism. *SE*, 21:152–157.

■ BULIMIA

See ANOREXIA NERVOSA.

■ CASTRATION

□ Castration Anxiety

□ Castration Complex

Although most dictionaries define *castration* as deprivation of the testicles (or ovaries), Freud (1923) noted, "It is remarkable . . . what a small degree of attention the other part of the male genitals, the little sac with its contents, attracts in children. From all one hears in analyses, one would not guess that the male genitals consisted of anything more than the penis" (p. 142). More recently, however, Anita Bell (1961) has described a complex associated with absence, loss, or fear of injury to the testicles. In general psychoanalytic usage, therefore, *castration* refers to real or fantasized loss of or injury to the genitals of either sex, but more specifically to loss of the parts where the most sexual pleasure is experienced—the penis and the clitoris. Castration may be symbolically expressed in many ways.

From the time of an early genital phase at about sixteen to twenty-four months (Roiphe, 1968), attention becomes focused on the genitals and the differences between the sexes. Beginning at about two and a half years, sexual excitement becomes concentrated in the genitals concomitant with the development of the oedipus complex, and genital masturbation acquires major significance. One of Freud's crucial discoveries was the universality of the unconscious fantasy that women are castrated and inferior since they do not possess the phallus. Castration, associated with the idea of forbidden wishes, takes on the meaning of punishment; fear of losing the penis is the source of *castration anxiety*. Such anxiety is an integral part of oedipal fantasies and together with the associated ideas and emotions constitute the *castration complex*. Boys' castration anxiety is focused on the penis; girls fear having their genitals penetrated, torn, or otherwise injured. The girl may develop the fantasy that she has already been castrated because she lacks a penis; penis envy characterizes the female castration complex. Penis envy is not simply a wish to have a penis; it has significant defensive and reactive aspects. Restitutive fantasies may include what is essentially an illusory penis.

Though there are important oral and anal precursor anxieties, the castration complex should be confined to the excitations and consequences bound up with the genitals in both sexes. In adults, fears of genital injury are usually displaced to other parts of the body—an exaggerated fear of loss of, injury to, or penetration of any part of the body is based to some degree on castration anxiety. Severe castration anxiety may lead in both sexes to narcissistic overestimation of the phallus and may interfere with independence, autonomy, and healthy pride in masculinity and femininity.

See ANXIETY; FANTASY; GENITALITY; PENIS ENVY.

References

Bell, A. (1961). Some observations on the role of the scrotal sac and testicles. *JAPA*, 9:261–286.

Blum, H. P. (1976). Masochism, the ego ideal and the psychology of women. *JAPA*, 24 (suppl.):157–192.

Clower, V. (1975). Significance of masturbation in female sexual development and function. In *Masturbation from Infancy to Senescence*, ed. I. Marcus & J. Francis. New York: Int. Univ. Press, pp. 107–143.

Freud, S. (1923). The infantile genital organization. *SE*, 19:141–145.

——— (1925). Some psychical consequences of the anatomical distinction between the sexes. *SE*, 19:248–258.

Lerner, H. E. (1976). Parental mislabeling of female genitals as a determinant of penis envy and learning inhibitions in women. *JAPA*, 24 (suppl):269–284.

Nunberg, H. (1955). *Principles of Psychoanalysis*. New York: Int. Univ. Press.

Roiphe, H. (1968). On an early genital phase. *PSOC*, 23:348–365.

■ CATHEXIS

A term derived from Greek, invented by the English translators of the *Standard Edition* to render *Besetzung*, an everyday German word that has no English equivalent, although "occupation" comes close. Although Freud never defined *Besetzung*, he used it in formulating a concept of mental energy capable of increase, diminution, displacement, and discharge, which may be spread over the memory traces of ideas somewhat as an electric charge is spread over the surface of a body. This is a metaphorical quantitative conception and does not refer to any actual measurable force; rather, it represents the relative intensity of unconscious mental activities. Thus *cathexis* means interest, attention, or emotional investment. *Libidinal cathexis* specifies taking an erotic interest in a specific person or item.

Freud used descriptive images quite differently in various contexts, and though his figures of speech were vivid and clear, the editors of the English edition of his works apparently thought that the inconsistency of his terminology was unscientific. They apparently felt that the terms of a science should be standardized and distinct from everyday language. Freud's English editors also sought to reconcile and integrate the various terms. They made *cathexis*, *cathectic energy*, and *psychic energy* into synonyms, saw *anticathexis* or *countercathexis* as one way of introducing psychic conflict into the quantitative metaphor, and defined *withdrawal of cathexis* or *decathexis* as detachment of interest, attention, emotional involvement, or energy from one person or problem so that it can be reinvested in oneself or in another area.

Free cathexis refers to relatively raw kinds of energy or nascent abilities, similar to what Freud called *drive components* involved in primary processes. During human development many immediate desires are frustrated and one must make increasingly differentiated compromises. Fantasy, language, and thinking emerge from such adjustments. Some analysts describe a person's specific areas of interest or attention to a certain activity as *bound* rather than *free*. Thus an enduring love for a steady partner is bound as compared to the intense but momentary loving feelings attributed in the past to the newborn infant.

When several different impulses or needs contribute to the development of a single common interest—for example, if erotic love, jealous hate, fear of guilt, pride in mastery, and driven curiosity combine to motivate watching over a toddler's safety—some analysts describe the vigilant attention as due to *hypercathexis* (*Überbesetzung*). Here, activity stemming from several sources takes on an overdetermined psychological organization that integrates or even sublimates the elements.

Current research has begun to clarify some differences between Freud's own flexible conceptions and others' later attempts at precise metapsychological accounts often based on Strachey's edition of Freud's works. The validity of the economic viewpoint has been increasingly brought into question, especially since so many kinds of cathexis or energy have been described. Those who still use these terms often imply that they are making a relative description or rough comparison of one or another kind of interest or investment. Current usage has therefore come to resemble Freud's plain German metaphor.

See INSTINCTUAL DRIVE; LIBIDO THEORY; METAPSYCHOLOGY; PSYCHIC ENERGY.

References

Freud, S. (1915). Das Unbewuste. *Gesammelte Werke*, 10:264–303.

Kubie, L. S. (1947). The fallacious use of quantitative concepts in dynamic psychology. *PQ*, 16:507–518.

Ornston, D. G. (1982). Strachey's influence. *IJP*, 63:409–426.

Strachey, J. (1962). The emergence of Freud's fundamental hypotheses. *SE*, 3:62–68.

■ CENTRAL EGO

See FAIRBAIRN'S THEORY.

■ CHANGE OF FUNCTION

A behavior form that originates in one context early in life may, in the course of development, appear in an entirely different context and serve a different function. Thus a means (for example, a defense in the form of a reaction formation such as an altruistic attitude) may become fixated and turn into a goal in its own right (Hartmann, 1939). In a developmental sense the term refers to any progression from more primitive and instinctual behaviors and organizations to more mature or socially accepted, age-appropriate ones.

The term *sublimation* has been applied when instinctualized behavior (that is, behavior charged with libidinal or aggressive energy) changes to less primitive and more controlled, socially adaptive forms (especially when displacement in aim is involved). The energies are said to be transformed and redirected into areas that are relatively autonomous and conflict-free, especially into creative efforts. The concept of sublimation presents many theoretical problems that do not, however, affect the validity of change of function.

See GENETIC FALLACY; PSYCHIC ENERGY; SUBLIMATION.

References

Hartmann, H. (1939). *Ego Psychology and the Problem of Adaptation*. New York: Int. Univ. Press, 1958.

Kaywin, L. (1966). Problems of sublimation. *JAPA*, 14:313–334.

■ CHARACTER

The enduring, patterned functioning of an individual. As perceived by others, it is the person's habitual way of thinking, feeling, and acting. Understood psychodynamically, character is the person's habitual mode of reconciling intrapsychic conflicts. Character stands beside, but may be differentiated from, other terms for global aspects of personality, such as *identity, self*, and *ego*.

A person's character is made up of an integrated constellation of *character traits*, each a complex admixture of drive derivatives, defenses, and superego components. Character traits, like neurotic symptoms, are compromise formations. But character traits are more stable than symptoms, are better able to bind anxiety, and are experienced more as part of one's self (ego-syntonic). Character traits can be thought of as behavioral patterns that develop over time as the result of an attempt at resolution of intrapsychic conflict. Character is most closely related to the concept of an individual's defensive style.

Character organization, a somewhat more abstract term than *character trait,* is primarily a descriptive entity, an outside observer's synthesis of the traits he or she infers from the person's behavior and attitudes. *Character organization* is more concrete and less metaphorical than the term *ego,* however; and therefore it does not occupy a place in the metapsychological tripartite model of the mind. The term is useful in clinical discourse, but it has little explanatory specificity.

Character formation is a developmental process, not unlike some aspects of ego development, whereby stable patterns of thinking, feeling, and acting are consolidated as compromise formations, coming to represent some measure of resolution of the intrapsychic struggle between drive impulses and the various inhibiting, modifying, and gratifying forces. The manner in which the ego admits, repels, or modifies instinctual demands is influenced by the developing child's environment. The environment (initially the parents) enforces specific frustrations, blocks certain modes of reaction to these frustrations, and facilitates others, suggesting ways of dealing with the conflicts between instinctual demands and fear of further frustrations. Furthermore, through the identifications and the values and ideals that evolve as the oedipal conflict is resolved (the process of ego-ideal and superego formation), the environment even creates desires by setting up specific goals; and it influences the values the individual attaches to particular ways of adjusting inner need to external reality. The parents serve as models for ego development and ego-ideal and superego formation through the processes of introjection and identification. How a person's developing character is affected by his or her parents depends upon the stage of development at which crucial situations involving trauma and conflict arise. It also depends upon whether the child adopts the parents' affirming or prohibiting attitudes and whether he or she seeks to be like or unlike the parents. Inborn potentialities, including a disproportion between the sexual and the aggressive drives, as well as other genetic and dynamic factors, help determine whether conflicts are solved by reality-adjusted, well-integrated, and flexible behavior; or, in contrast, whether fixation and regression influence a neurotic compromise resulting in overt symptomatology or the inflexible behavior of pathological character traits.

Although not all of character is the result of conflict, most analytic work deals with traits that are the outcome of intrapsychic conflict. There is some disagreement about when character formation begins. There are differences among newborns, but it has been difficult to predict which traits endure as part of the individual's stable mental structure. New infant-observation studies continue to clarify the understanding of development. One could say that character formation starts in utero, but that a stable character organization does not really emerge until the resolution of the oedipal conflict and the formation of a discrete, organized superego. This process is largely completed during the individuation and remolding processes of adolescence. But later life events, both positive and negative, can still have significant modifying effects on an individual's character.

Character disorders are a heterogeneous group of pathological character disturbances involving habitual inflexibility of behavior patterns without marked subjective discomfort. Whereas persons with neurotic symptoms themselves complain, in cases of character disorder it is usually the person's family, friends, and work associates who complain. Neurosis involves discrete symptoms, but in character disorder the entire personality is usually affected, especially those ego functions determining frustration tolerance, drive regulation, affective responses, and object relationships. The closely related term *character neurosis* was more often used in the past in referring to these "asymptomatic neuroses." The similarities between character disorders and psychoneuroses are further evidenced by the use of the same name for the character type and the corresponding symptomatic neurosis: for example, obsessional character, phobic character.

Individuals with character disorders have resolved intrapsychic conflict through the formation of stable reaction patterns that either permit partial gratification of instinctual wishes under limiting conditions or necessitate total renunciation of instinct and result in severe inhibitions in work and play. These rigid character formations are required to maintain a constant defense against instinctual impulses and the affects connected with them, such as anxiety, guilt, anger, depression, and humiliation. The need for love, security, enhancement of self-esteem, or the satisfaction of passive longings may also be involved. The typical reactions may be elicited only by certain situations, or the attitudes may be nonspecific and indiscriminately exhibited toward anyone at any time. The individual's rationalization of his or her motives and idealization of his or her behavior may obscure the underlying pathology of the attitudes, traits, and reaction patterns. The total result may be adaptive and may secure important realistic gains for the individual, so that he or she sees the behavior as justified, reasonable, appropriate, and consciously determined. Because character disorders are usually ego-syntonic (unlike neurotic symptoms), the individual is little motivated to change. The character may permit sufficient satisfaction of instinctual needs without guilt or anxiety, and the individual's behavior may be less troublesome for him- or herself than for others. However, people with character disorders betray themselves by their chronic fatigue and dissatisfaction with life, by their specific or generalized inhibitions, by the cramped and rigid nature of their adaptations, or by the occasional breaking through of warded-off impulses directly or in distorted form. If the individual repeatedly feels the personal and social consequences of his or her actions, he or she may seek treatment.

Analysis of the character distortions is necessary for change to take place, but such analysis leads to anxiety and strong resistance before the individual can recognize the nature of the instinctual impulses and reconstruct the childhood situations that provided a genetic basis for intrapsychic conflict. When anxiety is aroused, a phase of neurotic symptomatology may precede successful resolution of the conflicts.

The treatment of character disorders is often long and complicated. The character resistances must be brought into the analytic process as transference resistances in order for interpretation to be effective. This often requires active confrontation from the analyst, because the analysand tends not to see his or her character traits as the problem. This process is sometimes referred to as *character analysis*, although the term is less often used now that most analyses are considered to involve the analysis of the stable patterns which make up character.

The classification of character traits and disorders into *character types* has not been satisfactorily resolved. Confusion results from the mixing of terms that derive from different levels of abstraction. They may be listed according to the libidinal phase involved (e.g., anal character), the defenses expressed (e.g., compulsive character), or the behaviors exhibited (e.g., passive-aggressive character). Character types are loose descriptive entities, having no inherent explanatory value but useful nevertheless for conceptualizing patterns of psychopathology. Character disturbance does not occupy a well-defined place on the line between health and pathology. For example, some narcissistic character traits, indicative of severe pathology, may not interfere with adaptation within a particular individual's chosen milieu; whereas traits of shyness or feelings of inferiority, based on much higher-level conflicts, may cripple a person. Abnormality is an ambiguous concept when it comes to character traits, because it requires consideration of the sociocultural setting in which the given behavior occurs. Both internal factors (for example, the flexibility of the trait) and external ones must be considered. Adaptation is not identical with conforming behavior. Sometimes rebellion is a sign of overall strength and autonomy.

Specific character types will be discussed separately, but several are mentioned briefly here as examples. Seemingly contradictory character traits may arise in the same person depending on which part of the compromise formation is being expressed. For example, *oral characters* may exhibit either optimism and self-assurance or depression and hostile dependency, according to whether a gratified or a frustrated oral need is being expressed. Such persons may induce others to take care of them by behaving passively, or they may exhibit cannibalistic aggressive voraciousness. They may be generous, as an identification with the feeding mother, or ungenerous, out of an identification with a frustrating mother.

Whereas the character traits developed from conflicts in the oral phase seem more or less defined by their need-satisfying function, those arising during the anal phase are more readily identified by their defensive pattern. The *compulsive character,* roughly equivalent to one form of the *anal character,* is described in terms of a set of characteristics that result from defensive reaction formations. Typically these include orderliness, parsimony, and perfectionistic strivings. *Urethral characters* are described as ambitious, competitive, and prone to shame. *Phallic-narcissistic* characters tend to be reckless (counterphobic), self-assured, and exhibitionistic. The *genital character,* a psychoanalytic concept of the ideal level of psychosexual development, is a person who has achieved the full primacy of genitality in psychosexual development, has resolved the oedipal complex, and is capable of postambivalent object love.

Character traits that derive from reaction formations or phobic avoidance block instinctual gratification. Character traits in which the predominant defensive mode is sublimation allow some aim-inhibited and adaptive gratification and are viewed as more or less normal. Thus, according to one view, the aim of character analysis is to replace reactive character traits with sublimatory ones.

In addition to character types described on the basis of libidinal phases and defenses, some typological terms primarily describe pathological constellations, including those derived from the partial instincts. This group includes the as-if, borderline, depressive, histrionic, masochistic, narcissistic, neurotic, paranoid, phobic, psychotic, sadistic, schizoid, schizotypal, and sociopathic characters. Finally, there are several character types that do not fit into such classifications but are known by such descriptive terms as "the exceptions," "those wrecked by success," and the related "fate neurosis."

See character types mentioned above. See also COMPROMISE FORMATION; DEFENSE; DEVELOPMENT; EGO-ALIEN; IDENTITY; LIBIDO THEORY; SELF; STRUCTURAL THEORY; SYMPTOM.

References

Abraham, K. (1921). Contributions to the theory of the anal character. *Selected Papers*. New York: Basic Books, 1953, pp. 307–392.

——— (1924). The influence of oral erotism on character formation. *Ibid.*, pp. 393–406.

Baudry, F. Character. *PMC*. Forthcoming.

——— (1983). The evolution of the concept of character in Freud's writings. *JAPA*, 31:3–31.

Fenichel, O. (1945). Character disorders. In *The Psychoanalytic Theory of the Neurosis*. New York: Norton, pp. 463–540.

Freud, S. (1908). Character and anal erotism. *SE*, 9:167–176.

——— (1916). Some character types met with in psychoanalytic work. *SE*, 16:309–337.

——— (1931). Libidinal types. *SE*, 21:215–222.

Panel (1983). Clinical aspects of character. M. Willick, reporter. *JAPA*, 31:225–236.

Panel (1983). Theory of character. S. M. Abend, reporter. *JAPA*, 31:211–224.

Reich, W. (1933). *Character Analysis*. New York: Orgone Press, 1949.

■ CHILD ANALYSIS

Treatment aimed at the internal revision of psychic structure and function. Its method is based on the same concepts and principles as adult analysis: an overall emphasis on the patient's intrapsychic life entailing interpretation of resistance, defense and transference, reconstruction and working through. The child analyst also avoids, insofar as possible, the promotion of gratification and advice, including intervention in the patient's environment.

The techniques of child analysis, although designed for compatibility with the analytic method, are adapted to the level of ego development the child has attained. They are based on considerations of the child's ability to free-associate, cognitive development, modes of communication, and the vulnerabilities attendant on a relatively immature ego. Caution is required in dealing with defenses and assessing the child's degree of tolerance for frustration; the analyst must underscore the ego aspect when addressing areas of conflict so as to appear as an ally in combating the forces of the id and to augment the reinternalization of externalized conflicts. He or she must attend to, and verbalize, the child's feeling states, whether these are expressed directly or through play characters and stories. These adaptations of technique are not to be confused with modifications (or parameters) of technique which may obstruct or disrupt the analytic process.

Intimately connected with the question of variations in technique between child and adult analysis are some of the conditions under which child analysis takes place. The child is still dependent on his or her parents, who decide whether he or she should undertake analysis. The preadolescent child may enter treatment under protest. In addition, most child analysts have some regular, continuing contact with the parents of the prelatency and latency-age child and obtain information through this contact. Caution is required lest this extra-analytic information prejudice understanding of the analytic material at hand. Although even young latency-age children can often provide the necessary material for the analysis, to exclude the parents from the treatment situation would be tantamount to neglect of the child's developmental needs—the younger he or she is, the more he or she needs to feel that the parents are in accord with the analysis. Equally important is the need to preserve the parents' alliance in order to maintain the child's analysis in the face of his or her own resistance. Nonetheless, with advances in ego development and the concomitantly greater stability of the therapeutic alliance, child analysts have learned that they can count increasingly on the older child to maintain the analysis.

Transference plays an important role in child analysis, although it is not the equivalent of transference in adult analysis. The parents—that is, the original objects, with whom the child's infantile relationships were formed, and around whom his or her infantile fantasies were woven—are still very much a part of the child's life. Coupled with this is the fact that the child's ego structure lacks the cohesiveness of the adult's; thus the processes of internalization are not so stable. Intensity and duration of transference manifestations vary, however, not only from child to child but also in the same child during different phases of analysis. The frequency of alternating cathectic shifts between analyst and parents also varies. Likewise, although there is fairly general agreement that the child may form a transference neurosis, it is usually more sporadic and of shorter duration than its adult counterpart.

Inasmuch as the techniques of child analysis are determined by the child's developmental level, it is clear that as he or she advances these techniques change. The child analyst moves progressively from a predominant use of play to verbalization and finally to free association proper. Interpretations move from the simple and concrete to higher levels of conceptualization. Their timing and content are influenced by the changing character of specific areas of conflict and special sensitivities as one developmental phase merges into the next. As the child analyst deals with successive stages of development, he or she can observe transitions and make appropriate technical adaptations. At adolescence certain aspects of adult techniques are combined with techniques utilized with preadolescent patients. For late adolescents (college age), the techniques in general are those of adult analysis.

References

Harley, M. (1967). Transference develoments in a five-year-old child. In *The Child Analyst at Work,* ed. E. Geleerd. New York: Int. Univ. Press, pp. 115–141.

——— (1986). Child analysis, 1947–1984, a retrospective. *PSOC,* 41:129–153.

Sandler, J., Kennedy, H. & Tyson, R. L. (1980). *The Technique of Child Psychoanalysis.* Cambridge: Harvard Univ. Press.

■ CHILDHOOD NEUROSIS

A psychological disorder of childhood in which the immature ego resolves intrapsychic conflicts via pathological compromise formations that interfere with normal development. The visible components of the compromise formations are disturbances in affect, behavior, or cognition. Symptoms or symptomatic behavior may consist of anxiety, depression, phobias, inhibitions, hysterical paralyses, tics, rituals, and other obsessions; or they may manifest in eating or excretory problems, antisocial behavior, learning disabilities, and so on. Commonly there is a cluster of symptoms, sometimes with one dominating the complex clinical picture. The disorder may appear any time between the development of internal psychic structures and the onset of puberty. Although the unconscious conflicts and fantasies in a childhood neurosis are organized and structured around sexual and aggressive impulses in the oedipal phase, the psychopathology bears witness to developmental interferences and conflicts from the preoedipal period.

In children, although the manifest symptomatology of neurosis may resemble that of adult neurosis, the underlying conflicts and personality organization are often quite different. Conversely, the same constellation of intrapsychic conflicts in children and adults may lead to different symptoms. The immaturity of the child's ego functions, tendency toward action rather than reflection, and continuing dependence of intrapsychic functioning on the objects toward whom the conflictual impulses were originally directed contribute to this difference. For example, it is not uncommon for a neurotic child with phobic symptoms to develop obsessive-compulsive symptomatology in adolescence or adulthood. In addition, what may appear to be a severe obsessional neurosis in childhood may develop into psychotic or borderline pathology in later life.

Childhood neurosis, which is based on internal conflict, should be distinguished from conditions resulting from external conflict; the latter may be due either to traumatic influences in the environment (*developmental interferences*) or to maturational forces within the child which bring him or her into conflict with the environment (*developmental conflicts*). Although such conditions may lead to symptoms or behavioral changes similar to those seen in childhood neurosis, the symptoms are more transient, do not have the same symbolic function in terms of unconscious content, and do not represent an unconscious compromise formation, as neurotic symptoms do. However, keep in mind that "a neurotic conflict is frequently the continuation of a developmental conflict that has not resolved itself properly at the appropriate time" (Nagera, 1966, p. 49). Childhood neurosis must also be differentiated from infantile neurosis, which is a metapsychological construct rather than a clinical entity.

The self psychology school challenges the traditional psychoanalytic explanation of neurosis, including childhood neurosis. Its position is that there are no normal intrapsychic conflicts and that symptoms classically ascribed to them are better explained as breakdown products of empathic failure with a consequent lack of self-cohesion.

See COMPROMISE FORMATION; CONFLICT; INFANTILE NEUROSIS; METAPSYCHOLOGY; PSYCHONEUROSIS; SELF PSYCHOLOGY; STRUCTURAL THEORY; SYMPTOM.

References

Blos, P. (1972). The epigenesis of the adult neurosis. *PSOC,* 27:106–135.

Freud, A. (1970). The infantile neurosis. *WAF,* 7:189–203.

——— (1965). *Normality and Pathology in Childhood.* New York: Int. Univ. Press, chap. 5.

Nagera, H. (1966). *Early Childhood Disturbances, the Infantile Neurosis, and the Adult Disturbances.* New York: Int. Univ. Press.

Tolpin, M. (1970). The infantile neurosis. *PSOC,* 25:273–305.

■ CHOICE OF NEUROSIS

See PSYCHONEUROSIS; SYMPTOM.

■ COGNITION

The psychic acquisition, transformation, coding, and storage of knowledge. Cognition encompasses perception, imaging, concept formation, thinking, judgment, and imagination. Although some definitions are quite circumscribed (for example, cognition is equated with information processing), others are overinclusive (for example, Kessler's 1970 definition: "all processes above the reflex level which produce some change in behavior"). Holt's (1964) statement that cognition deals with all aspects of symbolic behavior reflects the vastly broadened content of the term as well as the scope of cognitive psychology over the last few decades.

In the psychoanalytic literature, the term is usually restricted to the individual's intellectual functions, and it often refers specifically to the processes of child development (especially developmental epistemology) studied by Jean Piaget. Piaget wrote extensively on the construction of the object (sensorimotor intelligence); the preconceptual, operational, and formal stages of intelligence; play; symbol formation; and the reciprocal influences of intelligence and affect. Only a small area of this work, that referring to infancy (Piaget's sensorimotor period), has been adequately studied from a psychoanalytic perspective.

More recently, cognitive studies on mental representation with reference to the enactive, iconic (imagistic), and verbal modes of representation (Bruner, 1966) have gradually been integrated into psychoanalytic theory. In particular, language development has always attracted a great deal of interest among psychoanalysts.

See PSYCHOLINGUISTICS.

References

Bruner, J. E., Olver, R. R. & Greenfield, P. M. (1966). *Studies in Cognitive Growth.* New York: Wiley.

Erdelyi, M. H. (1985). *Psychoanalysis.* New York: W. H. Freeman.

Holt, R. R. (1964). The emergence of cognitive psychology. *JAPA,* 12:650–665.

Leon, I. G. (1984). Psychoanalysis, Piaget and attachment. *Int. Rev. Psychoanal.,* 11:255–278.

Kessler, J. W. (1970). Contributions of the mentally retarded toward a theory of cognitive development. In *Cognitive Studies,* ed. J. Hellmuth. New York: Brunner/Mazel.

Peterfreund, E. & Schwartz, J. T. (1971). *Information, Systems, and Psychoanalysis.* New York: Int. Univ. Press.

■ COLLECTIVE UNCONSCIOUS

See ANALYTICAL PSYCHOLOGY TERMS.

■ COMPENSATORY STRUCTURES

See SELF PSYCHOLOGY.

■ COMPLEX

See ANALYTICAL PSYCHOLOGY.

■ COMPONENT INSTINCTS

The infantile elements (also called *partial instincts*) contributing to the sexual instinct, which ultimately becomes organized under the primacy of the genitals at puberty. By pointing out the infantile elements in sexuality, Freud (1905) was able to establish a simple correlation between health, perversion, and the neuroses.

Sexual excitations have their source primarily in the erotogenic zones, and the organ involved determines their independent aims: incorporation in the case of the oral zone, and active and passive aims and an "instinct" for mastery in the case of the anal zone. In addition to the preponderant influence of the erotogenic zones, other component instincts—scopophilia, exhibitionism, and cruelty—are observable in childhood but do not enter into the genital life until later. These lesser component instincts emerge for the most part as pairs of opposites, both of which are active and introduce new sexual aims: for example, the scopophilic instinct pairs with exhibitionism, and there are active and passive forms of the instinct for cruelty. Though these appear somewhat independent from the erotogenic zones, in scopophilia and exhibitionism the eye corresponds to an erotogenic zone, while in those components involving pain and cruelty the same role is assumed by the skin (although Freud also postulated that cruelty arises from the anal-sadistic stage and the instinct for mastery).

These component (or partial) instincts make up the sexual constitution of children (who are thus said to be *polymorphously perverse*). The oral and anal elements undergo a first, or pregenital, sexual organization during which the sexual activity is autoerotic. At puberty the individual attempts to combine all of the components into a unity under the primacy of the genital zone, producing an impulsion under the sway of the reproductive function with the drive directed toward an object outside the self. In the course of development, shame, disgust, pity, and the morality and authority of society are restraining influences. Repression of certain constituents of the infantile disposition and subordination of the remaining ones under the primacy of the genital zones results in normal sexual functioning; in this process certain components are eliminated, restricted, or modified and confined to sexual foreplay. Unsuccessfully repressed components may become vehicles of sexual activity in perversions. With partial but insufficient repression, neuroses may result in which a considerable proportion of sexual energy is attracted to the components, emerging as symptoms. The sexual life of neurotic individuals has remained in, or has been brought back to, an infantile state.

In describing component instincts Freud was in effect delineating the variety of routes through which libido and aggression may gain expression at various developmental levels. The designation of separate component instincts seems inconsistent with his efforts to subsume all motivated behavior under a dual instinct theory. Nevertheless, these early observations continue to have heuristic value, and in postulating the ontogenesis of an instinct, Freud presaged later concepts about the drives.

See EROTISM; EXHIBITIONISM; GENITALITY; INSTINCTUAL DRIVE; PSYCHOSEXUAL DEVELOPMENT; SADOMASOCHISM; SCOPOPHILIA.

References

Freud, S. (1905). Three essays on the theory of sexuality. *SE,* 7:125–243.

■ COMPROMISE FORMATION

The ideational, affective, and behavioral resultants of attempts at solution of conflict among and between the psychic agencies and the outside world. Compromise formations occur because certain derivative manifestations of instinctual drives (wishes and fantasies) encounter ego restrictions or superego prohibition; the conflict results in their being barred from consciousness. The solution for such conflict involves reorganization of the internal forces in such a way as to provide some acceptable degree of expression for each of the competing interests in accordance with the principle of multiple function (Waelder, 1930). Compromise formations involve dynamically active contributions from each of the psychic agencies (id, ego, superego) as well as from external reality. For example, a fantasy expresses not only a wish but also feared dangers, defensive activities, and punishment—thus the fantasy can be tolerated in consciousness. Such formations may take many forms: character traits, identity, self-esteem, sublimated behavior, symbols, fantasies, symptoms or symptomatic acts, dreams, parapraxes, transference, or intrapsychic patterns that may achieve structural importance, such as components of the superego (see Brenner, 1982). They may have lasting significance or they may be only fleeting combinations observable during the analytic process. The role of compromise formations in the service of resistance to analysis means that identifying defense components against specific emerging drive derivatives is especially important.

But not all behavior results from compromise formation; Hartmann (1939) conceptualized a conflict-free sphere of the ego with relatively autonomous functions, and the resulting activities are not regarded as compromise formations.

See ANXIETY; CONFLICT; MULTIDETERMINISM.

References

Arlow, J. A. (1953). Masturbation and symptom formation. *JAPA,* 1:45–58.
Brenner, C. (1982). *The Mind in Conflict.* New York: Int. Univ. Press.
Coen, S. J. & Bradlow, P. A. (1982). Twin transference as a compromise formation. *JAPA,* 30:599–620.
Freud, S. (1923). The ego and the id. *SE,* 20:3–66.
——— (1926). Inhibitions, symptoms, and anxiety. *SE,* 20:77–175.
Hartmann, H. (1939). *Ego Psychology and the*

Problem of Adaptation. New York: Int. Univ. Press, 1958.
Waelder, R. (1930). The principle of multiple function. In *Psychoanalysis*. New York: Int. Univ. Press, 1976, pp. 68–83.

■ COMPULSIONS

See OBSESSION.

■ CONDENSATION

See DREAMING, DREAMS.

■ CONFABULATION

See AMNESIA.

■ CONFIDENTIALITY

The principle that a provider of professional services should not violate an individual's right to privacy by revealing information obtained in the course of their association. This principle is intended to benefit the person. In medicine it is explicit in the Hippocratic oath; it is also applicable in insurance, health, employment, education, credit, business, and marriage. Some relationships—such as those between spouses, lawyers and clients, clergy and penitents, accountants and clients, doctors and patient, and psychotherapists and patients—are safeguarded by common law and/or statute. Communications between people in these relationships are said to be privileged, but only partially and subject to exceptions and qualifications.

The principle of confidentiality is of unique importance in psychoanalysis because some of the information actively sought in the relationship has been unconscious; that is, what is revealed is often not acceptable to the patient. Discussing such information with others through any breach of confidentiality would add to resistances already inevitably present. The duty to protect confidential communications extends to all those who learn of them in the course of administering professional services, such as colleagues (for example, in a consultation or teaching situation) and office or hospital personnel. In psychiatry and psychoanalysis, the identity of the patient is also considered confidential.

See PRIVACY; PRIVILEGE.

References

Lifschutz, J. E. (1976). A critique of reporting and assessment in the training analysis. *JAPA*, 24:43–59.
Marcovitz, E. (1973). On confidentiality in psychoanalysis. *Bull. Phila. Assn. Psychoanal.*, 23:1–7.
Panel (1972). Levels of confidentiality in the psychoanalytic situation. A. S. Watson, reporter. *JAPA*, 20:156–176.
Slovenko, R. (1973). *Psychiatry and Law*. Boston: Little, Brown.

■ CONFLICT

Psychic or *intrapsychic conflict* refers to struggle among incompatible forces or structures within the mind, *external conflict* is that between the individual and aspects of the outside world. (They often go together, however.) In his early writings Freud described conflict as occurring between unconscious wishes and the conscious dictates of morality, but he discovered later that conflict could be totally unconscious and formulated his tripartite structural model to account for it. Conflict is manifest in such observable phenomena as symptoms, actions, and thought; it may also be inferred from data obtained by the psychoanalytic method. Present theory sees the formation of conflict in terms of a sequence: instinctual wishes come into conflict with internal or external prohibitions; the ego is threatened and produces signal anxiety; defenses are mobilized; and the conflict is resolved via compromise formations in symptoms, character changes, or adaptation.

In normal early development, preoedipal conflicts arise between: the child and the environment; superego precursors and drives; and opposing wishes within the child's personality (aggression/passivity, dependence/independence, and conflicts of ambitendency and beginning ambivalence). Environmental events preventing fulfillment of the child's developmentally appropriate needs—for example excessive or insufficient stimulation—may constitute *developmental interferences*. These are to be distinguished from *developmental conflicts*—either appropriately timed external demands conflicting with the child's wishes (for example, toilet training) or conflicting inner wishes, such as the desire to please the mother and the urge to defecate immediately (Nagera, 1966). These conflicting inner wishes are prototypical of *internal conflicts,* which take shape as development proceeds; they are commonly classified as involving ambivalence, bisexuality, and activity/passivity. The threat to the child's ego in preoedipal conflicts is the danger of loss of the love object and loss of love.

Internalized conflicts occur when environmental forces that originally opposed the child's sexual or aggressive drives become, by internalization and identification, forces within the child's own psyche standing in opposition to his or her drives. The infantile neurosis, as a manifestation of infantile sexuality, and the oedipus complex ordinarily follow the establishment of internalized conflicts. As a result of defensive efforts in childhood and sometimes later, such internalized conflicts are often experienced as *externalized*—that is, the person perceives conflict with something outside himself or herself.

It is important to note that developmental interferences and internal conflicts are not necessarily antecedents of internalized conflicts (A. Freud, 1962). Either continuity or discontinuity in development may enable the developing psyche to master incipient conflicts. Parents who contribute to the child's internal incompatibility at one developmental level may aid in his or her mastery of problems at a subsequent level. Many conflicts are more or less resolved as development continues; others persist throughout life, leading to various degrees of pathology. The manifestations of conflict vary according to developmental level, the nature of the psychopathology, and cultural factors contributing to the makeup of the superego. Certain manifestations are typical for particular developmental stages of childhood—for example, reactions to conflicts over habit training are manifested in ritualistic behavior, while oedipal conflicts are often manifested by nightmares. Oedipal conflict is generally regarded as the core conflict in psychoneuroses. Its threat involves the danger of injury and mutilation (the castration complex).

Intrapsychic conflict may also be categorized as *intersystemic* or *intrasystemic,* a division based on the structural theory. Intersystemic conflict refers to clashes between wishes or forces originating in separate psychic systems. For example, an urge to gratify a sexual drive originating in the id may come in conflict with a prohibition deriving from the superego. Intrasystemic conflict refers to opposition between constituents within the same psychic structure, for example, between two incompatible ideals (in the superego); between drives (id); or between alternative choices or decisions to be made (ego). The tripartite structural model of the mind also allows us to distinguish between *opposition,* or *convergent conflicts*—as between a wish and a prohibition—and *dilemma,* or *divergent conflicts*—conflicts of decision or of ambivalence (Rangell, 1963; A. O. Kris, 1984). The latter appear first most clearly in the rapprochement phase of separation-individuation (Mahler, Pine, and Bergman, 1975).

"Conflicts are part of the human condition" (Hartmann, 1939, p. 12). Intrapsychic conflict is inevitable, universal, and one of the most important dynamic factors underlying human behavior. The outcome of intrapsychic conflict determines the basis both of neurotic symptoms and inhibitions and of a wide variety of character traits, normal and abnormal.

See AMBIVALENCE; ANXIETY; EGO; ID; INFANTILE NEUROSIS; OEDIPUS COMPLEX; SEPARATION-INDIVIDUATION; STRUCTURAL THEORY; SUPEREGO.

References

Beres, D. Conflict. *PMC*. Forthcoming.
Freud, A. (1962). Assessment of childhood disturbances. *PSOC,* 17:149–158.
Hartmann, H. (1939). *Ego Psychology and the Problem of Adaptation*. New York: Int. Univ. Press, 1958.
Kris, A. O. (1984). The conflicts of ambivalence. *PSOC,* 39:213–234.
Mahler, M. S., Pine, F. & Bergman, A. (1975). *The Psychological Birth of the Human Infant.* New York: Basic Books.
Nagera, H. (1966). *Early Childhood Disturbances, the Infantile Neurosis, and the Adulthood Disturbances*. New York: Int. Univ. Press.
Rangell, L. (1963). Structural problems in intrapsychic conflict. *PSOC,* 18:103–138.

■ CONSCIENCE

See SUPEREGO.

■ CONSCIOUS
□ Consciousness

A quality of mental awareness (consciousness) of external events and mental phenomena. Other such phenomena go unnoticed but nevertheless exert a dynamic influence.

Using a topographic point of view, Freud (1915) regarded the conscious (*Cs.*), preconscious (*Pcs.*), and unconscious (*Ucs.*) as dynamic systems with different functions, processes, energies, and ideational content. The conscious was the most peripheral, receiving information from both the outside world and the soma and psyche, but its functional distinction from the preconscious was less clear than it was from the unconscious. Freud sometimes referred to the first two entities as the preconscious-conscious system (*Pcs.-Cs.*), which has available a freely mobile energy (*attention cathexis*) to hypercathect certain mental contents, thereby making conscious what was preconscious. In contrast to the primary process of the Ucs., the Pcs.-Cs. system operates by secondary process, characterized by logical thought in verbal language form.

Consciousness represents a higher level of mental organization than perception. It involves awareness and integration of internal and external perceptions and readiness to respond to the environment. Consciousness is an individual, subjective experience, continuous except during sleep or dissociative states, but transitory in content. It is the product of what Freud designated the perception-consciousness system (*Pcpt.-Cs.*), which he regarded as the nucleus of the ego. The Pcpt.-Cs. system functions so that perceptions of outside stimuli received by the sense organs become a base for the function of reality testing. The system also perceives the quality (pleasurable or unpleasurable) of internal sensations, instinctual wishes, memories, fantasies, and thought processes—Freud compared it to a sense organ for the perception of psychic qualities. Some cognizance of time and place it usually present and may at times take into account past, present, and future.

What is in consciousness is evanescent. It varies, Freud thought, according to attention based on dynamic and reality considerations. What is latent can easily become conscious again. Consciousness is dependent on and influenced by the individual's present situation and past history, including such factors as motivation, affect, memory, and knowledge. Phenomena that may become conscious thus vary from person to person and from moment to moment. Though it is involved in psychic conflict and defense, consciousness is not itself an indication of conflict, since aspects of the ego and superego are unconscious, and conflicting ideas may be entertained consciously.

Altered states of consciousness may result from such psychological or physiological factors as sleep, fatigue, illness, hypnosis, and drugs. They usually involve either hyperalertness or diminished awareness of external stimuli and suspension of ego functions such as reality testing. Altered states of consciousness comprise somnolence in the classroom or on the highway; trancelike states during hypnosis, in analysis, or in acting out; mystical experiences; and states of depersonalization and derealization (usually regressive and defensive in nature).

See ALTERED EGO STATE; DEPERSONALIZATION; EGO; PRECONSCIOUS; TOPOGRAPHIC POINT OF VIEW; UNCONSCIOUS.

References

Dickes, R. (1965). The defensive function of an altered state of consciousness. *JAPA*. 13:356–403.

Freud, S. (1900). The interpretation of dreams. *SE*, 5:508–621.

——— (1915). The unconscious. *SE*, 14:166–204.

John, E. R. (1976). A model of consciousness. In *Consciousness and Self-Regulation*, ed. G. E. Schwartz & D. Shapiro. New York: Plenum Press, 1976, vol. 1, pp. 1–50.

Luria, A. R. (1978). The human brain and conscious activity. In *Consciousness and Self-Regulation*, ed. G. E. Schwartz & D. Shapiro. New York: Plenum Press, 1978, vol. 2, pp. 1–35.

■ CONSTANCY PRINCIPLE

See PLEASURE/UNPLEASURE PRINCIPLE; PSYCHIC ENERGY.

■ CONSTITUENTS OF THE SELF

See SELF PSYCHOLOGY.

■ CONSTRUCTION

See RECONSTRUCTION.

■ CONTAINER–CONTAINED (♀♂)

See BION'S THEORY.

■ CONVERSION

A process by which repudiated mental content is transmuted into physical phenomena. Symptoms take many different forms, including motor, sensory, and visceral reactions: anesthesias, pains, paralyses, tremors, convulsions, gait disturbances, incoordination, deafness, blindness, vomiting, hiccupping, and difficulty in swallowing.

Freud's earliest cases of hysteria provided him with conversion symptoms; and hysteria became his model for all psychopathology and for the theory of neurosis. He saw conversion as a hysterical phenomenon that attempts to resolve conflicts of the oedipal phase: "the incompatible idea is rendered innocuous by its sum of excitation being transformed into something somatic" (Freud, 1894, p. 49). Although conversion remains indissolubly associated with hysteria, Rangell (1959) and others have argued for widening its scope, citing clinical examples of conversion phenomena in a broad spectrum of psychopathology representing all levels of libidinal and ego development. The essence of conversion, Rangell says, "is the shifting or displacement of psychic energy from the cathexis of mental processes to that of somatic innervations in order for the latter to express in a distorted way the derivatives of repressed forbidden impulses" (p. 636). The somatic phenomena are symbolically meaningful, a "body language" that expresses in distorted form both forbidden instinctual impulses and defensive forces. The associated thoughts and fantasies can be retranslated through analysis into words.

The early cases upon which the concepts of hysteria and conversion were based are now believed to have been much more complex than originally thought. Such cases are overdetermined, with dynamic mechanisms stemming from multiple points of fixation and regression, including pregenital components as well as phallic and oedipal ones. But as Freud observed, favorable conditions are necessary for conversion to occur, although it may be based in a wide variety of conditions. He assumed a "capacity for conversion" or "somatic compliance" was required for the resolution of conflicts by conversion instead of phobic or obsessional symptoms; however, conversion phenomena are often intermingled with the latter syndromes.

Although Freud's concept was an economic one—psychic energy is displaced or transformed from the psychic sphere to the somatic—in the same paper he laid the groundwork for a different and currently more acceptable explanation. Just as obsessional ideas may be formed when affect is separated from an objectionable idea and reattached to a more acceptable substitute, so also may the affect be reattached to fantasies of physical disease as a compromise formation, resulting in the clinical picture of conversion (Freud, 1894, p. 52).

The relationship between conversion symptoms, as encountered in hysteria, and other psychosomatic manifestations remains unclear. In *organ neuroses,* for example, functional disturbances appear to have no psychic meaning of their own; they are not translations of specific fantasies or impulses into somatic terms. The same is the case with *pregenital conversions* (Fenichel, 1945), involving stuttering, tics, and asthma. To avoid including every shift from the psychic to the somatic, Rangell (1959) would restrict conversion to cases including the criteria mentioned above; he would exclude inevitable but nonspecific somatic sequelae of psychic tension and undischarged affect. But such distinctions are often difficult to make clinically.

See HYSTERIA; METAPSYCHOLOGY; OEDIPUS COMPLEX; PSYCHIC ENERGY; PSYCHONEUROSIS.

References

Fenichel, O. (1945). *The Psychoanalytic Theory of Neurosis.* New York: Norton.

Freud, S. (1894). The Neuro-psychoses of defence. *SE,* 3:45–61.

Rangell, L. (1959). The nature of conversion. *JAPA,* 7:632–662.

■ COUNTERPHOBIA

See PHOBIA.

■ COUNTERTRANSFERENCE

A situation in which an analyst's feelings and attitudes toward a patient are derived from earlier situations in the analyst's life that have been displaced onto the patient. Countertransference therefore reflects the analyst's own unconscious reaction to the patient, though some aspects may be conscious. The phenomenon is analogous to transference, which is of central therapeutic importance in analysis. Countertransference is narrowly defined as a specific reaction to the patient's transference. Others include all of the analyst's emotional reactions to the patient, conscious and unconscious, especially those that interfere with analytic understanding and technique. This broad purview might be better designated *counterreaction.*

Under the influence of countertransference, analysis takes on an unconscious, conflicted significance for the analyst instead of being a reality-adapted, conflict-free activity. The manifestations of countertransference are protean. It is likely to appear when the analyst identifies with the patient, reacts to material produced by the patient, or reacts to aspects of the analytic setting. In these circumstances unconscious strivings underlying character traits of the analyst are stimulated, and their derivatives appear in the analyst's thoughts, feelings, and actions.

Reactions emanating from the analyst's unconscious conflicts differ from reactions to the patient's personality and circumstances. The former can impede the analyst's neutrality, leading to "blind spots" that impair empathy and understanding; or in extreme cases, countertransference may lead to acting out. On the other hand, the analyst's scrutiny of countertransference feelings can provide clues to the meaning of the patient's behavior, feelings, and thoughts, thus facilitating perception of the patient's unconscious. This self-scrutiny is one of the cardinal purposes of the training analysis, which helps the analyst become aware of his or her conflicts and their derivatives.

The mechanism of identification is involved in both countertransference and empathy, but there are important differences. In empathy identification is transient, a temporary sharing of derivatives expressing the patient's unconscious fantasies. Through an affective resonance with the patient clues to understanding his or her conflicts may emerge. In identification arising from unanalyzed countertransference, however, the analyst is denied this insight inasmuch as he or she is caught up in conflicts identical to those of the patient.

In recent years countertransference has received increased attention in the psychoanalytic literature, perhaps as a result of greater focus on the analytic relationship. Some authors believe that both patient and analyst develop reactions to each other's transferences and that countertransference is a bipolar phenomenon. Analysis of children and of psychotic, borderline, and narcissistic patients seems to evoke more troublesome countertransference reactions; the increase in such work has also contributed to a greater interest in countertransference.

See EMPATHY; IDENTITY; TRANSFERENCE.

References

Arlow, J. A. (1985). Some technical problems of countertransference. *PQ,* 54:164–175.

Brenner, C. (1982). *The Mind in Conflict.* New York: Int. Univ. Press.

Freud, S. (1910). The future prospects of psychoanalytic therapy. *SE,* 11:139–151.

——— (1913). On beginning the treatment. *SE,* 12:121–144.

——— (1914). Observations on transference love. *SE,* 12:157–171.

Orr, D. W. (1954). Transference and countertransference. *JAPA,* 2:621–670.

Reich, A. (1951). On countertransference. In *Psychoanalytic Contributions.* New York: Int. Univ. Press, 1973, pp. 136–154.

■ CYCLOTHYMIC DISORDER

See AFFECTIVE DISORDERS.

■ DANGER SITUATION OF THE EGO

See ANXIETY.

■ DAY RESIDUE

See DREAMING, DREAMS.

■ DEAGGRESSIVATION

See PSYCHIC ENERGY.

■ DEFENSE

□ Defense Mechanism

Defense is a general term describing the ego's active struggle to protect against dangers—typically, loss of the love object, loss of the object's love, castration, and superego disapproval—and their attendant unpleasant affects during development and throughout life. A repressed wish, idea, or feeling that has become associated with some real or fantasied punishment threatens to erupt into consciousness. Painful feelings of anxiety, depression, shame, or guilt ensue as signal affects, impelling the ego to ward off the wish or drive. Defense operates unconsciously; the individual does not recognize the defense mechanisms he or she uses to ward off dangerous drives or wishes. The operation of defense mechanisms may delete or distort aspects of reality.

The term *defense* was first used by Freud in "The Neuro-Psychoses of Defense" (1894), but for many years he used *repression* and *defense* interchangeably. The term *defense mechanism* appeared for the first time in Anna Freud's classic *The Ego and the Mechanisms of Defense* (1936), which described ten activities or methods of ego functioning in the service of defense.

Defense mechanisms operate singly or occur together in everchanging and interrelating patterns, utilizing various behaviors, ideas, affects, aspects of character, other ego functions, and even drives. For this reason the usefulness of the concept of specific defense mechanisms has been questioned. Any aspect of ego functioning may be used in the service of defense, and a defense is so complex that delineating single mechanisms can be reductionistic and misleading (Brenner, 1981). Nevertheless, many analysts find it useful to employ defense mechanisms to describe the effect of the defenses in regard to the dangers to the ego. Brief descriptions of some principal defense mechanisms follow:

Repression. Withholds, expels, or forgets an idea or feeling. It may exclude from awareness what was once experienced consciously or may stop ideas and feelings from reaching consciousness at all. A person may, for example, be unaware of feelings of hatred directed at a parent or sibling. Repression operates throughout life, regularly occurring in respect to childhood events during the crucial period before six years of age (infantile amnesia).

Displacement. Shifts the focus or emphasis in dreams and behavior, generally by diverting the interest or intensity (cathexis) attached to one idea onto another idea that is associatively related but more acceptable to the ego. Thus exhibitionistic wishes may be displaced from the genitals to the body as a whole. In a dream the most important elements of the latent content may be represented by apparently insignificant details.

Reaction formation. Changes the unacceptable

to acceptable, thereby also ensuring the efficient maintenance of repression. A painful idea or feeling is replaced in conscious awareness by its opposite. For example, a child who has repressed feelings of hate toward mother may develop an extreme solicitousness and concern for her welfare.

Projection. Externalizes the objectionable impulse or idea by attributing it to another person or to some perhaps mystical force in the outside world. ("The devil did it.") The intolerable idea or wish may be transformed before it is projected—Freud inferred, for example, that paranoid ideas are based on unconscious homosexuality. First the feeling of homosexual love is transformed into hatred, then the hatred is projected onto the person who was the object of the unacceptable love. That person is then seen as a persecutor.

Isolation. Separates a painful idea or event from feelings associated with it, thereby altering its emotional impact. There are several types of isolation. Two or more related thoughts or feelings may be separated: for instance, the idea, "I am angry at her" and another thought, "She left me," are separated by time, and the causal connection is thereby lost. Or ideas may appear simply without the conscious presence of associated feelings. Fleeting aggressive thoughts—plunging a knife into someone, throwing a child out of a window, shouting obscenities in a public place—often occur without the emotion (anger) appropriate to such thoughts. Such isolation deprives the thought of motivational force and hence of intent; the thought seems alien, action is thwarted, and guilt is sometimes avoided.

Undoing. Ritualistically "removes" the offensive act, sometimes by atoning for it. Particularly in compulsive neuroses, a two-stage act may symbolize expression of an aggressive or sexual wish and its reversal or undoing. Some individuals habitually commit transgressions and try to undo them by religious or self-punitive expiations.

Many other defense mechanisms have been described. While the function of all these mechanisms is the same—to protect against painful affects—they achieve this aim in different ways. Regression works by effecting a retreat to an earlier phase of psychic organization; introjection and identification, by taking inside the self what is threatening; denial, by pretending a threatening situation is not there; sublimation, by changing the form of the unacceptable drive to one that is acceptable; and turning against the self, by redirecting the impulse from outside to inside, from another person to the self. (This defense is operative especially in depression and masochism.)

Defenses may also function constructively making action and thought more efficient. These might be called *adaptive mechanisms* or *autonomous ego functions.* For instance, isolation, by dissociating thinking from emotions, can facilitate the logical progression of ideas by avoiding the distraction associated emotions might cause.

See COMPROMISE FORMATION; CONFLICT; DENIAL, EGO; EGO FUNCTION; INTERNALIZATION; PROJECTION; REGRESSION; REPRESSION; SUBLIMATION.

References

Blum, H. P., ed. (1983). Defense and resistance. Foreword. *JAPA,* 31(suppl.):5–17.

Brenner, C. (1981). Defense and defense mechanisms. *PQ,* 50:557–569.

Fenichel, O. (1945). *The Psychoanalytic Theory of Neurosis.* New York: Norton.

Freud, A. (1936). *The Ego and the Mechanisms of Defense.* New York: Int. Univ. Press.

Freud, S. (1894). The neuro-psychoses of defense. *SE,* 3:45–61.

Rangell, L. (1983). Defense and resistance in psychoanalysis and life. *JAPA,* 31(Suppl.):147–174.

Wallerstein, R. (1983). Defenses, defense mechanisms and the structure of the mind. *JAPA,* 31(Suppl.):201–225.

■ DEFENSE NEUROPSYCHOSIS

Used early by Freud to distinguish psychological illnesses resulting from the need to defend against (repress) the memory of a childhood sexual seduction (the defense neuropsychoses) from illnesses believed to be the result of a constitutional degeneracy or, in the case of the *actual neuroses,* a physiological reaction to a current faulty sexual practice. With the replacement of the seduction theory of neurosogenesis by the theory of infantile sexuality, the term *defense neuropsychosis* was given up in favor of the term *psychoneurosis.*

See ACTUAL NEUROSIS; PSYCHONEUROSIS.

References

Freud, S. (1894). The neuro-psychoses of defence. *SE,* 3:45–61.

——— (1896). Further remarks on the neuro-psychoses of defence. *SE,* 3:162–185.

——— (1898). Sexuality in the aetiology of the neuroses. *SE,* 3:263–285.

■ DEFENSIVE STRUCTURES

See SELF PSYCHOLOGY.

■ DÉJÀ VU

□ Déjà Raconté

These terms belong to a group of subjective falsifications of experience; the common element is the erroneous belief that a current experience has already occurred at some earlier time. Other terms, derived from French nineteenth-century psychiatric nomenclature, refer to diverse yet related phenomena. These include *déjà raconté* (already communicated), *déjà entendu* (already heard), *déjà eprouvé* (already accomplished), *déjà fait* (already done), *déjà pensé* (already thought), and *déjà voulu* (already desired). Psychoanalytic interest has centered on *déjà vu* and *déjà raconté*.

Déjà vu in its fully developed form is associated with an unpleasant, unreal, dreamlike feeling and an uncanny prophetic sense of being able to foretell each element of the experience as it occurs. It is common in normal and pathologic states, both psychological and organic, and it appears frequently in childhood and adolescence as well as in adulthood.

Although still incompletely understood, déjà vu seems to represent a defensively altered regression in the sense of reality corresponding to the memory of a previously repressed unconscious fantasy or some concrete experience of the past associated with a forbidden wish. There are various explanations of the essential feature of erroneous familiarity. The most useful regards déjà vu as analogous to the manifest dream and to screen memories, with each manifest element in the experience richly determined by its latent and childhood connections. The defensive achievement is obscured by the concomitant unpleasant affect and consists of the consoling assertion: "Just as once before I was frightened and survived, so now too I will be unharmed." Déjà vu is thus a compromise formation evoked by a situation that both symbolizes and stimulates the revival of memories, wishes, or fantasies related to unpleasant affects. The compromise affords simultaneous partial gratification of these wishes, repudiation and punishment, and assuages psychic pain.

Déjà raconté describes an event as well as an experience in which a patient falsely asserts that he or she has already told something to the analyst. Its occurrence is a reliable signal of significant new communications in psychoanalytic treatment. It is unclear whether all such events should be included or whether the term should be restricted to those instances where the patient vehemently insists that he or she is correct. If one accepts the broader definition, déjà raconté occurs commonly. There is also clinical evidence of the advantages of the broader definition. Although déjà raconté has the same structure as déjà vu, the former is actually a special instance of this entire group of parapraxes, requiring the participation of the psychoanalyst, whereas déjà vu is an intrapsychic experience. Many would agree that transference must be included in any effort to understand déjà raconté. To the extent that transference is a universal phenomenon, it is not contradictory to include this form of parapraxis in events outside as well as within the psychoanalytic treatment situation.

Viewed as a parapraxis déjà raconté has been demonstrated to have the same structure as dreams and screen memories. The content of the disputed communication can be usefully analyzed just as dreams are analyzed. The defensive wishes expressed include the wish to pursue discussion of this topic as well as the reassurance that once again a danger situation evoked by transference wishes will be successfully mastered.

References

Arlow, J. A. (1959). The structure of the *déjà vu* experience. *JAPA,* 7:611–631.

Boesky, D. (1973). *Déjà raconté* as a screen defense. *PQ,* 42:491–524.

Freud, S. (1914). Fausse reconnaissance (*déjà raconté*) in psychoanalytic treatment. *SE,* 13:201–207.

■ DENIAL

A primitive or early defense mechanism by which an individual unconsciously repudiates some or all of the meanings of an event (sometimes called *disavowal*). The ego thus avoids awareness of some painful aspect of reality and so diminishes anxiety or other unpleasurable affects. Explicit or implicit denial is also an integral aspect of all defense mechanisms. Since the late 1970s the term has been used less to describe a discrete defense mechanism and more to describe the reality-repudiating aspect of defensive operations.

To help efface a perception of reality, a fantasy is often created that erases the disagreeable and unwelcome facts of the situation. For example, a child who feels helpless and frightened may create a fantasy in which he or she is powerful or omnipotent. Denial is frequently aided by means of action as well, though that too is based on an unconscious denying fantasy.

Denial plays a normal role in childhood, and some degree of transient denial is an expectable and usually normal reaction to stress, trauma, and the loss of loved ones at any age. Denial can involve massive or relatively minor and selective distortions of reality. At one extreme, a denial may be delusional (a mother believes that a doll is her dead baby), indicating psychosis. All neuroses distort and deny reality to some degree, and the persistence of denial often presents significant problems. On the other hand, in the sphere of feelings or affects persistent denial is sometimes normal and adaptive. (We continue to travel in airplanes although crashes are not infrequent; we also behave as if there were no danger of nuclear warfare.) The earlier psychoanalytic literature tended to emphasize the more pathological kinds of denial observed in the psychoses, but the recent trend has been toward a broader definition including normal and neurotic types of denial.

Strictly speaking, denial usually refers to external reality, while repression relates to internal representations. *Negation,* often considered synonymous with denial, manifests aspects of repression, isolation, and denial. Negation permits the repressed into consciousness but in the negative form. To use Freud's (1925) example, the patient who dreams of a woman might say, "You ask who the person in the dream can be. It's *not* my mother." The "negative judgment is the intellectual substitute for repression" (p. 236), enriching thinking but isolating it from affect and thereby denying its emotional impact.

See DEFENSE; REALITY; REPRESSION.

References

Breznitz, S., ed. (1983). *The Denial of Stress.* New York: Int. Univ. Press.

Dorpat, T. L. (1985). *Denial and Defense in the Therapeutic Situation.* New York: Jason Aronson.

Freud, S. (1925). Negation. *SE,* 19:235–239.

Moore, B. E. & Rubinfine, D. L. (1969). The mechanism of denial. *Kris Study Group Monographs.* New York: Int. Univ. Press, vol. 3, pp. 3–57.

Weisman, A. D. (1972). *On Dying and Denying.* New York: Behavioral Publications.

■ DEPENDENCE

The tendency to lean upon another for the purpose of gratification and/or adaptation. Though it has normative influences on development and is experienced as a need, dependence generally carries a pejorative meaning, implying the need to lean on others in an excessive and age-inappropriate way.

Excessive dependence has been most often associated with the "oral dependent" character and the chemically addicted. Some of the most severe disorders stem largely from defects in normal dependence. Autistic, schizoid, and some borderline conditions arise from a disastrously insufficient attachment to objects. The antisocial character may also center on disavowal of early object relations and rejection of early infantile needs for love and protection. In symbiotic childhood psychosis dependence is excessive and does not yield to the normal process of separation-individuation.

Dependence has a significant normative influence on the development of the psychic organization. Freud wrote of its importance for libido gratification, healthy attachments to objects, and ego and superego development; he also delineated its relations to anxiety, religious belief, and development of neurosis. Mahler (1963) said that the "libidinal availability of the mother, because of the emotional dependence of the child, facilitates the optimal unfolding of innate potentialities" in the child (p. 322). Parens and Saul (1971) recognize the normal place of dependence in human existence, psychic development, and object relations. Dependence, they proposed, has a greater influence in species whose psychophysiological differentiation is incomplete at birth. Immaturity and protracted helplessness highlight and stabilize the need for the object. So great is the importance of this determinant of personality development in humans that Anna Freud (1963) proposed a developmental line "from dependency to emotional self-reliance and adult object relationships." Central to this process is the internalization of object relations by which the child may be sustained from within. The better the earliest object relations, the more stable will be object cathexes leading to libidinal "inner sustainment." But dependence continues throughout life, and many pathological conditions in which it plays a key part arise within the context of insufficient, distorted, or failing human relationships. In these cases and in others, dependence on psychic representations such as transitional objects, religious ideas, and institutions may substitute for dependence on objects.

References

Freud, A. (1963). The concept of developmental lines. *PSOC,* 18:245–265.

Freud, S. (1940). An outline of psychoanalysis. *SE,* 23:141–207.

Mahler, M. S. (1963). Thoughts and development and individuation. *PSOC,* 18:307–324.

Parens, H. & Saul, L. J. (1971). *Dependence in Man.* New York: Int. Univ. Press.

■ DEPENDENCY

See BION'S THEORY.

■ DEPERSONALIZATION

An alteration in the perception of the self, such that the usual sense of one's reality is temporarily lost or changed. One's perception of oneself splits into a detached, observing self and a participating or experiencing self, together with a feeling of self-estrangement or unreality about the latter. The feeling of unreality is basic to the phenomenon. Parts of the body or the whole person may seem changed, unreal, not one's own; a feeling of conviction about personal identity is retained, but the sense of connection with the observing self is stronger than that with the participating self. Dizziness frequently accompanies these phenomena, which appear rapidly and disappear more gradually. The experience is nondelusional, dreamlike, and usually (though not always) unpleasant.

A variety of altered ego states may be associated with the phenomenon called depersonalization; some authors subsume all these states under depersonalization, while others attempt to make a distinction. In particular, *derealization,* a sense of estrangement from the environment, often occurs along with depersonalization, though one may be more prominent. In situations of realistic external danger, otherwise normal people may experience depersonalization and derealization. Both phenomena serve a denying fantasy—that the danger is not real or that the person is only a spectator, not involved in the danger situation.

In the literature there is apparent agreement that depersonalization is "the outcome of an intrapsychic conflict in which the ego utilizes, in a more or less unsuccessful way, various defenses against anxiety" (Arlow, 1966, p. 459). Earlier authors explained the experience in economic terms—it resulted from massive shifts of libidinal cathexis, either countercathexis against one's own feelings or a withdrawal of cathexis from external objects.

Jacobson (1959) postulated that the stability and sense of familiarity of the self image depend on the compatibility, harmonious interplay, and collaboration of ego-superego and narcissistic identifications. While Oberndorf suggested intersystemic conflict involving a superego antithetical to the body ego, Jacobson viewed the conflict as intrasystemic, occurring within the ego between incompatible identifications. Unacceptable exhibitionistic or aggressive wishes, sadomasochistic trends and seductions, and identification with a degraded object image are among the aspects of the self rejected by detachment and disavowal.

See ALTERED EGO STATES; CONFLICT; DEFENSE; DEREALIZATION; EGO FUNCTION; METAPSYCHOLOGY; REGRESSION.

References

Ackner, B. (1954). Depersonalization. *J. Ment. Sci.,* 100:838–853.

Arlow, J. A. (1966). Depersonalization and derealization. In *Psychoanalysis—A General Psychology,* ed. R. M. Loewenstein, L. M. Newman, M. Schur & A. J. Solnit. New York: Int. Univ. Press, pp. 456–478.

Bradlow, P. A. (1973). Depersonalization, ego splitting, non-human fantasy and shame. *IJP,* 54:487–492.

Jacobson, E. (1959). Depersonalization. *JAPA,* 7:581–610.

Panel (1964). Depersonalization. W. A. Stewart, reporter. *JAPA,* 12:171–186.

■ DEPRESSION

A mood or affect manifested by subjective phenomena such as feelings of sadness, hopelessness, helplessness, guilt, self-critical thoughts, and diminished interest in outside activities. Concomitant with this mental content, psychomotor activities slow and patients experience general lassitude, fatigue, diminished sexual drive, anorexia, constipation, and insomnia (especially in the early morning). In some affective disorders insomnia may be replaced by an increased need for sleep, and overeating may replace anorexia. These physical manifestations are labeled vegetative signs of depression and are the basis for the long-held assumption of a psychosomatic element in causality. Another frequent symptom, very disturbing to the patient, is difficulty in thinking clearly or effectively; it can be severe enough to be mistaken for organic dementia.

An increased concern with the self and diminished interest in outside activities and people accompany depression. The individual is frequently convinced that some aspect of the self is worthless, defective, or diseased (hypochondriasis). Hypochondriacal anxieties are often prominent—sometimes primary. In agitated depression this narcissistic preoccupation includes fear of impoverishment and self-critical thoughts that can extend to suicidal ideation.

From the psychoanalytic perspective, a breakdown in regulation of self-esteem is a common, perhaps even universal, feature in depressions. Mahler (1966) has described a developmental basis for this narcissistic vulnerability in the mother's lack of acceptance and emotional understanding during the rapprochement subphase of separation-individuation. This leads to ambivalence, repetitive aggressive coercion of the parents, and the affect of depression. The child fails to develop internal psychic structures that can regulate self-esteem; he or she requires a great deal of outside reassurance. Individuals with fragile self-esteem become depressed when they lose the external supports they need to maintain a stable self image.

The breakdown of self-esteem regulation and consequent depression may result from loss of an object by death, hurt, neglect, or disappointment. Other causes include disillusionment over an idealized cause, failure to live up to ego ideals, or a sense of helplessness and powerlessness in the face of insurmountable odds. Normal grief over object loss does not usually involve diminution of self-esteem or self-accusations. Melancholic overreaction to the loss of an object usually occurs when such objects had narcissistic value (that is, possessed traits coinciding with some aspect of the vulnerable individual's self representation). Loss of such an object is tantamount to loss of part of the self image; the depressed person may identify with the lost object in an attempt to recapture what has been lost. In that case his or her self-criticisms are derived from criticisms originally directed toward the emotionally significant person, either the one lost or one connected with the loss. The self-criticism is therefore an expression of anger that was part of the original ambivalent attitude toward the object when it was present. Guilt is superimposed on sadness. Through a fusion of self and object representations, aggression originally directed toward the object has been turned against the self. Depression in such instances is the result of intersystemic conflict (between the superego and the id).

In other cases, however, guilt is absent, and the conflict appears intrasystemic. Bibring (1953) describes depression as an ego-psychological phenomenon involving tension between highly charged narcissistic aspirations (ego ideals) and the ego's awareness of its incapacity to fulfill them. While Jacobson (1971) stresses the intensity of aggression and the degree of ambivalence as important psychodynamic factors in depressed persons, Bibring regards depression as essentially independent of the vicissitudes of aggression and oral drives. In his view, the breakdown of self-esteem regulation, frustration, and aggression are inevitable results of the feeling of helplessness and powerlessness.

When the term depression is used as a diagnostic category, it refers to a mental illness in which the affective disturbance is the predominant feature. But depression occurs in a wide spectrum of nosological entities with varying etiology and psychopathology. In these conditions Freud's view still holds true—there is a complementary series of causal factors, including constitutional and hereditary factors, even in the transference neuroses. Understanding of depression therefore depends on combined neurophysiological and psychological research after careful clinical diagnostic studies: Despite some phenomenological similarities, there appear to be significant differences in the depressions associated with neurotic, borderline, and cyclothymic and schizophrenic psychotic pathology (Jacobson, 1971). In the psychological sphere, the structure and nature of the conscious and unconscious conflicts, the specific defenses, and the level of object and self representations involved in conflict help determine variants of the depressive process (Asch, 1966).

See AFFECTS; AFFECTIVE DISORDERS; ANXIETY; MOOD.

References

Asch, S. S. (1966). Depression. *PSOC*, 21:150–171.

Bibring, E. (1953). The mechanism of depression. In *Affective Disorders*, ed. P. Greenacre. New York: Int. Univ. Press, pp. 13–48.

Brenner, C. (1974). On the nature and development of affects. *PQ*, 43:532–556.

Freud, S. (1917). Mourning and melancholia. *SE*, 14:237–258.

Goldberg, A. (1975). The evolution of psychoanalytic concepts of depression. In *Depression and Human Existence*. ed. E. J. Anthony & T. Benedek. Boston: Little, Brown, pp. 125–142.

Jacobson, E. (1953). Contribution to the metapsychology of cyclothymic depression. In *Affective Disorders*, ed. P. Greenacre. New York: Int. Univ. Press, pp. 49–83.

——— (1971). *Depression: Comparative Studies of Normal, Neurotic and Psychotic Conditions*. Madison, Conn.: Int. Univ. Press.

——— (1975). The regulation of self-esteem. In *Depression and Human Existence*, ed. E. J. Anthony & T. Benedek. Boston: Little, Brown, pp. 169–181.

Mahler, M. S. (1966). Notes on the development

of basic moods: the depressive affect in psychoanalysis. In *Psychoanalysis—A General Psychology,* ed. R. M. Loewenstein, L. M. Newman, M. Schur & A. J. Solnit. New York: Int. Univ. Press, pp. 152–168.

■ DEPRESSION TYPES

See SELF PSYCHOLOGY.

■ DEPRESSIVE CHARACTER

See DEPRESSIVE NEUROSES.

■ DEPRESSIVE DISORDERS

See AFFECTIVE DISORDERS.

■ DEPRESSIVE NEUROSES

Conditions corresponding psychodynamically to the psychoneuroses in which depressive affect is the predominant manifestation. There are several forms of depressive neurosis. Most involve the precipitating factors and personality features characteristic also of the major affective disorders, but in depressive neurosis reality testing is intact and symptoms are less severe than in the psychotic reactions.

Though *reactive depression* is now generally equated with *neurotic depression* or *situational depression,* the term originally designated the kind of psychotic depression that, unlike endogenous depression, develops in reaction to a precipitating event. An individual experiencing change or the threat of change in his or her life develops a depressive mood. The conscious or unconscious perception of the change as a personal loss is the important psychodynamic factor. The loss can usually be identified—defection of a lover, death of a spouse, divorce, or loss of a job—but in other circumstances it may be necessary to search out an unconscious symbolic meaning. For example, a promotion may be experienced as a loss rather than a gain if one's lower status has been employed to defend against oedipal conflict; unconsciously, the loss of a defensive adaptation results in guilt over the oedipal triumph—the promotion symbolically represents surpassing the father.

People who have developed object constancy often react strongly to change. They must loosen their investment in the past in order to adapt to a new situation, an exercise in loss followed by gain, which is typical of the process of mourning. A person may experience difficulty in mourning after a loss especially if he or she has been very dependent on others to maintain self-esteem. Such individuals are particularly prone to situational depression. They maintain an intense but ambivalent internal relationship with the mental representation of what is lost. Love for the object represented leads to the mechanism of identification in order to keep it within the self, while feelings of hate demand its destruction. Since the individual identifies with the representation of the lost object, he or she experiences these destructive forces as if directed toward the self. If the depressive symptoms are mild, the condition is called a depressive neurosis, but situational depression may also evolve into a major depression.

Cyclothymic disorders resemble manic-depressive disorder in their alternating swings of mood from elation to depression, but the episodes are neither severe enough nor sustained long enough to justify the diagnosis of major bipolar affective disorder. Feelings of inadequacy during depressive periods and elation during times of inflated self-esteem suggest a narcissistic personality organization. The fluctuations are short-lived and not a stable element of the personality. Psychoanalytic studies of persons suffering from cyclothymic disorder reveal experiences of rejection in childhood that alternated with experiences of fulfillment of narcissistic aspirations. Such an adult tends to relate to actual or imaginary stimuli according to his childhood model. For example, children who had several caretakers may be susceptible to cyclothymic disorder. Frustration with one mother leads to seeking another more gratifying, and the pattern is repeated each time the mother figure is "bad" or disappointing.

When the affect is limited to a depressed mood, accompanied by loss of interest and pleasure in activity over a period of years, the term *dysthymic disorder* is sometimes applied. The severity and psychodynamics, however, do not differ from that of depressive neurosis, with which it is equated.

The *depressive character* suffers chronically from a depressed mood; he or she either lacks the capacity for pleasure or experiences pleasure only briefly and with anxiety. This kind of depression is neither severe nor acute; it is not experienced as a symptom; the individual sees it simply as part of his or her personality. Such a person tends to have a pessimistic attitude: upon being told "Good morning!" he or she might typically ask, "What's good about it?" He or she is also passive-receptive and expresses grudging feelings of injustice, complaining that his or her ambitions cannot be attained.

Psychoanalytic studies suggest that hostile parenting, actual or fantasized, makes a child feel that he or she is being punished because he deserves punishment. The adult life of such an individual will reflect the early psychodynamics; he or she is likely to be self-deprecating and sacrificing of his or her pleasure in an effort to earn the affection of others.

The distinctions between these syndromes are by no means clear-cut. Cyclothymic and dysthymic disorders, for example, may be regarded as symptom neuroses or character neuroses depending on the clinical picture.

See AFFECTS; AFFECTIVE DISORDERS; DEPRESSION; MOURNING; PSYCHODYNAMICS; PSYCHONEUROSIS.

References

Abse, D. W. (1985). The depressive character. In *Depressive States and Their Treatment,* ed. V. Volkan. New York: Jason Aronson, pp. 47–69.
Berliner, B. (1966). Psychodynamics of the depressive character. *Psychoanal. Forum,* 1:244–251.
Fenichel, O. (1945). *The Psychoanalytic Theory of Neurosis.* New York: Norton.
Freud, S. (1917). Mourning and melancholia. *SE,* 14:237–258.
Volkan, V. D. (1981). *Linking Objects and Linking Phenomena.* New York: Int. Univ. Press.

■ DEPRESSIVE POSITION

See KLEINIAN THEORY.

■ DEPTH PSYCHOLOGY

Bleuler is generally credited with having originated this designation, which extended the scope of academic, rational, or organicist psychology to encompass Freud's newly discovered unconscious dimensions, motivations, and phenomenology.

Freud, Hartmann, Rapaport and Gill, among others, formulated and elaborated metapsychology ("beyond psychology") in part for the same reason—to cover, in a manner consistent with psychoanalytic theory, the full spectrum of phenomena, conflicts, and compromise formations, from the deeply unconscious to the fully conscious ones of rational, cognitive, and physiological psychology. Hence, depth psychology is sometimes used in everyday, nontechnical language to refer to what is encompassed by the theories of psychoanalysis.

Depth psychology is sometimes used interchangeably with *dynamic psychology* and applied retroactively to the contributions of those who, knowingly or unknowingly, wrote, described, or theorized about unconscious phenomena before the advent of or outside the confines of psychoanalysis.

See METAPSYCHOLOGY.

References

Freud, S. (1914). On the history of the psychoanalytic movement. *SE,* 14:7–66, p. 41.
——— (1915). The unconscious, *SE,* 14:166–215, p. 173.

■ DEREALIZATION

An experience involving a feeling that the external world is unreal and strange, no longer like it used to be. One's surroundings may appear flat, two-dimensional, colorless, drab, and without emotional significance. It does not involve failure in perception or impairment of judgment. The change may seem threatening. It may involve only the immediate situation or it may be global; fleeting or prolonged; isolated or recurrent.

Usually derealization occurs in association with depersonalization—both phenomena ward off anxiety by a denying fantasy, namely, that the situation is unreal ("This is not only not really happening to me, it is not even happening in the world, so there is absolutely nothing to worry about"; Bradlow, 1973, p. 488.) Sarlin (1962) suggests that depersonalization involves withdrawal of cathexis from the self representation, while in derealization the cathexis is withdrawn from object representations, resulting in the feeling of estrangement of the world.

See ALTERED EGO STATES; CATHEXIS; DEPERSONALIZATION; REPRESENTATION.

References

Arlow, J. A. (1966). Depersonalization and derealization. In *Psychoanalysis—A General Psychology,* ed. R. M. Loewenstein, L. M. Newman, M. Schur & A. J. Solnit. New York: Int. Univ. Press, pp. 456–478.
Bradlow, P. A. (1973). Depersonalization, ego splitting, non-human fantasy and shame. *IJP,* 54:487–491.
Sarlin, C. N. (1962). Depersonalization and derealization. *JAPA,* 10:784–804.
Stamm, J. L. (1962). Altered ego states allied to depersonalization. *JAPA,* 10:762–783.

■ DESEXUALIZATION

See PSYCHIC ENERGY.

■ DESOMATIZATION

See SOMATIZATION.

■ DEVELOPMENT

An ongoing process in which the psychic structures and functions determining the human personality gradually evolve from the experiences of a biologically maturing individual in interaction with his or her environment. Such interaction involves genetically determined maturational sequences and inherent potentialities, environmental influences, and personal experiences. In psychoanalytic usage the term is applied specifically to those growth processes directly dependent on interaction with the environment and through which the major psychic structures (id, ego, superego) form. *Maturation* refers to physical and psychic growth related to the inherent genetic potential and largely independent of external factors. This distinction has become less clear, however, with recognition that environmental interaction plays a role in both maturation and development.

Development has been viewed from a number of different psychoanalytic perspectives according to the *developmental schemas* utilized by particular investigators. Perhaps the best known is Freud's (1905) psychosexual frame of reference, which charted successive stages of the libidinal drive (oral, anal, and phallic phases) in the course of childhood development, each stage based on bodily areas and organs predominantly involved in sensual gratification at the time. When psychoanalysts realized the importance of objects in development, a number of authors devised means of recognizing stages in the response of the infant to the mother in relation to the constancy of her mental representation and developing ego and superego functions, such as indicators and organizers (Spitz); separation-individuation concepts (Mahler); and developmental lines (Anna Freud). Similar attempts have been to define developmental stages for the self, gender identity, and the sense of reality; but these are less clearly delineated and not so well accepted.

Employed in each of these schemas is the idea of predictable, sequential progressions in the developmental process; these are usually referred to as *stages* or *phases*. Psychosexual (or libidinal) development and Mahler's separation-individuation schema are usually described as *phases,* but there appears to be no consistency in the use of *phase* versus *stage* and no essential distinction in meaning between them. Both refer to a period in the course of normal development distinguished by the appearance of specific structures, functions, or clusters of behavior. At each stage the evolving elements are integrated with analogous elements of the previous stage, and these in turn are reorganized at the next stage.

Although Freud advanced his first developmental schema in terms of libido, in 1938 he expressed reservations about the idea of clear-cut stages in the development of libido, recognizing that stages may overlap and that behavior characterizing one stage may appear in others as well. Recent observations have led others to question the utility of a stage model altogether, at least for certain elements of the personality (Pine, 1985; Stern, 1985).

The stages of development related to libido, object relations, sense of self, and structures should be distinguished from *stages of the life cycle,* global constellations of physical and psychic attributes during periods at various points along a spectrum of dependence/independence and adaptation to the tasks and responsibilities of life. The current division is *infancy* (years 0–3), *early childhood* (years 3–6), *latency* (years 6–12), *adolescence* (years 12–18), and *adulthood.* These stages are often subdivided, and in the literature *infantile* often refers to the first five years.

Among the developmental schemas or theoretical frameworks for understanding development is Anna Freud's (1963–1965) concept of *developmental lines,* which she elaborated (from a phrase Freud often used) and refined. Anna Freud believed that more was needed to assess a child's personality than isolated perspectives such as those of libidinal or intellectual development. To capture the complexity of the developmental process, she viewed certain behavioral clusters metaphorically as structural units and the developmental trajectories of these units as lines. She then described development in terms of a series of predictable, interrelated and interlocking, overlapping, and unfolding lines. In this conceptualization, behavioral clusters defining the personality represent a complex interlocking of psychic units reflecting id, ego, and superego components as well as adaptive, dynamic, and genetic influences. In her view, sequences in specific parts of the child's personality portray this interaction among drive, ego, superego, and environment; when viewed collectively, these sequences paint a convincing picture of the individual's achievements or failures in personality development. Prototypical are the lines "from dependency to emotional self-reliance and adult object relations." Other lines lead "from irresponsibility to responsibility in body management" and "from the body to toy and from the play to work."

Since the developmental lines are viewed largely as inherent potentialities within the ego and the id, a general correspondence between lines is postulated. However, Anna Freud emphasized that lines often do not develop at the same rate, making personality distortions and incongruities more apparent. Such discrepancies result from a complex array of interacting factors such as environmental conditions, maturational rates, conflicts, defenses, and regressions.

See LIBIDO THEORY; METAPSYCHOLOGY; OBJECT; PSYCHOSEXUAL DEVELOPMENT; STRUCTURAL THEORY.

References

Freud, A. (1963). The concept of developmental lines. *PSOC,* 18:245–265.

——— (1965). *Normality and Pathology in Childhood.* New York: Int. Univ. Press.

Freud, S. (1905). Three essays on the theory of sexuality. *SE,* 7:125–243.

——— (1938). An outline of psychoanalysis. *SE,* 23:141–207.

Pine, F. (1985). *Developmental Theory and Clinical Process.* New Haven: Yale Univ. Press.

Stern, D. N. (1985). *The Interpersonal World of the Infant.* New York: Basic Books.

Tyson, P. & Tyson, R. L. Development. *PMC.* Forthcoming.

■ DEVELOPMENTAL ARREST
See FIXATION.

■ DEVELOPMENTAL CONFLICT
See CHILDHOOD NEUROSIS; CONFLICT.

■ DEVELOPMENTAL INTERFERENCE
See CHILDHOOD NEUROSIS; CONFLICT.

■ DIFFERENTIATION SUBPHASE
See SEPARATION-INDIVIDUATION.

■ DISAVOWAL
See DENIAL.

■ DISPLACEMENT
See DEFENSE; DREAMING, DREAMS.

■ DOMINANT
See ANALYTICAL PSYCHOLOGY: Archetype.

■ DREAMING, DREAMS
Dreaming is a universal and normal, regressive, psychophysiological phenomenon occurring periodically during sleep in regular cycles about ninety minutes apart. Rapid eye movements (REM), which occur in stage 1 of sleep, indicate dreaming. Children dream more than adults; at least 50 percent of the night sleep of an infant is occupied by REM sleep and dreaming. Penile erection and clitoral vasocongestion occur during the dreaming portions of sleep; this phenomenon is utilized to test whether cases of impotence have organic or psychological bases.

Anxiety dreams may awaken a person from the REM phase of sleep and be remembered. Anxious arousals may occur from any stage of sleep, however. Dreams that disturb stage 4 sleep are often accompanied by somnambulism, crying out, and obvious terror (*pavor nocturnus*), but they are seldom remembered. The forgetting of dreams seems to be related to both physiological factors, such as the immediacy of recall, and psychological factors, including repression, resistance, and censorship. Individuals often recall forgotten dreams when resistance is removed by analysis or even by hypnosis.

In *The Interpretation of Dreams,* Freud related the underlying or *latent content* of dreams to wish fulfillment, an understanding which led to some of his most important concepts in psychoanalytic theory. Others have suggested that dreams are attempts at problem solving—at working through and mastering of psychically traumatic experiences (both recent and from infancy). Dreaming is also seen as an information-processing mode to cope with emotional problems presented to the dreamer.

Thought processes and affects are represented in dreams in visual and (less frequently) auditory form. Other modes of sensory experience—touch, smell, taste, and kinesthetic sensation—also appear in dreams. According to Freud, dreaming and the formation of dreams are results of the *dream work,* a mental process characterized by archaic modes of thinking, particularly *displacement, condensation,* and *substitution,* which serve to transfer the latent dream thoughts into the *manifest dream.* Two other elements of the dream work are *plastic* and *symbolic representation,* that is, the transformation of thoughts into sensory symbols and images; and *secondary elaboration,* the linking together of the separate images and elements of the dream into a relatively coherent story or action. Sometimes secondary elaboration or revision does not occur and the dream is recalled as a disjointed, incoherent, or bizarre series of images or phrases.

The *manifest dream* content is the dream as it is recalled by the dreamer, with its associated images, speech, sensory content, and affect, as well as its specific *formal aspects,* including division into parts, commentaries on the dream occurring within the dream, and so on. Dreams occurring within one night or within the same sleep period are considered to belong to a single latent thought sequence: for example, a solution in one dream may lead to another problem in a second dream, or a single conflict can be addressed repetitively throughout the night.

The process of *dream formation* is generally conceived as follows: because of regression, motor inhibition, and the relaxation of conscious and unconscious censorship during sleep, an archaic form of functioning revives and is manifested in the dream work (which uses the primary process mode of thinking). The dream work interacts with the derivatives of infantile drives, defenses, and their related conflicts, as well as with their current representatives, to create during sleep predominantly visual images (dreams) that replace thought.

The *day residue* or precipitating stimulus is the dream's recent source material, that is, innocuous elements from daily life which contribute to the formation of the dream. When events, impressions, perceptions, ideas, and feelings from several preceding days appear in the dream as unimportant, they have acquired significance through their unconscious connections with deeply repressed infantile drives, wishes, and conflicts. The day residue connects with unconscious infantile drives and wishes of an erotic and aggressive nature, effectively disguising the infantile impulse that is the impetus for the dream. To this disguise is added a process of distortion (including secondary elaboration) accomplished by the dream work.

The term *dream screen* was introduced by Bertram Lewin to describe a dream without discrete or recognizable visual content. It consists of a blank background, not necessarily seen as such or mentioned by the dreamer. Such dreams are thought to relate to infantile sleep and to symbolize the mother or breast. They may also be the fulfillment of the wish to sleep. Some observers consider the dream screen to be the background or matrix of the dream; the visual content, the waking elements, appear on it.

Freud thought dreams were the "royal road to the unconscious." With the increasing importance attributed to ego psychology and the psychoanalytic process, analytic work with interpretation of dreams has become an important element in the analytic process. Therapeutic use of the dream thus means using the dream to help discover unconscious mental contents and integrate infantile fantasies, their underlying drives, and the resulting conflicts and defenses with the current latent content of manifest behavior and transference.

See PRIMARY PROCESS; REGRESSION; REPRESSION; SYMBOL.

References

Altman, L. (1969). *The Dream in Psychoanalysis.* New York: Int. Univ. Press.

Fischer, C. et al. (1965). Cycle of penile erection synchronous with dreaming (REM) sleep. *Arch. Gen. Psychiat.*, 12:29–45.

Fliess, R. (1953). *The Revival of Interest in the Dream.* New York: Int. Univ. Press.

French, T. & Fromm, E. (1964). *Dream Interpretation.* New York: Basic Books.

Freud, S. (1900). The interpretation of dreams. *SE,* 4 & 5.

——— (1901). On dreams. *SE,* 5:633–714.

——— (1917). A metapsychological supplement to the theory of dreams. *SE,* 14:222–235.

Grinstein, A. (1983). *Freud's Rules of Dream Interpretation.* New York: Int. Univ. Press.

Lewin, B. D. (1953). Reconsideration of the dream screen. *PQ,* 22:174–199.

Madow, L. & Snow, L. H., eds. (1970). *The Psychodynamic Implications of the Physiological Studies on Dreams.* Springfield, Ill.: Thomas.

Natterson, J. M. (1980). *The Dream in Clinical Practice.* New York: Jason Aronson.

Whitman, R. M. (1963). Remembering and forgetting dreams in psychoanalysis. *JAPA,* 11:752–774.

■ DYNAMIC VIEWPOINT

See METAPSYCHOLOGY.

■ DYSTHYMIC DISORDER

See AFFECTIVE DISORDERS; DEPRESSIVE NEUROSES.

■ ECONOMIC VIEWPOINT

See METAPSYCHOLOGY.

■ EGO

An important term in the history of the development of psychoanalytic theory, *ego* has an early and a later meaning, both still used to some extent. In his early writings, Freud sometimes used the term to refer to the total (mental) self; sometimes it meant an organized group of ideas. Certain of these ideas could be admitted to consciousness—these constituted the ego. Others were unacceptable and were relegated to the unconscious. Thus in his early conception of the ego Freud emphasized defense, one of its central functions.

In modern usage, the term most often refers to Freud's 1923 redefinition of the ego as one of the three major functional subdivisions of the mental apparatus. Though it has some conscious components, many of the operations of the ego are automatic, unconscious mechanisms. One aspect of the ego in its earlier meaning has now been replaced by the concept of the *self*. In reading psychoanalytic literature, one should determine the sense in which *ego* is used; this is often facilitated by noting the historical period to which the paper belongs.

The newborn infant exists in an undifferentiated psychic state from which the ego gradually evolves. The resulting ego-id matrix is based on constitutional factors (the genetically determined growth pattern of the central nervous system, the sense organs, and the body in general) and experiences in the surrounding world in relation to objects. The ego occupies a position between the primal instincts, based on physiological needs, and the demands of the outer world; as the internalized psychic representative of both, it serves to mediate between the individual and external reality. It perceives the physical and psychic needs of the self and the qualities and attitudes of the environment (including objects) and it evaluates, coordinates, and integrates these perceptions so that internal demands can be adjusted to external requirements; finally, it brings about relief from drive tensions and wishes through a discharge involving either reduction in the intensity of the drives (taming) or a modification of the external situation. The important task of the ego is to achieve optimum gratification of instinctual strivings while maintaining good relations with the external world and with the superego (the internal representative of the standards of behavior and moral demands imposed from without and the threats consequent to failure to meet them). For this task, protective devices must be available to reduce excessively strong stimuli, both internal and external. Physiologically, the sense organs are equipped to receive only certain stimuli and to ignore or reduce the intensity of others. This is especially important in infancy when many defenses have not yet developed adequately. (The infant's physiological mechanisms serving this purpose are referred to collectively as a protective shield or stimulus barrier.) Psychically, certain defensive functions are also developed and maintained to protect against conscious awareness of the conflicting demands of the id (primitive urges, impulses, biological needs, and so on) and superego insofar as these might arouse intolerable anxiety.

In order to function effectively, certain ego functions (for example, perception, motor capacity, intention, anticipation, purpose, planning, intelligence, thinking, speech, and language) need to mature in an environment relatively free of psychic conflict (Hartmann's concept of the primary autonomy of the ego) or need to develop so that they can function without undue conflict (secondary autonomy). Hartmann and others have theorized that the psychic energy devoted to such conflict is neutralized and by that means becomes available for the further development of the ego. As a part of its adaptation to reality, the ego must also develop the capacity for relatively stable relationships with objects, especially of the opposite sex, upon whom satisfaction of the instinctual needs depends. The individual must learn to form affectionate, friendly ties with others, ties involving a minimum degree of hostile expression that are maintained over a long period of time (object constancy).

The ego should not be thought of as an anthropomorphic executor or as a part of the brain. Rather, the term represents a useful way of thinking about basic aspects of human behavior. Traditionally, the ego has been defined as a group of functions, which grow, are subject to numerous disturbances, and may be made more effective through psychiatric, and especially psychoanalytic, treatment.

The functions of the ego are numerous; and few individuals learn to exercise them all effectively. Some individuals function very badly in some areas and with conspicuous success in others (the ambitious, high-powered, successful executive who cannot carry out the demands of parenthood; the dedicated and brilliant scholar who displays the most ludicrous ineptitude in the everyday affairs of life). There are, moreover, individuals whose disturbed egos allow them to achieve conspicuous success (the fanatical paranoiac may sway millions with the fire of his delusional convictions). Adaptation to reality, which is the outstanding function of the ego, may take strange forms indeed. The ego must therefore be evaluated in terms of its specific functions, not as a totality.

See ADAPTATION; DEFENSE; EGO DEVELOPMENT; EGO FUNCTIONS (including references); STRUCTURAL THEORY.

■ EGO AUTOMATISMS

Ego functions, usually involving motor activity, conducted without conscious attention directed at them. They have become preconscious, that is, they are not conscious but are easily made so. Examples include driving an automobile, using a typewriter, and swinging a tennis racket.

Pathological automatisms are determined by unconscious needs and do not appropriately conform to the reality of the situation. They occur in psychotic states such as schizophrenia (for example, *echolalia*—monotonous repetition of the same phrase or of what another person says) and in fugue states (altered states of consciousness during which an individual may unknowingly engage in elaborate patterns of action).

■ EGO DEFECT

Incapacity or impairment in one or more of the functions of the ego. The term usually refers to the result of a developmental event that adversely affects all the ego functions, but especially those concerned with psychic defense and adaptation. The focus of the dysfunction and the extent and severity of the impairment vary.

Ego defects may be based on constitutional, maturational, experiential, and developmental factors. These determinants generally come into play in the earliest years when the ego is evolving; thus they contribute to prestructural ego psychopathology—impairment of self–object differentiation; problems in identity formation; establishment of defensive and coping mechanisms; modulation of instinctual drives; and faulty perception, cognition, and reality testing. Although these defects are established early in life and may even be evident then, in some cases they appear clinically only as a result of subsequent psychic stress.

Though early dynamic conflicts (intrapsychic, intrasystemic, or interpersonal) may contribute to an ego defect, and the defect in turn may contribute to dynamically determined compromise formations, *ego defect* implies a nondynamic impairment in psychic structure and functioning. Ego defects are relatively permanent in contrast to the more transient ego distortions that result from the regressive alterations seen in neurotic and psychotic compromise formations.

■ EGO DEVELOPMENT

According to current theory, the psychic apparatus is in an undifferentiated state at birth, and the potentiality for id and ego development is determined by hereditary and constitutional (innate) factors. Development also depends greatly on the interaction between the infant and the environment. Certain events mark the growth of the ego and are reflected not only in external behavior but also in psychic states.

The infant is flooded by external stimuli, which might be intolerable if not for the stimulus barrier. The infant is physiologically less sensitive to pain and other stimuli than is an older individual. The primitive state of the ego also helps protect the infant from awareness of unpleasurable stimuli arising both from within and from without. The capacity to differentiate between pleasurable and painful states exists almost from the beginning, however, and memory traces record such experience. The body image is gradually built up via an amalgamation of these memory traces, some from the physiological processes of the body and some from the ministrations of the first emotionally charged object, the mother. Psychic representations of other people are at first only partial: the breast, face, hands, and bodily warmth represent the mother. Self and object representations are poorly differentiated—even in adult life they remain somewhat fluid and interchangeable.

The mother's gratification of the infant's physiological needs establishes memory traces of satisfaction which are reactivated in wish-fulfillment when, as inevitably happens, the mother is unable to satisfy needs immediately. This progression from appreciation of need to the psychic state of satisfaction, even when the need has not been met (via hallucinatory wish fulfillment), has the anticipatory quality of a conditioned reflex, but it is also the beginning of fantasy and thought. The mother comes to recognize the meaning of her infant's motor activity and emotions, and her appreciation of and response to these preverbal signals establish a primitive affectomotor form of communication between them. The degree of satisfaction in this interchange probably contributes to the capacity for empathy in later life as well as to other character traits. The infant smiles in response to the smile of the mother, and this imitation is the precursor of the later psychic process of identification, the basis of much ego development.

The infant associates repeated experiences of pleasure and pain with human beings, especially the mother. The child begins to recognize the mother as a separate individual toward the end of the first year. At first her absence brings discomfort (accompanied by separation anxiety) and the presence of strangers frightens the child (stranger anxiety). These phenomena mark important stages of ego growth. Objects begin to appear; memories are differentiated from current perceptions; and the precursors of defense against painful stimulation develop. In its primitive functioning the ego follows the model of bodily functions: the mind introjects (that is, takes in, as in nursing) what is need-satisfying and pleasurable as it seeks to deflect or ward off awareness of what is noxious or unpleasant or to eject, evacuate, or externalize the impressions that have been unavoidably received.

From the latter half of the first year through the third year, the child passes through a phase described by Mahler as "separation-individuation." The psychic conception of the self as separate from the object is established. During the second year the infant begins to develop the capacity to be alone. The child no longer requires the constant presence of mother because she has, so to speak, become a part of his or her personality: object constancy has achieved representation in the child's mind. Object constancy and mutually satisfactory object relations exert a powerful influence on ego development and vice versa. But satiation still brings fusion of self and object representations and a return to a psychic state similar to the earlier unity with mother, while deprivation heightens the sense of separation. If the mother has not provided the infant with an optimal degree of instinctual gratification and frustration for the needs and strengths of the child's developing mind, individuation and the development of a sense of self and identity are impaired. The very identity of the individual is therefore in part determined by the degree of instinctual gratification others give him or her, especially mother and father. The conflicts connected with such gratification may interfere with or facilitate identification with the parent of the same sex. All individuals have some admixture of masculine and feminine qualities derived from identification with both parents.

Early in life the infant cannot know how helpless he or she is; his or her needs are satisfied as if by magic as beings not yet differentiated from him or herself, come and go; it is as if the child were omnipotent. Later, when the child becomes aware of his or her separateness and helplessness, he or she attributes this omnipotence to the parents and idealizes them. As the child learns how dependent he or she is on others, he or she begins to crave their affection and becomes willing to renounce certain satisfactions in return for being loved—a precursor of the ability to give love as well as to receive it. This marks the beginning of a change from passivity to activity—facilitated by the development of motor skills through which the child is able to attain some degree of mastery over the surroundings.

The development of speech in the middle of the second year and its maturation in the third to fifth years are accompanied by great strides in thought processes. Primary process thinking is replaced by secondary, but the latter remains fragile for a long time; magical thinking and omnipotence of thought continue to exert influence in many situations. Through the psychic representations of object introjects, some control over impulses is achieved. However, the child still operates more from fear of punishment and wish for the reward of love than through guilt and self-approval. These come only gradually, achieving their greatest development when oedipal wishes are renounced and the child develops an identification with the father (the boy forms a superego as a result of resolving the oedipus complex).

Following the oedipal period and the formation of the superego is a stage of diminished sexual manifestations from about the sixth year of life to puberty (the latency period). Reorganization of the ego's defensive structure, partly via superego development, brings instinctual drives under better control; they are less disruptive of the ego's tasks, contributing to affect stabilization. The psychic orientation is directed outward; teachers and peers are used as objects for oedipal displacement and identification. Thinking becomes less egocentric, less personalized, and more concrete; rational thinking and fantasy are increasingly separated. Exposure to cultural and educational influences provides opportunities for sublimation and intellectual growth, and behavior becomes more consistent as habitual modes of reacting become character traits.

In the development of ego functioning, differentiation of the self from the object world is succeeded by object constancy and finally, in adolescence, by the capacity for object love. Object love requires relinquishing infantile objects and extreme self-love (narcissism). If the environment is suitably benign, the individual masters reality, learns to think objectively, increasingly engages in autonomous activities, and achieves reasonably efficient regulation of the drives. However, specific ego functions continue to mature well into adult life as the individual increases his or her capacity to love, to work, and to adapt to the world about him.

See ACTIVITY/PASSIVITY; ADAPTATION; CHARACTER; DEFENSE; DEVELOPMENT; EGO; EGO FUNCTION; PSYCHIC APPARATUS; PSYCHOSEXUAL DEVELOPMENT; REALITY.

■ EGO-DYSTONIC
□ Ego-Syntonic

Drives, affects, ideas, or behavior subjectively experienced by the observing ego as foreign to the self are *ego-dystonic* or *ego-alien*. The opposite of ego-dystonic is *ego-syntonic*. These terms use the word ego in its earlier ambiguous sense to refer to what would now be called the self, not as an agency of the mind as in the structural concept. However, *self-alien* or *self-dystonic*, though semantically logical, are not used.

See EGO.

■ EGO FUNCTION

In order to carry out ego tasks, a host of psychic functions must be performed. To some extent they overlap, but it is convenient to categorize them as perceptive, object and reality related, defensive, regulative, synthetic and integrating, autonomous, and executive. This section discusses aspects of these functions that have received particular attention in psychoanalysis and psychiatry.

Relationship to reality. Comprises not only adaptation to reality, requiring the functioning of the total person, mediated by the ego, but also reality testing and the sense of reality. Adaptation to reality means adjusting to the changing external world, whether it involves things, objects, or situations. Some individuals find it difficult to cope with such changes in their normal routines as job transfer, economic setback, or unfulfilled promise. Some parents never adjust to the marriage or departure of grown children; some children find it difficult to transfer their allegiance from their families to their spouses. Reality testing refers to the capacity to appraise correctly the external world and its generally accepted meanings. A conspicuous example of its failure is the paranoid delusion, the conviction that neutral and innocuous people are determined to harm the self. If a person feels as if this were so but knows rationally that it cannot be true, reality testing is preserved despite severe emotional disturbance.

In general, the preservation of reality testing distinguishes relatively normal and neurotic individuals from psychotic ones, although in many instances the distinction is difficult. The sense of reality is definitely disturbed in very abnormal mental conditions, such as schizophrenia. In such cases the entire appearance of the outside world may seem changed—the sky looks dark and foreboding, buildings loom ominously, the person feels unreal, his or her body strange, with parts seemingly detached. The sense of reality may be transiently compromised in conditions of lesser pathology when strong affects distort the accuracy of perceptions. The sense of reality can, however, remain intact in the face of faulty reality testing—some brilliant paranoiacs go about their daily business without any loss of reality sense, but maintain delusions that are impervious to reason.

Regulation and control of drives. Manifested in the ability to withstand anxiety, frustration, depression, disappointment, postponement of expected satisfactions, and so on. The individual can hold in check and distribute harmoniously the numerous demands for the expression of urges, needs, and wishes that come from within. Drive control implies the ability to wait, to delay satisfactions, and not to be overcome by unexpected situations. It also implies the ability to suit the action to the intention, to find appropriate outlets for relief and satisfaction, and to engage in constructive, satisfying, and socially acceptable forms of activity (that is, sublimations).

Object relations. There are two aspects to this ego function. The first is the ability to form affectionate, friendly ties to other individuals, involving few inappropriately hostile feelings. This ability is closely tied to the formation of positive mental images of these objects. The second aspect is the ability to maintain positive object relationships, and their corresponding mental representations, consistently over time while engaging in few mutually hostile interchanges. Disturbances in object relationships take the forms of emotional coldness and detachment; inability to fall in love and to sustain love; self-centeredness; helpless dependency on others, or the necessity to dominate them ruthlessly; and perversions. A childishly dependent person often tries to make his or her spouse behave like a parent. Sadomasochistic relationships (such as are portrayed in *Who's Afraid of Virginia Woolf?*), involving years of endless bickering, may bring morbid satisfactions to each partner. Perversions are characterized by abnormal object relationships of varying degress and types or the absence of object relationships. The psychotic's relationship to objects is at such a faulty, primitive, and often—strangely enough—hypersensitive level that psychotic individuals tend to avoid human relationships.

Thought processes. The ability to perceive what is going on around one and to coordinate, classify, and make sense of the perceptions; to think, to arrive at conclusions, to detect similarities and differences; to remember, to concentrate, to learn, to make judgments, to plan for the future—all these and other activities which we loosely call thinking, the ego function which distinguishes man from the lower animals, are subject to far-reaching disturbances. Thus, with respect to mathematics and the physical sciences, Newton and Pascal were geniuses beyond measure, but in their beliefs and their evaluation of human motives and behavior their thinking was contaminated by serious pathology. Individuals tend to be influenced in their appraisals of political situations much more by background, economic state and class, prejudices, and personal animosities than by cool, objective, impersonal considerations. Very young children and people in undeveloped cultures often attribute human motives to nonhuman and inanimate objects; consequently they live in a world of fear and superstition where consequences can be dealt with only by magical means. For ages human beings believed that disease was caused by demons or sorcerers; not until they became capable of dissociating themselves from such faulty thinking dominated by fears and wishes was it possible to make progress in conquering disease. Thought disturbances related to adolescent preoccupation with masturbation have ruined the academic careers of many gifted children.

Defensive functions. The earliest ego function defined by Freud, repression marked the beginning of psychoanalytic theory. Freud's ideas about the ego changed markedly, and his emphasis on its defensive functions varied over the years. At first he conceived of the ego as the conscious part of the personality, and defense—an attempt to ward off unacceptable sexual impulses and wishes—as a more or less conscious process. Ultimately, however, the present concept of ego defenses evolved from the recognition that they, like the instinctual drives, operate at an unconscious level.

Defenses are mechanisms utilized by the ego (as well as by other agencies of the mind) to force out of awareness sexual and aggressive impulses that would arouse anxiety in the individual. (Someone may be enraged at the sight of young people necking in public, and unaware that he or she is sexually aroused by this sight, jealous of this free expression of sexuality, and threatened by an anxiety-provoking impulse.) The ego, perceiving an impulse being aroused, experiences small amounts of anticipatory anxiety and attempts to protect itself by instituting defenses. Among the more important defense mechanisms are intellectualization, rationalization, identification (used as a defense, it most frequently takes the form of identification with an aggressor), introjection, projection, denial, repression, reaction formation, isolation, undoing, displacement, and regression.

Autonomous functions. Although most ego functions are easily disturbed by instinctual impulses, autonomous ego functions have been conceptualized (primarily by Hartmann) as relatively resistant to such forces. These functions are perception, motility (walking, use of the hands, and so on), intention (planning, anticipation, purpose), intelligence, thinking, speech, and language. These primary autonomous functions are thought to develop relatively independent of the powerful forces of sexuality and aggression—unlike such functions as object relations, defenses, and so on. Secondary autonomies are forms of behavior that begin as defenses against instinctual drives but become relatively free of such influences in the course of development. (An individual who rebels against an authoritarian parent, to whom he or she unconsciously wishes to submit, transforms the rebelliousness into constructive social criticism. In the effective form the rebellion finally takes, it becomes emancipated from the passivity and reaction formation in which it was nourished.)

Synthetic, integrative, or organizing function. The ego's capacity to unite, organize, and bind together various drives, tendencies, and functions within the personality, enabling the individual to feel, think, and act in an organized and directed manner. This function reveals itself in numerous individual experiences, which satisfy drives, ego interests, social demands, and so on, in a harmonious way. It may also bring together various forces in a way not completely adaptive to life but the best possible solution for the individual and the situation. The formation of a symptom that represents the amalgamation of two opposing tendencies, while unpleasant, is preferable to either yielding to a dangerous impulse or stifling it completely. (A hysterical conversion combines a forbidden wish and its punishment in a physical symptom. On examination, the symptom turns out to be the only compromise possible under the circumstances.)

See AUTONOMY; COMPROMISE FORMATION; CONFLICT; DEFENSE; INSTINCTUAL DRIVE; OBJECT; PSYCHOSIS; STRUCTURAL THEORY; SUBLIMATION.

References

Arlow, J. A. (1977). Affects and the psychoanalytic situation. *IJP*, 58:157–170.

Arlow, J. A. & Brenner, C. (1963). *Psychoanalytic Concepts and the Structural Theory*. New York: Int. Univ. Press.

Brenner, C. (1983). Defense. In *The Mind in Conflict*. New York: Int. Univ. Press, pp. 72–92.

Freud, A. (1936). *The Ego and the Mechanisms of Defense*. New York: Int. Univ. Press, pp. 28–65.

Freud, S. (1923). The ego and the id. *SE*, 19:3–66.

——— (1926). Inhibitions, symptoms, and anxiety. *SE*, 20:75–175.

Hartmann, H. (1952). The mutual influences in the development of ego and id. *PSOC*, 7:9–30.
______ (1956). The development of the ego concept in Freud's work. *IJP*, 37:425–438.
Hartmann, H. & Loewenstein, R. M. (1962). Notes on the superego. *PSOC*, 17:42–81.
Kris, E. (1951). Ego psychology and interpretation in psychoanalytic therapy. *PQ*, 20:15–30.
______ (1956). On some vicissitudes of insight in psychoanalysis. *IJP*, 37:445–455.
Loewald, H. W. (1951). Ego and reality. *IJP*, 32:1–18.
Nunberg, H. (1948). The synthetic function of the ego. In *Practice and Theory of Psychoanalysis*. New York: Int. Univ. Press, vol 1, pp. 120–136.
Sandler, J. & Rosenblatt, B. (1962). The concept of the representational world. *PSOC*, 17:128–145.

■ EGO IDEAL

Originally used by Freud (1914, 1921) in much the same way as he later used *superego:* to refer to a mental agency with specialized functions including setting up a system of moral codes otherwise known as the conscience (involving self-observation and self-criticism), dream censorship, reality testing (eventually viewed as an ego function), and the formation of an exemplar or ideal view of oneself.

Today most analysts consider the ego ideal as one set of functions within the structure of the superego. A number of authors name "ideal concepts of the self" and "idealized features of the love objects" as two main, original parts of the ego ideal; self psychologists take cognizance of these two aspects of the ego ideal with the terms "grandiose self" and "idealized object (selfobject)." Still others stress that *ego ideal* refers to a number of ideal representations which are differentiated from the beginning and throughout life: (1) the *ideal object*—the image of an admired, idealized, and omnipotent object; (2) the *ideal child*—the parents' ideal of a desirable and lovable child, as perceived by the child (later on, this representation becomes part of "the self I ought to be"); (3) the *ideal self*—a wishful concept, the "self I want to be," one which will elicit the most object approval, provide the greatest narcissistic gratification, and minimize aggressive discharge against the self; (4) the *ideal relationship*—a representation of a wished-for, optimal relationship. To this fourth aspect of the ego ideal belong representations of actions that either ought to be done or ought to be avoided so that the desired relationship can prevail. These various representations provide yardsticks for measuring how well the individual fulfills expectations of him- or herself vis-à-vis others; they also help determine the nature of the unpleasant affects attending failure.

The primary affects associated with the functioning of the ego ideal or superego—shame and guilt—often overlap, but some distinguishing generalizations may be made about them. Shame protects an integral image of the self; guilt, the integrity of the object. Thus shame relates primarily to failure, weakness, or flaws in the self—to the inability to see one's self as one wants others to see one. Guilt refers to some attack upon the other—a violation of a personal code of actions based on the "ideal relationship."

The representations held by the ego ideal are based on identifications—both with the idealized parent and with earlier images of the self. Yet strong influences may also lead to an ego ideal radically opposed to such identifications. Such *disidentification* or *negative identity* reflects intrasystemic conflicts between parts of the superego (ideals, values) or parts of the ego. When severe, such conflicts may lead to pathology, for example, identity conflicts. Split identity often involves impulsive action and more rarely multiple personality or symptoms of depersonalization.

Although the ego ideal forms over the course of the ego's development, in some pathological conditions the earliest images associated with primitive drive manifestations (merger fantasies, grandiose ambitions) appear to persist and even to impede the formation of ideals at later stages. Such pathology renders the individual vulnerable to severe *narcissistic injury* and to the experience of intense and archaic affects such as rage, shame, depression, and anxiety, as well as to the more derivative narcissistic affects such as envy, jealousy, spite, and scorn. A. Reich (1954) pointed out the role of sadistic superego forerunners and archaic forms of the ego ideal in pathological states involving crude sexual ideals, unstable ego boundaries, and confusion between wish and reality.

See CONFLICT; DEPERSONALIZATION; GUILT; IDEALIZATION; IDENTITY; INTERNALIZATION; SHAME; SUPEREGO.

References

Erikson, E. H. (1956). The concept of ego identity. *JAPA*, 4:56–121.
Freud, S. (1914). On narcissism. *SE*, 14:67–102.
Hartmann, H. & Loewenstein, R. M. (1962). Notes on the superego. *PSOC*, 17:42–81.
Holder, A. (1982). Preoedipal contributions to the formation of the superego. *PSOC*, 37:245–272.

Jacobson, E. (1964). *The Self and the Object World*. New York: Int. Univ. Press.
Kohut, H. (1971). *The Analysis of the Self*. New York: Int. Univ. Press.
Piers, G. & Singer, M. B. (1953). *Shame and Guilt*. Springfield: Thomas; new ed., New York: Norton, 1971.
Reich, A. (1954). Early identifications as archaic elements in the superego. *JAPA*, 2:218–238.
——— (1960). Pathologic forms of self-esteem regulation. *PSOC*, 15:215–232.
Sandler, J., Holder, A. & Meers, D. (1963). The ego ideal and the ideal self. *PSOC*, 18:139–158.
Wurmser, L. (1981). *The Mask of Shame*. Baltimore: Johns Hopkins Univ. Press.

■ EGO IDENTITY

Erikson's (1956) term for a psychosocial extension of the psychoanalytic concept of identity. It denotes "certain comprehensive gains which the individual, at the end of adolescence, must have derived from all of his pre-adult experience in order to be ready for the tasks of adulthood" (p. 56). The term was chosen to indicate the role of the ego (as an agency) in maintaining a genetic continuity of self representation through "the selective accentuation of significant identifications throughout childhood; and the gradual integration of self-images in anticipation of an identity" (p. 103). That identity "connotes both a persistent sameness within oneself . . . and a persistent sharing of some kind of essential character with others" (p. 57). Involved are a sense of individual identity, unconscious striving for a continuity of personal character, ego synthesis, and maintenance of an inner solidarity with a group's ideals and identity.

Ego identity is manifest in the individual's views, ideals, standards, behavior, and role in society. It is characterized by "the more or less actually attained but forever to-be-revised sense of the reality of the self within social reality, [while] . . . the ego ideal represents a set of to-be-strived-for but forever not-quite-attainable ideal goals for the self" (p. 105).

Erikson viewed identity as only one concept applicable to a gradual unfolding of the personality through phase-specific psychosocial crises. At the end of adolescence identity must be integrated as a relatively conflict-free psychosocial arrangement. If such integration does not occur, a syndrome of *identity diffusion* appears, usually when circumstances demand simultaneous commitment to physical intimacy, occupational choice, energetic competition, and psychosocial self-definition.

See CHARACTER; EGO; IDENTITY.

References

Erikson, E. H. (1956). The problem of ego identity. *JAPA*, 4:56–121.

■ EGO INSTINCT

A term frequently used by Freud, particularly before he formulated the structural hypothesis. For the most part it seems synonymous with self-preservative instincts. But Freud's (1912) comment, "We learn . . . that the sexual instincts find their first objects by attaching themselves to the valuations made by the ego instincts" (p. 180), suggests that ego instinct plays a role in the formation of object relations. In the context of the structural hypothesis, which holds that the ego's role is to modulate the expression of instincts in accordance with the exigencies imposed by the environment and superego, *ego instinct* became self-contradictory. Hartmann (1937), for example, clearly distinguished between the instinctual functions of the id and autonomous ego functions.

Modell (1975) has reintroduced the term in connection with his effort to reconcile structural theory with object relations theory. He proposes a second order of "quieter" instincts—in effect gene-derived propensities—not associated with id function. Modell feels these instincts account for such phenomena as the development of attachments and object relations. They are distinguished from Freudian instincts in that they do not have a definable physiological source; they do not seek to resolve tension via discharge; they derive gratification from interaction with the object rather than from consummating an object-directed impulse; initiation of behavioral patterns depends on timely and appropriate stimulation from the environment.

See INSTINCT; INSTINCT THEORY; INSTINCTUAL DRIVE.

References

Freud, S. (1912). On the universal tendency to abasement in the sphere of love. *SE*, 11:179–190.
Hartmann, H. (1937). *Ego Psychology and the Problem of Adaptation*. New York: Int. Univ. Press.
Modell, A. (1975). The ego and the id. *IJP*, 56:57–68.

■ EGO PSYCHOLOGY

Covers all areas of study, research, theory building, and clinical application that place major emphasis on, and are presented from, the vantage point of the ego. Early psychoanalysis focused mainly on drive or id psychology, the unconscious, and conflict, with more or less *pari passu* references to the ego as personality, self, or defense (repression). In the early 1920s Freud's structural theory and delineation of resistances established ego psychology as a major focus of the new science of psychoanalysis. Anna Freud's study of ego defenses and Hartmann's elaboration of ego adaptation followed. These developments opened the theory to research into psychosocial and constitutional considerations, thus enhancing the claim that psychoanalysis is a general psychology of the mind.

See ADAPTATION; EGO; DEFENSE; METAPSYCHOLOGY; STRUCTURAL THEORY.

References

Blanck, G. & Blanck, R. (1974). *Ego Psychology*. New York: Columbia Univ. Press.

Freud, A. (1936). *The Ego and the Mechanisms of Defense*. New York: Int. Univ. Press, 1966.

Hartmann, H. (1951). Technical implications of ego psychology. *PQ*, 20:31–43.

Kris, E. (1951). Ego psychology and interpretation in psychoanalytic therapy. *PQ*, 20:15–30.

Loewenstein, R. M., Newman, L. M., Schur, M. & Solnit, A. J., eds. (1966). *Psychoanalysis—A General Psychology*. New York: Int. Univ. Press.

■ EGO REGRESSION

See REGRESSION.

■ EGO STRENGTH

□ Ego Weakness

Commonly used clinically to designate an overall assessment of an individual's psychic functioning in relation to the self, objects, and environment. Such global impressions may overlook strength or weakness in specific areas of functioning. A strong ego might be defined as one that has developed substantial competence in dealing with internal impulses and the external world. Mastery over these forces, developed over time, may enable some individuals with tendencies toward major psychopathology to emerge psychologically healthy.

Elements that together make up global ego strength or competence include the individual's ability to tolerate anxiety; the capacity for modulating and channeling instinctual urges and superego demands; adequate reality testing and judgment; a sense of the reality of world and self; adequate frustration tolerance and impulse control; the ability to conceptualize and to utilize abstract thinking; and the capacity to utilize appropriate ego defenses. In turn, these capacities are derived from specific functions of the ego—perceptive, integrative, defensive, and so on. Ego strength involves the ability to deal with stress, an adequate work and social history, the pleasurable pursuit of hobbies and interests, and a capacity for humor.

Ego weakness refers to failures or deficits in the above ego capacities. It may result from childhood psychological trauma. Factors contributing to ego weakness include genetic inheritance and intrauterine insults affecting cerebral functioning. Freud first suggested that unusually strong instincts on a constitutional basis might arrest development and thus lead to ego weakness.

The concept of weakness or strength of the ego has particular relevance in the assessment of patients for analysis, since a certain degree of ego strength and capacity for impulse control, frustration tolerance, intelligence, and reality testing is necessary for successful analysis. Analysis of severely disturbed patients with profound ego weaknesses is sometimes possible but necessitates some modification of classical technique. Patients that may benefit from analysis include those suffering from borderline personality disorders but retaining specific and relatively stable pathological ego structures despite significant ego weaknesses (poor impulse control, lack of tolerance for anxiety, lack of sublimatory channels, impairment in self–object differentiation, predominantly primitive defense mechanisms such as splitting and projective identification).

See DEFENSE; EGO FUNCTION.

References

Fenichel, O. (1954). Ego strength and ego weakness. *Collected Papers*. New York: Norton, vol. 2, pp. 25–48.

Kernberg, O. F. (1967). Borderline personality organization. *JAPA*, 15:641–685.

White, R. W. (1963). *Ego and Reality in Psychoanalytic Theory*. *Psychol. Issues*, 3:136–150.

■ EIGHT-MONTH ANXIETY

See STRANGER ANXIETY.

■ EJACULATIO PRAECOX

See IMPOTENCE.

■ EJACULATIO RETARDATA

See IMPOTENCE.

■ ELATION

An abnormally elevated, incongruous mood, often constituting the affective component of states of mania and hypomania. The elevated mood is related to the primary defense of denial; it is usually accompanied by marked physical and mental hyperactivity.

Viewed as an affect, even though incongruous, elation is not always pathological. It occurs in children's fantasies and in dreams, which employ denial. Young children use denial as a defense, and elation is a primary affect of infancy, but under ordinary conditions the role of denial in adulthood is minimal and elation does not normally occur. Such animated states of mind that do occur—enthusiasm, for example—are formally and dynamically related to elation, but they are moderate, more oriented toward reality, and more adaptive than elation.

See AFFECTS; HYPOMANIA; MANIA; MOOD.

References

Greenson, R. R. (1962). On enthusiasm. *JAPA,* 10:3–21.

Lewin, B. D. (1950). *The Psychoanalysis of Elation.* New York: Norton.

Pao, P.-N. (1971). Elation, hypomania and mania. *JAPA,* 19:787–798.

■ ELECTRA COMPLEX

See OEDIPUS COMPLEX.

■ EMOTIONAL REFUELING

See SEPARATION-INDIVIDUATION.

■ EMPATHY

A mode of perceiving by vicariously experiencing (in a limited way) the psychological state of another person. Literally, it means "feeling into" another person, as contrasted with *sympathy,* which means "feeling with." It has its origin in nineteenth-century aesthetics and psychology, where it was equated with motor mimicry and inference from the observer's own kinesthetic sensations as a way of knowing and understanding the object.

The capacity for empathy is thought to be developmentally related to preverbal mother–infant interactions in which there is a concordance of wish, need, and response. It is an essential prerequisite for the practice of psychoanalysis. In the analytic situation empathy derives in part from the analyst's evenly suspended attention and the developed autonomy that is part of his or her work ego. Analysts do not view empathy as a mystical or transcendent experience. The patient's verbal and nonverbal activities and affects impinge on the analyst at work, producing resonating, parallel states. The analyst's self-perceptions or introspections then become a source of information about the analysand. Empathy, therefore, is a temporary, partial ego regression in the service of the analytic process, permitting an easily reversible trial identification with the analysand. It may occur during a loss of verbal communication and understanding—and may constitute a reaction to the resulting experience of loss in the analytic relationship.

Empathy is preconscious, silent, and automatic. It coexists with more objective ways of gathering information about feelings and behavior. Immediate, first-hand empathic data need to be reviewed and integrated with other information to yield full analytic insight. Empathy thus includes many components—affective, cognitive, inferential, and synthetic—which, taken together, constitute a substrate of psychoanalytic treatment.

Empathy does not substitute for analysis of transference and resistance, though it can yield information about these processes. It is relatively neutral and nonjudgmental, unlike the related phenomena of pity and *sympathy,* from which it should be rigorously distinguished. Pity and sympathy lack objectivity, encourage overidentification, and sometimes lead to enactment of rescue fantasies. Empathy can become a source of countertransference if lingered over, fearfully avoided, or overvalued at the expense of other modes of analytic observation and comprehension.

Within the perspective of psychoanalytic self psychology (Kohut, 1959), *empathy* signifies a fitting and appropriate perception of and response to the patient's feelings and needs. Within analysis generally, empathy implies a consistent focus on the patient's inner experience. Thus we speak of empathic aspects of understanding, interpretation, or intervention, without giving empathy a superordinate position in psychoanalytic technique.

See ANALYSIS; INTERNALIZATION; INTERPRETATION; INTUITION; REGRESSION; SELF PSYCHOLOGY; WORK EGO.

References

Basch, M. F. (1983). Empathic understanding. *JAPA,* 31:101–126.

Buie, D. H. (1981). Empathy. *JAPA,* 29:281–308.

Greenson, R. R. (1960). Empathy and its vicissitudes. *IJP,* 41:418–424.

Kohut, H. (1959). Introspection, empathy, and psychoanalysis, *JAPA,* 7:459–583.

Levy, S. T. (1985). Empathy and psychoanalytic technique. *JAPA,* 33:353–378.
Lichtenberg, J., Bornstein, M. & Silver, D., eds. (1984). *Empathy,* vols. 1–2. Hillsdale & London: Analytic Press.
Olinick, S. L. (1980). *The Psychotherapeutic Instrument.* New York: Jason Aronson.

■ EMPTINESS

A subjective mental state characterized by a painful sense of impoverishment of inner feelings, fantasies, and wishes, as well as lack of response to external stimuli or mere mechanical response. Convictions, enthusiasms, and relatedness to others all seem lost and are replaced by feelings of deadness, boredom, and superficiality. The person complaining of emptiness often feels changed, different from others, without hope for future happiness, unable to love or care about others or to appropriately respond to affection and attention. Feelings of emptiness may be fleeting, periodic, or—especially in some borderline and narcissistic patients—may define basic subjective self-experience. Emptiness often appears alongside depression, boredom, and depersonalization; at times it may seem to be the entirety of experience, painfully precluding any other feeling.

There are several psychoanalytic hypotheses for the subjective experience of emptiness. Emptiness is explained as the unconscious avoidance of intolerable or otherwise unacceptable feelings (they are replaced by the conscious experience of emptiness); as a demand to be filled up or as a covert complaint against an unsatisfying object; as the result of deteriorated internalized object relations (Kernberg, 1975)—especially the absence of stable and reliable good internal objects; and as a reflection of self-fragmentation in patients with narcissistic personality disorders (Kohut, 1977).

References

Greenson, R. R. (1953). On boredom. *JAPA,* 1:7–21.
Kernberg, O. F. (1975). *Borderline Conditions and Pathological Narcissism.* New York: Aronson.
Kohut, H. (1977). *The Restoration of the Self.* New York: Int. Univ. Press.
Levy, S. T. (1984). Psychoanalytic perspectives on emptiness. *JAPA,* 32:387–404.

■ ENVY

Discontent over another's possession of what one would like for oneself. It is characterized by a sense of uneasiness about the other's good fortune, animosity toward that person, chagrin or mortification over one's own presumed deficiency, and longing for the missing attribute. Because the objective is often unattainable, envy can usually be resolved only by relinquishing the wish and accepting reality. The psychoanalytic prototype of envy is penis envy, but envy may be directed at many attributes. Young boys, in preoedipal identification with mother, may wish to incorporate into their own body image certain favored female attributes; they experience breast envy. Older children may envy the unattainable talents or physical characteristics of siblings or others—height, color of hair or eyes, or physical strength, for example.

Although envy is often combined with rivalry and jealousy, the three phenomena should be differentiated.

See JEALOUSY; KLEINIAN THEORY: Envy; PENIS ENVY; RIVALRY.

References

Neubauer, P. B. (1982). Rivalry, envy, and jealousy. *PSOC,* 37:121–142.

■ EROTISM
□ Erotogenicity
□ Erotogenic Zones

Derived from *Eros,* the Greek word for sexual love and the God of love (Freud used the terms *eros* to designate the life instinct and *libido* to designate its energy), *erotism* is essentially equivalent to sexuality in a broad sense—not limited to genital function. It includes the capacity (*erotogenicity*) for a special type of pleasure that is experienced in anticipation of and during excitation of parts of the body (especially the skin and mucous membranes) in activities that conform to specific memories and fantasies based on the arousal and response patterns of those parts. Freud postulated erotogenicity as a quantitative factor, capable of increase or decrease and displacement from one part of the body to another. Perceptions, feelings, ideas, or actions may, because of this erotogenicity—that is, because of their readiness to be a source of sexual excitation—activate the sexual system. Such excitement spreads to other mental and biological systems, leading to states of mind in which self concepts, object concepts, and aims for physical contact with another are colored by sensuality.

While various perceptions, symbols, or fantasies may be erotogenic, certain anatomical areas of the body—the *erotogenic zones*—are biologically determined components of the sexual system. The craving for sexual gratification is related to these body parts, and their stimulation usually triggers sexual excitation. They are used both for autoerotic satisfaction and for sexual contact with others. The psychobiological patterns and functions of these zones influence both character development and symptom formation. The determination that a particular part of the body will be erotogenic, and the psychosexual functioning of the erotogenic zone, are influenced by developmental and cultural factors. Any area of the body (not just the oral, anal, and genital zones) may become secondarily invested as an erogenous zone. Body parts or areas that become erotogenic are usually those that provide satisfying contact with the mother in infancy through the attention, care, and stimulation given by her. Such contact is the source of the component elements (partial instincts), which later determine sexual aims and are organized, to a greater or lesser degree, under the primacy of the genital zone at puberty.

See COMPONENT INSTINCTS; PSYCHOSEXUAL DEVELOPMENT.

References

Freud, S. (1905). Three essays on the theory of sexuality. *SE,* 7:135–243.

——— (1920). Beyond the pleasure principle. *SE,* 18:7–64, p. 49ff.

——— (1914). On narcissism. *SE,* 14:73–102, p. 84.

Laplanche, J. & Pontalis, J.-B. (1973). *The Language of Psycho-Analysis.* London: The Hogarth Press.

Stoller, R. (1985). *Observing the Erotic Imagination.* New Haven: Yale Univ. Press.

■ EROTOGENIC MASOCHISM

See MASOCHISM.

■ EUPHORIA

A state of physical and emotional well-being, without pain, accompanied by joyous or triumphant high spirits. It is usually artificially induced. Euphoria is often an attempt to regain an experience of happiness or joy that no longer occurs spontaneously. Like elation, the state of euphoria is incongruous with the individual's external or intrapsychic reality, but euphoria is not accompanied by hyperactivity, as is the elation characteristic of mania or hypomania.

Euphoria may be produced normally by diversion or amusement, by the resolution of a difficult life situation, or by the lifting of a heavy responsibility; artificially, it is induced by alcohol and mood-elevating drugs (amphetamines, cocaine, etc.). Extreme forms of euphoria appear in organic, toxic, or traumatic brain syndromes. An "indifferent euphoria," a kind of cheerfulness without emotional depth, has been described in schizophrenia.

See ELATION; MOOD.

References

Bleuler, E. (1911). *Dementia Praecox or the Group of Schizophrenias.* New York: Int. Univ. Press, 1951.

Freud, S. (1905). Jokes and their relation to the unconscious. *SE,* 8:219–236.

■ EXCEPTIONS

See CHARACTER.

■ EXCITING OBJECT

See FAIRBAIRN'S THEORY.

■ EXHIBITIONISM

In the broadest sense, the act of attracting attention to the self. One of the paired component or partial instincts that Freud (1905) described as part of infantile sexuality, exhibitionism is evident in the child's wish to exhibit the body, especially the genitals, particularly during the phallic phase. It is closely related to and usually associated with scopophilia—exhibitionism involves turning the looking impulse onto the self. Other parts of the body or the body as a whole may replace the genitals, or achievements and behavior may be displayed instead.

In a narrower sense exhibitionism is used to refer to the adolescent or adult perversion (almost exclusively male) in which exposure of the genitals is the preferred means of achieving final gratification in orgasm. Exhibitionism first received a perverse or psychopathological meaning in 1877 when Lasegue described the syndrome.

In psychoanalysis the term is used mostly in its nonperverse meaning. The perverse exhibitionist is usually not amenable to psychoanalytic treatment.

See COMPONENT INSTINCTS; SCOPOPHILIA; PERVERSION.

References

Allen, D. W. (1980). Psychoanalytic treatment of the exhibitionist. In *Exhibitionism, Description, Assessment and Treatment,* ed. D. Cox. New York: Garland STPM Press, pp. 59–82.

Lasegue, C. (1977). Les exhibitionnistes. *L'Union Medicale, Troisieme Serie,* 23:225–273.

■ EXPRESSIVE THERAPY

See PSYCHOTHERAPY.

■ EXTERNALIZATION

A general heading for mental processes that result in the individual's attributing inner phenomena to the external world. It can be viewed as the counterpart to internalization. Instinctual wishes, conflicts, moods, and ways of thinking (cognitive styles) may be projected. Thus, angry feelings and aggressive impulses may lead young children to be afraid of monsters in the dark, the savage to believe the jungle is populated by evil spirits, or the paranoiac to see persecutors everywhere.

Freud (1911) described paranoid projection in the Schreber case, which has served as a prototype: love is transformed into hate, which is then externalized; subject and object are changed in the process. Novick and Kelly (1970) describe other types of externalization: *generalization,* a developmentally normal mode of thinking that enables the child to assume that others experience the world in the same way he or she does; and defensive externalizations, in which aspects of the self are projected and causality attributed to others. Child analysts in particular have emphasized the importance of distinguishing between the various types of externalization (Furman, 1980; Sandler, Kennedy & Tyson, 1980). They suggest that the externalizations seen in work with children can also be found in adults.

Anna Freud (1965) cautions that externalization can be confused with transference. Extending her views, Berg (1977) and Novick (1982) have distinguished between *externalizing transference* and *differentiated transference.* In the externalizing type, a part of the patient's internal world—an id impulse, superego prohibition, self representation, or even ego function (e.g., reality testing)—is attributed to the analyst. Pathological family relationships are also among the elements externalized. A differentiated transference basically displaces infantile aims toward earlier objects to the analyst.

Externalization encompasses a range of normal and pathological phenomena, and the processes involved may be either adaptive or defensive. The capacity for externalization may be used constructively in art, poetry, literature, and other cultural activities. It is also the basis for such psychological tests as the Rorschach. The concept provides a way of unifying seemingly disparate theoretical orientations: the Kleinian concept of *projective identification,* for example, can be understood as a special type of externalization; and Kohut's *mirror* and *idealizing transferences* are forms of externalizing transference.

See DEFENSE; INTERNALIZATION; PROJECTION; TRANSFERENCE.

References

Berg, M. D. (1977). The externalizing transference. *IJP,* 58:235–244.

Freud, A. (1965). Normality and pathology in childhood. *WAF,* 6.

Freud, S. (1911). Psycho-analytic notes on an autobiographical account of a case of paranoia. *SE,* 11:3–82.

Furman, E. (1980). Transference and externalization. *PSOC,* 35:267–284.

Novick, J. (1982). Varieties of transference in the analysis of an adolescent. *IJP,* 42:139–148.

Novick, J. & Kelly, K. (1970). Projection and externalization. *PSOC,* 25:69–95.

Sandler, J., Kennedy, H. & Tyson, R. L. (1980). *The Technique of Child Psychoanalysis.* Cambridge: Harvard Univ. Press.

■ EXTRAVERSION

See ANALYTICAL PSYCHOLOGY TERMS: Typology.

■ FACE-BREAST EQUATION

A phenomenon whereby the human face and breast may unconsciously become identified or fused with each other, or they may screen each other. The identification between the eyes and the nipples is essential and particularly prominent. This phenomenon was discovered by R. J. Almansi (1960) in several clinical cases in which actual or threatened loss of the object (such as birth of siblings, termination of analysis), brought to the surface intense oral longings and feelings of aggression connected to oral deprivation. Other instances of this phenomenon were also found in humorous drawings, ancient artifacts, and linguistics.

This material is strong evidence for the hypothesis that this equation may embody perceptual experiences harking back to the nursing situation. The infant sees the mother's face while nursing, and the nipple upon her withdrawal of the breast; the infant's eyes deviate from the mother's face in the general direction of the breast in a period when the dividing line between the "I" and the "non-I" is not yet sharply drawn. These ideas are consistent with Spitz's hypothesis that the Isakower phenomenon and Lewin's dream screen represent the visually perceived human face and Spitz's studies on the importance of the gestalt of the mother's face in the child's early mental life and in the formation of object relations.

See ORALITY; PRIMAL CAVITY.

References

Almansi, R. J. (1960). The face-breast equation. *JAPA,* 8:43–70.

Spitz, R. A. (1946). The smiling response. *Genet. Psychol. Monagr.,* 34:57–125.

——— (1955). The primal cavity. *PSOC,* 10:215–240.

——— (1957). *No and Yes.* New York: Int. Univ. Press.

■ FAIRBAIRN'S THEORY

The theoretical contributions of W. Ronald D. Fairbairn were clinically based on the study of dreams and on work with hysterical and schizoid individuals. Underlying the pathology of the latter he discovered traumatic experiences in infancy that caused them to feel unloved for themselves "as persons." When innate strivings for interaction, especially those based on incorporative wishes, were not lovingly responded to, these infants came to feel that their love was bad or worthless. Deprivation had not only intensified their oral needs but had also imparted an aggressive quality to them, and frustration due to the mother's lack of love had made such patients experience their own love as demanding and aggressive. As a result, they withdrew from spontaneous relations with the mother and overinvested in an "inner world," thus splitting the ego into two parts, one dealing with external figures and another linked to internal objects.

Melanie Klein, whose work greatly influenced Fairbairn, postulated a critical first structural achievement whereby the infant could preserve his or her internalized mother as a whole person from the destructive impulses of the death instinct. This phase, with its anxieties about losing the good object, she named the *depressive position.* Fairbairn concluded that an essential prerequisite for what Klein described involved gaining a structured security within the self from which to relate to the good mother. Anxieties related to this earlier phase were aroused not by loss of the good object but by dread of losing the emerging self, that is, distintegrating into fragments equivalent to death or madness. In keeping with Klein's choice of terms he adopted the term *schizoid position* for this primary critical phase. The depressive and schizoid positions were closely linked, and Fairbairn regarded failure in their developmental functions to be the two ultimate disasters that could threaten the ego. He followed Klein in telescoping all structural developments in these two early positions, but he did not accept her concept of a death instinct. Rather, he stressed environmental factors—namely, the quality of the mother's loving care—as crucial to early development.

Fairbairn concluded that the libido theory should be replaced by one founded on purely psychological factors in the relations with the mother and later the father, not on hypothetical instinctual energies and the zonal discharge of tension. In short, Fairbairn asserted that psychoanalysts' fundamental concern was not the vicissitudes of instinct but events within relationships of dependence on others, without which there could be no development.

His clinical observations led Fairbairn to develop what he called an *object relations theory of the personality.* This reinterpretation of psychoanalysis had two substantial departures from Freud. First, Fairbairn conceived of the ego as a structure present from birth rather than developed from the id as a result of its relations with reality. The ego had an energy of its own, not acquired from the id; it was a *dynamic structure.* This idea was consistent with the view in modern physics that energy cannot be conceived as independent from matter or structure. Since he conceptualized libido as a function of the ego and aggression as a reaction to frustration or deprivation, Fairbairn's formulation dispensed with an independent id.

His second departure relates to energy itself, for which he retained the term *libido.* Fairbairn's libido is object-seeking, not pleasure-seeking; its aim is not the relief of tension but the establishment of satisfactory relationships. In seeking to satisfy the basic human need to relate to others, the infant is oriented toward reality from the start. This viewpoint coincides with the modern biological conception of the infant organism as a functioning totality existing in a specified environment. Fairbairn questioned Freud's view that the infant was activated by a number of instincts or forces anchored in the erotogenic zones. Instead he saw the infant as oriented toward the mother and the erotogenic zones as merely means to reach a satisfactory relationship; they were "techniques" or "channels" available for the expression of libidinal needs related to objects, not the sources of libidinal stimuli or the primary determinants of libidinal aims.

Fairbairn gradually developed a revised model of the structure of the mind. Using Klein's concept of an inner world of fantasy relations, Fairbairn evolved a systematic theoretical framework for normal development and psychopathological conditions in terms of dynamic structures within the self. He replaced the structural model of id/ego/superego with the *basic endopsychic structure,* a unitary, all-embracing psychic structure, for which he retained the term *ego.* Itself a source of energy, the ego is from the start oriented toward reality, seeking a relationship with a primal object, the breast or mother. The structure of the mind develops from this pristine ego through the processes of internalization, splitting, and subsequently repression of the maternal object.

Necessary dissatisfactions and frustrations in the relationship between mother and infant, especially those activated by separations, result in the internalization of an object which is both satisfying and unsatisfying. The infant's response is ambivalent, anxiety is evoked, the sense of security is disturbed, and defensive operations are elicited. Aggression serves as the energy of repression, and splitting is the result. *Splitting*—which Fairbairn postulated as a universal mental phenomenon necessary to cope with the frustration and overexcitement of early human relationships—is a normative (although sometimes pathological) defense mechanism that divides and organizes the ego (self). Objectionable aspects of the object are split off and repressed, constituting an internal world. Some internal objects represent whole persons, others such parts as breasts or penises. These whole or part objects can be repressed or projected onto outside objects. Extreme qualities of a precursory, undivided object-representational structure called the *original object* are split into two "bad" partial objects: the *rejecting object,* a frustrating, withholding, persecutory component; and the *exciting object,* an alluring, seductive component (preoedipally a maternal part object, the breast, and oedipally the penis, the father regressively treated as a part object). The remaining nucleus is a desexualized, accepted *ideal object* that is originally internalized as the comforting, gratifying aspect of the breast. The original object receives the infant's love and hate. It is later dichotomized into an *accepted object* (an early term for the ideal object) that receives the infant's love and a *rejected object,* an internalized bad object with two components or *subsidiary objects*—the exciting object and the rejecting object—held in repression by the central ego. In his early writings Fairbairn considered the *accepted* (*ideal*) *object* "the nucleus of the superego."

Fairbairn conceived of the ego as attached libidinally to objects; hence the splitting of the object involves the splitting of parts of the ego associated with it. The inner world eventually reaches a more or less stable constellation with the ego linked to a number of internal objects. From the precursor *original* or *undivided ego,* a tripartite structuring emerges.

1. The *central ego,* the "residue of the undivided ego," serves as the agent of repression. Fairbairn called it the *I* and thought it comprised conscious, preconscious, and unconscious elements, although he emphasized its conscious nature. Rinsley (1982) considers it analogous to Freud's *reality ego* and emphasizes its whole objectlike nature.
2. The *libidinal ego* is the split-off, repressed part of the original ego that comes into libidinal relationship with the exciting object. Fairbairn thought of this as analogous to the classical id; Rinsley compares it to Freud's purified pleasure ego.
3. The *antilibidinal ego* (originally called the *internal saboteur*) is the split-off, repressed part of the original ego that comes into libidinal relationship with the rejecting object. Identified with attacking parent(s), the antilibidinal ego represents a primitive persecutory structure that later merges in part with the inhibiting aspects of what Freud conceptualized as the ego ideal and the superego. The antilibidinal ego aroused fear, however, rather than the guilt elicited by Freud's structures.

Thus what Freud described as the superego Fairbairn (1963) considered a "complex structure comprising (a) the ideal object or ego-ideal, (b) the antilibidinal ego, and (c) the rejecting (or antilibidinal) object" (p. 224). What he called a *moral defense* was an effort by the superego to maintain good object relations with bad objects by reinforcing the internalization of the split-off, bad (frustrating and exciting) object.

The early splitting could be intensified or modified by the parents' attitudes. Fairbairn regarded this structure as the universal pattern from which development proceeds and therefore called it the *basic endopsychic situation,* though it is essentially the same as the schizoid position. It arises from the central ego's "aggressive attitude" toward the libidinal ego and the antilibidinal ego, which it splits off from itself and represses. Fairbairn did not accept the primacy of the oedipus complex, which in his theory is a derivative of the earlier structure. He regarded longing for genital relations with oedipal objects and corresponding fears and prohibitions as a consequence of regression from total and integrated relations to part-object relations with oedipal parents.

Fairbairn defines repression as either *direct* or *indirect*. The former consists of the central ego's "attitude of rejection" toward the exciting object and the rejecting object and secondarily toward their affiliated libidinal ego and antilibidinal ego. Indirect repression is the antilibidinal ego's "uncompromisingly hostile attitude toward the libidinal ego" and its affiliated exciting object. The subsidiary (rejecting and exciting) objects and subsidiary egos (libidinal and antilibidinal) are repressed and therefore unconscious, but Fairbairn does not account for how repressed (that is, split-off) mental contents become unconscious—indeed, repression and splitting seem to be essentially the same process.

Fairbairn replaced Abraham's schema of libidinal development and its phases—oral, anal, phallic—with a model for the development of object relationships based on the vicissitudes of dependence on the mother. Three stages were postulated:

Stage 1, *infantile dependence,* is marked by absolute, inescapable dependence, with the mother's breast as a natural biological object to which the infant's mouth relates. But a predominant attitude of incorporation, or "taking in" from the object, characterizes this stage rather than libidinal investment of the mouth, resulting in internalization of the breast. This stage involves *primary identification,* by which Fairbairn meant something akin to fusion with an object not yet fully differentiated from the self. Infantile dependence, primary identification, and narcissism are thus connected in Fairbairn's model. This stage is divided into an *early oral (preambivalent) phase* in relation to the maternal breast (as part object) and a *late oral (ambivalent) phase* in relation to the mother-with-the-breast, that is, a whole object treated as a part object.

Stage 2, *quasi independence,* is a long intermediate or *transitional stage* that has no specific, natural biological object. The infant establishes firmer relationships with external objects, which are progressively better differentiated, and organizes his or her internal world with the internal representations of the objects. Discrimination, acceptance, and rejection characterize this stage. The whole object is treated as bodily contents, and "bad" parts of the object are expelled. This is why this stage is tinted with "excretory" attitudes, according to Fairbairn—not because of libidinal endowment of the anus or feces.

Fairbairn found that all of his schizoid patients exhibited, at some stage of analysis, the patterns of each of the common psychoneuroses as defensive measures against the basic disaster of loss of the self. Hence he believed that psychoneuroses could not be regarded as pathological entities, each with a specific origin in one of the libidinal phases. Instead, he regarded them as *transitional stage techniques* of internalization and externalization resulting from common family patterns. These techniques enable the child to regulate or "deal with" the accepted object and rejected object and to renounce stage 1 (oral) relationships based upon primary identification in favor of relationships based upon differentiated objects. As these techniques persist into later life, however, they become pathological mechanisms for warding off regression to schizoid and depressive states and are recognizable in phobic, hysteric, obsessional, and paranoid behavior.

Stage 3, *mature dependence,* reflects the achievement of full self–object differentiation and a give-and-take relationship with whole objects. The natural biological object is the genital of a nonincestuous partner (thus the stage corresponds to the classical concept of genitality). However, an attitude of sharing or cooperation between equals is characteristic of this stage, and the biological aspect is only part of the whole relationship.

Fairbairn also introduced to psychoanalytic theory an object relations approach that some analysts consider more appropriate than Freud's scheme (which was founded on nineteenth-century views of free energies as forces apart from structures). Klein's findings were essential to the development of Fairbairn's concepts, but he worked out—in relative isolation and with remarkable cogency—a contribution whose value has been increasingly recognized, especially by Kernberg, Rinsley, and others who treat the more serious disorders that were once deemed unsuitable for analysis. Guntrip (1961) greatly widened appreciation of Fairbairn's work by providing clinical material in support of it and helping make Fairbairn's highly condensed exposition more understandable.

References

Fairbairn, W. R. D. (1954). *An Object-Relations Theory of the Personality*. New York: Basic Books.

______ (1963). Synopsis of an object-relations theory of the personality. *IJP*, 44:224–225.

Greenberg, J. R. & Mitchell, S. A. (1983). *Object*

Relations in *Psychoanalytic Theory*, pp. 151–187. Cambridge: Harvard Univ. Press.
Guntrip, H. (1961). *Personality Structure and Human Interaction*. New York: Int. Univ. Press.
______ (1968). *Schizoid Phenomena, Object-Relations and the Self*. London: Hogarth Press.
Kernberg, O. F. (1980). Fairbairn's theory and challenge. In *Internal World and External Reality; Object Relations Theory Applied*, pp. 57–84. New York: Jason Aronson.
Rinsley, D. B. (1982). Fairbairn's object relations and classical concepts of dynamics and structure. In *Borderline and Other Self Disorders: A Developmental and Object-Relations Perspective*, pp. 251–270. New York: Jason Aronson.

■ FAMILY ROMANCE

Designates a variety of fantasies expressing a corrective revision of the identity of the subject's parentage. The child becomes disenchanted by the discrepancy between the idealized image of the parents he or she held in childhood and the more fallible portrait that emerges in later years. In one version of the fantasy the child entertains the notion that he or she is the offspring of another couple, persons of noble or exalted rank, from whom the child has been separated in infancy, and with whom he or she will be one day reunited. Although this transparent wish to augment self-esteem may be viewed as a repudiation of the true parents, on a deeper psychological level it is an attempt to reinstate them to their erstwhile idealized status, recalling "those happy vanished days," as Freud put it, when the father "seemed the noblest of men and the mother the dearest and loveliest of women."

The family romance may also serve to mitigate oedipal guilt by denying the incestuous quality of libidinal feelings toward the true parents. Additionally it may permit a repudiation of kinship with envied siblings, who, by means of the fantasy, are reduced to bastardy.

Family romance fantasies tend to be abandoned in later years. They sometimes persist into adult life, however, and may play an important role in the fictitious autobiography of the imposter.

Variations on the theme are common in mythology, fiction, drama, and opera. The Christ legend in which Jesus is depicted not as the child of Joseph, the humble carpenter, but as the Son of God, is an expression par excellence of the family romance. Rank (1909) widened the scope of the family romance fantasy as described by Freud by associating it with rescue fantasies—found not only in such fairy tales as Cinderella and in myths related to the birth of the hero but also in apocryphal versions of the early life of the creative artist, as noted by Ernst Kris (1952). According to a stereotypical formula, the future artist is a simple peasant child who, engaged in some rudimentary artistic effort, is accidently discovered by an established master. The master rescues the youth from obscurity and forthwith becomes his or her teacher and mentor. In another variant of the idealized parent of the family romance fantasy, the rescuer, a personage of near-divine stature, becomes the progenitor of a genius.

See FANTASY.

References

Freud, S. (1909). Family romances. *SE*, 9:237–241.
______ (1910). A special type of choice of object made by men. *SE*, 11:171–172.
______ (1939). Moses and monotheism. *SE*, 23:11–16.
Kris, E. (1952). *Psychoanalytic Explorations in Art*. New York: Int. Univ. Press, pp. 69–72.
Rank, O. (1909). *The Myth of the Birth of the Hero*. New York: Nerv. Ment. Dis. Monogr., 18.

■ FANTASY

The commonsense specimen for the psychoanalytic concept of fantasy is the *daydream*, a storylike piece of mentation which is usually a transparent gratification of sexual, aggressive or self-aggrandizing wishes—a form of wish fulfillment enacted in the imagination. When conscious and in its purest form, fantasizing occurs in an altered state of mind resembling the state before falling asleep. This state is sometimes called *reverie*. Almost everyone is also familiar with brief fragments, at least, of personal "stories" that occur during full engagement with another person or situation in the external world.

Common types of conscious fantasy, familiar to most people from their own experience, are fantasies of gratification (sexual conquest or particular sexual activities), which may or may not accompany masturbation; fantasies of revenge, reparation, or the undoing of a blunder or humiliation ("what I should have said"); fantasies of great wealth, resounding success, accomplishment, recognition, power, fame, or adulation; and fantasies of violent or destructive acts.

Freud (1905) pointed out that certain functions related to survival become attuned to "what is there," to reality; other functions, especially those having to do with the production of pleasure, remain relatively free of such adjustments until much later in development—sometimes permanently. Such self-stimulating pleasurable activities as thumb sucking may at first be carried out without associated mental content, but later in development they are usually accompanied by thoughts about activities with other persons. Fantasizing is thought to arise in this way, as a result of the combination of pleasurable sensations and memories of experiences with others. These memories are not necessarily connected strongly with immediate external events. Kleinian analysts also maintain that fantasies may be inherited.

There is a vast amount of evidence that most mental activity is unconscious. This is especially true of fantasy. Fantasies may be created afresh or recalled from memory; they may be freely conscious, conscious only under special circumstances, or warded off (defended against) more or less firmly. In addition, the kind of thinking characteristic of daydreams, in which satisfaction pushes aside reality and imagined action replaces reflection, goes on continuously during waking and sleeping hours.

Probably what we are aware of as conscious fantasy is in fact a derivative of unconscious patterns or structures that generate a variety of conscious fantasies and have other, important organizing influences on our mental life as well. For example, in attempting to explain why much dream content apparently occurs almost instantaneously, Freud (1900) suggested that the dream work may include an unconscious fantasy which is then opened up in remembering the dream. Unconscious fantasies can be responsible for the particular form or content of psychological symptoms and for the lifelong patterns known as character traits.

Unconscious fantasy is descriptively connected to conscious daydreams and theoretically connected to the concept of instinctual drives. Drives involve aim, object, and strength (impetus); *impulses* are mental phenomena directly related to drives or drive derivatives. They may involve simple action sequences such as preferred kinds of sexual foreplay. But drive derivatives are more commonly organized by experience and memory into more complex mental structures in which action, aims, and other people are discernible as experienced or desired. Acts often vary, incorporating a number of aims into one scenario and using the memory image of a person as a model or type rather than in its original form. These unconscious *templates* or unconscious fantasies become factors in the organization of new experience as well as in the reproduction of patterns of previous pleasure.

The formation of unconscious fantasies is partially determined by psychosexual developmental level, and fantasies are grouped around certain basic wishes. The child organizes perceptual experiences according to his or her cognitive capacities. If the child witnesses parental coitus during the anal/sadistic phase of development, for example, he or she may understand the act—and thus organize the memory—as the father's sadistically assaulting the mother. This organization, the beginning of what we call a "primal scene fantasy," may or may not remain unconscious—even at the time it is experienced. Subsequently it is almost certain to be defended against. The structure of the fantasy is modified by the defensive activity, so that the unconscious fantasy becomes a compromise formation. In addition, when internal or external stimuli activate the fantasy, it does not become conscious in its "stored" form. Rather, defensively modified derivatives of the fantasy may appear in consciousness—a further alteration of the fantasy in the form of compromise formation. Both the unconscious fantasies and their conscious derivatives are ultimately products of the interaction of wishful impulses, cognitive capacities, defensive operations, and superego functioning.

An orderly taxonomy of unconscious fantasies and/or their derivatives has yet to be developed. Some types of fantasies, however, appear across cultures and are perhaps universal. These include birth, pregnancy, primal scene, spanking (beating), incest, castration, bisexuality (in which one plays both roles in the sexual act), and being the secret descendent of exalted parents (family romance). Many of these fantasies were first introduced by Freud (1908) in the essay "On the Sexual Theories of Children." Fantasy content can be related developmentally or regressively to each of the stages of psychosexual organization. Some types of fantasies seem closely connected with psychopathology; for example, bisexual fantasies are common among hysterical personalities; fantasies of fusing or merging with someone else often appear in severe forms of mental illness.

Fantasy serves many functions other than the production of dreams, psychological symptoms, and character traits. Because of the cross-cultural similarities of physiological and early life experience, many elements of fantasy life are shared across cultures. This communality establishes a basis for empathy and for the production and enjoyment of creative works (Arlow, 1969a; Sachs, 1942). Fantasy is also used defensively (A. Freud, 1936). Ever-present, ongoing fantasy thinking partly determines the "set of mind" with which we perceive external stimuli and organize them into life events. Thus "what is consciously apperceived and experienced is the result of the interaction between the data of experience and unconscious fantasy" (Arlow, 1969a, p. 23).

See BEATING FANTASY; BISEXUALITY, CHARACTER, FAMILY ROMANCE; INSTINCTUAL DRIVE; KLEINIAN THEORY; PRIMAL SCENE; PSYCHOSEXUAL DEVELOPMENT, TOPOGRAPHIC POINT OF VIEW.

References

Arlow, J. A. (1969a). Unconscious fantasy and disturbances of mental experience. *PQ,* 38:1–27.

——— (1969b). Fantasy, memory and reality testing. *PQ,* 38:28–51.

Blum, H. P., Kramer, Y., Richards, A. K. & Richards, A. D., eds. (1988). *Fantasy, Myth, and Reality: Essays in Honor of Jacob A. Arlow.* Madison, Conn.: Int. Univ. Press.

Freud, A. (1936). *The Ego and the Mechanisms of Defense.* New York: Int. Univ. Press.

Freud, S. (1900). The interpretation of dreams. *SE,* 4–5.

——— (1905). Three essays on the theory of sexuality. *SE,* 7:130–243.

——— (1908). On the sexual theories of children. *SE,* 9:209–226.

——— (1919). "A child is being beaten." *SE,* 17:179–204.

Sachs, H. (1942). *The Creative Unconscious.* Cambridge, Mass.: Sci-Art Publishers.

■ FATE NEUROSIS

See REPETITION COMPULSION.

■ FEMALE PSYCHOLOGY

Freud (1926) called female psychology a "dark continent" (p. 212). His original formulation, based primarily on reconstructive data obtained from the psychoanalysis of adults, was that male and female development is identical until the child discovers the anatomical differences between the sexes. During the phallic phase both boys and girls behave as if there is only one kind of genital organ—the penis. Ultimately the girl must transfer the dominant erotogenic zone from clitoris to vagina; but in the phallic phase neither boys nor girls are aware of the vagina, and girls use the clitoris to obtain masturbatory gratification. Girls' discovery of their lack of a penis gives rise to feelings of inferiority, penis envy, "masochistic" surrender to a second-class status, and anger at the mother, who is blamed for the deprivation. As the girl loosens her ties to mother as a love object and relinquishes masturbation out of a narcissistic sense of humiliation at the smallness of her clitoris, she gives up her wish for a penis in favor of a wish for a child, now equated with father's penis. For this purpose the girl takes her father as a love object and her mother becomes an object of jealousy. In girls, Freud postulated, the operations of the castration complex precede and prepare for the oedipus complex. In boys, the phallic phase coincides with the oedipus complex, which succumbs to the threat of castration and gives rise to superego formation. The realistic possibility on which the castration threat is based does not apply to girls, and their oedipus complex is different from that of boys. It may be slowly abandoned or eliminated by repression, or it may persist into adulthood, modifying superego development. According to Freud, the castration complex may lead the girl to give up sexuality, cling to masculinity, or develop the "normal" feminine attitude.

More recent research, however, contradicts the hypothesis that femininity is a reactive phenomenon, secondary to a disappointed masculinity. Without testosterone to modify the structure of the external genitals and organization of the brain, the fetus will be female in nature and structure despite its genetic sex. After birth, the parents' assignment of a sex to the child and their rearing are major factors in determining gender orientation. Gender identity is formed in the first three years of life. Innate differences between the sexes have been found from birth. Infant observational research provides evidence for girls' primary femininity before castration anxiety, penis envy, and the oedipus complex, and indicates that feminine fantasies accompany clitoral masturbation. Penis envy and feminine "masochism" may arise secondary to the discovery of the anatomical differences between the sexes, but the intensity of these traits is influenced by the stability of the girl's preexisting feminine identity. Observational as well as reconstructive data suggest that girls can be conflicted about their primary feminine identity, and by shifting focus from their internal organs to the phallus they can use penis envy and feminine masochism as parts of a defensive operation.

See GENDER IDENTITY; MASCULINITY/FEMININITY; PENIS ENVY.

References

Blum, H. P., ed. (1976). Female Psychology. *JAPA,* 24 suppl.: no. 5.

Freud, S. (1923). The infantile genital organization. *SE,* 19:139–145.

——— (1925). Some psychical consequences of

the anatomical distinction between the sexes. *SE,* 19:248–258.

——— (1926). The question of lay analysis. *SE* 20:212.

——— (1931). Female sexuality. *SE,* 21:225–243.

Moore, B. E. (1976). Freud and female sexuality. *IJP,* 57:287–300.

■ FEMININE MASOCHISM

See MASOCHISM.

■ FEMININITY

See MASCULINITY/FEMININITY.

■ FETISH

□ Fetishism

A natural or artificial material object, supposed to be the temporary abode of a supernatural spirit and to possess magical powers capable of achieving the designs of the owner and protecting him or her from injury or disease. Idols and talismans were fetishes and important in primitive religions. The psychoanalytic term is used to describe an inanimate object or a part of the human body that a *fetishist* needs in order to attain sexual arousal and orgasm. Many fetishists can engage in sexual relations with a partner provided they can see, touch, or smell a fetish, or at least engage in a fantasy involving it. Some demand that their partner display or wear certain objects, for instance specific pieces of clothing. Even bodily deformities may become fetishlike prerequisites for the sexual act. For other fetishists, the presence or fantasy of a fetish is all that is needed for sexual arousal and orgasm through masturbation.

The vast majority of fetishists are men. The most common fetishes are feet, hair, women's undergarments, and shoes. Leather articles may serve as fetishes, especially among homosexuals. Fetishistic practices and fantasies may also be combined with such other perversions as sadomasochism and transvestism.

Freud elucidated the dynamic and unconscious aspects of fetishism in two monographs (published in 1905 and 1927). He discovered that the fetish represents in concrete form an unconscious fantasy that defends against awareness of the woman's lack of a penis; the fetish is the woman's—usually mother's—phallus. A split in the ego between realistic conscious perception and the unconscious, contradictory fantasy maintains denial of the "castration" of women, mitigates or eliminates the fear of castration, and allows the individual to engage in intercourse and achieve sexual gratification.

The memory of arousal by a fetish may go back to the oedipal period. It is usually a screen memory, however, concealing early traumas and intense preoedipal castration fears (Greenacre, 1970). Recent observations indicate that the fetish may unconsciously symbolize not only the fantasied female phallus but also the breast, buttocks, and even feces and urine. The relation of the transitional object to fetishism can be considered genetically in terms of "different stages of a similar process" (Dickes, 1983). The infantile fetish appears during the first two years of life as the result of inadequate object relations and defective drive and ego development. It may be the antecedent of the adult fetish (Roiphe & Galenson, 1981).

See CASTRATION; DEFENSE; PERVERSION; SPLITTING; WINNICOTT'S THEORY: Transitional Object.

References

Dickes, R. (1963). Fetishistic behavior. *JAPA,* 11:303–330.

Freud, S. (1905). Three essays on the theory of sexuality. *SE,* 7:125–243.

——— (1927). Fetishism. *SE,* 21:149–158.

Greenacre, P. (1970). The transitional object and the fetish. In *Emotional Growth.* New York: Int. Univ. Press, pp. 335–352.

Roiphe, H. (1968). On an early genital phase. *PSOC,* 23:348–365.

Roiphe, H. & Galenson, E. (1981). *Infantile Roots of Sexual Identity.* New York: Int. Univ. Press, pp. 189–209.

■ FIGHT/FLIGHT

See BION'S THEORY.

■ FIXATION

The persistence of archaic modes of achieving satisfaction, relating to objects, and reacting defensively to danger, as if remnants of functioning at a particular earlier stage of development are "fixed" in the psyche, ready to play a significant role in a later situation. Freud first applied the concept to perversions, which involve the persistence of anachronistic sexual traits related to some aspect of childhood sexuality. Later he used it in describing trauma and various neurotic conditions. For example, he thought the obsessional neurosis was based on fixation at the anal stage.

Freud also mentioned fixation in regard to memories and symptoms, the instinctual drives, and specific ego and superego functions. He listed a number of factors that interfere with development and contribute to points of fixation: constitutional predisposition, circumstances contributing to an unusual amount of pleasure or frustration, accidental events having the effect of trauma, and a postulated "adhesiveness" of the libido that militates against giving up any position the libido has taken up. The idea of fixation thus contributed to the concept of a compulsion to repeat.

Regression to points of fixation readily occurs under certain types of stress. For instance, a child who has reached the oedipal stage may, under the influence of anxiety, regress to the earlier oral or anal stage and behave in a manner characteristic of that period.

More serious is *developmental arrest,* which may result from certain fixations. The child fails to progress, either fully or in part, to a more advanced developmental level. If libidinal development has become severely fixated, the child may not enter the oedipal stage at the usual age and may remain fixed at the oral or anal stage. If ego development is arrested, the child may not achieve age-appropriate reality testing. A person may not sufficiently distinguish self and object, thus using projection and identification excessively as defenses. Inadequate moral development may result from superego arrest. Arrests also occur along developmental lines in which ego, id, and superego work in tandem.

Individuals may stop at some point along a normal developmental line or may be arrested at a pathologically distorted stage. For example, a child suffering from autism may retain early disordered traits.

See DEVELOPMENT; PSYCHOSEXUAL DEVELOPMENT; TRAUMA.

References

Fenichel, O. (1945). *The Psychoanalytic Theory of Neurosis*. New York: Norton.

Freud, S. (1915–17). Introductory lectures on psycho-analysis. *SE,* 16:273–285, lecture 18.

Sandler, J., with A. Freud (1985). *The Analysis of Defense*. New York: Int. Univ. Press.

■ FOREPLEASURE

The emotional response to sexual stimulation preceding sexual intercourse. *Foreplay* may include looking, exhibiting, kissing, fondling, and any action which stimulates the erotogenic zones and heightens erotic tension. Such activity prepares the individual for intercourse by intensifying desire and inducing physiological responses conducive to intromission. The pleasure may result from stimulation of the genitals or nongenital organs such as the breasts, mouth, anus, buttocks, or any other part of the body. Freud (1905) observed that forepleasure may be so great as to preclude sexual intercourse itself. He also used the term to refer to techniques used to prepare a person for the enjoyment of a joke or aesthetic experience.

References

Freud, S. (1905). Three essays on the theory of sexuality. *SE,* 7:125–243.

■ FORMAL ASPECTS

See DREAMING, DREAMS.

■ FREE ASSOCIATION

The basic procedure of psychoanalysis and psychoanalytic psychotherapy. Freud replaced hypnosis with free association in the 1890s and regarded it as the methodological key to all the results of psychoanalysis.

The word *free* in this term refers only to the relative suspension of conscious control. The patient in psychoanalytic treatment is asked to express in words all thoughts, feelings, wishes, sensations, images, and memories, without reservation, as they spontaneously occur. This requirement is called the *fundamental rule of psychoanalysis*. In following the rule, the patient must often overcome conscious feelings of embarrassment, fear, shame, and guilt. His or her cooperation is motivated in part by knowledge of the purpose for which he or she is in analysis—to deal with conflicts and overcome problems.

The nature of the associations, in the regressive state facilitated by the analytic situation, permits the analyst to infer the determinants of the sequences, patterns, and content of the patient's productions, including their unconscious influences and the conflicts between them. The analyst's interventions, especially the interpretations of unconscious determinants, aim at expansion of the patient's freedom of association, that is, the elucidation and mastery of resistances (unconscious interferences), which are expressed in a myriad of ways.

Emphasis on the intimate connection between language, reason, consciousness, and the ability to make decisions has been an explicit feature of the psychoanalytic method from the beginning. Although not all of mental life can be put into words, free association allows the patient to do so as much as possible under conditions in which he or she can integrate the experience of its effects in the analytic process. The analyst's interventions—including silence—aid in sustaining the patient's balance between expression and reflection.

References
Freud, S. (1900). The interpretation of dreams. *SE*, 4–5.
——— (1924). A short account of psycho-analysis. *SE*, 19:189–209.
Kris, A. O. (1982). *Free Association*. New Haven: Yale Univ. Press.
Mahony, P. (1979). The boundaries of free association. *Psychoanal. Contemp. Thought*, 2:151–198.

■ FREE-FLOATING ANXIETY
See ANXIETY.

■ FRIGIDITY
A woman's lack of responsivity during the sexual act. The term has acquired a pejorative connotation and has been largely replaced by *anorgasmia* or *orgasmic dysfunction*. There are varying degrees of unresponsiveness, from lack of erotic feeling to full participation and enjoyment of the sexual act but with apparent inability to achieve orgasm through intercourse. Inadequate vaginal lubrication is sometimes involved; sometimes the involuntary contractions of orgasm are not accompanied by excitement and pleasure. Anatomical and hormonal factors as well as aberrations in drive and ego development have been adduced to explain the inability of some women to achieve "vaginal" orgastic release. This capacity was once accepted as the hallmark of sexual and psychological normality despite its absence in many normal, happy women and intense vaginally experienced orgasms in some severely neurotic and psychotic women. Now, however, frigidity, like all behavioral phenomena, is viewed as multiply determined; specific conflict resolutions may figure in its development. Vicissitudes of development contribute to the representation of different genital parts and the level of their cathexis, determining whether sensation is associated with the clitoris or vagina. Unconscious fantasies may interfere with conscious sexual pleasure and result in inhibitions. These fantasies may equate sexual intercourse with oedipal fulfillment, associate the penis with castration, or conceive of intercourse as an attack by a huge (paternal) phallus that could injure or mutilate. Aggressive fantasies may cast the vagina in the role of a castrating (or devouring) organ that will take back the penis. One's sexual partner, adequacy of stimulation, and the social and cultural conditions under which intercourse takes place are other important determinants of the degree of orgastic response.

See FEMALE PSYCHOLOGY; MASCULINITY/FEMININITY; PENIS ENVY.

References
Greenacre, P. (1950). Special problems of early female sexual development. In *Trauma, Growth and Personality*. New York: Int. Univ. Press, pp. 237–258.
——— (1952). Pregenital patterning. *IJP*, 33:410–415.
Moore, B. E. (1964). Frigidity. *PQ*, 33:323–349.
——— (1975). Freud and female sexuality. *IJP*, 57:287–300.
——— (1977). Psychic representation and orgasm. In *Female Psychology*, ed. H. P. Blum. New York: Int. Univ. Press.

■ FUNDAMENTAL RULE
See FREE ASSOCIATION.

■ FUSION
See PSYCHIC ENERGY.

■ GAIN, PRIMARY (PARANOSIC)
□ Gain, Secondary (Epinosic)
The unconsciously motivated advantages derived from neurotic symptoms and illness. The *primary (paranosic) gain* relates to the motives that lead to symptom formation and to the first appearance of symptoms. It has two components. The *internal* component refers to the advantages of the symptom as a compromise formation between conflicting instinctual and repressive (superego) motivations. Freud (1905) described this internal element as a "saving of psychical effort . . . economically the most convenient solution where there is a mental conflict" (p. 43). (We speak of a "flight into illness.") The *external* component of the primary gain relates to the symptom's usefulness in alleviating the interpersonal conflicts or other external threats that triggered the internal conflict.

The *secondary (epinosic) gain* is the advantage derived from already formed symptoms, advantages that could not have been foreseen or sought after (unconsciously) at the time of initial symptom formation. This gain did not enter into symptom formation but contributes to the establishment of an illness and to resistance to treatment. Secondary gain may also be thought of as having an external and an internal element (Katz, 1963, p. 48), although the external element is more often focused on in analytic discussions. It relates to advantages in interpersonal relationships and life circumstances. The internal element relates to exploitation of the possibilities the illness holds for regressive, narcissistic satisfactions. Freud's (1926) example is of an obsessional individual gaining narcissistic satisfaction from the idea that he is cleaner and more conscientious than other people.

The examples adduced by Freud and others to illustrate secondary gain illustrate the concept's ambiguity. It is generally impossible to determine whether a given factor regarded as secondary gain was present when the symptom first formed. The timing of superego and narcissistic gains from illness are even more difficult to localize temporally after the fact. The distinction between primary and secondary gain on the basis of a sharp distinction between symptom formation and illness also needs to be replaced. As Katz (1963) points out, gains from illness elaborate, defensively and adaptively, upon the gains from symptom formation in a continuous process as neverending as the ego's defensive efforts.

See MULTIDETERMINISM; SYMPTOM.

References

Freud, S. (1905). Fragment of an analysis of a case of hysteria. *SE,* 7:7–122.

——— (1917). Introductory lectures on psychoanalysis, lecture 24. *SE,* 16:378–391.

——— (1926). Inhibitions, symptoms, and anxiety. *SE,* 20:87–174.

Katz, J. (1963). On primary gain and secondary gain. *PSOC,* 18:9–50.

■ GENDER IDENTITY
□ Gender Behavior
□ Gender Role

The basic sense of maleness or femaleness, including the conviction that one is male or female. Gender identity formation is a normal developmental milestone. The first evidence of the process appears in the late preverbal and early verbal periods, as early as sixteen to seventeen months. Gender identity is often clearly demarcated around age two and is relatively unmodifiable by age four. The biological contribution to gender identity is uncertain, but hormonally induced fetal brain differentiation may be involved. Psychologically, gender identity formation is part of the separation-individuation phase and is probably consolidated with the achievement of object constancy.

The precursors of gender identity are the body ego, the early body image, and the dyadic "me/not-me" sense. Gender identity is developed from the extension, elaboration, and integration of these precursors into a male or female self representation. It normally includes a basic internalization of the distinctions between the sexes, identification with one's own sex, and recognition of the two sexes' complementary reproductive functions: to make babies or to have babies.

Gender identity is sometimes considered to be synonymous with or a subcategory of *sexual identity.* It is preferable, however, to distinguish between the terms on the basis of their correlations with specific phases of development. Gender identity refers to the initial preoedipal integration of anatomy, sexual distinctions, and complementary reproductive functioning into a male or female identity. Sexual identity, on the other hand, refers to the phallic-oedipal and oedipal integration of childhood sexual "research," castration anxiety, penis envy, and triangular object relations into a personal erotism. In other words, sexual identity is a later refinement of basic gender sense. The development of sexual identity in the oedipal phase is marked by the elaboration of the concepts of masculinity and femininity (as distinct from basic maleness or femaleness) and by a personal erotism expressed in sexual fantasies and object choices.

Clinical conditions help to illustrate the distinctions between gender identity and sexual identity. For example, in some homosexual men the gender identity is male while the sexual identity, in terms of fantasy and object choice, is female. The etiology of abnormalities of gender identity, as seen in *transsexualism* and some *perversions,* is controversial. Money has suggested a biological etiology (Money & Green, 1969); Stoller (1975) has outlined a nonconflictual symbiotic phase abnormality; and Meyer (1982) has described a process of conflict, fixation, and regression.

Gender identity is different from the terms *gender role* and *gender behavior,* which refer to the culturally determined, stereotypical behavior patterns characteristic of males and females.

References

Galenson, E. & Roiphe, H. (1976). Some suggested revisions concerning early female development. *JAPA,* 24:29–57.

——— (1980). The preoedipal development of the boy. *JAPA,* 28:805–827.

Meyer, J. (1982). The theory of gender identity disorders. *JAPA,* 30:381–418.

Money, J. & Green, R. (1969). *Transsexualism and Sex Reassignment.* Baltimore: Johns Hopkins Univ. Press.

Stoller, R. (1975). *Sex and Gender,* vol. 2. New York: Jason Aronson.

■ GENDER IDENTITY DISORDER

See TRANSSEXUALISM.

■ GENETIC FALLACY

The false assumption that a current function or meaning can be equated with or reduced to its historical precursors, as if genetic continuity is inconsistent with change of function. For example, it might be assumed that manifest oral behavior necessarily derives from or represents a regression to the oral phase of development, or that complex later functioning (for example, surgical skill) is derived from a drive component (such as anal sadism). The belief that some form of adult behavior has the same meaning when it occurs in a child is similarly erroneous.

Allport (1937) stated the essence of the genetic fallacy metaphorically: the life of a tree is continuous with that of its seed, but the seed no longer nourishes the full-grown tree. Earlier purposes lead into later purposes but are abandoned in favor of the latter. Allport used the term *functional autonomy* to emphasize that a historical tie is not necessarily a functional one. Hartmann (1964) agreed and pointed out that *change of function* is inherent in the structural point of view and is part of *secondary autonomy*. Genetic continuity is consistent with a change of function, and many sublimations are examples of this process of change.

See AUTONOMY; CHANGE OF FUNCTION.

References

Allport, G. (1937). *Personality*. New York: Henry Holt, p. 194.

Hartmann, H. (1964). *Essays on Ego Psychology*. New York: Int. Univ. Press, pp. 123, 152, 221–222.

Levy, D. (1983). Wittgenstein on the form of psychoanalytic interpretation. *Int. Rev. Psychoanal.*, 10:106.

■ GENETIC VIEWPOINT

See METAPSYCHOLOGY.

■ GENITALITY

Psychic qualities, phenomena, and concepts associated with the genitals. Analogous to orality and anality, *genitality* is a broad, general term. Libido theory posits a biological progression of ascendency of the sexual zones (oral, anal, urethral, phallic), with associated ego organization referred to as *stages*. These stages are theoretical developmental constructs, not to be confused with sensual functioning.

The *genital stage* is the final stage in instinctual libidinal development. Earlier phases and their conflicts are integrated and subsumed under a genital orientation, representing the attainment of what has been called *genital primacy* or psychosexual maturity. Fixations and regressions to earlier phase levels interfere with the attainment of genital primacy and with genital phase functioning.

The theoretical and clinical usefulness of the concept of genital primacy has been questioned by many authors. Ross (1970), Berezin (Panel, 1969), and Lichtenstein (1970) fault any definition of genital primacy that simply equates it with the capacity for orgastic functioning. Orgastic capacity often bears little relationship to the maturity of object relationships or ego abilities. Clinically, it is common to see sexual genital functioning with orgasm that serves almost entirely the goals of orality or anality. Sarlin (1970) adds to the concept of genital primacy later developments in ego psychology, such as developmental crises, maturity of identifications, control of libidinal and aggressive drives, neutralization processes, and sublimation. Kernberg (1977) shares this view. In his discussion of love, he speaks of the "normal integration of genitality with the capacity for tenderness and a stable, deep object relation" (p. 82). Freud's libido theory was based on reconstruction from the analyses of adults. The data of child and adolescent analysts, obtained directly from children, is more accurate with respect to the chronology of development and the delineation of subphases. Additional data, requiring modification of Freud's original formulations, have been derived from (1) direct observation of children; (2) recent developments in ego psychology and object relations theory; and (3) narcissism and self psychology.

Erikson (1950) assumes an early bisexual disposition for both sexes—he believes full differentiation for the genital modes of male intrusion and female inclusion occurs only at puberty. He therefore prefers to substitute the term *infantile genital stage*, which implies a combination of both intrusive and inclusive modes and modalities, for the more common *phallic phase*.

Kestenberg (1968) posits an early infantile *inner genital phase*, during which genital sensations inside the body cause anxiety leading to externalization of these sensations to the surface of the body or to a substitute such as a doll. This phase precedes the phallic. At puberty, the inner genital phase ends as all component drives, including the phallic, are integrated in the sex-specific genital primacy.

Parens (1980), believing that the term *phallic phase* implies and emphasizes masculine development as primary, proposes the term *first infantile genital phase* for the period between 24 and 36 months. This term is consistent with the concept that boys and girls develop from an earlier primary masculinity or femininity, respectively.

Roiphe (1968) describes an *early genital phase*, emerging between the fifteenth and nineteenth months in boys and girls alike. Children in this phase were observed to repeatedly stimulate their genitals, either directly with the hand or an object or indirectly through rocking, thigh pressure, etc. From the direct observation of toddlers he concluded that genital cathexis and awareness of the genital differences between males and females emerge earlier than had been thought previously. From these observations children appeared to separate and differentiate the genitals from the excretory organs, although the immaturity of the body image precludes a high degree of differentiation. The girl is likely to hold a unitary cloacal concept of the area, which may persist into adolescence (Shopper, 1979). Accordingly, the definition of what is "the genital" varies with the degree of clarity and differentiation of the body image.

See PSYCHOSEXUAL DEVELOPMENT; SYMBOL.

References

Erikson, E. H. (1950). *Childhood and Society*. New York: Norton.

Freud, S. (1905). Three essays on the theory of sexuality. *SE*, 7:123–243.

Kernberg, O. F. (1977). Boundaries and structure in home relations. *JAPA*, 25:81–114.

Kestenberg, J. S. (1967). Phases of adolescence. *J. Amer. Acad. Child Psychiat.*, 6:577–614.

Lichtenstein, H. (1970). Changing implications of the concept of psychosexual development. *JAPA*, 18:300–318.

Panel (1969). The theory of genital primacy in the light of ego psychology. M. Berezin, reporter. *JAPA*, 17:968–987.

Parens, H. (1980). Psychic development during the second and third years of life. In *The Course of Life*, ed. S. Greenspan & G. Pollock. Washington: Nat. Inst. Health, pp. 459–500.

Roiphe, H. (1968). On an early genital phase. *PSOC*, 23:348–365.

Ross, N. (1970). The primacy of genitality in the light of ego psychology. *JAPA*, 18:267–284.

Sarlin, C. N. (1970). The current status of the concept of genital primacy. *JAPA*, 18:285–299.

Shopper, M. (1979). The (re)discovery of the vagina and the importance of the menstrual tampon. In *Female Adolescent Development*, ed. M. Sugar. New York: Brunner/Mazel, pp. 214–233.

■ GOOD ENOUGH MOTHER

See WINNICOTT'S THEORY.

■ GRANDIOSE SELF

See SELF PSYCHOLOGY.

■ GRIEF

A psychophysiological response to loss characterized by decreased interest in the external world, preoccupation with unbidden, poignant reminiscences sometimes of a near hallucinatory intensity, sleep disturbance, sadness, intermittent regret, and weeping.

Although *Trauer*, used by Freud in *Mourning and Melancholia* (1917), can be translated as either "mourning" or "grief," there is clinical and theoretical advantage to considering mourning as the process and grief as the attendant affective response to loss. Freud's concept of grief encompasses response to loss of a loved one or to loss of some representation in the abstract, such as an ideal. Hence it is advantageous to differentiate *bereavement*, specifically loss of a loved one (an interpersonal object), as a subclass of the affect of grief (Pollock, 1978).

The process of mourning an ideal or a loved person takes a sequential course which, when successful, enhances the ego, as has been detailed in many studies of mourning as an adaptive process. The psychopathological counterpart of grief associated with disturbed mourning has been extensively described and is closely associated with the psychodynamic understanding of various kinds of depression.

See DEPRESSION; MOURNING.

References

Bowlby, J. (1961). Process of mourning. *IJP*, 42:317–340.

Freud, S. (1917). Mourning and melancholia. *SE*, 14:243–258.

Jacobson, E. (1957). Normal and pathological moods. *PSOC*, 12:73–113.

Pollock, G. H. (1961). Mourning and adaptation. *IJP*, 42:341–361.

——— (1978). Process and affect. *IJP*, 59:255–276.

Welmore, R. J. (1963). The role of grief in psychoanalysis. *IJP*, 44:97–103.

■ GROUP PSYCHOLOGY

The study of the reciprocal psychic processes involved in behavior of a group and its individual members. Such behavior is greatly affected by the degree of structure provided by the group's leadership, particularly in terms of its effect on the extent of the regressive phenomena typical of groups, on group identification and cohesiveness, and on the ability of the group to function rationally and morally toward stated or alleged goals. A group that functions rationally toward a goal is called a *work group;* the coexistence of regressive mental activity will affect (positively or negatively) the achievement of the group's goals depending on the degree of group structure implemented via interpretations, clarification of goals, the setting of limits, and so on. Freud (1921) explained the regressive emergence of unconscious phenomena in unstructured groups topographically, claiming it arose from the removal of repression: "As we should say, the mental superstructure, the development of which in individuals shows such dissimilarities, is removed and the unconscious foundations, . . . so similar in everyone, stand exposed to view (74)." Moreover, Freud saw the group phenomena as a revival among a collection of individuals of the phylogenetically inherited memory of the primal horde (a small band of people) under the sway of its revered, just, but terrifying father-chief. The bond among the group members evokes the wish for the primal chief as the group ideal, who governs their egos in the place of their ego-ideal and renders them all equal. By reaction formation, the rivalry among group members for the chief's attention is put in the service of preserving justice and equality among the members.

While Freud stated his views largely in oedipal terms, others have seen such group regression as extending well into early primitive object relations (oral, undifferentiated, psychotic). Primitive, seemingly chaotic constellations of behavior frequently emerge—the so-called *Basic Assumptions* of Bion (1961). Through a mutual process of introjection and projective identification, the group focuses these Basic Assumptions upon the leader, who can facilitate the formation of a collective superego among the individual members (depending on their receptivity or "valency"). This allows the individuals to feel identified with one another, creating a group spirit.

See EGO IDEAL; INTERNALIZATION; PRIMAL HORDE; SUPEREGO.

References

Bion, W. R. (1952). Group dynamics. *IJP,* 33:235–247.

——— (1961). *Experiences in Groups.* New York: Basic Books.

Freud, S. (1921). Group psychology and the analysis of the ego. *SE,* 18:67–143.

Ganzarain, R. Group psychology. *PMC.* Forthcoming.

Greenacre, P. (1972). Crowds and crisis. *PSOC,* 27:136–155.

■ GUILT

Refers, like shame, to a group of affects including fear of retribution both from outside and within the self, feelings of remorse, contrition, and penitence. Its core is a form of anxiety with the underlying ideational content: "If I hurt somebody else, I shall be hurt in turn." In addition to this fear of outer or inner retaliation for one's sexual or aggressive acts or wishes, one may hold the depressive conviction that one has already hurt the other and is being punished for it; therewith goes the hope that, by atonement through mental or physical suffering, one can attain forgiveness, that is, regain acceptance and love.

Both guilt anxiety and the depressive affect of guilt become internalized during development in the form of complex sequences of inner processes subsumed under the functions of the superego. One of the functions of conscience is measuring one's wishes and actions against standards of what one ought and ought not do. Other functions include internalized processes of self-evaluation, self-criticism, and self-punishment in various forms, such as inflicting pain or deprivation upon oneself. These functions direct the guilt-arousing aggression against the self in the hope of attaining atonement and forgiveness through remorse and self-mortification. The defense of turning against the self is part of guilt as well as a way of dealing with guilt.

Among the defenses against guilt are reaction formations, either in the form of emphasized nonaggressiveness (exaggerated kindness and benevolence, passivity and refusal to compete, submissiveness) or, conversely, a lack of caring about hurting others or violating their needs. Another reaction formation turns passive behavior into active (making others feel guilty instead of or after feeling guilty oneself). Through projection, one either accuses others of intents or acts about which one feels guilty or treats others as figures of silent reproach who have to be removed or attacked.

The full internalized affect of guilt requires, like shame, the establishment of the superego, but precursors of guilt exist long before the superego is developed. How early in development one relates aggressive wishes or acts to fantasies and fears of retaliation is the subject of controversy.

Various forms of aggression against others lead to characteristic fears of retribution, hence to various fantasies about punishment and different attributes of guilt. But throughout its history, psychoanalysis has ascribed particular importance to the role of *castration anxiety* in the development of guilt.

One of the major manifestations of unconscious guilt is the *negative therapeutic reaction*. The motive for such paradoxical deterioration lies in "a sense of guilt, which is finding its satisfaction in the illness and refuses to give up the punishment of suffering" (Freud, 1923, p. 49). A parallel form of negative therapeutic reaction is attributable to unconscious shame; every success has to be "paid for" at once by a kind of preemptive self-disparagement, provoked humiliation, and failure.

See AFFECTS; DEFENSE, NEGATIVE THERAPEUTIC REACTION; SHAME; SUPEREGO.

References
Freud, S. (1923). The ego and the id. *SE,* 19:3–66.
Jacobson, E. (1971). *Depression.* New York: Int. Univ. Press.
Piers, G. & Singer, M. B. (1953). *Shame and Guilt.* New York: Norton.
Wurmser, L. (1981). *The Mask of Shame.* Baltimore: Johns Hopkins Univ. Press.

■ GUILTY MAN

See SELF PSYCHOLOGY.

■ HALLUCINATION

The apparent perception of a sensory stimulus from an external object not actually present. Though usually indicative of psychosis, hallucinations may occur in hysteria, while falling asleep or waking up (hypnagogic and hypnopompic phenomena), in febrile conditions, and in toxic states. Hallucinations may be experienced in any of the senses and take on a wide variety of forms. Freud viewed hallucinations as evidence of the return of the repressed. He considered their occurrence in psychoses as an attempt at restitution, that is an endeavor to bring libido back to objects that had been lost. In schizophrenia, auditory hallucinations can be traced to formerly loved objects, with whom the patient attempts to recreate not only persecutory but also loving and protective relations.

See PSYCHOSIS; RESTITUTION; SCHIZOPHRENIA.

References
Freud, S. (1924). Neurosis and psychosis. *SE,* 19:149–153.
——— (1924). The loss of reality in neurosis and psychosis. *SE,* 19:183–187.
Modell, A. (1958). The theoretical implications of hallucinatory experiences in schizophrenia. *JAPA,* 6:442–480.

■ HALLUCINATORY WISH FULFILLMENT

The capacity of the mental apparatus to gratify a wish by means of a hallucination is, according to Freud, one of its fundamental characteristics. He also considered regression to hallucinations the most essential part of the dream work, understanding the visual dream image as carrying with it, because of its perceptual nature, a belief in its reality. According to this view, the dream process is the result of a topographic regression, and dreaming is analogous to the earliest stages of mental development. Hallucinatory gratification is of course illusory, and by virtue of its failure to provide real satisfaction it contributes to the origins of reality testing.

See DREAMING, DREAMS; MEMORY; REALITY; REGRESSION.

References
Freud, S. (1895). Project for a scientific psychology. *SE,* 1:295–391.
——— (1900). The interpretation of dreams. *SE,* 4–5.
——— (1917). A metapsychological supplement to the theory of dreams. *SE,* 14:222–235.

■ HETEROSEXUALITY

Sexual interest in and erotic focus on persons of the opposite sex. Heterosexual organization of the personality is based upon a gender identity concordant with anatomy and a sexual identity complementary to that of the opposite sex. There is strong animal evidence that hormonal central nervous system (CNS) organizing effects play a major role in establishing stereotypic courtship and mating behaviors. While similar CNS conditioning in human beings seems likely, it has not yet been convincingly demonstrated.

Postnatal psychological factors play an unambiguous role in determining sexual orientation. This is demonstrated in the development of the oral, anal, and phallic drives, together with their cathected object and self representations and their later organization under genital dominance. The initial milestone seems to be the development of *gender identity* during the second year of life at the height of the rapprochement crisis of separation-individuation. Gender identity includes a basic internalization of the distinctions between the sexes, an identification with the like sex, and a complementary identification with the opposite sex through which the two sexes' reciprocal reproductive roles—to make babies and to have babies—are recognized. For boys successful establishment of gender identity requires a disidentification from mother as well as an identification with father. This process is not necessary for girls, leading to the speculation that the extra step involved for boys contributes to their greater vulnerability to disorders of gender and sexual identity.

The second major juncture in the development of sexual orientation is the establishment of *sexual identity* during the oedipal phase. Heightened drive pressures directed toward incestuous objects, realignment of dyadic into triadic object ties, the accentuation of castration anxiety, and the consequent structuring of the psyche make this period critical for the development of sexual orientation. Boys who develop a heterosexual identity identify with the father despite his fantasied role as a potential castrator, because the threat is translated into superego and ego-ideal structures. In the same vein, these boys repress their incestuous wishes toward the mother without replacing erotic interest in females with identification. The residue of these conflicts and compromises is reflected not only in heterosexual identity but also in the personal erotism expressed in foreplay, the appeal of particular members of the opposite sex, and the choice of a particular sexual and marital partner.

In female heterosexual development, the girl continues to identify with the mother despite her feelings of genital inferiority and fantasies that the mother has deprived her of a penis. A solid gender identity helps here. The girl's narcissistic wound, outrage, and guilt at fantasied castration is sufficiently ameliorated for her to develop libidinal interest in the father rather than compensatory identification with him. Since the fantasied penis is already lost, girls do not experience the castration threat as strongly; hence incestuous libidinal investments in the father and father substitutes are more tolerable to girls than the analogous situation is to boys.

Boys, but not girls, disidentify from their primary object in forming a gender identity. On the other hand, during the oedipal phase heterosexual girls shift their phallic libidinal interest in the mother to a more genitally receptive orientation toward the father. Some have suggested that this extra step means that women are more likely than men to experience failure of sexual interest and satisfaction.

Among heterosexual individuals the negative oedipal complex is not strong. Nevertheless, residual, unconscious homosexual wishes persist to some degree after the major resolution of the oedipus complex and foster the process of complementary identification with the opposite sex begun with gender identity formation. A man, for example, can appreciate how a woman could love a man; he can also show a genuine but sublimated femininity in the qualities of tenderness, care, and concern.

Heterosexuality is most often compared and contrasted to homosexuality. The critical difference between the two is that heterosexuality preserves libidinal interest in the opposite sex and self representations complementary to the opposite sex despite compromise formations that may affect sexual practices. This is the case, for example, in heterosexual perversions, even though sexual expression may be compromised.

See GENDER IDENTITY; HOMOSEXUALITY; OEDIPUS COMPLEX; PSYCHOSEXUAL DEVELOPMENT.

References
Freud, S. (1925). Some psychical consequences of the anatomical distinction between the sexes. *SE,* 19:243–258.
Galenson, E. & Roiphe, H. (1976). Some suggested revisions concerning early female development. *JAPA,* 24 (suppl.): 29–57.
______ (1980). The preoedipal development of the boy. *JAPA,* 28:805–827.
Meyer, J. (1985). Ego-dystonic homosexuality. In *Comprehensive Textbook of Psychiatry,* 4th ed., ed. H. Kaplan & B. Sadock. Baltimore: Williams & Wilkins, pp. 1056–1065.
Panel (1970). The development of the child's sense of his sexual identity. Virginia L. Clower, reporter. *JAPA,* 18:165–176.

■ HOLDING

See WINNICOTT'S THEORY.

■ HOMOSEXUALITY

Choice of an object of the same sex to achieve sexual arousal and gratification. The homosexual inclination may be *overt* (that is, manifest in consciously accepted sexual activity with a partner or fantasies accompanied by masturbation and orgasm), latent, or unconscious. In *latent homosexuality* the erotic preference is dormant but has the potential to achieve expression; the term is used to refer to those individuals who do not engage in homosexual activity because of social restraints or internal conflict that sometimes temporarily blocks acceptance or conscious awareness of one's homosexuality. *Unconscious homosexuality* may be recognized in disguised form in the analysis of characterological disturbances, neuroses, dreams, and psychoses, though such patients rarely become overt homosexuals. This distinction may have potentially useful implications, but it has not been generally accepted; *latent* and *unconscious* are often used interchangeably. Unconscious homosexuality exists to a greater or lesser degree in all heterosexual individuals.

Freud thought that homosexual libido is diverted from the physical to socially accepted objectives (sublimation) or directed toward service of an admired person or cause (bound by the ego ideal). It may appear in dreams and other regressive states and arouse anxiety. Conversely, overt homosexuals retain elements of heterosexuality.

Freud (1905) described three subgroups of homosexuals: *absolute, amphigenic,* and *contingent.* Absolute, exclusive, or obligatory homosexual individuals are aroused exclusively by their own sex; they are indifferent or hostile to the opposite sex. Amphigenic individuals can engage in sexual relations with both sexes. The term *bisexual* has now largely replaced *amphigenic* to describe such overt sexual behavior—it does not necessarily refer to what Freud considered a general bisexual predisposition in human beings. Rado (1949) called this *variational* homosexuality.

Contingent homosexual people (Rado's *situational*) are those capable of accepting homosexual gratification when objects of the opposite sex are unavailable to them (for example, prison inmates). Less easily categorized are individuals whose sexual orientation is basically heterosexual, but who may for various reasons transiently engage in homosexual activity. They include adolescents (homosexual activity defends against anxieties of that stage) and those motivated by opportunistic considerations.

These classifications differentiate homosexuality according to manifest sexual behavior. They are useful descriptively but do not address the psychogenic and psychodynamic factors, largely unconscious, that lead to heterosexual or homosexual object choice. The psychoanalytic view is that any overt manifestation of human sexuality is overdetermined by a multitude of developmental factors and accidental environmental events. Those occurring in the preoedipal and oedipal stages of development usually succumb to repression and become unconscious, not subject to recall under ordinary circumstances. Thus some insist that we know nothing about the early factors determining object choice. Some observers and clinicians suggest, for example, that many heterosexual individuals have family constellations identical to those considered to produce homosexuality, and that many homosexual people had "average expectable" parenting (Isay, 1986). The relevant dynamic factors can be recovered only through the consistent application of psychoanalytic technique.

Attempts to establish somatic (chromosomal and hormonal) factors in sexual orientation have not been convincing. While somatic factors determine the anatomical sex, especially prenatally, object choice appears to be environmentally determined. Psychoanalysts have postulated that conflict either during the separation-individuation stage or during the oedipal stage may lead to identification with the parent of the opposite sex and to homosexual object choice.

Until the 1950s the outcome of the oedipal phase was considered the essential explanation for the origin of homosexuality and heterosexuality. Many homosexual men experienced an overly strong attachment to the mother during the early oedipal relationship. Remaining "faithful" to her, they were unable to transfer sexual feelings to other women without experiencing incest fantasies and accompanying prohibitions—thus they changed their orientation from women to men. Castration fears also contribute to a negative oedipal resolution with partial regression to oral and anal levels of integration and fixation. Though the boy fears penetration (or castration) by the more powerful male (father), he may also wish to incorporate the father's strength, orally or anally, and he may long for security based on dependency on the father. The negative oedipus complex favoring a homosexual outcome is also usually related to problems in the early preoedipal relationship to the mother that contribute to overattachment to the father.

More recent studies of sexual orientation and early childhood development have emphasized preoedipal determinants that result in failure to progress from the mother–child unity of earliest infancy to individuation. Although some cases may present a predominantly oedipal or preoedipal configuration, most involve mechanisms stemming from multiple levels of fixation or regression. Similar correlations with various degrees of psychopathology depending on points of fixation or developmental arrest, level of ego functions, and use of primitive defenses could be applied to heterosexuals as well as homosexuals. Hence, while psychoanalytic observations that consider childhood sexuality, conflict, defense, and compromise formation have furnished basic data on psychosexuality, the determinants of homosexual object choice are not yet clearly delineated. Unconscious bases for homosexual and heterosexual object choice differ. They are not necessarily correlated with a particular clinical picture but are recognizable only through psychoanalytic investigation.

Many homosexual individuals appear capable of living well-adjusted lives and show no evidence of significant psychopathology. The homosexual act may defend against conflict and anxiety in such a way as to permit a high degree of personal development and achievement in other areas. One line of development may be affected without impairing other lines to a superficially recognizable degree. Thus object relations are probably determined by the kinds of psychopathology that may coexist with homosexuality in a way analogous to the heterosexual situation. Homosexual men and women, like heterosexual, are capable of mature, lasting attachments, although individuals of both sexual orientations may be masochistic, narcissistic, depressed, borderline, or psychotic. In this connection, Freud (1905) wrote,

> 1. Inversion [a term he preferred to homosexuality] is found in people who exhibit no other serious deviations from the normal.
> 2. It is similarly found in people whose efficiency is unimpaired, and who are indeed distinguished by especially high intellectual development and ethical culture [pp. 138–139].

Female homosexuality (*lesbianism*) has been much less explored and reported by analysts than has male homosexuality, and the formulations regarding it are more questionable. As with male homosexuality, early theories focused on conflicts of the phallic-oedipal phase, on the girl's incestuous wishes toward the father (and brothers) and her hatred and rivalry toward the mother (and sisters), both of which generate guilt and anxiety and may result in defensive regression to the preoedipal mother–daughter relationship. Real or fantasied primal scene exposure and a sadomasochistic conception of intercourse often contribute to the intensity of such conflicts. Severe castration anxiety and penis envy, fear of passive wishes and penetration, and disappointment with the father are associated with an increased tendency to masculine identification. The girl may idealize her mother, but the mother is sometimes revealed during analysis to have been aloof, intrusive, controlling of bodily functions, and prohibiting of infantile sexual gratifications, including masturbation. In this context the partner becomes a substitute "good mother," and the homosexual activity is thought to act out a blissful symbiotic relationship that attempts to deny the oedipal conflict: the daughter does not hate her mother but loves her, and her mother gratifies sexual wishes rather than frustrating them. This solution is often unstable, however, as intense closeness may also be threatening, and a masculine identification may be needed to defend against anxiety based on fantasies of merging with the mother.

More recent formulations continue to recognize the importance of oedipal conflict but place more emphasis on disturbances in the mother–child relationship during the preoedipal separation-individuation phase. Congenital defects, repeated medical procedures, and the mother's physical or emotional absence may contribute to such disturbances and may distort sexual identity. These result in fixation and make regression from the oedipal conflict more likely. In situations of maternal deprivation and neglect, the homosexual partner may represent a transitional object, loss of which may cause severe anxiety or depression or may threaten the integrity of self or sexual identity. Excessive physical or mental pain tends to increase the child's dependence on mother and accentuates hostility and aggression toward her; a defensive masochism sometimes results. If the mother encourages dependence or deprecates the girl's body, castration fantasies and fears are intensified. Significant contributions to a homosexual orientation may be found in a father who shows contempt and criticism toward men who take an interest in his daughter, frightening or painful heterosexual encounters, disappointments in heterosexual love experiences or marriage, or the unavailability of heterosexual objects. Thus, a complex interaction of biological, developmental, intrapsychic, and cultural influences are believed to be involved.

See BISEXUALITY; CASTRATION; DEFENSE; FEMALE PSYCHOLOGY; FIXATION; GENDER IDENTITY; HETEROSEXUALITY; MULTIDETERMINISM; OBJECT; OEDIPUS COMPLEX; TOPOGRAPHIC POINT OF VIEW.

References

Male Homosexuality

Freud, S. (1905). Three essays on the theory of sexuality. *SE*, 11:159–137.

Isay, R. A. (1986). Homosexuality in homosexual and heterosexual men. In *The Psychology of Men*, ed. G. Fogel, F. Lane & R. Liebert. New York: Basic Books.

Rado, S. (1949). An adaptational view of sexual behavior. In *Psychosexual Development in Health and Disease*, ed. P. H. Hoch & J. Zubin. New York: Grune & Stratton, pp. 159–189.

Socarides, C. W. (1978). *Homosexuality*. New York: Jason Aronson.

——— (1982). Abdicating fathers, homosexual sons. In *Father and Child,* ed. S. H. Cath, A. R. Gurwitt & J. M. Ross. Boston: Little, Brown, pp. 509–521.

Wiedeman, G. (1962). Survey of psychoanalytic literature on overt male homosexuality. *JAPA,* 10:386–409.

Female Homosexuality

Bacon, C. (1956). A developmental theory of female homosexuality. In *Perversions,* ed. S. Lorand & M. Balint. New York: Gramercy, pp. 131–159.

Deutsch, H. (1932). Homosexuality in women. *PQ,* 1:484–510.

Freud, A. (1965). *Normality and Pathology in Childhood.* New York: Int. Univ. Press.

Freud, S. (1920). Psychogenesis of a case of homosexuality in a woman. *SE,* 18:145–175.

——— (1931). Female sexuality. *SE,* 21:223–247.

——— (1933). The psychology of women. New introductory lectures on psychoanalysis. *SE,* 22:112–135.

Panel (1987). Toward the further understanding of homosexual women. A. Wolfson, reporter. *JAPA,* 35:165–173.

Roiphe H. & Galenson, E. (1981). *Infantile Origins of Sexual Identity.* New York: Int. Univ. Press.

Socarides, C. (1963). The historical development of theoretical and clinical aspects of female homosexuality. *JAPA,* 11:386–414.

——— (1978). *Homosexuality.* New York: Jason Aronson.

■ HORIZONTAL SPLIT

See SELF PSYCHOLOGY.

■ HOSPITALISM

A catastrophic symptom picture that develops during the first year of life when infants are raised in institutions or otherwise severely deprived of mothering for extended periods of time. Symptoms include physical deterioration, extreme susceptibility to infection, illness, and mortality, and deterioration, arrest, and dysfunction of psychological functioning. Survivors have a high incidence of psychiatric disturbance, mental retardation, and antisocial tendencies.

The psychiatric consequences of hospitalism were first studied in the 1930s, but Spitz (1945) was the first to systematically study infants with the intent of discovering the pathogenic factors responsible for this syndrome. He studied infants who received adequate nursing, hygienic, and nutritional care, but who were lacking in the normal affective supplies usually provided by the mother. From the third month on, physical and psychological deterioration with extreme susceptibility to infection and illness was noted, and the mortality rate from usually nonfatal disease was very high. The infants suffered from depression and exhibited motor retardation, complete passivity, vacuous facies, and defective eye coordination. From the second year on, the children were profoundly physically and psychologically retarded—unable to sit, stand, walk, or talk. The effects of hospitalism are long-term and generally irreversible.

Spitz's pioneering study demonstrated that adequate mothering is absolutely essential for healthy physical and psychological development. Spitz distinguished *hospitalism,* brought about by total emotional deprivation, from *anaclitic depression,* which occurs when a previously normal mother–child attachment is disrupted and the child is deprived of affection.

Recently the term hospitalism has been extended to include severe maternal deprivation regardless of setting: for example, Leon Kreisler (1984) uses *intrafamilial hospitalism* to describe a situation in which the mother is incapable of emotionally responding to her baby.

See ANACLITIC DEPRESSION.

References

Kreisler, L. (1984). Fundamentals for a psychosomatic pathology of infants. In *Frontiers of Infant Psychiatry,* ed. J. D. Call, E. Galenson & R. L. Tyson. New York: Basic Books, vol. 2, pp. 447–454.

Provence, S. & Lipton, R. (1962). *Infants in Institutions.* New York: Int. Univ. Press.

Rutter, M. (1972). *Maternal Deprivation.* Baltimore: Penguin Books.

Spitz, R. A. (1945). Hospitalism. *PSOC,* 1:53–74.

——— (1946). Hospitalism: A follow-up report. *PSOC,* 2:113–117.

——— (1965). *The First Year of Life.* New York: Int. Univ. Press.

■ HYPOCHONDRIASIS

A type of symptom complaint focusing on bodily concerns. Such unpleasant bodily sensations as pulling, fullness, and bloating receive exaggerated attention in the absence of manifest illness, while pain and other symptoms of actual physical illness cause insistent, nagging, even persecutory anxiety. The patient is convinced that he or she has a major organic disease, such as cancer, tuberculosis, or syphilis. He or she is distressed and demands relief. The symptoms are especially likely to involve the skin, abdomen, nose, rectum, and genitals; at times they assume the quality of a somatic delusion, for example, the patient believes that something is growing inside the body or that a body part is changing shape.

The hypochondriacal patient is typically reclusive and self-preoccupied, with prominent narcissistic traits. Anxiety may lead him or her to seek one consultation after another with medical specialists. He or she may seek a career in medicine, become a food faddist, or, in a reaction formation, neglect his or her health and well-being. States characterized by hypochondriasis mark a transition between neuroses, primarily hysterical and obsessional, and delusional, depressive or schizophrenic psychotic disorders.

Psychoanalytically, hypochondriasis has been understood as due to a relative withdrawal of object cathexes and a parallel intensification of bodily or organ cathexes. The intensified organ cathexes may be associated with organic changes in the affected part(s), which in turn may give rise to hypochondriacal sensations.

See ACTUAL NEUROSIS; AFFECTIVE DISORDERS; OBSESSION.

References

Engel, G. L. (1962). *Psychological Development in Health and Disease*. New York: Saunders.

Fenichel, O. (1945). *The Psychoanalytic Theory of Neurosis*. New York: Norton.

Freud, S. (1914). On narcissism. *SE*, 14:83–102.

■ HYPOMANIA

A pathological mental state characterized by high spirits and inflated self-esteem inappropriate to the patient's reality circumstances, and by hyperactivity and a hunger for stimuli and new experiences. Hypomania is a moderate form of mania and occurs in a broad range of psychiatric conditions, including borderline and neurotic disorders. Mania represents a phase of manic-depressive illness and only rarely appears as a symptom. In *cyclothymic personalities* or disorders, considered by some as the neurotic counterpart of the manic-depressive psychosis, hypomania may alternate with depression but these phases are not severe enough to impair seriously reality testing and hence do not justify the diagnosis of a manic-depressive condition. Hypomania can be severely pathological or closer to a fairly adaptive state. For instance, a cyclothymic artist may be extraordinarily productive during the hypomanic phase of his or her condition.

Although the fantasies and ego defenses characteristic of mania—denial, idealization, and fusion of self and object—are also assumed to underlie the condition of hypomania, their effect on behavior is moderated by a relatively healthy ego. Thus, hypomania does not usually involve a complete loss of boundaries, a compromised sense of reality, dissolution of the superego, or complete loss of critical self-awareness.

See ELATION, MANIA, MOOD.

References

Lewin, B. D. (1950). *The Psychoanalysis of Elation*. New York: Norton.

Jacobson, E. (1971). *Depression*. New York: Int. Univ. Press.

■ HYSTERIA

A class of neuroses, recognized since the time of Hippocrates and attributed in ancient times to a malfunctioning uterus (*hysteron*). Janet and Charcot directed medical attention to hysteria at the end of the nineteenth century. Freud, influenced by Charcot, began investigations with Breuer into the psychic mechanisms involved in hysteria. He discovered in the course of his studies unconscious fantasy, conflict, repression, identification, and transference, marking the beginning of psychoanalysis. Freud explained hysterical symptoms as the result of repressed sexual memories and fantasies that were converted into physical symptoms.

Freud divided the psychoneuroses into two categories, hysterical and obsessional neuroses. He distinguished these from *anxiety neurosis*, which he felt had a physiological basis in current improper sexual practices—he thought the psychoneuroses were psychic and related to early childhood conflicts. Freud also distinguished two types of hysteria: *conversion hysteria* and *anxiety hysteria*. In both, oedipal conflict defended against by repression is a cardinal feature. Conversion hysteria deals with mental conflict by converting it into bodily symptoms or by dissociation; in anxiety hysteria the ego does not overcome anxiety despite obsessive and primarily phobic mechanisms. Anxiety hysteria is now more often labeled *phobic neurosis* or *mixed psychoneurosis*.

Conversion hysteria is characterized by (1) bodily symptoms, protean in nature but related to mental functions and meanings rather than to anatomical or physiological pathology; (2) an appearance of affective indifference to the allegedly serious nature of the symptom ("la belle indifference"); and (3) episodic mental states, either separate from or together with the foregoing, known as *hysterical spells.* These involve dissociation of certain mental functions that may coexist with or exclude normal consciousness, resulting in such disturbances as multiple personalities, fugue states, somnambulism, major amnesia and so on. The hysterical spells often pantomime complicated fantasy stories that can be analyzed in the same way as can the elements of the manifest dream; both phenomena are products of the distortion resulting from mechanisms utilizing the primary process.

The bodily symptoms of conversion hysteria may involve motor, sensory, or visceral phenomena—anesthesia, pain, paralysis, tremors, deafness, blindness, vomiting, hiccoughing, and so on. They conform to lay concepts of disease rather than to the facts demonstrated by anatomical pathways and physiology. Nevertheless—and despite an affective reaction inappropriate to the alleged severity of the symptom—hysterical patients are convinced that their symptoms are due to objective physical disease.

Hysterical symptoms occur when conflicts associated with the oedipal period of psychosexual development are reawakened. The wish for the incestuous love object represents the chief danger. Since Freud's time it has become evident that pregenital determinants, particularly oral conflicts, are also important in certain types of hysteria. The major defenses used are repression, regression, and identification, leading to dissociated bodily and affective symptomatology that acts as a distorted substitute and compromise for the original infantile sexual gratification.

The symptoms therefore represent an expression in "body language" of specific unconscious fantasies that have developed as a compromise in the conflict between an anxiety-provoking instinctual wish and the defense against that wish. The syndromes differ from one individual to the next, and analysis demonstrates that they are historically determined by specific repressed experiences in the individual's past. The choice of symptom (including the organ or body zone affected) is predominantly based on the content of the unconscious fantasy, the erotogenicity of the area, early identifications, and the organ's capacity to symbolize the forces involved. These symptoms are, par excellence, an example of the "return of the repressed"—both the instinctual wish and the defense against it are reenacted in the symptom. The suffering or deprivation involved in the symptom represents masochistic punishment for the partial gratification of the forbidden fantasy.

Oedipal conflicts may also contribute to the formation of a *hysterical character*. Persons with this type of character structure are histrionically exhibitionistic, seductive, labile in mood, and prone to act out oedipal fantasies, yet fearful of sexuality and inhibited in action.

Psychoanalysis is the treatment of choice for hysteria and offers a good to excellent prognosis.

Defense hysteria, retention hysteria, and *hypnoid hysteria* are archaic terms employed in Breuer's and Freud's early work; they have no modern significance.

See ANXIETY DISORDERS; CHARACTER; CONVERSION; DEFENSE; OEDIPUS COMPLEX; SYMBOL.

References

Breuer, J. & Freud, S. (1893–95). Studies on hysteria. *SE,* 3:1–306.

Fenichel, O. (1945). *The Psychoanalytic Theory of Neurosis.* New York: Norton.

Freud, S. (1905). Fragment of an analysis of a case of hysteria. *SE,* 7:1–122.

Rangell, L. (1959). The nature of conversion. *JAPA,* 7:632–662.

■ ID

An agency (or structure) in the tripartite division of the mind Freud (1923) advanced in a major revision of his theory of the psychic apparatus. The id is a concept that encompasses the mental representations of the instinctual drives and some but not all of the contents of the system *Unconscious* from Freud's earlier topographic theory. (Certain functions of the ego and superego are also unconscious.) Broadly speaking, the id includes all wishes that result from the perception and memories of gratification of basic physiological needs. Freud's view of the id and of the individual's biological inheritance underwent modifications, but in his "Outline of Psycho-analysis" (1940) Freud considered that the id "contains everything that is inherited, that is present at birth, that is laid down in the constitution—above all therefore, the instincts, which originate from the somatic organization and which find a first psychical expression here [in the id] in forms unknown to us" (p. 145). In the same work, however, Freud postulated an undifferentiated matrix from which the id and ego both evolve. This and other ambiguities are reviewed by Schur (1966) in his exhaustive monograph on the id concept.

In his "New Introductory Lectures on Psychoanalysis," Freud (1933) stated that the id "is the dark inaccessible part of our personality. . . . We approach the id with analogies: we call it a chaos, a cauldron full of seething excitation" (p. 73). However, in that work and throughout his other important writings on the subject, Freud alludes to impressions which have sunk into the id by repression and which are immortal except through the therapeutic effect of analytic treatment (p. 74). This led to the dictum that the goal of analytic treatment is to make the repressed conscious, so that "where id was there ego shall be" (1933, p. 80).

The relationship between the id and the ego is also described in the famous metaphor of a rider and his horse in which the superior strength of the horse has to be guided and held in check (Freud, 1923). The superego is also described as merging into the id and gaining its strength from the forces of the id. From this it is apparent that Freud regarded the boundary between id and the other agencies as less rigid than the boundaries he postulated for the systems Ucs. and Pcs.-Cs.

Some of Freud's other important assumptions about the id were that it functions with primary process mentation, that it contains freely mobile energy, and that it operates entirely according to the pleasure principle. These assumptions subject the id to all the controversy surrounding the concepts of instinct theory, psychic energy, and the economic viewpoint. There is disagreement about whether the id has any mental contents at all or is totally composed of biological forces (Panel, 1963); whether its contents should include repressed unconscious memories and fantasies or only what has never reached consciousness or achieved representability; and how awareness of events relating to the id should be delineated. Gill (1963) concluded that the id and the ego are conceptually very similar unless the id is reduced to a nonstructured energy concept. More recently, Slap and Saykin (1984) note that while psychoanalysts in general claim allegiance to the structural model, the concept of the id appears to be in chaos. They point out that not a single paper containing the term *id* in its title had been published in the analytic literature in a decade.

Thus, though spoken of by Freud in the "Outline" as "the most important psychological apparatus . . . throughout life," the id is now a concept in relative disuse and is generally regarded as subsidiary to the ego. Nevertheless, as Schur (1966) points out, the mutual relationship between the id and the other psychic structures is still the cornerstone of the concept of psychic conflict.

See EGO; METAPSYCHOLOGY; STRUCTURAL THEORY; SUPEREGO; TOPOGRAPHIC POINT OF VIEW.

References

Freud, S. (1923). The ego and the id. *SE,* 19:12–66.

——— (1933). New introductory lectures on psycho-analysis, *SE* 22:5–182.

——— (1940). An outline of psycho-analysis. *SE,* 23:144–207.

Gill, M. M. (1963). *Topography and Systems in Psychoanalytic Theory. Psychol. Issues,* monogr. 10. New York: Int. Univ. Press.

Panel (1963). The concept of the id. E. Marcovitz, reporter. *JAPA,* 11:151–160.

Schur, M. (1966). *The Id and the Regulatory Principles of Mental Functioning.* New York: Int. Univ. Press.

Slap, J. & Saykin, J. (1984). On the nature and organization of the repressed. *Psychoanal. Inquiry,* 4:107–123.

■ ID RESISTANCE

See RESISTANCE; WORKING THROUGH.

■ IDEAL OBJECT

See FAIRBAIRN'S THEORY.

■ IDEALIZATION

Unrealistic exaggeration of an object's personal attributes. Contradictory qualities, related to either libidinal or aggressive cathexes, can be attributed to an individual, who is elevated to the point of perfection, aggrandized, and exalted. Accompanying feelings include admiration, awe, veneration, worship, adoration, and enthrallment. Freud first described the process in connection with the phenomenon of falling in love. The self as well as the object may be idealized.

Freud postulated a state of infantile narcissism, involving feelings of omnipotence, that coincided with a stage of primary identification or oneness with mother. According to his theory, this state is lost when the child becomes aware of his or her separateness, aloneness, and helplessness; the child's original feelings of omnipotence are then attributed to the parents via idealization. When the parents fail to live up to expectations, the child's frustration leads him or her to withdraw some of the idealizing libido onto the subject (self), providing energy for identification and the acquisition of drive-controlling and tension-regulating ego structures during the preoedipal stage. During this essentially *anaclitic* period, when the relationship is based on need for a satisfying object, exaggerations of the parents' importance are related to the child's need, and the all-fulfilling parent is a reflection of the child's experience of satisfaction. Idealization fluctuates in relation to the vicissitudes of satisfaction, frustration, and anger. Subsequently, when the parent becomes important irrespective of needs (object constancy), idealization becomes increasingly suited to defensive needs. The mother, who has been ideally irresistible and attractive, paradoxically can also be ideally virginal and untouchable. The father, who is exaggeratedly powerful and terrible, can be experienced simultaneously as humane and judicious.

During the phallic-oedipal stage, selected aspects of the idealized images of the parents are internalized as the superego, which functions as the parents did in regard to setting standards, prohibiting misconduct, and meting out punishment. Freud originally described the superego in anthropomorphic terms as the ego's ideal. Current usage distinguishes two constituents of the superego. The *ego ideal* is based on narcissistically enhanced elements of the parent–child interaction and is related to values, strivings, and aspirations. Failure to meet these internal standards generally leads to shame. The idealized aggressive and prohibitive figures are internalized in the part of the superego relevant to conscience, initiating the affect of guilt and punishing transgressions. Internalization of these idealized aspects of the parental images has lasting benefit to the psychic economy; it protects the personality from narcissistic regression during a period of great vulnerability (the phallic-oedipal phase) by taming the object-directed drives and thereby increasing the ego's dominance over the drives.

Internalization is accompanied by a continuing need to idealize or glorify the actual parents (especially the parent of the same sex) to maintain association with a powerful figure. Frustration of this need—loss, unresponsiveness, deprivation, or disappointment—may interfere with the basic structuring of the ego ideal and superego proper. Even after internalization, disappointment with the parents may undo a precariously established idealization and initiate renewed search for an ideal external object, to bolster what has been weakened internally.

Idealization continues throughout life. It is particularly noticeable in adolescents. The patient frequently idealizes the analyst during psychoanalytic treatment. While traditional analysts believe that understanding the origins of such attitudes is indispensable to proper analysis, self psychology theorists hold that idealization of the analyst is necessary to replace the functions of a segment of the mental apparatus that has not been securely established in childhood or infancy; they argue that idealization must be allowed to exist until it has served the function of a delayed internalization.

See EGO IDEAL; INTERNALIZATION; NARCISSISM; OEDIPUS COMPLEX; SUPEREGO.

References

Freud, S. (1914). On narcissism. *SE,* 14:69–102.
______ (1923). The ego and the id. *SE,* 19:3–68.
Jacobson, E. (1964). *The Self and the Object World.* New York: Int. Univ. Press.
Kernberg, O. F. (1967). Borderline personality organization. *JAPA,* 15:641–685.
Kohut, H. (1971). *The Analysis of the Self.* New York: Int. Univ. Press.
Reich, A. (1960). Pathologic forms of self-esteem regulation. *PSOC,* 15:215–232.

■ IDEALIZING TRANSFERENCE

See SELF PSYCHOLOGY.

■ IDENTIFICATION

See INTERNALIZATION.

■ IDENTITY

The relatively enduring, but not necessarily stable, experience of the self as a unique, coherent, entity over time. The *sense of identity,* a subjective experience, begins with the child's awareness that he or she exists as an individual in a world with similar outer objects, but that he has his own wishes, thoughts, memories, and appearance distinct from that of others. Thus "the term identity . . . connotes both a persistent sameness within oneself . . . and a persistent sharing of some kind of essential character with others" (Erikson, 1956, p. 57).

The development of the body image is at the core of identity formation, which gains momentum as the process of separation-individuation unfolds but is not completed until after adolescence. The earlier stages may be thought of as the evolution of a psychological self, while identity is achieved later once the individual is defined in a variety of social contexts. Identification with both parents gives a bisexual quality to the self-representations and schemas, and self-concepts of children of both sexes. Eventually, however, an integrated self-organization is created out of the multiple former identifications contributing to character traits. With respect to gender and sexual identity these self-concepts usually represent a predominant identification with the parent of the same sex.

The sense of identity achieves relative stability when bisexual identifications are resolved and adolescence completed. The consciously available sense of identity is derived from the current self concept, while an abiding sense of identity over time is derived from supraordinate self schemas, which integrate various subordinate self concepts and personal roles for relating with others. The conscious sense of "I" or "me" includes only some aspects of self organization; other organizing forms for appraising self are unconscious.

Personality is the impression others perceive of the individual's physical appearance, affective expressions, modes of speech, and behavior. It may differ in certain ways from the person's inner working model of his or her identity.

See CHARACTER; GENDER IDENTITY; IDENTIFICATION; OBJECT; SELF; SEPARATION-INDIVIDUATION; TOPOGRAPHIC POINT OF VIEW.

References

Abend, S. Identity. *PMC*. Forthcoming.

——— (1974). Problems of identity. *PQ*, 43:505–637.

Erikson, E. H. (1956). The problem of ego identity. *JAPA*, 4:56–121.

Galenson, E. & Roiphe, H. (1981). *Infantile Origins of Sexual Identity*. New York: Int. Univ. Press.

Lichtenstein, H. (1961). Identity and sexuality. *JAPA*, 9:179–260.

Panel (1958). Problems of identity. D. L. Rubinfine, reporter. *JAPA*, 6:131–142.

■ IDENTITY DIFFUSION; IDENTITY CRISIS

See EGO IDENTITY.

■ IMAGO

See ANALYTICAL PSYCHOLOGY TERMS.

■ IMPOSTOR

One who assumes an identity or title not his own. In psychoanalysis, the "true" impostor, one who so misrepresents himself, has been the subject of a limited number of studies, notably by Abraham (1925), H. Deutsch (1955), and Greenacre (1958). Typically such an individual has a severe character disorder; he or she engages in delinquent, psychopathic, sociopathic acts or other criminal behavior with the conscious and deliberate intention to deceive in ways facilitated by his false identity.

Imposturous tendencies occur in a variety of personality disturbances and situations, from the least to the most pathological. At the least pathological end is the promotion of illusion and disguise within the bounds of creative art and play.

The "as-if" personality has been subsumed under imposturous conditions. It is seen as an identity disturbance characterized by unstable and unintegrated identifications. While the "true" impostor pretends under the literal cover of someone else's name, the "as-if" personality, lacking a cohesive identification, unconsciously takes on the color and style of admired individuals through mimicry and imitation.

Affirmation of the *false self* (a term introduced by Winnicott) by a real or imagined audience that can be fooled, duped, or deceived has been regarded as an important aim of imposture, serving defensive, integrative, narcissistic, and self-cohesive functions, as well as gratifying instinctual drives.

See "AS-IF" PERSONALITY; IDENTITY; WINNICOTT'S THEORY: True Self, False Self.

References

Abraham, K. (1925). The history of an imposter in the light of psychoanalytic knowledge. In *Clinical Papers and Essays on Psychoanalysis*, New York: Basic Books, 1955, vol. 2, pp. 291–305.

Deutsch, H. (1955). The impostor. In *Neuroses and Character Types*. New York: Int. Univ. Press, 1965, pp. 319–338.

Greenacre, P. (1958). The relation of the impostor to the artist. In *Emotional Growth*. New York: Int. Univ. Press, 1971, vol. 1, pp. 93–112.

Ross, N. (1967). The "as-if" concept. *JAPA*, 15:59–82.

■ IMPOTENCE

Genital dysfunction in the male, usually an inability to achieve erection or to sustain it sufficiently for intercourse. Diabetic neuropathy and other physiological bases for impotence exist, but most cases are psychologically determined. *Premature ejaculation, retarded ejaculation,* and relative lack of pleasure despite orgasm (*psychic impotence*) involve the same underlying psychic problems. The same individual may suffer from any or all of these dysfunctions. Ideas, attitudes, or actions that serve to deny or minimize what the patient is doing may be used defensively with reasonably good results. Anything that provides emotional or physical distance may permit some degree of potency by neutralizing the danger of closeness and commitment, which often has an oedipal meaning. In some cases the physical position of intercourse has special meaning, as when potency is possible only when intercourse takes place from the rear. Potency may also be possible with women who are considered "bad" or "degraded" but impossible with a "good" woman, who is loved and respected but cannot be regarded sexually since she represents the pure mother of childhood. Women from foreign countries, different races, or religions may not be associated with the oedipal significance of the act.

Control over ejaculation is associated with sexual and emotional maturity and reflects consideration of the needs and welfare of the sexual partner. Patients with premature ejaculation usually have important psychopathology in their relationships with women, often viewing them unconsciously as dangerous, dirty, or degraded. Anxiety and hostility exert a decisive influence—a man may be potent with a woman when relations are good, but impotent with her when hostility has been aroused. Transient episodes of impotence may also be related to alcohol, a threatening situation, or distraction by other problems.

Serious psychopathology may affect only some functions, leaving others relatively unimpaired. Multiple forces determine whether the choice of symptom is psychic or sexual—phobias and obsessions or impotence or premature ejaculation. Character traits may express in a nonsexual way the meaning of the impotence; for example, social anxiety and hesitance reflect the same fear of injury or sense of shame as does impotence. Or the individual may be restricted in his capacity to feel warmth toward and sympathy with other people. Social conformity, excessive politeness, introversion, and difficulty in self-assertion are frequently associated with impotence. Impotent men may be shy, anxious, passive, and dependent around women, or may develop Don Juanism in reaction to such characteristics, engaging in shallow, short-lived relationships. They may avoid open clashes with men or may prefer to compete intellectually rather than physically, or these attitudes may be covered by an overcompensatory rivalry.

The childhood background of such patients often includes a mother who is pampering, smothering, guilt-promoting, and sexually provocative, while the father is apathetic, rejecting, absent, or brutally punitive, so that no real attachment develops between father and son. Proximity to the mother and distance from the father exaggerate oedipal wishes and fears, which are defended against by repression, inhibition, and character restriction. During youth a stronger sexual drive may override inhibitions that cause impotence in middle age.

References

Abraham, K. (1917). Ejaculatio praecox. In *Selected Papers*. New York: Basic Books.

Curtis, H. C. (1969). Psychoanalytic understanding and treatment of impotence. In *Sexual Function and Dysfunction,* ed. P. J. Fink & V. B. O. Hammett. Philadelphia: F. A. Davis.

Hastings, D. W. (1963). *Impotence and Frigidity.* Boston: Little, Brown.

Noy, P., Wollstein, S. & Kaplan-de-Nour, A. (1966). Clinical observations of the psychogenesis of impotence. *Brit. J. Med. Psychol.,* 39:43–53.

■ IMPULSE

The psychic awareness that a desire toward some action is welling up. The desire and the associated thoughts may be transitory, like a flash phenomenon, or they may evolve gradually. In either case, an impulse has an irresistable and impelling quality, and if action is inhibited a state of extreme tension may result. Impulses are usually id-derived fantasies, though the superego-derived need for punishment may find similar expression. Impulses are more likely to emerge into consciousness when repression is weakened or when the content of the fantasy finds a close match in conscious thoughts, relationships, or situations. Thus the psychoanalytic setting and the transference facilitate increased awareness of impulses.

Impulses are basically erotic or aggressive in nature. In the uncomplicated daily lives of ordinary people, an impulse may simply lead to an action that achieves the desired goal. Extreme, unbridled forms of this impulse-action sequence are seen in the *impulse disorders.* On the other hand, most impulses have a more complicated fate, interacting with defense mechanisms and resulting in various compromise formations, such as delayed gratification or neurotic symptoms. This sequence does not necessarily carry the impulse through to action; instead, it may result in obsessions or phobias. For example: one patient, who complained of an intense fear of heights, came to realize through an increased awareness of her impulses that her fear of heights arose because she had defensively turned upon herself the angry, aggressive impulse to push her mother out of the upstairs window.

■ IMPULSE DISORDERS

More appropriately designated "disorders of impulse control," a heterogeneous group of conditions involving impairment of normal mental functions that delay, modify, or otherwise restrict the behavioral expression of primitive impulses. The relative lack of control permits original, usually repressed, impulses to be acted out in a minimally distorted fashion.

Impairment in the ability to control impulses may be organically or psychologically determined. The nonorganic impulse disorders are divided into two large groups: the *symptom disorders* and the *character disorders*. The former are characterized clinically by the expression of specific impulsive acts, which are more or less discrete, sometimes isolated, frequently recurring. This group includes the simple impulsive act, the impulsion neurosis, the impulsive sexual disorders (perversions), the catathymic crisis, and the intermittent explosive behaviors. The character impulse disorders, or impulse-ridden characters, are typified by an overall impulsive quality permeating the personality and by diffuse, unpatterned impulsive behavior.

Most disorders of impulse control have several features in common: minimal distortion of the impulse, ego syntonicity, and a pleasurable component. Because sexual and aggressive wishes are less distorted than in classical neurotic symptoms, the meaning of the impulse and the action are more easily understood, both by the experiencer and the observer, than is the sometimes bizarre behavior of compulsive and hysterical neuroses. Although impulsive behavior may be used as a defense, the distortion is usually minimal, with the result that the impulse is generally expressed in a consonant act: anger results in aggressive assault, and sexual urges result in sexual acts. Furthermore, impulse and action may be experienced at the moment as being in harmony (ego syntonic) with the immediate conscious state and aims of the individual. That is, it feels like his or her own wish, and the individual usually experiences pleasure at the moment of expression, even though later he or she may criticize and despise his or her enjoyment of the act. This is in contradistinction to the compulsive person, who feels compelled to do something that he or she does not primarily enjoy.

In general, except for those whose difficulty is organic in origin, the individuals suffering from impulse disorders are fixated at pregenital and preverbal stages of development. The lack of tolerance for drive frustration is often the result of identification with parental objects who provided inadequate models for the development of ego controls and superego standards and prohibitions. When disorders of impulse control permeate the entire personality they resemble the severe character disorders in structure. Persons in this group are usually infantile, immature, and intolerant of tension and anxiety. They have more difficulty in seeing their behavior as unacceptable than do those referred to as suffering from symptom disorders. Their frustration tolerance is low, and they tend to react explosively in the face of deprivations.

Although disorders of impulse control and acting out may seem similar from a behavioral standpoint, it is important to distinguish between the two because of different treatment needs. The impulse disorders stem from insufficiency of the control apparatus, without prominence of an organized fantasy. Acting out represents a higher level of development and is a means of dealing with an organized fantasy through substitutive action, thereby avoiding recognition of the content of the fantasy. For individuals with impulse disorders, treatment plans must take into consideration the lack of capacity for delay of response to impulses. On the other hand, acting out calls for exploratory therapy utilizing clarification, confrontation, and interpretation.

See ACTING OUT; FIXATION, INSTINCTUAL DRIVE.

References

Frosch, J. (1977). The relation between acting out and disorders of impulse control. *Psychiatry*, 40:295–314.

Greenacre, P. (1950). General problems of acting out. *PQ*, 19:455–467.

Monroe, R. R. (1970). *Episodic Behavior Disorders*. Cambridge: Harvard Univ. Press.

Panel (1957). Acting out and its relation to impulse disorders. M. Kanzer, reporter. *JAPA*, 5:136–145.

Roughton, R. Acting out. *PMC*. Forthcoming.

■ INCORPORATION

See INTERNALIZATION.

■ INDIVIDUATION

See ANALYTICAL PSYCHOLOGY; SEPARATION-INDIVIDUATION.

■ INERTIA PRINCIPLE

See PSYCHIC ENERGY.

■ INFANCY

Although Freud used the term *infantile* to refer to phenomena throughout childhood, *infancy* is now regarded as the period of life from conception to three years of age. During this time the infant develops from a state of total psychological and physical dependency into an individual with an autonomously regulated sense of self and other, the capacity for verbal articulation and communication of inner reality, and independence in multiple areas of psychic functioning. By the end of infancy, important achievements in psychic structure should have been made: the child should clearly differentiate between self and object representations and should be able to integrate good and bad part objects into whole object and self representations. Ego and id should also be differentiated and defense mechanisms developed for dealing with conflictual feelings and impulses. The capacity for compromise formation should exist, as should the ability to generate anxiety internally and develop neurotic symptoms. With these advances, the ego is capable of intentionality, inhibition of discharge, resistance against regression, and beginning tolerance of frustration, anxiety, and ambivalence. The child then becomes increasingly able to tolerate a wide range of complex affectual experiences with the animate and inanimate environment.

During infancy the differentiation and integration of functions proceeds rapidly, reflecting a complex interaction among constitutional givens, the genetically determined maturational pathway, and the environment (both before and after birth). Infant development has been described via a number of theoretical models; although the emphasis of each differs, all models postulate that each new level of functioning (affect expression, motor skills, sensory perception and retention, impulse control, etc.) emerges as the infant interacts with the environment. Experience becomes organized in increasingly complicated patterns, first at a neurophysiological level, then at a psychological representational level.

The most important of these theoretical frameworks are Piaget's model of sensorimotor development; Freud's drive theory and conceptualization of psychosexual development, along with later psychoanalytic ego and object relation theories; Mahler's model of the process of separation-individuation; human ethology (the study of observable behavior); learning theory; and the infant observation research of Spitz, Wolff, Emde, Stern, and others.

During the first year of life maturation (genetics) wanes in influence as experience comes to the fore as a determinant of behavior. The rate of development is uneven. The most rapid development is marked by *biobehavioral shifts;* that is, new capacities and functions, including new affective behavior, that appear suddenly, reflecting a new level of psychological and physiological organization.

These shifts are manifested by dramatic changes in the social life of the infant. The so-called *smiling reponse* at two to three months of age leads to a new type and intensity of interaction with the human environment, while *stranger anxiety*, occurring between six and eight months, indicates the emergence of a capacity for fearfulness.

The third discernable biobehavioral shift occurs at eighteen to twenty-four months, when the "no" gesture signals rapid language acquisition, the development of autonomy, the capacity for social relations, a shift from sensorimotor to representational intelligence (Piaget), the rapprochement crisis (Mahler), and the anal phase of psychosexual development (Freud). After eighteen months the emerging sense of self is seen in the infant's awareness that he or she is the person in the mirror. The child also begins to speak of him or herself in the first person.

One way to conceptualize the shifts in the level of psychological organization is that after two months the infant remembers the mother at times of recognition, after seven to nine months when he or she experiences biological and psychological needs and after eighteen months as a consequence of evocative memory with relative autonomy from external stimuli or internal need. These shifts in behavioral capacity make the process of development appear at times discontinuous, for the achievement of a new level of integration and organization leads to a type of functioning that was not previously possible.

Periods of behavioral change to a more complex level of organization are the times of greatest vulnerability in the infant's capacity to handle stress. The potential for growth and mastery may alternate with the possibility of disorganization and decompensation, and both are affected by the child's constitutional endowment. For example, an infant who learns early to move about will have a different type of object relationship than will a relatively sedentary infant who explores the world with his or her eyes. The latter may move further into the process of individuation before beginning to separate physically from his or her caretaker. Similarly, the infant's vulnerability to stress will reflect the environment.

The infant's perceptual apparatus is innately capable of directing attention to part objects (the configuration of the human face, mother's voice, smell, etc.). These biologically determined perceptual predilections toward the object, which foster bonding, occur even in the absence of any nurturing or drive-reducing experience with the object. Hence the infant by endowment is socially interactive, seeks both arousing and soothing stimuli, and is able to stimulate others (especially mother) to evoke a response; thus the infant can make changes in the environment from the moment he or she arrives in the world. As development is part of an interactional system, both the infant's and the caretaker's behavior will increase in complexity over time. One current hypothesis is that the genetically determined, object-related behavior of the infant serves to engage the investment of the mother (or primary caretaker) at a time when the child is completely dependent on her for survival.

See EGO DEVELOPMENT; OBJECT CONSTANCY; PSYCHOSEXUAL DEVELOPMENT; SEPARATION-INDIVIDUATION; SMILING RESPONSE; STRANGER ANXIETY.

References

Call, J., ed. (1979). *Basic Handbook of Child Psychiatry*. New York: Basic Books.

Emde, R., Gaensbauer, T. & Harmon, R. (1976). *Emotional Expression in Infancy*. New York: Int. Univ. Press.

Greenspan, S. & Pollock, G., eds. (1980). *The Course of Life,* Vol. 1. Washington, D.C.: U.S. Government Printing Office.

■ INFANTILE AMNESIA

See AMNESIA.

■ INFANTILE DEPENDENCE

See FAIRBAIRN'S THEORY.

■ INFANTILE NEUROSIS

Introduced by Freud to describe the psychic disturbances that he considered to be the common fate of all human beings when confronted with the oedipus complex. At the height of what Freud originally called the "infantile genital organization" (the phallic phase), "interest in the genitals and in their activity acquires a dominating significance which falls little short of that reached in maturity" (Freud, 1923, p. 142). Accompanying this genital ascendency are the universal fantasies of possessing the object of the opposite sex; envy, jealousy, and anger toward the object of the same sex; and alternating conflicts and wishes for attachment to the same-sex object, who is also idealized. Penis envy, castration anxiety, fear of loss of love, low self-esteem, and guilt may appear as manifestations of this nuclear conflict.

The concept of infantile neurosis has been central to psychoanalysis since Little Hans and the Wolf-Man (Freud, 1909, 1918). Currently, it has two meanings: (1) the prototypical source of intrapsychic conflict during the oedipus complex, and (2) a metapsychological construct referring to the inner structure and organization of the infantile personality as a result of such conflict. Used in the latter sense, infantile neurosis is characterized by internalized conflict that arouses anxiety and by an ego structure capable of responding to the anxiety signal with appropriate defenses and compromises. With or without manifest symptoms, this intrapsychic organization forms the basis for a later adult neurosis.

Neurosis begins with intrapsychic conflict. Historically there has been a tendency to underestimate the potentiality of the ego and superego precursors to create intrapsychic conflicts at early levels of development. Current assumptions are that internalization of conflict begins as early as the second half of the second year (Mahler, 1975). The outcome of the rapprochement crisis significantly influences the mastery of oedipal conflicts. The phase-specific difficulties of the oedipus complex, combined with the demands of the emergent superego, increase the potential for neurotic conflict.

The infantile neurosis, however, implies not only internalized conflict but also a particular stage of psychic structuring. Increasingly the superego supports the ego in the battle against instinctual drives. Once the superego acquires greater consolidation, an organized set of standards and a source of punishment or reward exist internally, and infringement of internal standards arouses internal disapproval, that is, guilt. Reward for meeting internal standards or goals comes in the form of pride and elevation of self-esteem. Accordingly, inner turmoil and compromise solutions are less likely to be externally influenced, and the ego increasingly functions independently of external support. In other words, the classical formula for the formation of neurosis is now applicable: "conflict, followed by regression; regressive aims arousing anxiety; anxiety warded off by means of defense; conflict solution via compromise; symptom formation" (A. Freud, 1971, p. 80).

While historically the concept of infantile neurosis has been utilized to describe oedipal conflict, symptoms, and a metapsychological construct, it seems desirable to restrict the definition to the metapsychological construct. As noted, internalized conflict begins before the wishes and conflicts of the oedipus complex—thus patients with preoedipal conflicts may nevertheless be neurotic, and patients thought to be not neurotic (borderline, narcissistic, character disorder, or even schizophrenic) have oedipal wishes and conflicts. Likewise the infantile neurosis is not a clinical entity—the term should not be used to refer to a constellation of observable symptoms. Indeed, symptomatology usually thought to indicate the infantile neurosis, such as phobic or obsessional manifestations, may have a variety of dynamic configurations.

See CONFLICT; CHILDHOOD NEUROSIS; DEVELOPMENT; OEDIPUS COMPLEX; PSYCHOSEXUAL DEVELOPMENT; SEPARATION-INDIVIDUATION

References

Freud, A. (1965). Assessment of pathology, part 2. *WAF*, 6.

——— (1971). The infantile neurosis. *PSOC*, 26:79–90.

Freud, S. (1909). Analysis of a phobia in a five-year-old boy. *SE*, 10:3–149.

——— (1918). From the history of an infantile neurosis. *SE*, 17:1–123.

——— (1923a). The infantile genital organization. *SE*, 19:141–145.

——— (1923b). The ego and the id. *SE*, 19:3–66.

Mahler, M. S. (1975). On the current status of the infantile neurosis. *JAPA*, 23:327–333.

Ritvo, S. (1974). Current status of thc concept of infantile neurosis. *PSOC*, 29:159–181.

Tolpin, M. (1970). The infantile neurosis. *PSOC*, 25:273–305.

■ INFANTILE SEXUALITY

The manifestations of psychosexual development prior to adolescence. These reflect the phasic maturation of the sexual drive (itself subject to developmental influence) and the gradual development of the capacity for object relationships.

During development different areas of the infant's body (erotogenic zones) become important sites of tension, gratification, and distress (that is, pleasure-unpleasure). First the oral (mouth, lips, tongue), then the anal, the urethral, and finally the genital areas become endowed with heightened capacity to provide pleasure and discharge tension. However, the developmental time frame is so brief that even when one phase is dominant, the others are still active and capable of providing erotic gratification. Hence no one zone is cathected to the exclusion of others.

The genetic endowment of the infant includes the capacity at birth to begin affectual bonding to another human object. As basic bodily needs (such as hunger) are satisfied through contact with the object, gratifying stimuli from the various erotogenic zones increase attachment to the object and contribute an impulsion (the component instincts) toward further gratification. Pleasure becomes associated intrapsychically with the presence of the object. But it is also possible for the infant to gratify him- or herself (for example, by thumb-sucking or retention of stool). Gratification of drive derivatives can therefore be either object related or autoerotic.

As the ego develops, the child begins to evoke the mental representation of an unavailable object to increase the pleasure of autoerotic activity. With further development and experience, sexual fantasies gradually increase in complexity, leading to the conflictual fantasies of the oedipal period with or without accompanying genital masturbation. These are further elaborated in adolescent and adult masturbatory fantasies. During latency (a sexually quiescent period from the end of the phallic-oedipal phase until the beginning of adolescence) sexual impulses are significantly repressed. However, this repression is incomplete, and evidence of infantile sexuality continues, either displaced onto other activities, expressed through symptom formation or in character structure, or expressed via masturbation.

With adolescence it becomes possible to gratify sexual fantasies via an external object. The individual must then confront the nature of his or her fantasies and wishes, some of which are derivatives of the component drives hitherto unacceptable consciously. These residuals of infantile sexuality are expressed normally through foreplay (looking, touching, kissing, sucking, etc.) after the sexual elements have been organized under the primacy of the genitals. The maturation of the sexual organization is usually associated also with a taming of the aggressive drive, increased control over instinctual expression, and a fusion of tender love and sexual desire in one object relationship. Some individuals, however, because of either constitutional or developmental difficulties or intrapsychic conflict, do not achieve adult genital organization. Their sexual activities resemble those of infantile sexuality in regard to the conditions or mode of discharge required for gratification or the nature of the object relationship (for example, attachment to part objects).

See ADOLESCENCE; COMPONENT INSTINCTS; INFANTILE NEUROSIS; OBJECT; PERVERSION; PSYCHOSEXUAL DEVELOPMENT.

References

Freud, S. (1905). Three essays on the theory of sexuality. *SE,* 7:130–243.
Ritvo, S. (1971). Late adolescence. *PSOC,* 18:159–194.

■ INHIBITION

A restriction of an area of ego functioning. It may be normal or may denote the presence of some pathological process, in which case it may be a symptom as well. Inhibitions can range from specific to general and can involve any ego function. Examples are sexual performance, eating, locomotion, and work. Inhibitions may be the results of a need for self punishment or may be directly linked to unacceptable wishes. Some inhibitions are conceived to be the result of an impoverishment of available energy in the ego due to extensive utilization of energy elsewhere, as in the maintenance of defenses or in the work of mourning.

See CONFLICT; EGO FUNCTION; SYMPTOM.

References

Fenichel, O. (1945). *The Psychoanalytic Theory of Neurosis*. New York: Norton, pp. 168–186.
Freud, S. (1926). Inhibitions, symptoms, and anxiety. *SE,* 20:87–90.
Waelder, R. (1967). Inhibitions, symptoms and anxiety: forty years later. *PQ,* 36:1–36.

■ INSIGHT

The capacity or act of apprehending the nature of a situation or one's own problems. In psychiatry the term is often applied to recognition of one's own mental illness, characteristically absent in the psychoses but present in the neuroses. In psychoanalysis it has a broader implication—understanding of the dynamic factors contributing to conflict resolution—and it is regarded as an important achievement, essential for therapeutic change. Such understanding requires a degree of freedom of association, self-observation, contemplation, and discernment in a setting conducive to objectivity (which the psychoanalytic setting provides). It is a product of the synthesizing and integrating ego functions.

In ordinary usage *insight* connotes clear and immediate understanding, achieved seemingly intuitively. In psychoanalytic treatment it may occur as a sudden flash of recognition and understanding, called the "aha" experience, whereby the determining factors and connections of an idea or bit of behavior, or more global aspects of one's way of thinking and feeling, are seen in perspective. More commonly, however, insight follows a slow, gradual accretion of self-knowledge about oneself. As resistances are interpreted, repressed ideational content returns and is now accepted by the ego, so that psychic reorganization is facilitated. The resulting insight has two significant components, affect as well as cognition, for cognitive awareness alone does not lead to therapeutic change. Often the cognitive awareness of insight is repressed again in the process of psychic reorganization, but the new emotional freedom is maintained.

See ANALYSIS; PSYCHOANALYSIS.

References

Abrams, S. (1981). Insight. *PSOC,* 36:251–270.
Blum, H. (1981). Forbidden quest and the analytic ideal. *PQ,* 50:535–556.
Freud, A. (1981). Insight. *PSOC,* 36:241–250.
Neubauer, P. B. (1979). The role of insight in psychoanalysis. *JAPA,* 27:29–40.
Panel (1981). Insight. K. H. Blacker, reporter. *JAPA,* 29:659–672.

■ INSIGHT THERAPY

See PSYCHOTHERAPY.

■ INSTINCT

A term introduced by biologists, mainly students of animal behavior, which has been widely applied to the behavior of humans. The broadest definition is a species-specific behavior pattern, based mainly on potentialities determined by heredity (innate givens) and therefore relatively independent of learning. The term has been applied to a great variety of behavior patterns (e.g., maternal instinct, nesting instinct, the instinct of seasonal migration). These phenomena appeared to defy both further analysis into component behaviors and physiological explanation. As a consequence, the term has had a strong teleological connotation. This is reflected in the use of the term *instinctual aim,* which refers to an intended goal inherent in the instinctual behavior. The implication of prior purpose is seen, for example, in the concept of an "instinct for self-preservation," which played a major role in earlier hypotheses.

Modern instinct theory has been influenced by developments in a number of related fields. Observations, in particular those of the ethological school (e.g., Lorenz, Tinbergen, and others), but also those of sociobiologists (E. O. Wilson) and neurobiologists (E. Kandell), have cast considerable doubt on the validity and the heuristic value of the concept of instinct. Close observation of ostensibly purposeful instinctual behaviors allows scientists to analyze them into component patterns of interlocking and sequential reactions. Elements in these sequential patterns have proven vulnerable to environmental manipulations that pervert their apparent (i.e., teleologically plausible) purposes in the natural state (Hassler, 1960). The tendency of such patterns to persist in nature is generally explained in evolutionary terms: sequences of behavior will be favored to the extent that they promote survival better than competing sequences. But a third possibility exists: genetically encoded patterns of behavior that are neutral (i.e., that neither foster nor jeopardize survival) will also persist. Thus most biologists today follow T. C. Schneirla in critizing the concept of instinct. They prefer to speak of *species-typical patterns of behavior,* presumed to be rooted in innate, gene-determined equipment. The behavioral expression of such patterns, however, is almost always dependent on some degree of reaction with the environment. It can be taken as a general principle that the role of the environment increases as the nervous system becomes more complex.

While the term *instinct* was originally used in psychoanalysis to describe the motivational forces of human behavior, today these forces are usually referred to as *instinctual drives.*

References

Hassler, A. D. (1960). Guideposts of migrating fish. *Science,* 122:785–792.

Kandell, E. (1976). *Cellular Basis of Behavior.* San Francisco: W. H. Freeman.

Schneirla, T. C. (1959). An evolutionary and developmental theory of biphasic processes underlying approach and withdrawal. In *Nebraska Symposium on Motivation,* ed. M. R. Jones. Lincoln: Univ. Nebraska Press, pp. 1–49.

Solnit, A. J. & Ritvo, S. Instinct theory. *PMC.* Forthcoming.

Wilson, E. O. (1978). *On Human Nature.* Cambridge: Harvard Univ. Press.

■ INSTINCT THEORY

Central to the psychoanalytic perspective is the hypothesis that human behavior is actuated by endogenous sources of motivation. These have been referred to as *instincts.* In Freud's (1915) words, instincts are "the measure of the demand made upon the mind for work in consequence of its connection with the body" (p. 122). As the prime movers of behavior, they are assumed to transcend their idiosyncratic manifestations in particular individuals. That is, it is assumed that instincts reflect the operation of biological forces that are inherent, somatically rooted, and characteristic of all humans and indicate those aspects of humanness directly continuous with related species. Such biological imperatives can only be characterized in the most general terms. Although Freud's classification of instincts changed with the development of psychoanalysis, he consistently adhered to the conception that they take the form of polar opposites—that is, Freud felt that motivation is ultimately reducible to two broadly defined tendencies that are in opposition to one another. Over time the groupings he proposed went through three or four phases:

1. Sexual / self-preservative (ego)
2. (a) Object love / self love
   (b) Sexual / aggressive
3. Life / death.

While the importance of endogenous sources of motivation remains a cornerstone of psychoanalytic psychology, according to some analysts the heuristic value of the concept of *instinct* is in doubt.

See INSTINCT; INSTINCTUAL DRIVE.

References

Freud, S. (1915). Instincts and their vicissitudes. *SE,* 14:121–122.

■ INSTINCTUAL DRIVE
□ Instinctual Aim
□ Instinctual Object

The hypothesis that human behavior is actuated by endogenously derived motivational forces (among other things) was one of Freud's earliest assumptions, and it has remained a cornerstone of psychoanalytic theory. Freud used the German word *Trieb* to refer to such sources of motivation. Of his many definitions perhaps the most cogent is "an instinct [*Trieb*] . . . appears to us as a concept on the frontier between the mental and the somatic, as the physical representative of the stimuli originating from within the organism and reaching the mind, as a measure of the demand made upon the mind for work in consequence of its connection with the body" (Freud, 1915, pp. 121–122).

English-speaking readers of Freud were thrown

into confusion by Strachey's decision to translate *Trieb* as "instinct." Instincts, as they have been conceptualized by biologists and students of behavior, are characterized by a motivational force that always results in a specific pattern of behavior. Freud's concept of *Trieb,* by contrast, postulates that a motivational force may operate without relation to a particular mode of expression. While his definition refers to the psychic representations (conscious, preconscious, or unconscious) of stimuli that originate in physiological processes, it does not imply—as does the definition of instinct—a specific pattern of behavioral response. Freud appears to have had in mind the sum total of the mental representations that might be associated with a given somatic process. As defining characteristics he listed *source, aim,* and *object.* It should be noted that at least one of these, *object,* implies the presence of some degree of self–object differentiation. To this extent the concept of the instinctual drive has developmental as well as maturational connotations. *Aim* poses a related problem. While it may be possible to define aim in terms that refer only to the *need* to relieve somatic tension, many authorities (e.g., Hartmann, Kris & Loewenstein, 1949) consider action upon an object to be inherent in the definition of instinctual drive. Some authorities (e.g., Brenner, 1982) consider instinctual drives to be inborn, although they may be expressed only as they have been modulated by experience. Others (e.g., Jacobson, 1964) assume that instinctual drives are the products of development. Freud assumed that *Triebe* are based on innate givens, gene-determined potentials present from birth. This was one of the reasons why Strachey, and others before him, chose *instinct* as a translation. The term *instinctual drives* emphasizes the biological aspect of the word *Trieb* while at the same time avoiding the semantic pitfalls of the word *instinct.* It has been favored, therefore, by such theorists as Hartmann (1948) and Schur (1966).

It has never been settled how to specify the innate givens that are the gene-determined substrata (components) of instinctual drives. Freud's conceptualization underwent several modifications. Ultimately he distinguished between two very general tendencies which he referred to as *libido* or *Eros,* on the one hand, and *aggression,* which he formulated in terms of the *death instinct* (*Thanatos*), on the other. Libido or Eros is manifest in all processes, both physiological and psychological, that impel toward synthesis; it also exists in all the positive aspects of human relationships and is the constructive element in the motivation of most human activities. In a narrower sense, libido is usually associated with the "energies" expressed in erotic or sexual aims; in this sense it is sometimes referred to as the *sexual instinct.*

The death instinct is perhaps Freud's most controversial assumption. It has been severely criticized by both psychoanalysts and others, and it remains a highly speculative formulation, thus far unconfirmed by any biological investigation. Freud did recognize and discuss extensively the fact that the death instinct can be observed only in aggressive, destructive actions directed either toward the environment or against one's own person. Today most psychoanalysts, in both their clinical approach and their writings, use the concepts of the libidinal and aggressive instinctual drives. They also generally agree that instinctual drives are not seen in pure culture. Human behavior is usually conceptualized as reflecting the operation of libidinal and aggressive impulses (whether in conflict or in collaboration) under the modulating influences of already internalized regulatory agencies (superego) and the individual's perception of him- or herself and his or her relation to the environment. Expression of the instinctual drives will, therefore, always be subject to vicissitudes reflecting both the idiosyncratic history and the current circumstances of the individual. They undergo "fusion" very early in life and "defusion" as a regressive phenomenon in special situations.

References

Brenner, C. (1982). *The Mind in Conflict.* New York: Int. Univ. Press.

Freud, S. (1915). Instincts and their vicissitudes. *SE,* 14:111–140.

Hartmann, H. (1948). Comments on the theory of instinctual drives. *PQ,* 17:368–388.

Hartmann, H., Kris, E. & Loewenstein, R. M. (1949). Notes on the theory of aggression. *PSOC,* 3/4:9–36.

Jacobson, E. (1964). *The Self and the Object World.* New York: Int. Univ. Press.

Schur, M. (1966). *The Id and the Regulatory Principle of Mental Function.* New York: Int. Univ. Press.

Solnit, A. J. & Ritvo, S. Instinct theory. *PMC.* Forthcoming.

■ INTELLECTUALIZATION

The psychological binding of the instinctual drives to intellectual activities, especially in order to exert control over anxiety and reduce tension. This mechanism typically occurs in adolescence and is exemplified in abstract discussions and speculations about philosophical and religious topics that tend to avoid concrete bodily sensations or conflictual ideas or feelings. The adaptive use of ideas under favorable circumstances may enrich knowledge and intelligence, but pathological distortions lead to the creation of obsessive and paranoid symptoms. During psychoanalytic treatment intellectualization is often employed defensively, by separating and isolating ideas from their affects, to resist achieving emotional insight.

See INSTINCTUAL DRIVE, PSYCHIC ENERGY, OBSESSION.

References

Freud, A. (1936). *The Ego and the Mechanisms of Defense*. New York: Int. Univ. Press, 1966.
Sandler, J. & Freud, A. (1985). *The Analysis of Defense*. New York: Int. Univ. Press, pp. 500–507.
Stone, L. (1967). The psychoanalytic situation and transference. *JAPA,* 15:3–58.
Wieder, H. (1966). Intellectuality. *PSOC,* 21:294–323.

■ INTERNAL OBJECTS

See KLEINIAN THEORY.

■ INTERNAL SABOTEUR

See FAIRBAIRN'S THEORY.

■ INTERNALIZATION

In its broadest biological sense, a process by which aspects of the outer world and interactions with it are taken into the organism and represented in its internal structure. In the psychoanalytic frame of reference, the process is intrapsychic and usually object-related, taking place by three principal modes: incorporation, introjection, and identification. Projection and action are correlated externalizing phenomena. Though these terms have been loosely applied and used interchangeably in the literature, there have been various attempts to define them specifically in relation to levels of psychological and psychosexual development (Meissner, 1981).

Internalization, a generic term for all of these modes, is assumed to be the means by which aspects of need-gratifying relationships (Hartmann, Kris & Loewenstein, 1949; Hartmann, 1950; A. Freud, 1952) and functions provided for one individual by another (Loewald, 1962; Tolpin, 1971) are preserved by making them part of the self. Internalization is the primary contributor to psychological development, occurring throughout the life cycle whenever relations with a significant other are disrupted or lost. Perception, memory, mental representations, and symbol formation encode within the self aspects of objects and interactions with them, gradually building the structures of the mental apparatus, so that the individual can assume the functions originally supplied by others. A variety of different representational modes—sensorimotor or enactive, imagistic, lexical, or symbolic—may be involved (Piaget, 1937; Bruner, 1964; Horowitz, 1972; Blatt, 1974). The mental apparatus is thus capable of recording and retaining the history of the individual's personal and cultural experience, and this record reflects both the phase of psychosexual and ego development and the mode of information processing.

Freud (1917) postulated an early form of internalization, immediate and direct and not related to object loss, called *primary identification.* This occurs before self–object differentiation and must therefore be distinguished from internalization at other developmental levels, in which something previously experienced as external becomes internal (Sandler, 1960; Loewald, 1962; Jacobson, 1964). These *secondary internalizations* have been discussed as occurring at progressively higher developmental levels—incorporation, introjection, and identification. Some authors (e.g., Meissner, 1979, 1981) conceptualize these three levels of internalization as involving different psychological processes, while others (e.g., Behrends & Blatt, 1985) consider the mechanism of internalization to be the same at all levels but to involve different gradations of self and object differentiation and complexity.

Incorporation may be conceived of as internalization at a relatively undifferentiated level, in which the basic distinction between self and object has been achieved only in the most global form. Since there is at that stage little sense of part properties, internalizations are global, undifferentiated, and literal. The sense of the self often gets confused with the sense of the other. Implied is a fantasy of oral ingestion, swallowing, and destruction of the object. Incorporation as a mode of internalization is encountered in the fantasies and dreams of patients with psychoses, impulse disorders, and severe oral characters; it is also found in neurotic individuals during states of severe regression in analysis.

Introjection lacks the quality of destruction through ingestion implicit in incorporation, and there is no reference to body boundaries. It is a somewhat more differentiated process in which part properties and functions of the object are appropriated but not fully integrated into a cohesive and effective sense of self. Introjected components, however, do become a part of the self representation or of the structures of the mental apparatus (of the ego, superego, or ego ideal). Thus, object representations are transformed into self representations when boundaries between the two are indistinct, with the result that the individual may lose his or her sense of separateness or even his or her identity. This occurs when the child psychically takes in parental demands as his or her own, reacting in the same way whether or not the object is present. The regulating, forbidding, and rewarding aspects of the superego are formed by the introjection of parental directions, admonitions, and praise.

Identification is often used in a generic sense to refer to all the mental processes by which an individual becomes like another in one or several aspects, and so its meaning overlaps with that of the other terms discussed here. Now, however, analysts tend to reserve the term for a type of internalization more advanced than those previously described. This more mature level of internalization involves greater object–subject differentiation, and the process is more selective of the traits internalized. Various attitudes, functions, and values of the other are integrated into a cohesive, effective identity and become fully functional parts of the self compatible with other parts. Thus, identification differs from the other modes of internalization in terms of the degree to which the internalization is central to the individual's basic identity or ego core (Loewald, 1962). The transformed self representations are stable and enable the individual to establish an increasing sense of identity, mastery, and intentionality (Schafer, 1968).

The various modes of internalization are related to the stages of maturation and mental development and are influenced by the traumas, conflicts, arrests, and regressions to which each stage is subject. Optimally, they aid in the learning process (including the acquisition of language), as well as in the development of character traits, such as mannerisms, interests, and ideals. Identifications with either loved and admired persons or feared ones provide adaptive and defensive reaction patterns.

See CHARACTER; DEVELOPMENT; EGO DEVELOPMENT.

References

Behrends, R. S. & Blatt, S. J. (1985). Internalization and psychological development throughout the life cycle. *PSOC,* 40:11–39.

Blatt, S. J. (1974). Levels of object representation in anaclitic and introjective depression. *PSOC,* 29:107–157.

Bruner, J. S. (1964). The course of cognitive growth. *Amer. Psychologist,* 19:1–15.

Freud, A. (1952). The mutual influences in the development of ego and id. *WAF,* 4:230–244.

Freud, S. (1917). Mourning and melancholia. *SE,* 14:237–258.

——— (1938). An outline of psycho-analysis. *SE,* 23:141–207.

Hartmann, H. (1950). Comments on the psychoanalytic theory of the ego. In *Essays on Ego Psychology.* New York: Int. Univ. Press, pp. 113–141.

Hartmann, H., Kris, E. & Loewenstein, R. M. (1949). Notes on the theory of aggression. *PSOC,* 3/4:9–36.

Horowitz, M. J. (1972). Modes of representation of thought. *JAPA,* 20:793–819.

Jacobson, E. (1964). *The Self and the Object World.* New York: Int. Univ. Press.

Loewald, H. W. (1962). Internalization, separation, mourning, and the superego. *PQ,* 31:483–504.

——— (1973). On internalization. *IJP,* 54:9–17.

Meissner, W. W. (1979). Internalization and object relations. *JAPA,* 27:345–360.

——— (1981). *Internalization in Psychoanalysis.* New York: Int. Univ. Press.

Piaget, J. (1937). *The Construction of Reality in the Child.* New York: Basic Books, 1954.

Sandler, J. (1960). On the concept of the superego. *PSOC,* 15:128–162.

Schafer, R. (1968). *Aspects of Internalization.* New York: Int. Univ. Press.

Tolpin, M. (1971). On the beginnings of a cohesive self. *PSOC,* 26:316–354.

■ INTERPRETATION

The central therapeutic activity of the analyst during treatment, a process whereby the analyst expresses in words what he or she comes to understand about the patient's mental life. This understanding is based upon the patient's descriptions of memories, fantasies, wishes, fears, and other elements of psychic conflict that were formerly unconscious or known to the patient only in incomplete, inaccurate, or otherwise distorted form. Interpretation is also based upon observation of the way the patient distorts the relationship with the analyst to meet unconscious needs and to relive old experiences.

An interpretation is the statement of new knowledge about the patient. Both patient and analyst may contribute to it, although it is usually initiated by the analyst. *Genetic interpretations* connect present feelings, thoughts, conflicts, and behaviors with their historical antecedents, often dating back to early childhood. *Reconstruction* is part of the process of genetic interpretation, consisting of the piecing together of information about psychologically significant early experiences. This information is gathered from dreams, free associations, transference distortions, and other sources of analytic data. *Dynamic interpretations* clarify conflicting mental trends that result in particular behaviors, feelings, and other mental activities. *Transference interpretations* reveal and explain distortions in the therapeutic relationship that are based upon the displacement onto the figure of the analyst of feelings, attitudes, and behaviors originally experienced with significant past figures, usually parents and siblings. *Anagogic interpretation,* usually involving dream material, uncovers and clarifies abstract ideas that, due to the difficulty of directly representing them in mental images, are represented in allegorical form by material somewhat loosely related to the abstract thoughts.

An interpretation usually involves additions and modifications by both analyst and patient as new material emerges. The process of interpretation allows the patient's to understand his or her past and present inner life in a new, less distorted, and more complete way, leading to the possibility of changes in feelings, attitudes, and behavior. *Working through* links the process of interpretation to therapeutic change.

See GENETIC FALLACY; RECONSTRUCTION; TRANSFERENCE; WORKING THROUGH.

References

Arlow, J. A. (1979). The genesis of interpretation. *JAPA,* 27 (suppl.):193–206.
Kris, E. (1951). Ego psychology and interpretation in psychoanalytic therapy. *PQ,* 20:15–30.
Levy, S. T. (1984). *Principles of Interpretation.* New York: Aronson.
Loewenstein, R. M. (1951). The problem of interpretation. *PQ,* 20:1–14.

■ INTERVENTION

A generic term for all of the analyst's communications to the patient. Interventions include instructions, explanations, questions, confrontations, clarifications, reconstructions, and interpretations.

■ INTROJECTION

See INTERNALIZATION.

■ INTROJECTIVE IDENTIFICATION

See KLEINIAN THEORY.

■ INTROVERSION

See ANALYTICAL PSYCHOLOGY TERMS: TYPOLOGY.

■ INTUITION

The faculty of quick apprehension or cognition. Intuition involves the ability to organize and integrate silently and with seeming effortlessness (i.e., preconsciously) many different observations made over time. The process arrives at understanding without conscious awareness of the intermediate mental steps involved; thus the knowledge acquired has a sudden, unexpected, and therefore surprising quality. Knowledge acquired via intuition requires validation by purposeful and objective cognitive effort.

Intuition is related to and sometimes not adequately distinguished from empathy. Usually *empathy* involves shared emotional experiences, whereas *intuition* refers to individual thoughts and ideas that may or may not be communicated at the time they are arrived at. Empathic responses are information upon which intuitive understanding often is based. Finally, empathy appears to be a function of the experiencing ego; intuition, of the observing ego.

See COGNITION; EGO; EMPATHY; PRECONSCIOUS.

References

Arlow, J. A. (1979). The genesis of interpretation. *JAPA,* 27 (suppl.):193–206.

■ INVOLUTIONAL DEPRESSION

A depressive psychosis occurring for the first time during the climacterium or involutional period of life (forty to fifty-five years for women, fifty to sixty-five years for men), when the activity of endocrine glands decreases, reproductive capacity is lost, and often the responsibilities of parenthood diminish; other changes in relationships and work also occur as a result of advancing age. This diagnostic entity was omitted from the third edition of the American Psychiatric Association's *Diagnostic and Statistical Manual* (*DSM-III*) because of the opinion that it is identical with other depressions (although not bipolar depression) and that to distinguish it by the age of onset is not clinically valid. Many psychiatrists and analysts, however, do consider involutional depression to be a distinctive nosological entity, with specific symptoms, course, and prognosis.

Patients so classified have their first episode of depression after the age of forty-five. The family history is not significant, as it is in other depressions. Agitation and intense anxiety commonly accompany the depression, and the danger of suicide is greater. Hypochondriacal concerns are more frequent, often dominating the clinical picture. Aside from these differences, the mental content and other symptoms are much the same as in other depressions. Although the illness tends to be self-limiting, usually lasting nine to eighteen months, it is debilitating and dangerous. Prognosis with treatment is very good. Response to somatic therapies, medication, or electroconvulsive therapy is effective in 85–90 percent of cases and shortens the recovery period considerably. Recurrences are less frequent than in other depressions and may be delayed ten to twenty years.

Prior to the depressive episode the affected patients have usually functioned very well. They tend to be intense, obsessional, perfectionist individuals whose self-esteem regulation requires excellent performance with approving responses from significant people. The depression seems to represent a decompensation of a previously successful obsessional life pattern. Precipitating factors may include cessation of menstruation, death of a relative toward whom the patient had ambivalent feelings, departure of children from the home, or promotion of others at work in preference to the patient. These rigid, achievement-oriented people are faced with the passage of time and the threat of unacceptable limitations in achieving goals set by their ego ideals. Self-esteem falters and depression is precipitated. A good response to treatment is related to lifelong, relatively intact ego functions, which also explain the good premorbid functioning of such patients until they are faced with the problems, restrictions, and self-devaluations characteristic of the involutional period.

See AFFECTIVE DISORDERS; DEPRESSION; MANIC-DEPRESSIVE SYNDROME; PSYCHOSIS.

References

Rosenthal, S. M. (1968). The involutional depressive syndrome. *Amer. J. Psychiat.*, 124:21–35.

■ ISAKOWER PHENOMENON

A group of perceptual experiences, first described by Otto Isakower (1936), that occur during states of ego regression such as falling asleep (hypnagogic states), less commonly while awakening, during febrile states, as part of epileptic auras, and in the recumbent position on the analytic couch. More recently the phenomenon has been noted in frequent drug users. The sensations reported are much different from those of ordinary waking life and principally affect the mouth, skin, and hands, often simultaneously and without precise localization.

The subject may feel giddy, as if floating or sinking. Parts of the body blend together—the mouth and the skin, the body and the outside world, the internal and the external. Something shadowy and indefinite, like a balloon or lump, is seen. Something round comes nearer and nearer, swells to gigantic size, and threatens to crush the subject before receding, becoming smaller and smaller, and shrinking to nothing. The subject may feel enveloped by the "object" or may know that it is close at hand. Sometimes the subject feels a soft, yielding mass in the mouth, at the same time knowing that it is outside him or her. The patient hears humming, rustling, babbling, or murmuring. The hand may feel swollen or crumpled and the mouth and skin jagged, sandy, or dry. These sensations may be experienced as pleasurable, unpleasurable, or (usually) neither, but they are often accompanied by a sense of alienation from the experience, which is not regarded as real.

These sensations occur during childhood and puberty but much less frequently during adult life. The features are similar to auras prior to seizures and to déjà vu phenomena, but they may be reproduced voluntarily when they are being recounted to the analyst.

The phenomena may be viewed as representing memory traces of the self and the world at a time of early ego organization, when boundaries have not been firmly established and there is no sharp distinction between the body and its parts and the outside world. They suggest a hypercathexis of the oral zone and other parts of the body involved in breast-feeding. As in other regressive ego states, the phenomena serve as defenses aimed at warding off anxiety against the revival of disturbing oedipal fantasies. In the analytic situation, they may represent a regression from a specific primal scene experience. The regressive oral gratification serves both to repudiate the oedipal wish and to gratify it, though on a more primitive level.

See DÉJÀ VU; DEPERSONALIZATION; REGRESSION.

References

Easson, W. M. (1973). The earliest ego development, primitive memory traces, and the Isakower phenomenon. *PQ*, 42:60–72.

Fink, G. (1967). Analysis of the Isakower phenomenon. *JAPA*, 15:281–293.

Isakower, O. (1938). A contribution to the patho-psychology of phenomena associated with falling asleep. *IJP*, 19:331–345.

Lewin, B. D. (1946). Sleep, the mouth, and the dream screen. *PQ*, 15:419–434.
Mahler, M. S. (1975). Discussion of Bernard L. Pacella's paper. *JAPA*, 23:327–334.
Pacella, B. (1975). Early ego development and the déjà vu. *JAPA*, 23:300–317.
Richards, A. D. (1985). Isakower-like experience on the couch. *PQ*, 54:415–434.

■ ISOLATION

See DEFENSE.

■ JEALOUSY

Implies envy of the actual or presumed advantage of a rival, especially in regard to the love of an object. Jealousy is often accompanied by suspicion that the loved person favors the other. Deriving from the oedipal constellation, jealousy is based on the wish for an exclusive relationship to the primary object, which later in life is referred to other objects. Love, not gratification of needs or attention alone, is the objective. There is also an unconscious wish for the elimination of the rival.

See ENVY; RIVALRY.

Reference

Neubauer, P. B. (1982). Rivalry, envy, and jealousy. *PSOC*, 37:121–142.

■ KLEINIAN THEORY

Melanie Klein is one of the most influential psychoanalysts in the world, though her work is less well known in the United States than elsewhere. She was born Melanie Reizes in Vienna in 1882, the youngest of four children. At 21 she married Arthur Klein, with whom she had three children. From 1910 to 1919 the family lived in Budapest. Melanie Klein had lost a sister when she was five and shortly thereafter a brother. "These losses, strongly revived when Klein's elder son died in an accident, probably account for the depressive streak that colored Klein's life and contributed to her sensitivity to the depressive position" (Katz, 1985, p. 210). Her chronic depressions brought her to treatment with Ferenczi. In 1921 she separated from her husband and lived with her children in Berlin. The separation eventuated in divorce in 1923. Karl Abraham became Klein's analyst and was very supportive of her work in child analysis. He died in 1925, and Melanie Klein moved to London in 1926 at the invitation of Ernest Jones, continuing there her clinical and theoretical contributions until her death in 1960, at the age of 78.

Melanie Klein was drawn to Sigmund Freud's ideas about objects, guilt, anxiety, fantasy, and the death instinct, which she reworked into a theory of early aggression. The direction she gave "placed a new emphasis on the study of early development as well as opened the door to psychoanalytic work with psychotics" (Turkle, 1986). The play technique she devised for children "discovered a rich inner world of the child, peopled by fantastic part objects and people. She discovered primitive unconscious fantasies, anxieties, and defenses. Her understanding of early primitive mechanisms opened the way to the analysis of borderline cases and psychotics by her pupils and collaborators" (Segal, 1986).

In her treatment of children Klein found that it is not the patient's relationship to the real parents that is transferred to the analyst but the relationship to internal fantasy figures, the inner parents. Hence she emphasized the importance of early internal object relations in normal and pathological development in children and adults. Superego formation, she believed, begins much earlier than originally thought, and aggressive impulses lead to the constellations described as the *paranoid-schizoid* and *depressive positions* and to manic defenses against anxiety. The two positions represent a conceptual step beyond the fixed ontogenetic models of Freud's instinctual phases. Assuming the coexistence of different stages of psychosexual development involves a contradiction in terms. Several object relations, however, may combine or alternate in the same person. Klein replaced the concept of stage with that of object relationship, and her positions refer to a mixture of drives, defenses, and relations to objects expressed in affectively colored behavior. While it is true that the paranoid-schizoid and depressive positions may be seen as phases of development, the term *position* emphasizes that the phenomena described are not simply manifestations of a passing stage but rather "a specific configuration of object relations, anxieties and defenses which persist *throughout life*. The depressive position never fully supersedes the paranoid-schizoid position; the integration achieved is never complete and defenses against the depressive conflict bring about regression to paranoid-schizoid phenomena, so that the individual *at all times may oscillate between the two*" (Segal, 1973, p. ix, italics added).

Melanie Klein's formulations have been criticized on the basis that, though stated in theoretical terms, they are actually mixtures of clinical and theoretical ideas that Klein felt could be applied directly in clinical work. In particular there were objections to her assumption that the negative transference and aggressive-destructive impulses of child and adult patients could and should be dealt with immediately upon their appearance without jeopardizing the development of a therapeutic alliance. There is also controversy about the following ideas of Klein:

- The concept of an inborn death instinct and its early expression as envy
- Vast innate knowledge attributed to the neonate
- The telescoping of intrapsychic development into the first year of life with relative neglect of the later developments of ego and superego
- Techniques that are applied to all levels of pathology, focusing almost exclusively on transference while minimizing reality
- Premature, deep interpretations of unconscious fantasies while overlooking character analysis
- The view that children's play may be considered the equivalent of the adult patient's free association

Melanie Klein's ideas corresponded very closely to those put forward by Ernest Jones and others in the British Society, especially with respect to the importance of pregenital and innate determinants as opposed to the influence of environmental stress, the early development of female sexuality, and the role of aggression in anxiety. A so-called Kleinian group grew up around her in the British Institute, but her theories about very early development of organized fantasies and mental processes remained controversial, especially after Anna Freud, whose views were quite different, also came to settle in London. There was a great deal of rivalry between these two child analysts. The British Institute has to this day avoided formal division, but the differences between those who followed Melanie Klein, those who followed Anna Freud, and a middle group (the "Independents") are clearly demarcated. The establishment and perpetuation of the Kleinian school are partially explained by the number of charismatic leaders associated with it, beginning with Klein herself. From the British Institute her influence flowed mostly to Europe and South America. The patients (both children and adults) of Klein and her followers, to judge from published works, were severely disturbed, even psychotic. Her ideas have thus aided understanding of a severely ill group of patients relatively neglected by non-Kleinian analysts. Moreover, Klein pursued the vicissitudes of the aggressive drive more assiduously than other psychoanalysts, and her approach has appealed to many in its return to the depths of the unconscious, to deep primitive drives and mental mechanisms, in opposition to the abstractions of ego psychology. Under the influence of Heinz Hartmann, Ernst Kris, Rudolph Loewenstein, and David Rapaport, ego psychology has had more appeal in the United States.

Klein's "devotion to her work in psychoanalysis was a leading characteristic. . . . Ambitious, highly intuitive, courageous, honest, she was uncompromising about her work and fierce in its defense. . . . Hers was a powerful personality which commanded almost universal respect" (Katz, 1985, p. 214).

□ Depressive Position

A major developmental step forward, succeeding the paranoid-schizoid position, that integrates love and hate for objects, their "good" and "bad" aspects, other partial representations of them (e.g., "oral" and "genital" mother), and external reality with intrapsychic reality or fantasy. Like the paranoid-schizoid position, the depressive position represents a configuration of object relations, anxieties, and defenses and is not equivalent to any of Freud's phases of psychosexual development. Both positions occur during oral primacy; Klein assumed that the depressive position develops in rudimentary form at approximately three to four months of age and that it continues throughout the life of the individual. Since the maternal object is now recognized as a whole object, Klein postulates that oedipal conflict begins to operate at this early age. Mother is the source of both good and bad, and the infant discovers helplessness, dependency, and jealousy vis-à-vis her. Though the child develops some tolerance for these feelings, ambivalence persists, and anxiety shifts to fears that the aggressive impulses within the self may destroy the object now recognized as needed, important, and loved. The possibility of losing the good object through such aggression leads to guilt. Whereas the principal affect during the paranoid-schizoid position is that of persecutory anxiety, the principal concern in the depressive position is for the object and its welfare. Introjection now prevails over projection. Since the person develops the capacity to repair the fantasied damages to loved objects, he or she gains confidence that love can prevail over hate for objects. Omnipotent fantasies are involved, not only in fears of destruction of the object, but also in the predominant effort to deal with the anxieties of this position by means of "reparation." That concept implies retrospectively experiencing guilt for all the projections of bad impulses into the object.

The ideal outcome of the depressive position, never fully achieved, would require abandoning omnipotent control over the object in favor of accepting the reality of dependence. As this point is gradually reached, gratitude toward the object for its role in creating and sustaining the infant's life becomes possible.

If the depressive anxieties are too great to be dealt with defensively, the depressive position cannot be consolidated and overcome. Manic defenses may then be employed, consisting of fantasies of controlling the object, with a sense of triumph over and contempt for the object that protects against the dependence of the depressive position. The infant may also regress to the paranoid-schizoid position.

See FANTASY; INTERNAL OBJECTS; PARANOID-SCHIZOID POSITION; REPARATION. Refer to Klein, 1940, 1957b; Segal, 1964, 1981, at the end of this section.

□ Envy

One of the most primitive and fundamental emotions, an expression of the infant's destructive impulses operative from the beginning of life. Klein believed envy has a constitutional basis as the mental manifestation of the death instinct. It is felt first in relation to the good breast, the reservoir of food, warmth, and comfort, in contrast to the infant, distressed by painful feelings of helpless dependence, who wishes to be the provider of well-being. The infant feels a destructive urge to remove the source of the envy, hence the object's qualities and possessions are "stolen" or "spoiled" through fantasied oral or anal-sadistic attacks. The infant's envious psychic attacks on the breast transform it into a denigrated and worthless object, thereby obviating the need for gratitude and dependence.

Intense envy can prevent the development of internal representations of good objects, because they are instantly devalued; such envy may thus interfere with attempts to overcome the paranoid-schizoid position. In such cases the images of the breast are transformed, via splitting and projective identification, into retaliatory internal objects, which may form the core of an "envious superego" that disturbs or annihilates attempts at reparation and creativeness. Another defense against envy is the fantasy of possessing all the valuable attributes of the objects; these defenses promote identification with idealized objects and may lead to narcissistic overestimation of the self.

Envy is contrasted with *greed,* which aims at the possession of all the goodness of the object. Greed is more libidinal in nature than is envy, which is suffused with the death instinct. Envy in particular impairs the development of object relations and the introjection of the power and goodness of objects. In normal development, gratitude eventually modifies envy and allows further development.

Jealousy pertains to a triangular relationship, which occurs after objects are recognized as whole; it aims at the possession of the loved object and the removal of the rival. By comparison, envy is a two-part relationship experienced toward part objects, whose possessions or qualities the subject wishes to have.

See FANTASY; IDENTIFICATION; INTERNAL OBJECT; PARANOID-SCHIZOID POSITION; SPLITTING.

□ Fantasy

A storylike form of mentation, whether conscious or unconscious (spelled *phantasy* in Great Britain). In Kleinian theory, fantasy is defined as the mental expression of instincts and consequently is presumed to exist from the beginning of life. From the earliest period, therefore, organized mental activity in the form of fantasy expresses the infant's primitive relationship to objects in reference to the instincts, which seek object relations. Fantasies are thought to be the principal component of unconscious mental life; they directly reflect primary process functioning, originally hallucinatory wish fulfillment. However, they may also express functions of an ego and superego much earlier than Freud thought. Developmental conflicts, including oedipal conflicts, and defenses against them; the drives; and affects—including denial, repression, omnipotent control, and reparation—are believed to be expressed in fantasies as early as the first year of life. *Fantasy-forming* occurs long before the development of formal language and continues to dominate the internal world throughout adulthood.

The earliest fantasies are omnipotent and concrete. They derive originally from bodily sensations and represent instinctual aims toward objects with affective interpretations of the sensory experiences. At their most basic, they seem to represent the infant's bodily urges or wishes to possess different parts of the mother's (or father's) body (part objects, e.g., breast or penis). Only slowly does the infant begin to distinguish between his or her fantasy desire for mother's body and the reality of her separateness. Recognition that wishes are fantasies, not actual deeds of acquisition, constitutes the infant's earliest orientation to reality.

Although fantasies are the basis of all mental defense mechanisms, the latter are more formalized, depersonified, and all-inclusive. For instance, while the mental mechanism of introjection is based on the oral fantasy of incorporating the mother's breast, it also comprises a more formal mechanism of taking in and processing information from the external world.

See IDENTIFICATION; INTERNAL OBJECTS.

□ Identification

An automatic, unconscious mental process whereby an individual becomes like another person in one or several aspects. It naturally accompanies maturation and mental development and aids in the learning process as well as in the acquisition of interests, ideals, mannerisms, and other attributes. An individual's adaptive and defensive reaction patterns are often based on identification with either loved and admired persons or feared and hated ones. Kleinian theory gives special emphasis to two types of identification.

In *projective identification* parts of the self and internal objects are split off and projected onto an external object, which then becomes "identified" with the split-off part as well as possessed and controlled by it. Its defensive purposes include fusion with the external object in order to avoid separation; control of the destructive, so-called bad object, which is a persecutory threat to the individual; and preservation of good portions of the self by splitting them off and projectively identifying them in the therapist for "safe-keeping." This mechanism begins in the paranoid-schizoid position, but it can continue throughout development.

Although Klein and her followers use the terms *projection* and *projective identification* virtually interchangeably, there is an implied distinction between the two: projection designates only a defense mechanism and projective identification involves a fantasied object relationship. Ogden (1982) elaborates this distinction whereas Grotstein (1981) eliminates it, believing that there can be no projection without a recipient (container) with which the projected part is to be identified.

Introjective identification is the counterpart of projective identification. The term implies the fantasy of orally incorporating the object, whereby identification with it occurs. Introjection and projection are conceptualized as continuous processes that result in the formation of an internal world. Introjective identification is balanced by projective mechanisms insofar as the infant incorporates what he or she has already identified as good (via projective identification) but also "spits out" (projects) bad or dangerous aspects of the object. This interrelationship was described by Freud (1915) following the coining of the term *introjection* (Ferenczi, 1909). Thus, introjection of the parents can be thought of as a selective process whereby the ego "samples" the objects of the external world, introjects certain aspects, and projects others (Heimann, 1952). Identification with the parents occurs via a combination of these two mechanisms and results in ego and superego development. Whereas projective mechanisms seem to dominate in the paranoid-schizoid position, introjective mechanisms prevail during the depressive position. The depressive position represents maturational progress; the object is now a whole instead of a part object, and the danger is no longer that the ego will be destroyed by the projected death instinct (that is, the bad object), but rather that the child's destructive impulses will destroy the loved object. In general, introjective processes are stronger in this position because of the need to possess the object, keep it inside, and thereby protect it from the infant's own destructiveness. On the other hand, introjective identification can also be employed as a defensive mechanism for taking in a bad object and identifying with it in order to preserve the goodness of the external object in fantasy.

See DEPRESSIVE POSITION; FANTASY; INTERNAL OBJECTS; PARANOID-SCHIZOID POSITION. Refer to Ferenczi, 1909; Grotstein, 1981; Heimann, 1952; Klein, 1952a, 1952b, 1957a; Ogden, 1982, at the end of this section.

□ Internal Objects

Are intrapsychic representations of aspects of relations with other persons. Fairbairn and others employed the term in relation to the fantasy of internalizing a "bad" (disappointing) image of the nurturing person in order to control it. This usage follows Freud's and Abraham's original descriptions of the internalization of objects; Kleinians, however, utilize the term more specifically to designate the internalization of objects following their initial "discovery" or "creation" via the projective identification of aspects of the infant's instinctual life. For example, greed would yield a demanding internal object.

In Kleinian theory it is assumed that, from birth onward, anxiety is created by conflict between the life and the death instincts. Both are projected onto the mother's breast; the death instinct causes the breast to be fantasied as an external *persecutory object*. But since introjection and projection are continuous processes, the persecutory object can also become an internal object. At the same time, in order to create a good object which will satisfy the instinct for preserving life and protect against the internalized persecutory object, the infant bestows libidinal attributes on the breast, thus making it into an *ideal object*. The primary fantasy activity is introjection of the good and projection of the bad to keep them apart. At other times the good may be projected to keep it safe from internal aggression, while (as mentioned above) the external persecutory object is often introjected, becoming an internal bad object.

There may be an "assembly of internalized objects," interacting with each other and with the self. They can be transferred to the analyst and "influence the individual's affective states and overt behavioral reactions" (Greenberg & Mitchell, 1983, p. 10). Also called *introjects,* they may be "understood as loose anticipatory images of what is to be expected from people in the 'real world'; as becoming closely entwined with the individual's experience of who he/she is; as persecutors . . . or as a source of internal security, invoked in times of stress and isolation. They constitute a residue (within the mind) of relationships with important people in the individual's life. Crucial exchanges with others leave their mark; they are internalized" (ibid., p. 11). Internal objects can be divided into good or bad, partial or whole, and assimilated (into the identity of the self) or unassimilated (not identified with the ego) (Heimann, 1952).

Kleinians and members of the object relations school have not clearly distinguished between internal objects and object representations, although this distinction may be implicit in the Kleinian concept of the development of symbol formation. In order to achieve the capacity to represent symbols, according to Klein, the infant must progress from the paranoid-schizoid position to the depressive position, so that the capacity to tolerate separation is achieved and, along with it, the capacity to imagine the object in its absence.

See DEPRESSIVE POSITION; FANTASY; IDENTIFICATION; PARANOID-SCHIZOID POSITION. Refer to Fairbairn, 1952; Greenberg & Mitchell, 1983; Klein, 1950b, 1957a, 1959; Segal, 1964, 1981, at the end of this section.

□ Paranoid-Schizoid Position

In Klein's view, the ego has at birth the capacity for some organization: it can experience anxiety, use defense mechanisms, and form primitive object relationships. The paranoid-schizoid position is the first and most primitive organization of the mental apparatus, distributing the emotional experiences in relation to internal and external objects into a dynamic framework that continues to exert influence throughout life despite modification by the attainment of its counterpart, the depressive position. The defensive mechanisms predominating in the paranoid-schizoid position are splitting, projective identification, magical omnipotent denial, and idealization. The infant projects love and hate onto the mother's breast, splitting it into a "good" (or gratifying) and a "bad" (or frustrating) object. The good object is "idealized," that is, perceived as capable of providing unlimited gratification. The bad object, by contrast, becomes a terrifying persecutor. This position is therefore characterized by persecutory anxiety: the infant fears being destroyed by the bad object. Since the ego lacks adequate integration, it must resort to omnipotent denial to divest the persecuting object of reality or power.

The term *schizoid* is employed, following Fairbairn, to indicate the splitting the infant's self undergoes in fantasy in order to achieve a suitable relationship to the goodness of the object. Anxiety over threatened, fantasied annihilation by persecutory internal objects is personified by the designation *paranoid*. The common denominator in the schizoid mechanisms is omnipotence. The infant, in an effort to exert omnipotent control over objects, bestows omnipotence upon them via projective identification and thereby is victimized by omnipotent persecutory objects. Exaggerated, split, persecutory, omnipotent aspects of the paranoid-schizoid position can be observed in such conditions as the borderline syndromes, other primitive mental disorders, and, to a lesser degree, in all human beings.

See DEPRESSIVE POSITION; IDENTIFICATION; INTERNAL OBJECTS. Refer to Klein, 1952b, 1957a; Segal, 1964, 1981, at the end of this section.

□ Reparation

One of the principal mental activities of the depressive position. It includes all the infant's efforts to spare the object from harm, particularly from the damage threatened by the infant's own destructive mechanisms stemming from hostility and envy. Reparations proceed from the infant's first experiences of gratitude, which follow acceptance of the reality of dependence upon the maternal object. These "restorative" attempts are also closely associated with creative capacities, which reparation and gratitude seem to enhance.

Refer to Klein, 1950a, 1957b; Segal, 1964, 1981, at the end of this section.

□ Splitting

Best understood by keeping in mind the basic Kleinian assumptions that instincts operate from birth in a differentiated form; that fantasy represents mental activity, also operating from birth in a differentiated form and expressing the vicissitudes of the instincts; that the instincts involve objects; and that there is a complex interaction between the infant and its objects, the term *internal objects* implying introjections and projections between parts of the infant's fantasy life and the objects.

In this theoretical framework, *splitting* may be defined as a primitive mental mechanism that helps infants to order their experiences out of primal instinctual chaos. From early on the ego has a relationship to the primary object, the breast, represented in two parts (that is, split) which distinguish its pleasurable (good) from nonpleasurable (bad) aspects. By means of this splitting the infant can distinguish between pleasurable (good or ideal) aspects of the breast and nonpleasurable (bad) aspects (the available object world). Kleinian theory postulates that when the infant is hungry, screaming may express a fantasy of persecutory attack on the inside of the body, where the hunger pain is experienced; the nonpleasurable aspect of the breast then becomes a persecutory object. When these good and bad objects are internalized, they remain split, although the infant tries to project the bad object experiences. The fantasy of the ideal object merges with, and is confirmed by, gratifying experiences of love and attention from the real external mother, while the fantasy of persecution by the bad object similarly merges with real experiences of deprivation and pain.

The ego, which is thought to be incipiently organized at birth, is split as a result of the infant's introjective identification with both the good and bad objects. This creates an incompatibility in the ego during the earliest stages of development, before the capacity for ambivalence has been attained. Because of this rupture in the ego itself, splitting and the projection of split-off ego parts dominate the perception of early objects and the external world. Splitting is characteristic of the paranoid-schizoid position. In normal development it enables the infant to order his or her experiences and make discriminations, and it also serves defensive purposes, becoming ultimately the basis for such mechanisms as repression, as a consequence of the resolution of the oedipal phase, and the acceptance of ambivalent feelings toward a single object, in the depressive position. In severe pathology, splitting may progress to fragmentation of objects into minute bits of violently hostile elements presumed to be projected and reintrojected. This results in gross forms of pathological dissociation.

See DEPRESSIVE POSITION; INTERNAL OBJECTS; PARANOID-SCHIZOID POSITION. Refer to Grotstein, 1981; Klein, 1952b; Segal, 1964, 1981, at the end of this section.

□ Symbolic Equation

A mental process by which the mind chooses what could be an appropriate symbol for an object but uses it concretely and literally as if it were identical with the object. For example, a schizophrenic violinist is no longer able to play for an audience because he equates his violin with his genitals; hence playing would be like masturbating in public. Segal (1957) associated the symbolic equation with the paranoid-schizoid position, in which the capacity to mourn has not yet been developed and consequently the lost object is neither given up nor replaced by a symbol. By contrast, in the depressive position the loss of the object is acknowledged. Giving up the object stimulates the wish to recreate the object within the self. A creative process begins whereby multiple representations of the object are developed; some of these are symbols or abstract substitutes. Affects linked to the original object are displaced to these substitutes, but a clear distinction remains between the substitutes and the object they represent—the confusion characteristic of the symbolic equation no longer exists. The varied internal representations of the object are used to overcome, not to deny, its loss. Loss is thus followed by creative reparation freely using distant, multiple substitutes to recover the lost object internally. Creativity and sublimation are therefore enhanced when working through the depressive position.

See DEPRESSIVE POSITION; IDENTIFICATION; INTERNAL OBJECTS; PARANOID-SCHIZOID POSITION. Refer to Segal, 1957, 1981, at the end of this section.

References

Fairbairn, W. R. D. (1952). *Psychoanalytic Studies of the Personality*. London: Routledge & Kegan Paul.

Ferenczi, S. (1909). Introjection and transference. In *Sex in Psychoanalysis*. New York: Basic Books, pp. 35–93.

Freud, S. (1921). Group psychology, chapter 7: identification. *SE,* 18.

Greenberg, S. A. & Mitchell, J. R. (1983). *Object Relations in Psychoanalytic Theory*. Cambridge: Harvard Univ. Press.

Grosskurth, P. (1986). *Melanie Klein*. New York: Alfred Knopf.

Grotstein, J. S. (1981). *Splitting and Projective Identification*. New York: Jason Aronson.

Heimann, P. (1952). Certain functions of introjec-

tion and projection in early infancy. In Klein et al. (1952), pp. 122–168.
Isaacs, S. (1952). The nature and function of phantasy. In Klein et al. (1952), pp. 67–121.
Katz, J. (1985). Book review of *Melanie Klein* by Hanna Segal. New York: Viking Press, 1980. *JAPA*, 33 (suppl.):209–214.
Klein, M. (1948). *Contributions to Psycho-Analysis, 1921–1945*. London: Hogarth Press.
——— (1950). *Narrative of a Child Analysis*. New York: Basic Books.
——— (1957a). On identification. In *New Directions in Psycho-Analysis,* ed. M. Klein, P. Heimann & R. Money-Kyrle. New York: Basic Books, pp. 3–22.
——— (1957b). *Envy and Gratitude*. New York: Basic Books.
——— (1932). *The Psycho-Analysis of Children*. London: Hogarth Press.
——— Heimann, P., Isaacs, S. & Riviere, J., eds. (1952). *Developments in Psycho-Analysis*. London: Hogarth Press.
Ogden, T. (1982). *Projective Identification and Psychotherapeutic Technique*. New York: Jason Aronson.
Segal, H. (1957). Notes on symbol formation. *IJP,* 38:391–397.
——— (1964). *Introduction to the Work of Melanie Klein*. London: Hogarth Press, 1973.
——— (1973). *Introduction to the Work of Melanie Klein*. London: W. Heinemann.
——— (1981). *The Work of Hanna Segal*. New York: Jason Aronson.
——— (1986). Illuminator of the dim, shadowy era. *Sunday Times,* London, May 11, 1986.
Turkle, S. (1986). A review of Grosskurth, P.: *Melanie Klein. New York Times Book Review,* May 18, 1986.

■ LATENCY

Freud (1905) observed that after a short period of efflorescence between the ages of two and five, the sexual activity of children is markedly diminished during a period of latency (a term he borrowed from Fliess) lasting until puberty. The term therefore applies to the time interval from approximately six to twelve years of age and to the psychic characteristics of that phase. Clinically, children of this age are usually relatively well behaved, pliable, and educable. Some theorists have proposed a biological diminution of the sexual drive as a basis for the modifications in behavior during the latency period, but there is evidence that intense sexual drive derivatives continue. Freud postulated that energy from sexual excitation is stored and is employed for nonsexual purposes, contributing to the development of defenses against sexual impulses, social feelings, and sublimatory activities.

A more modern view is that, with the structural development that results from introjective-projective mechanisms, the defensive structure of the ego reorganizes, resulting in an equilibrium between defenses and drives. In this state of relative psychic harmony, the child can direct attention to the outer world and the development of physical, cognitive, and social skills with peer objects. These activities provide gratifications which make sexual activity less imperative. In spite of the relative quiescence of erotic activity, however, there is evidence that masturbatory fantasies and activity are present in mid- to late-latency children and that masturbation may be important for the child's stability.

See DEVELOPMENT; PSYCHOSEXUAL DEVELOPMENT.

References

Freud, S. (1905). Three essays on the theory of sexuality. *SE,* 7:176ff.
Sarnoff, C. A. (1978). *Latency*. New York: Aronson.
Tyson, P. & Tyson, R. L. Development. *PMC*. Forthcoming.

■ LATENT CONTENT

See DREAMING, DREAMS.

■ LAY ANALYSIS

The practice of psychoanalysis by a nonmedical analyst, most frequently a clinical psychologist or other mental health professional.

References

Freud, S. (1926). The question of lay analysis. *SE,* 20:183–258.
Panel. (1982). Beyond lay analysis. N. Fischer, reporter. *JAPA,* 30:701–715.

■ LESBIANISM

See HOMOSEXUALITY.

■ LIBIDINAL EGO

See FAIRBAIRN'S THEORY.

■ LIBIDO THEORY

Freud used the term *libido* from the 1890s on, at first loosely, to refer to sexual desire or sexual appetite. Later he employed the term in a more technical sense as well, in connection with his concept of instinctual drives (1905). Libido came to designate the idea, central to psychoanalytic theory, that sexual interest or stimulation is continuous throughout life, revealed in a variety of behavioral and mental manifestations related to one another by their common sexual or—to indicate the broader, psychoanalytic sense of that idea—libidinal component. Thus, sexuality as an instinctual drive could be called a *libidinal drive;* a felt or inferred sexual impulse might be a *libidinal impulse;* the person or thing that is the target or agent of gratification of such an impulse would be called a *libidinal object*. Affection as well as lust is included in this concept. Affectionate or sexual ties to another person may be designated as *libidinal attachments*. These usages are intended to indicate the underlying unity of libidinal drives, objects, and attachments.

In 1914 and 1915 Freud formally described his *libido theory*. Libido now came to be seen also as a form of mental "energy" (analogous to physical energy) that might be invested in various mental representations or structures of the mind. Freud called this investment *cathexis*. Seen as a form of energy, libido might be discharged at times of instinctual drive gratification or might cathect (be invested in) a mental structure. Failure to discharge libido adequately might result in a "dammed-up state," thought to be related to the formation of acute neurotic symptoms. Freud postulated a reciprocal relation between the amount of libido invested in oneself (self representation) and the amount invested in one's objects (object representations). These allocations of libido Freud referred to as *ego libido* and *object libido*.

Still later Freud described some broad clinical situations in libidinal terminology. Persons who readily formed transferences and who responded well to psychoanalytic treatment were described as having *plastic libido;* those who were insusceptible to such change, despite appearances to the contrary, were thought of as having *adhesive libido* (1937). Freud also made an attempt to classify character according to *libidinal types* (1931).

The libido theory is often confused with the related but distinct theory of instinctual drives. Libido is sometimes taken only in the "energic" sense; in that form it has become controversial. The most important feature of libido theory, however, is the idea of a causal factor common to a variety of pleasure states and personal attachments throughout life. That causal factor also helps explain quantitative changes in mental life (more or less intense feelings, impulses, attachments, etc.). It is important to remember that libido is only analogous to physical energy, not a form of physical energy. No way to measure it has been even remotely approached.

See CATHEXIS; CHARACTER; INSTINCTUAL DRIVE; SYMPTOM.

References

Fenichel, O. (1945). *The Psychoanalytic Theory of Neurosis*. New York: Norton.
Freud, S. (1905). Three essays on the theory of sexuality. *SE*, 7:130–243.
——— (1914). On narcissism. *SE*, 14:73–102.
——— (1915). Instincts and their vicissitudes. *SE*, 14:117–140.
——— (1931). Libidinal types. *SE*, 21:217–220.
——— (1937). Constructions in analysis. *SE*, 23:257–269.

■ LOVE

A complex affective state and experience associated with primarily libidinal investment of objects. The feeling state is characterized usually by elation and euphoria, sometimes ecstasy, and on occasion pain. Freud referred to it as a "refinding of the object," and it could be considered an affective recall of the state of symbiotic union. The child probably first experiences love in the form of attachment to and longing for the mother during and after differentiation of self and object representations. The development of love during infancy largely depends upon the reciprocal loving attachment of the mother or primary caregiver. Originally, the child loves both a narcissistic object and the self; this early love has prominent oral and narcissistic aims and features.

There are three important dimensions to love: narcissistic versus object love, infantile versus mature love, and love versus hate. The degree of concomitant hate, of aggressive versus affectionate aims (and thus of ambivalence), is an important factor in love's quality and stability. The development of object constancy, necessary for later mature love, depends upon numerous factors. Among these are the resolution of intense ambivalence, consolidation of stable, cohesive self and object representations, and resistance to ego regression and loss of attachment in the face of frustration and separation from the object. Self-constancy and sound secondary narcissism are necessary in order to feel loved, thus to reciprocity in a love relationship. The ability to find in each other means of repairing previous losses or traumas and the establishment and continuation of a sense of unique shared intimacy are important elements in love relationships. Satisfaction of sexual desire is usually a mutual wish, but love must be distinguished from the concept of "genital primacy," which now implies the capacity for orgasm without specifying the level or nature of the object relationship involved.

Freud discovered that all love is based upon infantile prototypes. Transference love is a revival of the patient's real and fantasied infantile love relationships; its analysis permits the patient to understand how infantile aims and attachments impede adult functioning and relationships. Even relatively consistent and constant adult love is subject to regression and infantile fixation. In severe regression or in cases of developmental arrest the individual may be unable to love. This incapacity is often associated with primitive aggression, self-hate, and hate of the object.

Love takes many aim-inhibited forms and directions once the psychosexual, primary object attachment has been established. Structurally considered, love involves the id, ego, and superego. Parental love, approval, and comfort are internalized in the benign, mature superego, while a harsh, primitive superego impairs the ability to love and be loved. Love may be displaced from the original objects onto collective objects and causes; to religion; to artistic, intellectual, and athletic sublimations; to pets; and to highly personal interests. While it is difficult to delimit love as a concept, all adult love has both mature and unconscious infantile features, and it always involves tendencies to identify with and idealize the love object.

References

Altman, L. L. (1977). Some vicissitudes of love. *JAPA,* 25:35–52.

Bergmann, M. S. (1980). On the intrapsychic function of falling in love. *PQ,* 49:56–77.

Kernberg, O. F. (1977). Boundaries and structure in love relations. *JAPA,* 25:81–114.

Panel (1969). The theory of genital primacy in the light of ego psychology. M. Berezin, reporter. *JAPA,* 17:968–987.

■ MANIA

A pathological mental state, usually representing a phase of manic-depressive illness. Mania is characterized by inappropriately high spirits, hyperactivity, and an inflated self-esteem often rich in paranoid grandiosity. A hunger for stimulus and new experience is exhibited in the patient's "pressure of speech" and "flight of ideas."

The patient's elation and inflated self-esteem are incongruous with reality, for he or she is actually experiencing (usually unconsciously) a sense of loss and defeat. The individual maintains a false mood of well-being by denying in fantasy the reality and impact of traumatic experiences, both present and past. In this way, the patient counteracts the pain and danger of the depression underlying his or her condition—but at great cost to self-awareness and critical judgment, and only temporarily, because the manic episode eventually gives way to depression.

The patient disposes of the potential rage over his or her trauma, which threatens both the self and the object, by merging (in fantasy) with the object; that is, the patient internally combines the image of the self with the image of the object of his or her rage and love. In classical theory this is viewed as a primary identification with the object, a return to a perfect state of harmony with the object, involving a regressive fusion of ego and superego. The resulting failure in superego function causes the patient's lack of self-judgment and uninhibited behavior.

Thus, psychoanalytic theory emphasizes that mania results from the defense (denial) that the ego predominantly resorts to in the face of its conflict with external reality. On the other hand, research has provided evidence in support of the cathecholamine hypothesis—neurotransmitter substances are found to be significantly above or below their normal concentrations in the central nervous system in cases of mania and depression. This hypothesis serves as a basis for the continuing investigation of the neurophysiological aspects of mania and depression, but little has been done to integrate physiological and psychoanalytic findings.

See AFFECTS; ELATION.

References

Freud, S. (1914). Mourning and melancholia. *SE,* 15:237–258.

Katan, M. (1940). The role of the word in mania. *Bull. Phila. Assn. Psychoanal.,* 22:4–34, 1972.

Lewin, B. D. (1950). *The Psychoanalysis of Elation.* New York: Norton.

Jacobson, E. (1971). *Depression.* New York: Int. Univ. Press.

■ MANIC-DEPRESSIVE SYNDROME

A pathological condition characterized by alternating phases of depression and mania or recurrent episodes of depression alone. Psychogenic and neurophysiological components are present in varying degrees; one or the other tends to dominate.

In current psychiatric nosology the condition is viewed as a single *bipolar disorder*. Genetic, familial, and neurophysiological aspects are stressed; the psychological factors are considered irrelevant or secondary. The psychoanalytic view, on the other hand, emphasizes the fact that the condition is often triggered by the experience of loss or personal defeat in a patient who from childhood has reacted catastrophically to separation. While acknowledging traumatic psychological experience in some cases, some clinicians claim it only serves to trigger a neuroendocrine metabolic disorder. Nevertheless, a clear-cut psychogenic condition, such as a borderline or narcissistic character disorder, is often in the background of the manic-depressive syndrome. The alternating mania and depression appear to be related to the predominant defense the ego resorts to in the face of conflict with external reality. Depression results from the use of introjection as defense, mania from the use of denial.

Freud believed that two different manic-depressive conditions exist, one primarily psychological, the other primarily physiological. This view is still held by many analysts. The fact that some patients respond to psychotherapy and others only to medication appears to support this hypothesis.

All investigators emphasize the existence of a predisposition to the condition, but they disagree as to whether it is constitutional or acquired in infancy. There is some evidence to suggest that very early traumatic experience may disturb neuroendocrine metabolism or cause a propensity for such disturbance.

See AFFECTS; DEPRESSION; ELATION; MANIA.

References

Abraham, K. (1924). Manic-depressive states and the pre-genital levels of the libido. In *Selected Papers*. London: Hogarth Press, 1949, pp. 418–480.

Freud, S. (1917). Mourning and melancholia. *SE*, 15:237–258.

Jacobson, E. (1953). Contribution to the metapsychology of cyclothymic depression. In *Affective Disorders*, ed. P. Greenacre. New York: Int. Univ. Press, pp. 49–83.

Wolpert, E. A. (1980). Major affective disorders. In *Comprehensive Textbook of Psychiatry*, ed. H. I. Kaplan, A. M. Freedman & B. J. Saddock. Boston: Williams & Wilkins, vol. 2, pp. 1319–1331.

■ MANIFEST CONTENT

See DREAMING, DREAMS.

■ MANIFEST DREAM

See DREAMING, DREAMS.

■ MASCULINE PROTEST

Using the terms *masculine* and *feminine* as metaphors for strength and weakness, Adler (1924) postulated masculine protest as a cluster of traits in both sexes overcompensating for feelings of inferiority and predisposing to neurosis. Later he used the term in a more limited way to refer to women's protesting the feminine role. Adler considered Freud's concept of penis envy too literal and biological, asserting women feel inferior not because of a conviction of physical deficiency but because of culturally ordained male dominance. This early critique of Freud's psychology of women grew from Adler's focus on power as a dominant influence in human psychology. Arguing against the term, Freud (1914) equated masculine protest with castration anxiety, which he defined as the boy's anxiety concerning his penis and the girl's envy of the penis.

Adler's divergent views marked his explicit disagreement with Freud's biologically oriented drive psychology. Ultimately he gave a detailed criticism of Freud's concepts and the two men parted ways.

See ANXIETY; CASTRATION; PENIS ENVY.

References

Adler, A. (1924). *Individual Psychology*. New York: Harcourt, Brace.

Ansbacher, L. & Ansbacher, R. (1956). *The Individual Psychology of Alfred Adler*. New York: Basic Books, pp. 44–69.

Freud, S. (1914). On narcissism. *SE*, 4:67–102.

——— (1937). Analysis terminable and interminable. *SE*, 23:216–253.

■ MASCULINITY/FEMININITY

Overall designations for the constellation of traits characteristic for each sex, including anatomy, appearance, gender identity, gender roles, sexual object preference, and culturally determined social behavior. Despite their historical and cross-cultural variability, it was long assumed that such characteristics were innate, biological in origin. The insight that the differences required psychological explanation was a major intellectual leap, for which Freud must be credited.

At first Freud equated the polarity of masculinity/femininity with that of activity/passivity, viewing activity in women as masculine and passivity in men as feminine. He was later forced to recognize that both men and women presented admixtures of activity and passivity as well as other masculine and feminine traits. As a result, he and others both within and outside psychoanalysis dramatically modified his original formulation. The terms have been further redefined as more questions have arisen about the traditional equations of biological sex with sex role assignment and psychological characteristics. A very complex development of characteristics designated as masculine and feminine is now posited, with emphasis not just on oedipal development, but on preoedipal development, identification, internalization, and learning.

As well as the anatomical and hormonal distinctions between the sexes, three major psychological differences have been established: (1) core gender identity: the sense of belonging to one sex or the other, established by three years of age once the separation-individuation is complete and the child has achieved autonomy; (2) sexual behavior, overt and fantasied, expressed both in choice of object and nature of activity; and (3) culturally determined and institutionalized nonsexual attributes and behavior, such as physical appearance, dress, mannerisms, speech, emotional responsiveness, aggressiveness, etc. Identifications with both father and mother mean that both sexes acquire a bisexual disposition, but by age three one sexual orientation prevails over the other. Though both gender identity and gender role behavior may reflect the masculine/feminine polarity, gender role identity refers to a psychological self-image that can be defined as the individual's self-evaluation of his or her maleness or femaleness as measured against societal standards for masculine or feminine behavior. This process is continuously monitored consciously and unconsciously. Gender role behavior, in contrast, refers to those traits designated by observers as either masculine or feminine.

See GENDER IDENTITY.

References

Freud, S. (1933). Femininity. *SE,* 22:112–135.

Person, E. & Ovesey, L. (1983). Psychoanalytic theories of gender identity. *J. Amer. Acad. Psychoanal.*, 2:202–226.

Spence, J. T. & Helmrich, R. L. (1978). *Masculinity and Femininity.* Austin and London: Univ. of Texas Press.

Stoller, R. J. (1968). *Sex and Gender.* New York: Science House.

Wiedeman, G. Sexuality. *PMC.* Forthcoming.

■ MASOCHISM

A propensity to seek physical or mental suffering in order to achieve sexual arousal and gratification. Masochism has been regarded as both a precondition and a source of pleasure. In the *masochistic perversion,* sexual gratification is contingent upon physical or mental pain from beatings, threats, or humiliations, imagined or actually experienced at the hands of the partner. Masochism appears early in childhood, usually coupled with sadism, as a component or partial instinct. Freud (1924) postulated that there is some degree of pleasure in pain (*erotogenic masochism*), and a small degree of masochism is assumed to be part of everyone's psychological makeup. Remnants of it persist in adult life as an attenuated component in forepleasure. Except in masochistic perversion, however, either the pursuit of suffering or the pleasure or both are usually unconscious. Also unconscious is the "beating fantasy" that is frequently a substrate of the clinical picture (Freud, 1919).

Freud (1924) distinguished three forms of masochism: erotogenic, feminine, and moral. He assumed the first to be biological and constitutional. The *feminine form* was so named because, although it occurred in men as well as in women, it is accompanied by fantasies that place the person in a characteristically female situation: being castrated, being penetrated, or giving birth to a baby. Freud also noted an infantile component—such masochists want to be treated like helpless, naughty children, and their manifest fantasies include being gagged, bound, beaten, dirtied, debased, and forced into submission. The guilt also present in these cases provides a transition to the third form. *Moral masochism* involves an unconscious need for punishment, based on a sense of guilt, which leads to neurotic symptoms or unconsciously self-inflicted suffering via accidents, financial loss, unhappy relations, failure, or disgrace. This form has apparently lost its connection to sexuality and an object, but Freud adduces that the superego takes the place of a sadistic object, and being punished is the equivalent of being beaten by father and therefore represents a hidden wish to have a passive, feminine, sexual relationship with him. The strength of moral masochism may lead to serious resistance to treatment, since the patient's reluctance to give up neurotic suffering can bring on a *negative therapeutic reaction.*

Moral masochism is a primary feature of the *masochistic character,* or *behavioral masochism,* though depressive moods and a tendency to complain about being a victim of fate and of malevolent people are also commonly involved in the latter condition. The pathogenesis involves an unconscious regressive sexualization of guilt feelings and, in men, unconscious passive homosexual wishes as a result of oedipal conflict and disturbed early object relations. In both men and women masochism is a compromise formation providing a means of undoing childhood fears of castration, rejection, and abandonment.

In his earlier papers Freud assumed that masochism was derived from a previous sadism. In the 1924 paper "The Economic Problem of Masochism" he took the position that there is a *primary erotogenic masochism,* a residue of fused life and death instincts left in the organism after projecting a portion out toward objects in the external world (sadism proper). In some circumstances the projected sadism is introjected, turned inward on the self, producing a *secondary masochism.* Sadistic and masochistic traits are invariably associated in the same individual.

See BEATING FANTASY; COMPROMISE FORMATION; CONFLICT; NEGATIVE THERAPEUTIC REACTION; PERVERSION; SADISM; SADOMASOCHISM.

References

Brenner, C. (1959). The masochistic character. *JAPA,* 7:197–216.
Freud, S. (1919). 'A child is being beaten.' *SE,* 17:179–204.
——— (1924). The economic problem of masochism. *SE,* 19:159–170.
Loewenstein, R. M. (1957). A contribution to the psychoanalytic theory of masochism. *JAPA,* 5:197–234.
Panel (1981). Masochism. W. Fischer, reporter. *JAPA,* 29:673–688.

■ MASTURBATION

Usually volitional rhythmic self-stimulation of the genitals which produces sexual pleasure with or without orgasm. An individual may masturbate him- or herself or another person, alone or in the presence of others, and sexually exciting self-stimulation may focus on erogenous zones other than the genitals; these can become the site of precursors of perversions. Masturbation occurs throughout the life cycle. It may be accompanied by a variety of feelings and both conscious and unconscious fantasies. Freud expressed the opinion that masturbation is the "primary addiction"; addictions to alcohol, morphine, tobacco, and other such substances enter into life as substitutes for it.

Infantile masturbation or *genital play* is one of the various types of autoerotic activity of infancy. It is a normal, developmentally progressive activity providing an outlet for tension: fostering early differentiation, learning, self-exploration, and self-awareness; and indicating satisfactory relations with the caretaking environment. Boys usually masturbate by manipulating the penis. Girls may manually stimulate the clitoris, but more often they use objects or engage in thigh rubbing. Clitoral sexuality is no longer seen as masculine in character, and its repression is no longer seen as a necessary prelude to establishing vaginal supremacy or feminine identity.

A relatively mature ego is necessary before true masturbatory fantasy is associated with the activity. Only after object constancy is established can very young children have a complete fantasy of the need-satisfying object. Oedipal fantasies are object-related and concerned with conquest or with the dread of retaliation (castration anxiety). Latency is associated with struggles against masturbation and its connected fantasies, reflecting the developing superego. Such defenses as repression, regression, and reaction formation provide early character changes in this phase. The struggles with masturbation continue into adolescence. On the one hand, masturbation serves to assist development, bringing pregenital drives under the regulation of the genital function. Masturbation fantasies herein foster object relatedness. However, the regressive aspects of the activity must be counteracted by new achievements in ego development.

Some undistorted masturbation is necessary for the normal development of the child. Throughout the life cycle masturbation can serve multiple functions, and it can have different meanings, both normal and pathological.

Compulsive masturbation or its equivalent may occur when (castration) anxiety and guilt accompany the activity so that the individual requires continued reassurance that the genitals are intact. Masturbation is pathological when the individual prefers it exclusively to available partners. Masturbation may also be part of such pathologies as transvestism, voyeurism, and exhibitionism. Pathological masturbation is sometimes associated with severe sadomasochistic perversion. *Psychic masturbation* involves a fantasy sufficiently intense to produce complete discharge of sexual excitation without physical stimulation.

Masturbation and its associated fantasies provide another avenue by which psychoanalysts can approach the complicated, multidetermined mental activities of the ego.

The *pregenital masturbatory equivalent* is the persistence of sexual excitement, without masturbation, when sexual feelings and fantasies are defended against unconsciously and disguised with a variety of defenses. The sexual nature of the feeling may not be recognized, becoming associated with nonsexual activities such as gambling, dangerous games, or reckless driving. The struggle against masturbation or associated fantasies may manifest itself in nail biting, scratching, head banging, trichotillomania (pulling the hair, eyebrows, or eyelashes), or trichophagy (biting, chewing, or swallowing hair). The fantasy associated with oral, anal, or urethral components of sexuality becomes totally unconscious and is displaced onto certain ego activities. The same elements may become linked to character traits, expressing masturbation fantasies through quarrelsomeness, criminal activity, exaggerated interest in anxiety-provoking events such as accidents, compulsive talking, and other compulsive or obsessional symptoms. Freud observed neurotic symptoms, as seen in hysteria, early; he viewed them as resulting from the struggle against masturbation and associated fantasies. Obsessive symptoms such as self-prohibition, self-punishment, and punishment-seeking (masochism) may also be connected to early parental prohibitions against masturbation. The (castration) anxiety and guilt associated with masturbatory behavior and/or fantasies cause a defensive regression to pregenital phases. These wishes are then expressed in typical compromise formations, producing a variety of symptoms serving multiple functions.

See AUTOEROTISM.

References

Arlow, J. A. (1953). Masturbation and symptom formation. *JAPA,* 1:45–58.

Freud, A. (1965). *Normality and Pathology in Childhood.* New York: Int. Univ. Press.

Freud, S. (1905). Three essays on the theory of sexuality. *SE,* 7:125–243.

Marcus, I. M. & Francis, J. J. (1975). *Masturbation.* New York: Int. Univ. Press.

■ MATURATION

See DEVELOPMENT.

■ MATURE DEPENDENCE

See FAIRBAIRN'S THEORY.

■ MEMORY

A function of the mental apparatus by which impressions once perceived or learned are retained and reproduced. The term is also applied to the capacity to remember and to the content of what is recalled. The processes employed are very complex, involving perception, apperception, recognition, encoding, retrieval, and activation or read-out. Different kinds of memory have been described. Memories may be of short or long duration, are reinforced by emotions, sustained attention, and repetition, and may be evoked by the various senses and verbal associations.

Memory and its disturbances have occupied a central place in psychoanalytic theory since Freud's earliest observations. His studies of hysteria led him to believe that his patients were suffering from "reminiscences" and that their symptoms could be understood as symbolic representations of traumatic memories, the recall of which was prevented by the quantity of emotion involved. When this disguised form of remembrance was replaced by a direct memory, accompanied by the appropriate emotions, the symptoms disappeared. Treatment consisted largely of attempts to recover the traumatic memories and to discharge through speech the affect associated with them (abreaction). Exclusion of the memories from consciousness was believed to be due to repression (the term referred to what is now called defense).

In "Project for a Scientific Psychology" (1895), Freud ascribed perception and memory to separate systems of the mind and conceived of memory as the persisting force of an experience. He saw memories as linked by emotional association, chance association, and the processes of symbolization. In the topological model, first described in 1900, Freud postulated a model of the mind consisting of the systems Conscious, Preconscious, and Unconscious. Consciousness represented in this schema only a small area of the mind and its activity. Thoughts and memories within the system Preconscious became conscious by receiving sufficient "attention cathexis," while those within the system Unconscious were assumed to be charged with intense sexual energies and forcibly kept out of consciousness. Because of their intensity, however, they seek expression, which is prevented by a hypothetical "censor," a defensive agent that distorts and disguises the memories so that they can be consciously tolerated. Freud also hypothesized that the earliest perceptions are registered in the perceptual apparatus by a structural modification of the system, which he called a *memory trace.* This idea is consistent with present neurophysiological belief that memory is laid down by a permanent modification in the structure of the cortical neuron's DNA. Freud believed that these primitive memory traces were arranged associatively in the mnemonic system, representing preconscious elements recovered by the associative activation of their schema or networks in the process of retrieval. In this preconscious form the memory trace is already linked with a symbol.

With the introduction of the structural model of the mind (Freud, 1923), with its tripartite division into id, ego, and superego, and the second theory of anxiety (1926), repression was regarded as one of the means of defense against signal anxiety evoked by the threatened emergence into consciousness of id impulses in the form of memories or fantasies in conflict with superego standards. Memory was conceived of as a function of the ego, which was also assigned recall and integrating and synthesizing functions. Theoretically, in the earliest stages of ego development, memory traces of a gratifying experience (the thing itself) lead to an anticipation of renewed gratification when the instinctual need recurs. When gratification is deferred, the infant hallucinates fulfillment of the wish through a cathexis of the memory trace. The failure of this hallucination to relieve the need is the basis for development of a sense of reality. Thus the process of remembering and its vicissitudes has adaptive potential for the ego as well as implications for psychopathology.

It is still a fundamental psychoanalytic belief that repressed or forgotten memories are a principal source of intrapsychic conflict. The resolution of such conflict by compromise formation results in symptoms or characterological problems for which patients seek help. Retrieval of these repressed memories is aided by free association, by association to the latent ideas present in dream material, and by exploring the transference, in which forgotten feelings toward earlier figures are reenacted in the relationship to the analyst. Retrieval of the repressed memories attenuates conflict and helps create a more cohesive self representation.

See AMNESIA; CATHEXIS; DEFENSE; DÉJÀ VU; REPRESSION; SCREEN MEMORY.

References

Beres, D. (1960). The psychoanalytic psychology of imagination. *JAPA*, 8:254–268.

Fine, B. D., Joseph, E. D. & Waldhorn, H. F., eds. (1971). *Recollection and Reconstruction in Psychoanalysis*. Monograph 4, Kris Study Group. New York: Int. Univ. Press.

Fisher, C. (1957). A study of the preliminary stages of the construction of dreams and images. *JAPA*, 5:5–60.

Freud, S. (1895). Project for a scientific psychology. *SE*, 1:295–397.

______ (1900). The interpretation of dreams. *SE* 5:533–549.

______ (1923). The ego and the id. *SE*, 19:3–66.

______ (1926). Inhibitions, symptoms, and anxiety. *SE*, 20:77–178.

Joseph, E. D. (1966). Memory and conflict. *PQ*, 35:1–17.

Klein, G. S. (1966). The several grades of memory. In *Psychoanalysis—A General Psychology*, ed. R. M. Lowenstein, L. M. Newman, M. Schur & A. J. Solnit. New York: Int. Univ. Press, pp. 377–389.

Rapaport, D. (1942). *Emotions and Memory*. New York: Int. Univ. Press, 1950.

Reiser, M. (1984). *Mind, Brain and Body*. New York: Basic Books.

■ MERGER TRANSFERENCE

See SELF PSYCHOLOGY.

■ MERGING

See OCEANIC FEELING.

■ METAPSYCHOLOGY

Used by Freud to designate a view beyond conscious experience, literally "beyond psychology" as psychology was understood and applied in his time. Metapsychology represents the highest level of abstraction in the continuum from clinical observation to psychoanalytic theory (Waelder, 1962), and it serves as a conceptual tool for establishing an orienting and systematizing framework for clinical data and lower-level psychoanalytic propositions.

Metapsychology is conventionally presented through five broad frames of reference or *viewpoints:* dynamic, economic, structural, genetic, and adaptive. The first three were Freud's. The last two were implicit in his writings and in the works of later psychoanalytic theoreticians; Rapaport and Gill first explicitly called them viewpoints. The theoretical principles inherent in these viewpoints are sometimes conceived of in the form of models, theoretical systems that facilitate study and understanding.

The *dynamic viewpoint* postulates the existence of directed psychological "forces" within the mind, each of which has an origin, magnitude, and object. This viewpoint provides for the possibility of such theoretical considerations as impulsion and conflict (e.g., between instinctual drives and restraining influences).

The *economic viewpoint* postulates the deployment of psychological energy within the mental apparatus, providing for such theoretical considerations as excitation and the forms and nature of discharge. Essential to this viewpoint are the quantity and inherent nature of the energies, their thresholds, and the laws of their accumulation and discharge. The viewpoint also leads us to consider that laws other than intentionality operate within the mind.

The *structural viewpoint* postulates that recurring and enduring psychological phenomena achieve more or less organized representation in the mind, and that the nature of these representations can be characterized. They include character traits, defenses, habits, moral standards, attitudes, interests, memories, and ideals. Freud's original model, termed *topographic,* consisted of three systems: Conscious, Preconscious, and Unconscious. He saw the phenomenology of consciousness and unconsciousness as relevant to ideation and emotions, the focus of clinical interest and theory formation at that time. Because of limitations and contradictions in this model, Freud proposed the *tripartite* model in 1923. A primarily energic id was postulated as contending with an executive ego, which, in addition to balancing the id's drives and external reality, had to juggle tensions emanating from the superego, the repository and expression of conscience and ideals.

The tripartite model has been followed, although not superseded, by a number of other models. One, which might be designated the *superordinate ego,* focused on the ego as the preeminent executive and adaptive agency. This model has been espoused by Anna Freud, Heinz Hartmann, Ernst Kris, Rudolph Loewenstein, David Rapaport, and Erik Erikson, who have worked toward the development of a general psychology. *Melanie Klein's model* postulated very early pathological structures that are personalized and attributed to the self or others in confusing and destructive ways. *Object relations theory* subsumes a variety of primitive self nuclei which, because of their pathological nature, are not integrated into a single, cohesive, superordinate organization. In Kohutian *self psychology,* the functioning and cohesiveness of a consistent "bipolar self" are compromised by deficits in structuralization dating from childhood experiences with pathologically disappointing or unempathic parental figures.

The *genetic viewpoint* provides a temporal dimension to psychological phenomena within the mind. It emphasizes the progression from infancy to adulthood and assumes that the adult cannot be understood as a psychological being without comprehension of the facts and circumstances of his or her childhood. Equally important, this viewpoint also provides for consideration of regressive phenomena and present and future perspectives.

The *adaptive viewpoint* includes interpersonal, societal, and environmental phenomena that influence and are influenced by the individual mind.

In addition to the five viewpoints mentioned, certain assumptions are so pervasive that they are treated within the viewpoints rather than specifically cited. The metapsychology must provide for a theory of mind in which human beings are regarded as biopsychological entities, coping with their inner and outer environments with endowed and evolved capacities but also contending with the animal from which they evolved. The system must provide for psychologically determined mental phenomena, in contrast to those resulting from chance or from biological or physical laws; the system should employ a lawful sequential logic, causal rather than teleological. It should allow for multiple causation either converging upon or diverging from a given element. The laws and dimensions should be inherently impersonal; personal considerations are appropriate only at a level closer to observational data and clinical theorization.

Freud referred to his theories as a kind of conceptual "scaffolding," to be revised as mandated by new observations and deductions. Though controversial, in part because of its distance from clinical observation, metapsychology has seemed to most analysts a necessary, useful, and flexible theoretical system.

See INSTINCTUAL DRIVE; PSYCHIC ENERGY; STRUCTURAL THEORY; TOPOGRAPHIC POINT OF VIEW.

References

Frank, A. Metapsychology. *PMC*. Forthcoming.

Freud, S. (1923). The Ego and the Id. *SE* 19:12–66.

Rapaport, D. & Gill, M. M. (1959). The points of view and assumptions of metapsychology. In *The Collected Papers of David Rapaport.* New York: Basic Books, 1967, pp. 795–811.

Waelder, R. (1962). Psychoanalysis, scientific method, and philosophy. *JAPA*, 10:617–637.

■ MIRROR TRANSFERENCE

See SELF PSYCHOLOGY.

■ MOBILE ENERGY

See PSYCHIC ENERGY.

■ MOOD

A temporary but relatively enduring complex psychic state consisting of several components: a predominant coloring of the emotional tone (the affective component), a narrowing of mental content and alteration of certain aspects of secondary process thinking (the cognitive component), and a tendency to particular actions (the behavioral component). A mood arises in response to an internal or external, conscious or unconscious psychophysiological event; it is different and distinct from the individual's customary personality.

The affective component is generally the most prominent feature of a mood; it is both subjectively experienced and usually objectively observable. The mood's affective quality can be evanescent but usually lasts hours or days. On a feeling-state spectrum, simple affects can be conceptualized at one end, moods in the middle, and the more complex and enduring affective states such as love, patriotism, loyalty, and so on at the other end. Moods are dynamic psychic constellations that regulate, contain, bind, and express a complex mixture of affects. From the structural point of view, a mood can be seen as the ego's attempt to integrate and control affective responses related to id, superego, and reality demands. In an economic sense, the mood structure regulates the expression of repeated small quantities of affects and thereby prevents explosive, potentially overwhelming discharge. Like symptoms, moods serve a compromise function, simultaneously defending against and allowing modulated expression of powerful affects arising from conflict.

The cognitive component of the mood qualitatively colors secondary-process thinking and mental content. Structurally, a mood compromises the ego's functioning, especially its ability to assess accurately and deal with internal and external reality. It alters the nature of self and object representations. For example, a depressed person might see him- or herself as worthless and others as uninterested. The same individual, if elated, might believe him- or herself able to surmount any obstacle and might extend that unbounded optimism to the world at large. This selective perception impairs reality testing. Selective focus on ideas, memories, attitudes, beliefs, assessments, and expectations in harmony with the mood's tone and exclusion of dissonant mental content reinforce and perpetuate the mood. This contributes to moods' global and pervasive qualities.

The behavioral component of the mood is revealed by the individual's actions, inactions, or patterns of motor activity. The disorganized, hyperagitated activity of the manic, the pressured loquaciousness of the hypomanic, the psychomotor retardation of the depressed, and the determined productiveness of one "in the mood to work" are examples of the behavioral component. A mood can color an individual's entire behavioral repertoire, including character traits usually thought of as being rigid or fixed. The behavior also affects others, whose responses tend to confirm the validity of the mood.

Psychoanalytic thinking about the origins of early, basic moods and about an individual's characteristic mood has focused on both innate factors and experiential variables. Different infants apparently are predisposed to different moods, and phases of normal infant development are associated with characteristic moods (e.g., elation is associated with Greenacre's [1957] "love affair with the world" stage, from ten to eighteen months). There is a relationship between depression and early actual or fantasied object loss (occurring in the context of the mother–child relationship); this relationship is particularly pronounced during the separation-individuation subphases in the second and third years of life. Early repressed experiences of excessive frustration/deprivation or gratification, as well as certain other events or traumas, serve as archaic niduses (fixation points) around which powerful affective reactions become organized. When contemporary experiences become associated with these fixation points; the complex psychological responses that we designate as moods are induced. As Jacobson (1971) has pointed out, the emotional experience that triggers the mood may be entirely internal (via psychological or neuroelectrochemical processes) or external (through a contemporary life experience). It may or may not be conscious, and its focus may be on either current reality or association with conscious or unconscious memories.

See AFFECTS.

References

Jacobson, E. (1971). Normal and pathological moods. In *Depression.* New York: Int. Univ. Press, pp. 66–106.

Greenacre, P. (1957). The childhood of the artist. *PSOC,* 12:57–58.

Mahler, M. S. (1966). Notes on the development of basic moods. In *Psychoanalysis—A General Psychology,* ed. R. M. Loewenstein, et al. New York: Int. Univ. Press, pp. 152–168.

Panel (1970). Psychoanalytic theory of affects. L. B. Lofgren, reporter. *JAPA,* 16:638–650.
Weinshel, E. M. (1968). Some psychoanalytic considerations on moods. *IJP,* 51:313–320.

■ MOOD DISTURBANCE
□ Mood Disorder

Psychopathological conditions caused by the severe distortion of a mood's components. Marked exaggerations in the intensity, duration, variability, or nature of the mood's affective tone (its affective component) render the individual unable to act (behavioral component) or to think (cognitive component) flexibly and appropriately in response to the internal dictates of the ego or the external demands of reality. The terms are often used as synonyms of the more common *affective disorder,* which refers to one of a group of clinical conditions including, among others, pathological grief reaction, involutional melancholia, endogenous depression, reactive depression, neurotic depression, psychotic depression, hypomania, mania, and manic-depressive illness or bipolar mood disorder.

See AFFECTIVE DISORDERS.

■ MORAL DEFENSE

See FAIRBAIRN'S THEORY.

■ MORAL MASOCHISM

See MASOCHISM.

■ MOTHER–INFANT SYMBIOSIS

See SEPARATION-INDIVIDUATION.

■ MOURNING

The mental process by which one's psychic equilibrium is restored following the loss of a meaningful love object. Although mourning is typically thought of in connection with the death of a loved person (bereavement), it is a normal response to any significant loss. The predominant mood of mourning is painful and is usually accompanied by loss of interest in the outside world, preoccupation with memories of the lost object, and diminished capacity to make new emotional investments. Uncomplicated mourning is not pathological and does not require treatment. With time the individual adapts to the loss and renews his or her capacity for pleasure in relationships.

Although reality testing is preserved and confirms that the loved object no longer exists, in the internal process of mourning the aggrieved person initially is unable to withdraw attachment from the lost object. Instead, the mourner turns away from reality, through denial, and clings to the mental representation of the lost object. Thus, the object loss is transformed into an ego loss. Through the stages of the mourning process, this ego loss is gradually healed and psychic equilibrium restored. The work of mourning includes three successive, interrelated phases; the success of each affecting the next: (1) understanding, accepting, and coping with the loss and its circumstances; (2) the mourning proper, which involves withdrawal of attachments to and identifications with the lost object (decathexis); and (3) resumption of an emotional life in harmony with one's level of maturity, which frequently involves establishing new relationships (recathexis).

A person's capacity to complete the mourning process is, at any age, affected by such internal and external factors as the level of emotional maturity, the ability to tolerate painful affects, the autonomy of self-esteem regulation, the degree of dependence on the lost object, and the circumstances of the loss. In childhood, the outcome of mourning depends on developmental factors including the level of self and object constancy, the ability to grasp the concrete aspects of death, tolerance of painful affects, and supportive parental relationships.

The term *mourning* may also be applied to the mental processes following forms of loss other than death. For example, grief and mourning may result from the loss of some representation in the abstract of a meaningful entity, such as the freedom of one's country or the belief in an ideal. One may need to mourn for the loss of body parts through accident or surgery, or for the loss of physical abilities with age. Other losses that sometimes require mourning include highly invested inanimate objects (for example, a home), anything representing an important source of security (a job), and significant separations (divorce, friends moving away, children leaving home, terminating analysis).

Freud distinguished between normal mourning and depression, but many psychoanalysts do not clearly appreciate the finer distinctions between depression and pathological mourning. Some forms of depression have a biological etiology rather than being caused by object loss. Pathological mourning reactions include the defensive absence of mourning as well as the prolonged grief reactions, described by Volkan, that perpetuate the representation of the lost object through "linking objects."

See CATHEXIS; DEPRESSION; GRIEF; OBJECT.

References

Bowlby, J. (1961). Process of mourning. *IJP,* 42:317–340.

Deutsch, H. (1937). Absence of grief. *PQ,* 6:12–22.
Freud, S. (1917). Mourning and melancholia. *SE,* 14:243–258.
Furman, E. (1974). *A Child's Parent Dies.* New Haven: Yale Univ. Press.
Pollack, G. H. (1961). Mourning and adaptation. *IJP,* 42:341–361.
Volkan, V. (1981). *Linking Objects and Linking Phenomena.* New York: Int. Univ. Press.
Wolfenstein, M. (1966). How is mourning possible? *PSOC,* 21:93-123.

■ MULTIDETERMINISM

A construct stating that a psychic event or aspect of behavior may be caused by more than one factor and may serve more than one purpose in the psychic framework and economy.

Freud used the term *overdetermination* to refer to the causation of a symptom, dream, aspect of behavior, or any element of psychic life by a variable number of intersecting paths. The term is derived from geometry: two intersecting lines determine a point; three lines intersecting at a point overdetermine the point. However, in psychoanalytic usage the term implies several lines but does not always imply more than necessary; so that *multideterminism* is preferable to *overdetermination.*

The *principle of multiple determinism* states that all psychic acts and structures appear to be multidetermined. Thus, analysis may reveal that a particular thought or dream is determined both by the intent consciously perceived and by multiple unconscious factors, including drive derivatives, the defensive operation of the ego, and complex transference feelings. This is possible because every psychic act has multiple meanings. Thus a symptom's meanings may include gratification of wishes, the need for punishment, and various other secondary gains. Each meaning stands on its own and has its own individual pathway to consciousness, but the convergence of these multiple meanings is in the nature of a final common pathway.

Building on Freud's concept of overdetermination, Waelder (1936) observed that every psychic action reflects the influences of all the psychic agencies (id, ego, superego), the repetition compulsion, and the demands of the outside world. The ego attempts to find solutions for the problems posed by these forces. On this basis Waelder postulated a *principle of multiple function,* according to which "no attempted solution of a problem is possible which is not of such a type that it does not at the same time, in some way or other, represent an attempted solution of other problems" (p. 49). But some of these forces are at variance with the others and not all can be equally satisfied; thus each act must be a compromise that solves one problem more successfully than others. Multideterminism and multiple function therefore correspond to the multiple meanings, and the psychic structures themselves develop according to these principles. They are particularly useful in understanding clinical manifestations and hence problems of neurosis and character. The synthetic function of the ego brings together the various conflicting forces in the best way possible for the individual in his or her particular state.

The *principle of multiple appeal* is a corollary of the preceding principles. Delineated by Hartmann (1951), it refers to the observation that an interpretation made along a particular line has effects beyond that line. In appealing to a variety of aspects of the dynamic system, it can produce unanticipated effects.

See COMPROMISE FORMATION; EGO FUNCTION; PSYCHONEUROSIS.

References

Hartmann, H. (1951). Technical implications of ego psychology. *PQ,* 20:31–43.
Smith, F. H., ed. (1978). *Psychoanalysis and Language.* New Haven: Yale Univ. Press.
Stein, M. (1971). The principle of multiple function. *Bull. Phila. Assn. Psychoanal.,* 21:191–197.
Waelder, R. (1936). The principles of multiple function. *PQ,* 5:45–62.

■ MYTHOLOGY

Psychoanalysis has from the time of its inception been concerned with the study of mythology as an avenue to understanding the workings of the human mind. Freud (1926) explicitly stated that a knowledge of mythology was necessary to an analyst's work. As early as *The Interpretation of Dreams* (1900), he used the myths of Kronos and Zeus to illustrate the universality of the oedipus complex. Indeed, the name of this most famous of all complexes and stages of childhood development is taken from the Greek legend or myth of Oedipus, who illustrated an unconscious fantasy common among boys and men when he unknowingly killed his father and married his mother.

Psychoanalytic pioneers such as Rank (1909), working within the framework of the topographic theory and the new theories of infantile sexuality, tried to use myths to validate what psychoanalysis had postulated about the unconscious and infantile sexuality.

With the change from topographic to structural theory and other subsequent changes in psychoanalytic theory and technique, mythology came to be understood in broader ways. Arlow (1961) stressed the myth as a shared fantasy that serves multiple purposes of instinctual gratification, defense, and adaptation for the group and its individual members. In return for renouncing gratification of infantile instinctual wishes, which is necessary for civilized living, the individual is presented with communally acceptable versions of the wishes in the form of myth. A society's myths also help form the superego, in part by presenting a communally accepted ego ideal for the individual to identify with. In an individual, intrapsychic conflict leading to repression of childhood events often culminates in the creation of personal myths. Some common versions of personal myths are screen memories and family romances.

See FAMILY ROMANCE; FANTASY; SCREEN MEMORY.

References

Arlow, J. A. (1961). Ego psychology and the study of mythology. *JAPA*, 9:371–393.

Freud, S. (1900). The interpretation of dreams. *SE*, 4–5.

——— (1926). The question of lay analysis. *SE*, 20:179–258.

Rank, O. (1909). *The Myth of the Birth of the Hero*. New York: Robert Brunner, 1951.

■ NARCISSISM

Love of the self, a term coined by Näcke in 1899, based on Havelock Ellis's correlation of the Greek myth of Narcissus with a case of male autoerotic perversion. In psychoanalysis, however, the meaning of the term has been greatly expanded and such perversion is viewed as only a specific, dramatic illustration of something more general in the human psyche and behavior.

Freud's first reference to the subject, in a letter to Fliess in 1899, implies an inclination to use narcissism as an energic concept to explain the fate of libidinal energies in psychotic disturbances, an idea he developed further later. However, in the meantime he used it to explain various phenomena, such as the "unbounded self-love of children" and homosexual object choice. Later he used the term in a genetic sense, positing narcissism as a developmental stage between autoerotism and object love. In his seminal 1914 paper "On Narcissism," Freud described a *primary narcissism*—"an original libidinal cathexis of the self from which some is later given off to objects, but which fundamentally persists" (p. 75)—and a *secondary narcissism*, the cathexis attached to the precipitates of lost objects installed (by introjection) within the ego. This object-libido was desexualized (sublimated) when it was transformed into narcissistic libido, and it presumably supplied the energy for the development and operation of the ego. Elsewhere Freud defined narcissism as "the libidinal cathexis of the ego," but as Hartmann (1950) points out, Freud was here using *ego* to mean *self*. Freud also designated as *narcissistic* a mode of relating to the environment characterized by the lack of object relations. Finally, he outlined the narcissistic roots of the ego ideal and indicated that self-esteem intimately depends upon narcissistic libido.

In psychoanalytic literature *narcissistic* thus came to be applied to many things: a sexual perversion, a developmental stage, a type of libido or its object, a type or mode of object choice, a mode of relating to the environment, an attitude, self-esteem, and a personality type, which may be relatively normal, neurotic, psychotic, or borderline. In addition, the concept of a separate line of development for narcissistic libido and object libido became a fundamental theoretical basis for the self psychology school, which accounted for various personality features as "narcissistic structures" resulting from transformations of narcissism. Such broad usage led to confusion and it became apparent that a more restricted use of the term would be advantageous (Pulver, 1970).

In current literature the term is largely used in the context of self-esteem. Kernberg (1967), for example, states that narcissistic patients are characterized by "an unusual degree of self-reference in their interactions with other people, a great need to be loved and admired by others, and a curious apparent contradiction between a very inflated concept of themselves, and an inordinate need for tribute from others" (p. 655). Such patients are also characterized by a sense of entitlement and fantasies of omniscience, omnipotence, and perfection of the self or idealized objects to varying degrees depending on the severity of the psychopathology. Accompanying affects vary from elation, when the inflated self-estimate is supported, to disappointment, depression, or severe anger, called *narcissistic rage*, when self-esteem is injured.

Freud's 1914 views about narcissism were not revised after he developed the structural theory, although he did mention in several reviews that narcissism played a significant role in his formulation of the second instinct theory and his second topographical model (that of, ego, id, and superego). His ideas about primary and secondary narcissism, although expressed in economic terms, indicate an appreciation of the role of objects and projective/introjective mechanisms in the identificatory processes leading to ego formation (as a result of the interchange between mother and child). The current understanding of narcissism retains the idea of libidinal investment of the self but adds a structural perspective to the earlier economic emphasis, and recognizes aggressive as well as libidinal elements in narcissistic phenomena.

Normal narcissism is to be distinguished from *pathological narcissism* (Kernberg, 1975). The former depends upon the structural integrity of the self, the acquisition of self and object constancy, equilibrium between libidinal and aggressive drive derivatives, harmony between the self and superego structures, capacity for ego-syntonic expression of impulses, capacity to receive, gratification from external objects, and a state of physical well-being. Pathological narcissism involves a defensive self-inflation with a concomitant lack of integration of the self-concept and dissociation of aggressively determined self representations. Normal narcissism leads to sustained, realistic self-regard and mature aspirations and ideals; it is accompanied by the capacity for deep object relations. Pathological narcissism, on the contrary, is accompanied by archaic demands upon the self, inordinate dependence upon acclaim by others, and poor or deteriorated object relations. It is manifested by a sense of entitlement, relentless pursuit of self-perfection, and impaired capacities for concern, empathy, and love for others.

See CATHEXIS, EGO IDEAL; HOMOSEXUALITY; LIBIDO THEORY; METAPSYCHOLOGY; PSYCHIC ENERGY; PSYCHOSIS; SELF; SUBLIMATION; SELF PSYCHOLOGY: The Self.

References

Freud, S. (1914). On narcissism. *SE,* 14:69–102.
Hartmann, H. (1950). Comments on the psychoanalytic theory of the ego. *PSOC,* 5:74–96.
Kernberg, O. F. (1967). Borderline personality organization. *JAPA,* 15:641–685.
——— (1975). *Borderline Conditions and Pathological Narcissism.* New York: Aronson.
Moore, B. E. (1975). Toward a clarification of the concept of narcissism. *PSOC,* 30:243–276.
Pulver, S. (1970). Narcissism. *JAPA,* 18:319–340.

■ NARCISSISTIC NEUROSIS
See PSYCHONEUROSIS.

■ NARCISSISTIC RAGE
See SELF PSYCHOLOGY.

■ NARCISSISTIC TRANSFERENCE
See SELF PSYCHOLOGY.

■ NEED-SATISFYING OBJECT
A stage in the development of object relations in which the nature of the relationship is based primarily on the urgency of the infant's bodily needs and drive derivatives. Since the object relatedness is based on intermittent and fluctuating needs, the nature of the object tie varies as needs are gratified and frustrated. Using an energic concept, the object cathexis depends on the pleasure/unpleasure balance.

Developmentally, the stage of need-satisfying relationships precedes the stage of object constancy, in which a positive inner image of the object can be maintained whether drives are satisfied or frustrated. The developmental level of need-satisfying object relationships described by Anna Freud (1965) corresponds to Spitz's phase of part-object relationships and to Margaret Mahler's symbiotic phase.

See OBJECT CONSTANCY.

References

Freud, A. (1965). *Normality and Pathology in Childhood.* New York: Int. Univ. Press.
Hartmann, H. (1952). The mutual influences in the development of ego and id. *PSOC,* 7:9–30.

■ NEGATION
See DENIAL.

■ NEGATIVE THERAPEUTIC REACTION
A clinical response that sometimes occurs during the course of analysis. Following a period of what seems to be constructive and effective therapeutic technique and understanding, the patient's condition paradoxically worsens. Freud (1923) described the situation clearly: "every partial solution that ought to result, and in other people does result, in an improvement or a temporary suspension of symptoms produces in them for the time being an exacerbation of their illness" (p. 49). In some instances, a single correct interpretation increases symptoms.

Such a negative reaction has several possible causes. Typically it occurs with depressed, masochistic patients who have strong unconscious needs to suffer and induce punishment. Their guilt may derive from very early fantasies that presume the patient has committed a "crime" (for example, a patient feels responsible for the mother's castration as a result of his or her birth). The need for punishment was previously gratified by the suffering of the neurosis itself; when effective analytic work threatens to alleviate the illness with its attendant suffering, the patient resists and undermines treatment. Punishment then continues as symptoms worsen. Another determinant may be particular masochistic urges, involving an ego ideal formed from identification with a parent who seemed to idealize a life of suffering.

These features—a strong tendency to depressive affect, sadomasochistic orientation, negativism, and resistance stemming from the superego—are deeply rooted in the character structure of patients who develop negative therapeutic reactions.

Negative therapeutic reaction is not to be confused with negative transference—indeed, clinical evidence suggests that it occurs in the presence of a latent positive transference. But negative therapeutic reaction can evoke countertransference. Such a countertransference–transference impasse is usually based on both participants' sense of helplessness, guilt, and anger. Therapeutic zeal should be avoided with these patients, who tend to fear invasive influence. When effective analytic work, and the therapist's obvious expectation that symptoms will be relieved, threaten to upset the delicate balance the individual has established, he or she meets the threat masochistically with increased suffering and a flare-up of symptoms.

Maladaptive behavior patterns which seem related to negative therapeutic reaction and have similar psychopathology occur outside the analytic situation. Examples include Freud's categories of criminals who commit crimes out of a sense of guilt, those wrecked by success, "losers," and so on. For such individuals any positive, life-enhancing experience is threatening and may evoke a negative reaction.

See COUNTERTRANSFERENCE; DEPRESSION; GUILT; SADOMASOCHISM; SUPEREGO; TRANSFERENCE.

References

Asch, S. S. (1976). Varieties of negative therapeutic reactions and problems of technique. *JAPA,* 24:383–407.

Freud, S. (1923). The ego and the id. *SE,* 19:1–66.

——— (1924). The economic problem of masochism. *SE,* 19:159–170.

Olinick, S. (1964). The negative therapeutic reaction. *IJP,* 45:540–548.

——— (1980). *The Psychotherapeutic Instrument.* New York: Jason Aronson.

Panel (1970). The negative therapeutic reaction. S. L. Olinick, reporter. *JAPA,* 18:655–672.

Sandler, J., Dare, C. & Holder, A. (1973). The negative therapeutic reaction. In *The Patient and the Analyst.* New York: Int. Univ. Press, pp. 84–93.

■ NEURASTHENIA

See ACTUAL NEUROSIS.

■ NEUROSIS

The term is now almost always synonymous with *psychoneurosis.* It was first used by William Cullen in 1777 to designate functional physiological disturbances without structural basis in the afflicted organ. Sigmund Freud (1896) later described what he called *actual neurosis* (from the German *aktual,* meaning "present-day"), in which symptoms of nervous disorder, including anxiety and asthenia, were attributed to the stress of current disturbances in adult sexual functioning. He distinguished these actual neuroses from the *psychoneuroses,* in which mental conflict, largely unconscious and based on early childhood experiences, preceded the development of nervous symptoms. Freud also recognized admixtures of the two forms of neuroses and conceded that they often could not be distinguished clinically.

Freud attributed the anxiety in actual neurosis, like that in traumatic neurosis, to an overwhelming influx of stimulation. Without normal sexual discharge, it flooded the body with tension that found expression via emergency autonomic discharge. According to this first theory of anxiety, anxiety represented transformed libido. Freud's second theory of anxiety (1926) viewed anxiety as the ego's signal of danger. Since then, use of the term *actual neurosis* has diminished.

See ACTUAL NEUROSIS; ANXIETY; PSYCHONEUROSIS; TRAUMATIC NEUROSIS.

References

Cullen, W. (1777). *First Lines of the Practice of Physic.* Edinburgh: Bell, Brandfute.

Freud, S. (1896). Heredity and the aetiology of neuroses. *SE,* 3:141–156.

——— (1926). Inhibition, symptoms, and anxiety. *SE,* 20:77–175.

Krystal, H., ed. (1968). *Massive Psychic Trauma.* New York: Int. Univ. Press.
Schwartz, H. J., ed. (1984). *Psychotherapy of the Combat Veteran.* New York: SP Medical and Scientific Books.

■ NEUROTIC CHARACTER

See ANXIETY.

■ NEUTRAL ENERGY

See PSYCHIC ENERGY.

■ NEUTRALITY

The stance of the analyst generally recommended for fostering the psychoanalytic process. Central to psychoanalytic neutrality are keeping the countertransference in check, avoiding the imposition of one's own values upon the patient, and taking the patient's capacities rather than one's own desires as a guide. In structural terms, neutrality is described as taking a position equidistant from the demands of the id, ego, and superego. The concept also defines the recommended emotional attitude of the analyst—one of professional commitment or helpful benign understanding that avoids extremes of detachment and overinvolvement.

The analyst's neutrality is intended to facilitate the development, recognition, and interpretation of the transference neurosis and to minimize distortions that might be introduced if he or she attempts to educate, advise, or impose values upon the patient based on the analyst's countertransference.

Many consider *abstinence* an aspect of neutrality. It is, however, a separate technical principle directed to the same goals.

Avoiding the imposition of values upon the patient is an accepted aspect of psychoanalytic neutrality. However, there is increasing recognition that the analyst's values are always operative, especially those involving the search for truth, knowledge, and understanding, and those emphasizing orientation toward reality, maturity, and change. These attitudes affect the therapeutic process in complex ways, and an extensive literature exploring these matters has developed (Bornstein, 1983).

Greater diversity of opinion exists regarding the emotional attitude of the analyst—particularly such qualities as coldness, distance, responsiveness, sympathy, encouragement, and the like. One factor leading to this divergence of opinion is that Freud's statements about the analyst's attitudes seem contradictory or ambiguous. At times he advised setting aside human sympathy and adopting an attitude of emotional coldness (1912); elsewhere he recommended an attitude of sympathetic understanding (1913) or the role of a helpful ally (1940). Freud first used the term *neutrality* in "Observations on Transference Love" (1915), one of six papers on psychoanalytic technique published between 1911 and 1915. These papers, plus later writings (1940), must be considered as a whole in order to understand his meaning and stance on neutrality. Many of his comments focus upon specific technical problems, and taken in isolation do not adequately express his view. But current writers do not fully agree with Freud on this issue.

While many analysts consider interpretation and insight to be the sole therapeutic agents in psychoanalytic treatment, others consider aspects of the object or selfobject relationship with the analyst to be essential to the therapeutic process. The position one takes on this important point influences one's understanding of psychoanalytic neutrality and its relation to the principle of abstinence (Panel, 1984).

See ABSTINENCE.

References

Bornstein, M., ed. (1983). Values and neutrality in psychoanalysis. *Psychoanal. Inquiry,* 3:547–717.
Freud, S. (1911–15). Papers on technique. *SE,* 12:89–171.
——— (1940). An outline of psychoanalysis. *SE,* 23:144–207.
Panel (1984). The neutrality of the analyst in the analytic situation, R. J. Leider, reporter. *JAPA,* 32:573–585.

■ NIRVANA PRINCIPLE

See PSYCHIC ENERGY.

■ NORMALITY

An ambiguous concept nevertheless useful in attempts to distinguish between so-called healthy and pathological behavior. Its varying definitions in many disciplines contribute to a conceptual confusion that complicates its meaning in psychoanalytic theory and practice. Statistical norms are different from a definition of normality as an ideal or the way something should be. Developmental, cultural, and moral questions (value judgments) must be resolved or circumvented in any definition of normality. Attempts to define normality in terms of health are subject to the issues surrounding attempts to define health itself. Hartmann (1939) attempted to resolve that dilemma by proposing a definition of health as not merely the absence of disease and symptoms but the existence of vital perfection. Embracing that idea, psychoanalysts have tended to view behavior on a continuum from the pathological to an ideal of normality, or health. The result has been criticized as minimizing the differences between pathology and normality or health.

Normality (or positive mental health) is measured by studying the psychic structure and functioning of the individual and determining how effectively capacities are being used. Such dynamic studies are preferable to static or phenomenological descriptions because whether a phenomenon is a symptom depends on the place it occupies in the structure and functioning of the individual. It is perhaps for this reason that most definitions of normality reflect the influence of psychoanalysis.

It is generally agreed that a mentally healthy person should be relatively reasonable and balanced in his or her attitudes and behavior. Adaptive ego functioning should predominate over the chaotic and untamed drives of the id, but such predominance should not be excessive. The ego should recognize the irrational nature of other mental activities and exercise control over them, but should also be able to utilize them to advantage. The objectives of psychoanalysis are thus relevant to what is considered healthy (in an ideal sense of normality). Herman Nunberg (1954) thought psychoanalysis should allow id energies to become more mobile, the superego more tolerant, and the ego freer from anxiety and more able to exercise its synthetic function. In her definition of normality, Anna Freud (1965) emphasized the ego's achievement of greater harmony between id, superego, and the forces of the outer world. Ernst Jones (1931) felt the psychological norm should include not only efficiency in mental functioning, but also happiness and a positive social feeling. All of these qualities of health or normality are crystallized in Sigmund Freud's phrase "where id was there shall ego be."

Hartmann (1964) proposed that a portion of mental energy is not primarily drive energy, but belongs from the beginning to the ego, serving its functions in mediating between the agencies of the mind and the environment. More recently, however, Brenner (1982) has questioned this notion of primary ego autonomy and the idea of a conflict-free sphere of operation. He cites clinical evidence that conflict is ubiquitous and continuous and that successful, adaptive compromise formations, even though they contain some degree of conflict, are the hallmark of mental health.

It is doubtful that any human being can achieve complete harmony of motivations; given this limitation, health can be defined according to the frequency with which behavior is based on an optimal equilibrium. Such equilibrium is facilitated by a felicitous fusion of instinctual drives in the id and a positive orientation toward the ego ideal. Psychological equilibrium is always likely to be unstable, but the more solid ego functions become, the more they can cope with the demands of the drives and the rigidity of the superego.

From a developmental point of view, it appears that many individuals who do not possess reasonable equilibrium still cannot be classified as abnormal or mentally ill. Children and adolescents show characteristics that would be considered pathological in adults. Regression causes imbalance in adults, while incomplete development is responsible for the child's lability. Thus a mentally healthy child can be described as one whose progression is not hampered and will be completed as biological maturation proceeds.

Conflicts arise in the course of development because it is difficult to harmonize one's instinctual needs with one's desire to incorporate values set up by the cultural milieu. One's impulses may be too strong and the environment too rigid in its demands. The anxiety that ensues may hamper the ego's perceptions and value judgments. Under these circumstances, a flexible adaptation to the conflicts would be considered healthy or normal if the reaction safeguards fundamental instinctual needs, allows the individual to tolerate necessary frustrations and anxieties, and enables him or her to develop unhindered toward sustained, mature adaptation. Mechanical adaptation is not considered a requisite for mental health. Free and alloplastic adaptation may include temporary withdrawal from reality if it is necessary in order to gain increased mastery. Adaptation also includes the possibility of choosing or creating a new environment. A psychoanalytic definition of normality should therefore include exercising the option of modifying one's own behavior or the environment.

Freud (1937) stated that the outcome of psychoanalytic treatment may be limited by the constitutionally determined intensity of the drives, the severity of infantile trauma, and the degree to which a defensive struggle has altered the ego. Accepting the possibility of such limitations, the aim of psychoanalytic therapy is to strengthen the ego and make it more independent of the superego, to widen its field and extend its organization so that it can take over new portions of the id. The psychic life of a person who develops in a healthy way is also characterized by these qualities.

See ADAPTATION; ANALYSIS; CHARACTER; CONFLICT; EGO; EGO FUNCTION; METAPSYCHOLOGY; PSYCHIC APPARATUS; STRUCTURAL THEORY.

References

Brenner, C. (1982). *The Mind in Conflict.* New York: Int. Univ. Press.

Freud, A. (1965). Normality and Pathology in Childhood. New York: Int. Univ. Press.

Freud, S. (1937). Analysis terminable and interminable. *SE,* 23:209–253.

Hartmann, H. (1939). Psychoanalysis and the concept of health. In Hartmann (1964), pp. 3–18.

——— (1964). *Essays on Ego Psychology.* New York: Int. Univ. Press.

Jones, E. (1931). The concept of a normal mind. In *Papers on Psychoanalysis,* 5th ed., London: Bailliere, Tindall & Cox, 1948, pp. 201–216.

Krapf, E. E. (1961). The concept of normality and mental health in psychoanalysis. *IJP,* 42:439–446.

Nunberg, H. (1954). Evaluation of the results of psychoanalytic treatment. *IJP,* 35:2–7.

■ OBJECT

First defined by Freud as the thing through which an instinctual drive is able to achieve its aim. Freud used the term somewhat indiscriminately, however, to mean (1) a real, tangible, physical person or thing, as distinguished from a subject; (2) the mental image of some other person or thing—an experiential concept; (3) a theoretical construct, different from both real person and experiential content and implying some lasting organizational structure. At this time certain distinctions are indicated. The object is to be distinguished from the subject, or self, to whom it must be psychologically significant; it may be animate or lifeless, but it is external; its counterpart within the mind of the subject is an *internal object,* sometimes called an *object representation.* However, all external phenomena are represented within the mind; the internal object representation is an amalgam of various attributes of the external object—physical, intellectual, and emotional—whether real or imagined by the subject. For this reason some authors have preferred to use *object representations* as a term for representations of the individual traits of the object.

The terms *object relations* and *object relationships* are often used interchangeably to designate the attitudes and behavior of someone toward his or her object. The terms can refer to mental images or actual persons. In order to preserve the distinction between what is external and what is intrapsychic, however, it seems desirable to use *object relationship* for the interaction between a subject and another actual person (that is an *interpersonal relationship*), and to reserve *object relations* for the psychological phenomena relating to objects' representations within the mind. But object relations must be inferred on the basis of reported experience or observed conduct in object relationships. Both are influenced by unconscious fantasy, which is a product of the individual's developmental history.

The object concept developed in relation to Freud's instinct theory. He conceived of the goal of the instinct as the discharge of energy or the attainment of pleasure via the object. The first object, then, was a *part object,* the mother's breast, to which libido was directed during the oral phase because it gratified the instinct of self-preservation by providing nourishment. A later development involves the cathexis of the whole object. Autoerotism, or the use of parts of one's own body as objects for instinctual gratification, is characteristic of the pregenital phase of development. *Object cathexis* means investing the mental representation of another person with libidinal or aggressive drives or energy. *Libidinal object* refers to any part or whole object cathected with libidinal energy, but it is sometimes understood to imply aggressive cathexis as well. *Object libido* is the libidinal energy attached (cathected) to objects, while *object love* describes the self's complex of feelings and attitudes toward integrated whole objects that are the source of its pleasure.

Object choice refers to the process by which one renders someone else psychologically significant. It occurs as early as the phallic-oedipal phase as instinctual drives attach themselves to a single object; some gratification of drive demands is implied. The choice is conscious, though it is influenced by unconscious determinants—in particular, one's love object in adult life often shares qualities with a love object who gratified one in infancy and childhood. Two types were described by Freud. An *anaclitic object choice* is based upon passive, dependent needs and the wish to be symbolically fed and protected, as one was by mother. A *narcissistic object choice* is based either on the subject's own self—what he or she is, was, or would like to be—or on someone once experienced as part of oneself. Both types of object choice are overvalued in some respect, just as the parents were, and both are invested (cathected) more with libidinal than with aggressive interest; that is, they are *idealized objects*. This implies that the memory trace of an object may serve as a model for future object investments. But the internal object may also serve as a model for identification, a psychic process by which self representations are modified as one takes on aspects of an object. Evidence suggests that identification is often related to some sort of *object loss,* for example, death of or separation from a real, external object, loss of love in the subject's inner world (without actual or threatened real loss); the loss of body parts or physical functions. Freud postulated that fear of loss of the object or the object's love was a danger situation for the ego and led to anxiety. Mourning is a normal response to object loss, but pathological responses occur when there was significant conflict with the lost object. These pathological responses include depression, hypomanic flight, and identification with the lost object by development of mental symptoms or physical illness.

Internalization (introjection and identification) of the object or its attributes, is important to the development of psychic structure or mental functioning. This occurs in the course of object relations and in a developmental line progressing from the biological need–satisfying object of earliest infancy and a psychological need–satisfying object evidenced by social smiling at two to three months through the sobering reaction at five months, stranger anxiety at eight to twelve months, separation anxiety, the separation-individuation phase, the phallic-oedipal phase, latency, adolescence, and adulthood. An important step in this progression is the achievement of *object constancy*. Though variously defined, its essence is a libidinal cathexis of the object (mother) that persists even when she is absent or angry.

Winnicott observed that some infants, before they have learned to differentiate between self and object, must keep an inanimate object, such as a blanket or stuffed animal, at their side to avoid anxiety. These objects, which seem to represent both mother and child, are called *transitional objects,* and various other transitional phenomena have been described that allow the child some independence from the reality of the absence of the object. Some borderline patients tend to divide people into idealized, loving *good objects* and totally devalued, hateful *bad objects,* and they rapidly shift from one extreme to the other in their perceptions of the same object. The need for such separate, unambiguous categories appears to be related to a preambivalent developmental phase when the infant has not integrated the representations of the gratifying (good) mother on the one hand and the frustrating (bad) mother on the other. In normal development, this preambivalent phase gives way to a phase of ambivalence in which the infant can tolerate an integrated maternal object that both gratifies and frustrates and is the object of both libidinal and aggressive drives. Kernberg (1976) has postulated that the borderline patient's intense aggressive drive limits such integration, and defensive splitting occurs. Without such splitting, it is presumed, aggression toward the internal object would be so overwhelming as to destroy it.

Because of splitting and other pathological reactions, borderline, narcissistic, and psychotic individuals cannot engage in mature object relationships. They are unable to maintain a loving relationship in the face of frustration; and they are unable to accept the separateness of a loved object who has different needs. In contrast, mature object relationships and love imply recognition that the object is separate from the self and that his or her needs may at times conflict with those of the self; acknowledgment, acceptance, and tolerance of ambivalence toward the object; ability to accept some dependence as well as separation; and the capacity to experience and adapt to both one's own changing needs and requirements and those of the object. Both direct instinctual gratification and neutralization of the drives should sometimes be possible. Ego development and the maturation of object relationships are contingent upon one another and are central to evaluation of an individual's adaptive capacity and his or her suitability for psychoanalysis.

See CATHEXIS; INTERNALIZATION; MOURNING; OBJECT CONSTANCY; OBJECT RELATIONS THEORY; REALITY; SELF; SPLITTING; STRUCTURAL THEORY; WINNICOTT'S THEORY: Transitional Object, Phenomenon.

References

Beres, D. & Joseph, E. D. (1970). The concept of mental representation in psychoanalysis. *IJP,* 51:1–9.

Compton, A. Objects and relationships. *PMC.* Forthcoming.

Edgcumbe, R. & Burgner, M. (1972). Some problems in the conceptualization of early object relationships, part I. *PSOC,* 27:283–314.

Freud, S. (1915). Instincts and their vicissitudes. *SE,* 14:117–140.

——— (1917). Mourning and melancholia. *SE,* 14:243–258.

Jacobson, E. (1964). *The Self and the Object World.* New York: Int. Univ. Press.
Kernberg, O. F. (1976). *Object Relations Theory and Clinical Psychoanalysis.* New York: Jason Aronson.
——— (1980). *Internal World and External Reality.* New York: Jason Aronson.
Rangell, L. (1985). The object in psychoanalytic theory. *JAPA,* 33:301–334.

■ OBJECT CONSTANCY

Introduced by Hartmann (1952) to describe a quality of object relations in the developing child. Constancy is achieved when the relation to a love object endures and remains stable and permanent "independent of the state of needs" (Hartmann, 1953, p. 181). Prior to this achievement, the object is characterized as "need-satisfying." As used by Hartmann, object constancy implies a cognitive and a drive element. On the cognitive side, it requires the achievement of object permanence (Piaget, 1937), in which a mental representation of the object persists in the object's absence. Object constancy also presupposes some neutralization of the aggressive and libidinal drives (Hartmann, 1952, p. 163).

Different usages of the term are associated with different developmental schemes. The terms *libidinal object, object constancy,* and *libidinal object constancy* are used interchangeably. Spitz (1959) took the reactions to strangers that appear at six to eight months of age as an indication that the mother had become the "libidinal object," as the infant at this stage prefers the mother above all others. In Anna Freud's view (1965), object constancy has been achieved when the child's libidinal investment in the mother is preserved regardless of need satisfaction—that is, when mother becomes the libidinal object (Spitz's formulation). Before this point, the child is thought not to sustain a relationship with the object either in the absence of need or when experiencing frustration. Neither Spitz nor Anna Freud uses the term *constancy* in a cognitive sense; both use it in the sense of a libidinal attachment to the love object.

In contrast, Mahler combines both cognition and drives to describe object constancy as beginning only when some of the ambivalence of the anal phase is resolved, between twenty-four and thirty-six months. In her view, object constancy requires first of all a stable cognitive mental representation of the object. Following this, "good" and "bad" affects become integrated (Jacobson, 1964; McDevitt, 1975), and the predominantly positive feelings aroused by the representation of the mother produce in the child nearly the same sense of security and comfort as does the mother's actual presence. Mahler (1968) notes, "By object constancy we mean that the maternal image has become intrapsychically available to the child in the same way as the actual mother had been libidinally available—for sustenance, comfort, and love" (p. 222). To distinguish this additional libidinal aspect of the object representation from its purely cognitive representation, psychoanalysts have begun to use the term *libidinal object constancy*. Burgner and Edgcumbe (1972) add that with the achievement of libidinal object constancy, the relationship between mother and child becomes more stable and durable and persists despite frustrating or gratifying experiences.

See AMBIVALENCE; EGO DEVELOPMENT; OBJECT RELATIONS THEORY; STRANGER ANXIETY.

References

Burgner, M. & Edgcumbe, R. (1972). Some problems in the conceptualization of early object relationships. *PSOC,* 27:315–333.
Fraiberg, S. (1969). Object constancy and mental representation. *PSOC,* 24:9–47.
Freud, A. (1965). *Normality and Pathology in Childhood.* New York: Int. Univ. Press.
Hartmann, H. (1952). The mutual influences in the development of ego and id. In *Essays on Ego Psychology.* New York: Int. Univ. Press, 1964, pp. 155–182.
——— (1953). Contributions to the metapsychology of schizophrenia. In Hartmann, 1952.
Jacobson, E. (1964).*The Self and the Object World.* New York: Int. Univ. Press.
Mahler, M. S. (1968). *On Human Symbiosis and the Vicissitudes of Individuation,* vol. 1. New York: Int. Univ. Press.
McDevitt, J. B. (1975). Separation-individuation and object constancy. *JAPA,* 23:713–742.
Piaget, J. (1937). *The Construction of Reality in the Child.* New York: Basic Books, 1954.
Spitz, R. A. (1959). *A Genetic Field Theory of Ego Formation.* New York: Int. Univ. Press.

■ OBJECT RELATIONS THEORY

A system of psychological explanation based on the premise that the mind is comprised of elements taken in from outside, primarily aspects of the functioning of other persons. This occurs by means of the processes of internalization. This model of the mind explains mental functions in terms of relations between the various elements internalized.

Many theories fit this definition. In general they encompass: (1) the motivations for relationships;

(2) the development from primitive relatedness in the infant to complex mental functioning and relationships in the mature adult; and (3) the structured aspects or enduring and distinctive patterns of relationships that characterize individuals. The work of Klein, Fairbairn, Winnicott, and Balint first drew attention to such theories; their object relations theories have been said to constitute the British school. However, Kernberg, Loewald, Meissner, Modell, Schafer, Stolorow, Kohut, and Sandler have also contributed their own object relations theories. Aspects of such theories were derived from Freud's own observations of the influence of objects on ego development, and some theorists, notably Kernberg, have made attempts to integrate various aspects of object relations theories into classical Freudian theory.

See FAIRBAIRN'S THEORY; INTERNALIZATION; KLEINIAN THEORY; WINNICOTT'S THEORY.

References

Compton, A. Objects and relationships. *PMC*, Forthcoming.

Fairbairn, W. R. D. (1952). *Psychoanalytic Studies of the Personality*. London: Routledge & Kegan Paul.

Kernberg, O. F. (1976). *Object Relations Theory and Clinical Psychoanalysis*. New York: Jason Aronson.

Klein, M. (1959). On the development of mental functioning. In *Envy and Gratitude*. London: Delacorte Press, 1975, pp. 236–246.

Kohut, H. (1971). *The Analysis of the Self*. New York: Int. Univ. Press.

Sandler, J. & Rosenblatt, B. (1962). The concept of the representational world. *PSOC*, 17:285–296.

Winnicott, D. W. (1958). *Collected Papers*. New York: Basic Books, Inc.

■ OBSESSION
□ Obsessional Character
□ Obsessive-Compulsive Neurosis

These terms relate to the domination of a person's thoughts, feelings, or behavior by a persistent idea, image, wish, temptation, prohibition, or command. *Obsessions* are thoughts that are ego-dystonic, occurring against the person's will. Rumination and brooding are varieties of obsessions. Rumination involves meditation, reflection, musing, or pondering; its Latin root refers to cud-chewing animals. Thus the obsessional person may engage in vague and repetitious thinking of a philosophical nature: "What is the meaning of life? Who am I, really?" To brood means literally to sit upon and hatch eggs, as does a bird; hence, brooding is thinking, persistently, quietly, and anxiously about a problem. All these mental phenomena involve an effort made to solve an emotional conflict by thinking, but the conclusion or solution is avoided, and the person starts the process over again repeatedly.

Compulsions and *rituals* are persistent and irresistible urges to engage in apparently meaningless acts; they are the motor equivalent of obsessive thoughts and often accompany them in *obsessive-compulsive neuroses*. Other characteristics of such neuroses include magical thinking, doubting and indecision, digression, rambling, circumstantiality, procrastination, retraction, and repetitiousness. The person so afflicted usually knows that his or her acts and thoughts are unreasonable but is unable to control them.

The symptoms of neurosis typically occur in the context of an *obsessional character* structure. A wide range of personality types fit into this diagnostic category. At one end of the continuum are well-organized, productive, hard-working, conscientious people. They think logically and are able to carry out their ideas effectively. At the pathological end of the spectrum are severely afflicted persons who show the cardinal traits of the obsessional character (excessive orderliness, parsimony, and obstinacy), have marked difficulty in thinking, and are incapable of acting constructively because of ambivalence, doubt, indecision, and procrastination.

The essential conflicts of the obsessive-compulsive neurosis and character type involve superego guilt and anxiety surrounding phallic-oedipal impulses, affects, and ideas that take the form of fantasies. These unacceptable fantasies are defended against, leading to the fantasies and conflicts of the negative oedipus complex. The individual regresses to an anal-sadistic level and even stronger guilt is added to superego–id conflicts, especially in relation to anal-sadistic impulses. Conflict is further intensified by magical thinking; many obsessive individuals unconsciously or consciously believe that wishing makes it so and that thought equals deed. The obsessional neuroses are therefore aptly called *guilt neuroses*. The superego is severely turned against the impulses, affects, and ideas involved. These conflicts, along with ego mechanisms of defense (especially isolation, displacement, intellectualization, reaction formation, and undoing in action and thought) result in compromise formations manifested by the neuroses and character traits described.

See COMPROMISE FORMATION; CONFLICT; DEFENSE; OEDIPUS COMPLEX; RITUAL.

References

Fenichel, O. (1945). *The Psychoanalytic Theory of Neurosis*. New York: Norton.

Freud, S. (1909). Notes upon a case of obsessional neurosis. *SE*, 10:155–318.

Nagera, H. (1976). *Obsessional Neuroses*. New York: Aronson.

Pfeffer, A. Z. (1984). Modes of obsessional thinking. Presented at the New York Psychoanalytic Society, October 23.

■ OCEANIC FEELING

Originally introduced to Freud by Romain Rolland to describe an alleged mystical source of rich beneficent energy, the term has come to refer to ineffable experiences including a sense of extending beyond one's customary boundaries in space and time. The former is often described as merging; the latter as timelessness. The feeling is believed to relate to the psychic state of early infancy, in which the narcissistic infant experiences all of space and time as coextensive with his or her ego. Experiences of the oceanic feeling in adult life are manifestations of extreme regression, typically following a sense of having been abandoned or of being threatened by abandonment. The experience resembles a neurotic symptom insofar as a defense against the threat of overwhelming aggression coexists with a gratification, that is, the illusion of narcissistic bliss.

The closely related concept of *merging* is also based on assumptions about the nature of the relationship of the contented infant and his or her mother. The infant presumably returns repeatedly, when satiated and drowsy, to a psychic state in which coenesthetic perceptions of the mother's physiological and behavioral manifestations of affect are indistinguishable from his or her own. Efforts to recover this state in adulthood, often incorporated in mysticoreligious rituals, may lead to regressive behavior associated with the fantasy of psychic oneness with the mother.

References

Arlow, J. A. (1984). Disturbances of the sense of time. *PQ*, 53:13–37.

Freud, S. (1930). Civilization and its discontents. *SE*, 21:57–146.

Harrison, I. B. (1979). On Freud's view of the infant-mother relationship and of the oceanic feeling. *JAPA*, 27:399–421.

Masson, J. M. (1980). *The Oceanic Feeling*. Boston: D. Reidel Publishing Company.

■ OEDIPUS COMPLEX

A characteristic constellation (in both sexes) of instinctual drives, aims, object relations, fears, and identifications, universally manifest at the height of the phallic phase (two and a half to six years), but persisting as an unconscious organizer throughout life. During the phallic period the child strives for a sexual union (conceived variously according to the child's cognitive capacities) with the parent of the opposite sex and wishes for the death or disappearance of the parent of the same sex. Because of the child's inherent ambivalence and need for protection, there coexists with these positive oedipal strivings the so-called *negative oedipus complex;* that is, the child also wishes to unite sexually with the parent of the same sex and finds him/herself engaged for the latter's affections in a rivalry with the parent of the opposite sex. Typically, the *positive oedipus complex* holds sway over the negative in organizing the heterosexual orientation and identity of the well-adapted adult. However, at the unconscious level, the girl's tie to her mother, as well as the boy's wish to surrender to his father in the hope of passively receiving masculinity, everlasting love, and protection, continue to exert profound influences on psychological life and later object choice.

Jung used the term *Electra complex* to indicate the existence in the girl of wishes and attitudes toward the parents analogous to those of the boy's oedipus complex. Freud did not accept the usefulness of this term, however; and oedipus complex has been almost universally accepted to designate the triangular relationship between the child and his or her parents regardless of the child's sex.

The child fears retaliation (talion fear) for the forbidden incestuous and parricidal wishes associated with the oedipus complex. Specifically, the boy fears castration or penile ablation and the girl fears a less specific injury to the genital and procreative organs. This fear compounds more primitive fears in relation to the rival parent—object loss and loss of object love. The last may be more acute in girls, though psychoanalysts now dispute Freud's emphasis on the girl's alleged greater narcissistic vulnerability and dependency.

Genetically or developmentally, the oedipal position is a nodal point marking the coalescence or consolidation of the superego. As the child identifies with the oedipal objects, idealizations are transformed into an ego ideal, and fear of punishment into guilt. Topographically, the complex is usually partly conscious; it is evident in the child's speech, behavior, and other modes of communication. In later life, it is most often unconscious, but, dependent on the extent of its resolution, it is more or less evident in behavior, attitudes, and object choice. It also bears upon character structure, the nature of object relationships and sexual identity, fantasy formation, and later sexual patterns and activities.

The unconscious, infantile sexuality, and the oedipus complex are among Freud's fundamental discoveries. He first formulated the theory during the year following his father's death in 1896, though he formalized it a full fourteen years later in its present form. Freud developed the theory while struggling with the inconsistencies of his earlier theory of neurosis emphasizing adult seduction of children and with his doubts about the new science. Recognizing hysterical symptoms in his family and himself, he entered into a period of intense introspection, which he called his self-analysis. In a famous letter to William Fliess, dated October 15, 1897, Freud stated his finding: "I have found love of mother and jealousy of the father in my case too, and now believe it to be a general phenomenon of early childhood. . . . Every member . . . was once a budding Oedipus" (Freud, 1887–1902, p. 223). When he published this thesis for the first time in *The Interpretation of Dreams* (1900), Freud used his own dreams and those of others to correlate the myth of Oedipus with the unconscious wishes of every man.

The classic myth, as rendered in Sophocles' *Oedipus Rex,* tells of Laius, king of Thebes, who was warned by an oracle that a son yet to be born would kill him. When Jocasta, the queen, gave birth to a boy, the king ordered that the infant be exposed to die on a mountainside. A shepherd found the infant and brought him to King Polybus, who adopted the boy. As a young man, Oedipus left Corinth and chanced to meet Laius at a cross-roads; in a quarrel about the right-of-way, he slew the king, his father. Oedipus next came to the Sphinx, who blocked the road to Thebes and challenged every traveler to answer a riddle or die. Oedipus mastered the riddle and the Sphinx jumped to her death in mortification. The grateful Thebans made Oedipus king and married him to Jocasta. However, the gods would not tolerate incest, even without conscious participation, and a plague fell upon Thebes. According to the oracle, finding the murderer of Laius was the price for lifting the plague. As Sophocles' play unfolds, Oedipus, sworn to uncover the crime and thus save the city, finds he is the murderer, married to his own mother. In the tragic ending, Jocasta hangs herself and Oedipus blinds himself with the brooch used to fasten her dress.

Freud's knowledge of the variants of the myth remain uncertain, according to his biographers. However, subsequent applications of psychoanalysis highlight the father Laius' hubris—his arrogance in trespassing against the gods—which brought upon him his horrific fate. As a youthful heir to the throne of Thebes, Laius had fled a usurping uncle. During the course of his travels Laius found himself under the protection of King Pelops. When Laius abducted and sodomized the Pelops's illegitimate son, however, his erstwhile host exacted revenge at the assault upon his hospitality and paternity. Pelops, together with Zeus and Hera, cursed Laius for assaulting the sacred values of hospitality and paternity. They condemned him to his fate, to be murdered by a son and replaced by the son in his wife's bed. Freud's omission of this background in the retelling of the narrative may have led his followers to overemphasize the "positive" oedipal elements in the drama and the conflicts to which it pertained, underplaying its homosexual as well as the infanticidal motives that served as a counterpoint to the patricide. Freud later corrected himself, elaborating his understanding of the oedipal drama in his case histories and in autobiographical addenda to his dream book.

A number of terms are related to the oedipus complex. The *oedipal phase* is considered by some authors to be identical with the phallic phase of development (two and a half to six years), whereas others reserve the term for the period toward the end of the phallic phase when the oedipal complex is well formed structurally and dynamically. During this period, phallic aims are directed toward a specific object rather than subserving narcissistic preoccupations; they have become the subject of intrapsychic conflicts involving id, ego, and superego imperatives; and they are dealt with by way of higher-level defenses based on repression. Both phallic strivings per se and the triangulation of object relations and the psychic structures in which they become embedded have precursors earlier in development. Investigators have remarked upon a preoedipal genital organization, primary femininity and masculinity, parental ambitions, castration reactions, and the like, all emerging well before the phallic oedipal phase proper. Some have speculated about the presence during the second year of life of rivalry and prototypical conflicts involving differential and gender-specific reactions to and identifications with mother and father.

In addition, it must be noted that the individual's oedipal organization is subject to modification throughout the life cycle, especially during adolescence.

Oedipal conflict is a term applied to various conflicts characteristic of the complex. The urge for sexual union (id-derived) is in conflict with ego and superego restraints; castration anxiety results. There are, moreover, conflicts inherent in the antithetical positive and negative phases of the complex, the active and passive aims of the drives, and the masculine and feminine identifications in the fantasy of sexual union. These conflicts can feed off each other; for example, castration anxiety as fear of retaliation from the father may be superimposed on castration anxiety as a result of a wish to receive a baby from him. While it is possible heuristically to separate specific conflictual units, inter- and intrasystemic conflicts are in fact interwoven. In addition, earlier and later developmental pressures and deficits are always at issue, either obscured by or themselves serving to screen oedipal struggles. In all events, preverbal phenomena are given shape and made accessible via the oedipus complex and its attendant cognitive and linguistic formal modalities. Many believe oedipal conflict plays the central role in clinical analysis.

Of lesser conceptual importance are two terms frequently present in clinical discussions. *Oedipal triumph* is said to occur when the child has gained the major portion of love and attention from the parent of the opposite sex. For example, the mother may be the aggressive member of the family and adore her son, while demonstrating contempt for the masculinity of her husband. Another circumstance leading to oedipal triumph is the death of the parent of the same sex during the person's childhood. Many authors, especially Ernest Jones (1949) in *Hamlet and Oedipus,* stress the tragic and fateful consequences of the "gratification" of this repressed and consciously unacceptable wish. The term *oedipal situation* refers loosely to a conglomerate of the phase, conflict, and complex; it is specific for the psychic development of a particular person, as evidenced in his or her masturbatory fantasy and family romance. The term is also used to refer to a current life situation or event that reawakens fantasies, feelings, and behavior derived from the oedipal phase.

See INFANTILE SEXUALITY; PSYCHOSEXUAL DEVELOPMENT.

References

Atkins, N. (1970). The Oedipus myth, adolescence, and the succession of generations. *JAPA,* 18:860–875.

Blos, P. (1984). Son and father. *JAPA,* 32:301–324.

Devereux, G. (1953). Why Oedipus killed Laius. *IJP,* 34:132–141.

Freud, S. (1887–1902). *Letters to Wilhelm Fliess.* New York: Basic Books, 1954.

——— (1900). The interpretation of dreams. *SE,* 4–5.

——— (1924). The dissolution of the Oedipus complex. *SE,* 19:173–179.

Jones, E. (1949). *Hamlet and Oedipus.* New York: Norton.

Kanzer, M. (1948). The "passing of the Oedipus complex" in Greek drama. *IJP,* 29:131–134.

——— (1964). On interpreting the Oedipus plays. *Psychoanal. Study Society,* 3:26–38.

Loewald, H. W. (1959). The waning of the Oedipus complex. *JAPA,* 27:751–756.

Rose, H. (1928). *A Handbook of Greek Mythology.* London: Methuen.

Sophocles. *The Oedipus Cycle,* tr. D. Fitts & R. Fitzgerald. New York: Harcourt, Brace & World, 1969.

■ ON THE WAY TO OBJECT CONSTANCY

See SEPARATION-INDIVIDUATION.

■ ORALITY

A comprehensive term for all psychic interests, mechanisms, and inclinations (as well as their manifestations) that stem from the early libidinal and aggressive functions of the oral cavity.

Early in life the infant's needs, perceptions, and modes of expression are mainly centered in the mouth, the lips, the tongue, the pharynx, and the upper digestive tract. These convey the sensations of thirst and hunger, the pleasurable tactile stimulations evoked by the nipple or its substitutes, the sensations involved in the act of swallowing, and the feeling of fullness. The infant's earliest feelings of pleasure and manifestations of aggression originate in this area, referred to as the *oral zone,* and contribute to its outstanding importance in psychic development.

Throughout approximately the first eighteen months of life the oral zone maintains its dominant role in the organization of the psyche, leading to the designation of this period as the *oral phase* of libidinal development. Subsequently, with the ascendancy of the other erotogenic zones (anal and then phallic and genital), the role of the oral zone diminishes, although its effects on personality development remain profound throughout life.

The states of psychic excitation and tension caused by the libidinal and aggressive needs associated with the oral zone are conceptualized as the outgrowth of psychic forces known as the *oral drives*. These consist of two separate components; one directed toward the satisfaction of libidinal needs, which is the psychological basis of *oral erotism,* and the other to the satisfaction of aggressive needs. The individual acts to assuage oral tension; its subsidence is referred to as *oral satisfaction* or *oral gratification*. A typical example of such gratification is the infant's quiescence after nursing. This state has been conceptualized in terms of an *oral triad;* it consists of the wish to eat, to sleep, and to reach that feeling of relaxation and yielding that occurs after sucking and just before falling asleep. The latter wish is where ideas of being enveloped and devoured originate. These may present themselves later in life in fantasies, anxieties, phobias, and manifestations of the Isakower phenomenon; if displaced, they may become part of the castration complex.

While the libidinal needs (pleasurable sucking) are prominent in the earlier stages of the oral phase, the aggressive ones tend to emerge later, particularly after the eruption of teeth; they are the basis for *oral aggression* (also called *oral sadism*). This aggressive instinct expresses itself in chewing, biting, and spitting; it may also play an important role in such conditions as depressions, addictions, and perversions.

When oral drives are blocked by psychic forces (defenses) that interfere with their emergence, a state of *oral conflict* ensues. This may manifest itself in such symptoms as distaste for food, food idiosyncrasies, vomiting, jaw spasm, grinding of the teeth, or speech inhibitions. Oral conflicts and early life experiences related to orality (especially excessive indulgence or severe deprivation) may also manifest themselves in character traits and abnormalities. Excessive optimism or pessimism can be traced back to particularly intense oral gratification or to especially severe oral deprivation. When such oral character traits as greed, demandingness, excessive generosity or penuriousness, dependency, restlessness, impatience, and curiosity acquire importance in an individual's total makeup, we speak of an *oral character structure,* which may present itself in a wide variety of ways.

See EROTISM; FACE–BREAST EQUATION; INFANTILE SEXUALITY; ISAKOWER PHENOMENON; PRIMAL CAVITY; PSYCHOSEXUAL DEVELOPMENT.

References

Abraham, K. (1916). The first pregenital stage of the libido. *Selected Papers*. London, Hogarth Press, 1948, pp. 248–279.

______ (1924). *Selected Papers*. London: Hogarth Press, 1948, pp. 393–406.

Freud, S. (1905). Three essays on the theory of sexuality. *SE,* 7:172–206.

■ ORGAN NEUROSIS

Refers to a condition in which an unconscious psychic conflict expresses itself through a disturbance in the physiology of the organism: a particular organ or organ system malfunctions. Included under this heading are such "psychosomatic" entities as peptic ulcer or bronchial asthma as well as nonspecific psychic tensions, undischarged affects, and the chronic dammed-up state. The physiological changes fundamental to organ neurosis do not have a primary psychic meaning that can be interpreted. Thus, organ neurosis is differentiated from conversion reaction, which typically does not involve physiological changes. Conversion depends on the "misuse" of an organ or body part as a specific unconscious fantasy is translated into body language; it is directly accessible to psychoanalysis in the same way as a dream is.

The distinction between organ neurosis and conversion symptoms, however, is not as sharp as this narrow definition suggests because in some cases conversion may result in tissue damage; also, even a purely physiological disturbance secondarily acquires psychic meaning.

The term *organ neurosis* is approximately equivalent to the more recent term *psychophysiological disorder,* which has wider currency in the psychiatric literature.

See PSYCHOSOMATIC CONDITIONS; SOMATIZATION.

References

Engel, G. L. (1968). A reconsideration of the role of conversion in somatic disease. *Compr. Psychiat.,* 94:316–326.

Fenichel, O. (1945). *The Psychoanalytic Theory of Neurosis*. New York: Norton.

■ ORGASM

The third phase of the human sexual response cycle. It occurs when sexual excitement reaches a peak and the demand for release of tension results in an involuntary physiological response accompanied by a maximum of sexual pleasure. During orgasm in the woman the lower third of the vagina undergoes three to fifteen involuntary contractions, and the uterus also contracts powerfully. At the time the woman may or may not be aware of intensely pleasurable sensation in the clitoral and pelvic regions. Orgastic pleasure in men accompanies ejaculation along with partial loss of voluntary control. Some individuals of both sexes experience fusion with the other and a loss of ego boundaries.

Masters and Johnson (1966) demonstrated that the physiological changes in the woman's vagina and clitoris are essentially the same whether the orgasm is experienced as occurring in the vagina or clitoris and whether it results from vaginal, clitoral, or other stimulation. Psychologically, the differences in the ways women experience orgasm may have dynamic significance, but analysts no longer believe that clitoral orgasms are indicative of immaturity or psychopathology. Conversely, orgasms experienced vaginally are not necessarily associated with maturity or mental health. Sexual inhibitions that preclude intercourse or limit pleasurable orgasm to certain circumscribed situations are of course symptomatic of pathology in either sex.

References

Dickes, R. (1981). Sexual myths and misinformation. In *Understanding Human Behavior in Health and Illness,* ed. R. C. Simon & H. Pardes. Baltimore: Williams & Wilkins, pp. 313–322.

Glenn, J. & Kaplan, E. H. (1968). Types of orgasm in women. *JAPA,* 16:549–564.

Masters, W. H. & Johnson, V. E. (1966). *Human Sexual Response.* Boston: Little, Brown.

Moore, B. E. (1977). Psychic representation and female orgasm. In *Female Psychology,* ed. H. P. Blum. New York: Int. Univ. press, pp. 305–330.

■ ORIGINAL EGO

See FAIRBAIRN'S THEORY.

■ ORIGINAL OBJECT

See FAIRBAIRN'S THEORY.

■ OVERDETERMINATION

See MULTIDETERMINISM.

■ PAIRING

See BION'S THEORY.

■ PANIC

See ANXIETY.

■ PARAMETER

A departure from a hypothetical ideal baseline—the classical analytic technique in which interpretation is the exclusive technical tool. The term was introduced by Kurt R. Eissler (1953). A typical example is an analyst's advising a phobic patient to expose him- or herself to the situation feared. According to Eissler, a parameter should be introduced only under the following conditions: (1) the psychoanalytic process would otherwise come to a standstill; (2) a return to standard technique is possible; (3) the parameter is dispensable after fulfilling its usefulness; (4) the patient can gain insight into its function. Analysis of the parameter and interpretation of its meaning to the patient are important.

Since Eissler introduced the concept it has been observed that ideal analytic technique includes preparation for interpretation as well as interpretation itself. Further, parameters (which Loewenstein terms variations or interventions) occur regularly in successful and well-conducted analyses; the patient's ego is not usually seriously modified. The term does not include errors the analyst may make or a range of technical interventions indicated by various types of psychopathology.

References

Eissler, K. R. (1953). The effect of the structure of the ego on psychoanalytic technique. *JAPA,* 1:104–143.

Glenn, J. (in press). A parameter. In *Annu. Psychoanal.*

Loewenstein, R. M. (1982). Practice and precept in psychoanalytic technique. In *Selected Papers of Rudolph M. Loewenstein.* New Haven: Yale Univ. Press.

■ PARAMNESIA

See AMNESIA.

■ PARANOIA
□ Paranoid Character
□ Paranoid Schizophrenia

These terms refer to a spectrum of related and overlapping psychopathological disorders. The designation *paranoid* is also applied imprecisely to such group phenomena as passionate, unyielding zeal for a social cause in otherwise apparently normal individuals. Although such fervor may be productive and may be given up when an end result is achieved, it is sometimes difficult to distinguish from the pathological intensity that characterizes certain "cult" devotees. At the other end of the spectrum is paranoid schizophrenia.

The *paranoid character* or *paranoid personality* involves inflexible, enduring, and maladaptive patterns of perceiving, relating, and thinking. Traits such as hypersensitivity to slights and blame, suspiciousness, mistrust, pathological jealousy, and vengeful feelings are common. In addition, persons with this diagnosis appear aloof and cold and lack a sense of humor. They may function very well alone, but they usually have difficulty with authority figures and jealously guard their independence. They are well attuned to the motives of others and to the power structure of groups. The paranoid character is distinguished from paranoia and paranoid schizophrenia by thinking and behavioral patterns, by more intact reality testing, and by the absence of hallucinations and systematized delusions.

Paranoia is a psychotic syndrome usually occurring late in adulthood. Feelings of jealousy, of being spied upon, observed critically, maligned, or poisoned are the content of persistent persecutory delusions, and litigious tendencies are often evident. The affected individual believes that random occurrences are related in some patterned way to him (the concept of *centrality*). He or she may suffer from generalized delusions or circumscribed ones—for example, that one person seeks to harm the patient or to have relations with his or her spouse. Such ideas are not tempered by reality testing with the suspected person. Functioning may be impaired in only one area, such as work or marriage. A paranoid personality may precede and underlie paranoia.

Paranoid schizophrenics exhibit more pervasive disturbances in relation to the outside world, based on inadequate self and object constancy, poor organization of the psychic representations (identity), and impairment of such ego and superego functions as thinking, judgment, and reality testing. All the schizophrenias include psychotic features, symptoms, and deterioration. A prodromal phase characterized by withdrawal is followed by an acute phase involving delusions, hallucinations, thought disorder (loosening of associations), and disorganized behavior. Acute exacerbations may lead to a residual phase in which symptoms taper off but affective blunting and social disturbance persist. As in paranoia, frequently a premorbid schizoid or paranoid personality disorder regresses under intense conflict and decompensates into an acute psychosis. This course conforms to Freud's concept of the withdrawal and restitutional phases of psychosis.

The paranoid type of schizophrenia involves hallucinations and persecutory, grandiose, and somatic (hypochondriacal) delusions, as well as delusions based on jealousy. Depression, diffuse irritability, anger, and occasional violence may accompany transitivistic feelings (the belief that the patient's thoughts are being read or controlled or that the patient is controlling others). The rigidity of the paranoid character may mask a gross disorganization. In the paranoid form of schizophrenia, general functioning tends to be better preserved than in other forms; affects are less severely blunted and the patient may be able to work.

Although Freud occasionally used *paranoia* and *paranoid schizophrenia* interchangeably, he made distinctions based on (1) a specific psychodynamic conflict over repressed homosexual wishes and (2) the tendency of the ego to regress and erect paranoid defenses. The idea of ego regression related his concept of the etiology of schizophrenia to that of psychoses in general, while his emphasis on conflict in paranoia related to his "unitary" theory, which stated that paranoia is, like the neuroses, a defensive reaction (compromise formation). Specifically, denial, reaction formation, and projection are used. As formulated in the Schreber case (1911): a conflictual unconscious wish ("I love him") is denied ("I do not love him, I hate him") but returns to consciousness as a projection ("he hates me and persecutes me"). Freud also recognized that characterologically such patients were concerned with narcissistic issues of power, potency, and the avoidance of shame, so that they were especially prone to competitive conflicts with authority. Their delusions of grandiosity were related to the same issues. Freud postulated massive regression to earlier stages of development (fixation points), related to the reactivation of childhood conflicts. In paranoia the fixation was said to be at the narcissistic stage of psychosexual development and object relations, a more advanced level than that of schizophrenics, whose regression is to an objectless or autoerotic stage. Schizophrenic regression, marked by a tendency to give up objects, is followed by a restitutional phase involving formation of delusions; this represents a pathological return to the world of objects. With the development of the structural theory, Freud gave more emphasis to ego and superego factors. He said that the ego withdraws from a painful external reality, while superego aspects and ego ideals are externalized, resulting in feelings of being watched and criticized. He also gave more importance to the role of aggression in the pathogenesis of paranoia.

Post-Freudian contributions focus on how aggression affects early development, internalized object relations, and ego formation. The quality of emotional investment in self and object images and its impairment as a result of conflict have been studied; this has led to recognition of the pathogenic effect of pathological introjects. The effects of shame and of aggression in reaction to narcissistic injury are better understood as a result of recent work on the psychopathology of narcissism. Separation-individuation concepts have elucidated the development and effect of gender identity conflicts, which predispose to feelings of vulnerability and primary femininity in men (for example, Schreber's fear of being transformed into a woman) that may be even more basic than the derivative homosexual conflict. Studies seem to confirm that homosexual conflicts are prevalent in paranoid schizophrenia, and it is not uncommon for more than one case of paranoid schizophrenia to occur in a family. Finally, historical research has revealed that Schreber's father was quite tyrannical and sadistic in his rearing of the children. This indicates that Schreber's delusions contained a kernel of truth, which is now believed to exist in the childhood history of many paranoid patients.

See PSYCHOSIS; PSYCHOTIC PROCESS; SCHIZOPHRENIA.

References

Freud, S. (1911). Psycho-analytic notes on an autobiographical account of a case of paranoia. *SE*, 12:3–82.

______ (1924). Neurosis and psychosis. *SE*, 19:149–153.

Kernberg, O. F. (1984). *Severe Personality Disorders*. New Haven: Yale University Press.

Meissner, W. H. (1978). *The Paranoid Process*. New York: Aronson.

■ PARANOID-SCHIZOID POSITION

See KLEINIAN THEORY.

■ PARAPHILIA

See PERVERSION.

■ PARAPHRENIA

Initially used in the early nineteenth century to designate folly, this term was employed by Freud to distinguish between schizophrenia (paraphrenia) and paranoia. Later he used the term paraphrenia to include both schizophrenia and paranoia. It is now obsolete.

See PARANOIA; SCHIZOPHRENIA.

References

Freud, S. (1911). Notes on a case of paranoia. *SE*, 12:3–79.

______ (1913). On beginning the treatment. *SE*, 12:121–144.

______ (1914). On narcissism. *SE*, 14:73–102.

■ PARAPRAXIS

Errors, slips of the tongue, memory lapses, and the host of manifestations Freud discussed in his book *The Psychopathology of Everyday Life*. They constitute symptomatic acts that are determined by unconscious motives; they are compromise formations between forbidden impulses or ideas and the censorship imposed upon them. The principle of psychic determinism is particularly well illustrated in parapraxes.

Repression, which operates in parapraxes, rests on a countercathexis. Energy is shifted between ego and id functions, serving to regulate conflict involved in pleasure-seeking, as well as serving to discharge drives. Tendencies particularly subject to conflict involve sexuality, aggression, strength or weakness, and control or lack of control. Parapraxes, like all symptom formations, blend drive, defense, and adaptation.

See DEFENSE; INSTINCTUAL DRIVE; SYMPTOMS; SYMPTOMATIC ACT.

References

Eidelberg, L. (1960). A third contribution to the study of slips of the tongue. *IJP*, 41:596–603.

Freud, S. (1901). The psychopathology of everyday life. *SE*, 6.

Gill, M. M. & Rapaport, D. (1942). A case of amnesia and its bearing on the theory of memory. *Character and Personality*, 11:166–172.

Jaffe, D. S. (1970). Forgetting and remembering. *PQ*, 39:372–388.

■ PART OBJECT / WHOLE OBJECT

See KLEINIAN THEORY: Internal Object.

■ PATHONEUROSIS

Ferenczi described this specific neurosis, which could result from a disease or injury to highly cathected body organs or specific areas, for example, the genitals or the face. The pathogenic route is energic. Object libido is withdrawn and invested in the injured organ, and the process may be viewed as a narcissistic regression. The augmented, localized libido then participates in symptom formation when repression fails and repressed material returns.

See PSYCHONEUROSIS; PSYCHOSOMATIC CONDITIONS; TRAUMATIC NEUROSIS.

References
Ferenczi, S. (1916/17). Disease or patho-neuroses. *The Theory and Technique of Psychoanalysis*. London: Hogarth Press, 1950, pp. 78–88.

■ PAVOR NOCTURNUS

See DREAMING, DREAMS.

■ PENIS ENVY

A mental attitude reflecting discontent with one's own genitals and angry, aggressive, covetous wishes for the penis. Unconscious wishes to castrate the male and take over his penis are involved. Penis envy is based on a sense of deficiency and inferiority, a narcissistic sensitivity derived from many sources, and a desire to have the supposedly superior genital equipment and potency of men.

Freud conceived of femininity as first emerging from castration and oedipal conflicts. Penis envy was its primary organizer and therefore fundamental to female sexuality. In his view penis envy represented a wish for replacement of the penis, which the girl believed she lacked because of her misconduct (masturbation) or because of maternal neglect or evil intent. Desire for the father's penis or his baby were also involved. Horney attached significance to desire for the greater urinary, scopophilic, and onanistic gratification provided by the penis.

Contemporary analytic contributions, however, have convincingly demonstrated that normal femininity has its own developmental line and is not derived from a primary, disappointed masculinity and penis envy. Gender identity is established during the first year of life. Assignment of gender at birth, early gratifying experiences, positive identifications with the mother and the nurturant mothering role prior to and after the phallic phase, cognition, learning, and language are important contributors to satisfaction with gender identity.

The child discovers the differences between the sexes between eighteen and twenty-four months. At this time girls' penis envy is often acute and quite openly expressed, but it is a phase-specific and usually transient phenomenon. The girl displaces her envy from the beginning, and other parts of the her body, her whole self, or such attributes as intelligence or achievement may take on the significance of an "illusory phallus," thereby denying her lack of a penis. These observations indicate that although overt penis envy passes, affects and fantasies activated by awareness of sexual differences often have an important organizing influence on later development.

Persistent or intense penis envy indicates the existence of other problems, superimposed on the early developmental phase of genital awareness, which may be an impediment to the development of mature femininity. The severity of the castration complex appears to be determined by the child's previous vulnerability to the threat of object loss or body integrity. Loss of a parent, inadequate mothering (especially the mother's depression or neglect), illness creating severe disturbance in the sense of the body, congenital defects, or surgery may set the stage for serious distortions in self and object representations, a severe castration complex, and heightened penis envy (Galenson & Roiphe, 1976).

Unconscious derivatives sometimes interpreted quite literally as a desire for the male organ apparently have multiply determined meanings derived from various levels of development. Present opinion is that penis envy should be treated as a mental product, the manifest content of a compromise formation that greatly condenses critical concerns. Central conflicts may involve the sense of identity, narcissistic sensitivity, and problems of aggression that give rise to a sense of damage, deprivation, inadequacy, and worthlessness. Penis envy constitutes a reductionistic metaphor for general envy, concrete and understandable, but short-circuiting the basic issues (Grossman & Stewart, 1976).

Awareness of genital differences is meaningful to the child's self-esteem as he or she differentiates from the mother. A mutually pleasurable mother–child interaction gives the child a feeling of self-worth, which extends to his or her genitals. If such interaction is not pleasant, the girl may not value her self or her genitals and may wish for a penis as a substitute object assumed to be more gratifying. Later, penis envy may represent a regressive effort to resolve oedipal conflicts. The girl may devalue her own genitals in identification with a mother who does not regard her own femininity highly. Narcissistic concerns and the child's relations to both parents therefore contribute to penis envy. It may also defend against dependency on men when unconsciously wished-for closeness carries with it the danger of merging and losing one's sense of self. Sociocultural overevaluation of the male often serves to obscure the unconscious determinants.

Persistent and intense penis envy—a pathological

dynamic—often leads to strong rivalry with men, identification with them, and manifest sexual dysfunction in a variety of neurotic constellations. It masks other conflicts and characterological problems, although these may be intertwined and condensed with sociocultural determinants.

Phallic awe or *penis awe* is a less widespread accompaniment or variant of penis envy. It is characterized less by aggressive covetousness and resentment than by admiration, excitement, and fear. It has been connected with traumatic childhood experiences of seeing the erect adult penis.

Breast envy is considered the male equivalent of penis envy, but envy of the larger penis of another male also occurs in boys and men. This is called a *small penis complex*.

See AWE; BREAST ENVY; CASTRATION; COMPROMISE FORMATION; FEMALE PSYCHOLOGY; GENDER IDENTITY; MASCULINITY/FEMININITY; OEDIPUS COMPLEX.

References

Blum, H. P. (1976). Masochism, the ego ideal, and the psychology of women. *JAPA*, 24(5):157–191.

Freud, S. (1925). Some psychical consequences of the anatomical distinction between the sexes. *SE*, 19:243–258.

——— (1931). Female sexuality. *SE*, 21:223–243.

Galenson, E. & Roiphe, H. (1976). Some suggested revisions concerning early female development. *JAPA*, 24(5):29–58.

Grossman, W. E. & Stewart, W. A. (1976). Penis envy. *JAPA*, 24(5):193–212.

Horney, K. (1924). On the genesis of the castration complex in women. *IJP*, 5:1, 50–64.

——— (1926). The flight from womanhood. *IJP*, 7:324–329.

Karma, L. (1981). A clinical report of penis envy. *JAPA*, 29:427–446.

Moore, B. E. (1976). Freud and female sexuality. *IJP*, 57:287–300.

Stoller, R. J. (1976). Primary femininity. *JAPA*, 24(5):59–78.

■ PERSONA

See ANALYTICAL PSYCHOLOGY TERMS.

■ PERSONAL MYTH

A highly invested set of autobiographical memories an individual holds as an aspect of his or her self representation. It is used to obscure omissions or distortions in the history of that person's life experience. The firm sense of conviction in this personal account and the cohesiveness and detail with which it is constructed provide a protective cover that prevents certain impulses, memories, and fantasies from becoming conscious. While it maintains repression, the personal myth simultaneously replaces, or preserves and gives expression to, important unconscious fantasies that represent the individual's personal version of the "family romance" theme.

In the clinical setting of an ongoing psychoanalysis, the personal myth appears as a special type of resistance to explorations of the patient's personal history. As described by Kris (1956), the phenomenon is most clearly seen in individuals with obsessional character structure who demonstrate the anal triad of character traits and in whom precocious ego development promoted early internalization and flourishing of fantasy life. In such individuals, factors that further contribute to the formation and defensive utilization of the personal myth include traumatic experiences during the phallic-oedipal phase followed by similar conflicts during latency age or adolescence.

See ANALITY; DEFENSE; FAMILY ROMANCE; INTERNALIZATION; OBSESSION; PHALLUS; REPRESENTATION; SCREEN MEMORY.

References

Freud, S. (1909). Family romances. *SE*, 9:235–241.

Greenacre, P. (1949). A contribution to the study of screen memories. *PSOC*, 3/4:73–84.

——— (1958). The family romance of the artist. In *Emotional Growth*. New York: Int. Univ. Press., 1971, vol. 2, pp. 505–532.

Kris, E. (1956). The personal myth. *JAPA*, 4:653–681.

Potamianou, A. (1985). The personal myth. *PSOC*, 40:285–296.

■ PERSONALITY

□ Personality Disorder

The observable, customary, ego-syntonic and, under ordinary circumstances, relatively predictable behavior pattern that characterizes an individual's day-to-day life. The term has broad applications and subsumes the concepts of temperament and character. *Temperament* refers to constitutionally determined affectomotor and cognitive tendencies. *Character* denotes ego-syntonic, rationalized behavioral attributes originating in developmental experience. The terms *personality* and *character* are often used interchangeably. The latter is more frequent in psychoanalysis, perhaps because the metapsychological viewpoint can be applied to it more readily.

Personality disorder refers to rigid and maladaptive personality traits that either significantly impair social functioning or cause considerable subjective distress. The patient believes his or her distress, is caused by others (for example, a spouse or coworkers) and fails to recognize his or her contribution to the situation. In contrast, persons with character disorder cause problems for others but do not recognize that they do so. There is considerable overlap, however, and a clear distinction often cannot be made.

The term *personality disorder* is more frequently used in psychiatry than in psychoanalysis. The best-known example is the so-called *psychopathic personality*. Though this is no longer considered a discrete psychiatric entity, the designation is frequently applied to individuals who are excitable and impulsive and who exhibit antisocial behavior such as lying, cheating, and criminality, without feeling any moral inhibition or guilt. They are rebellious, nonconforming, and often abnormally aggressive and irresponsible. A variety of syndromes present these attributes.

See CHARACTER, including references.

■ PERVERSION

Fixed and urgent sexual behavior considered pathological because it deviates in object choice and/or aim from the accepted adult norm of heterosexual genital intercourse. In describing perversions, Freud (1905) noted that aspects of such sexual practices almost always exist in the sexual life of a healthy person. Under certain circumstances such activity may substitute for or coexist with "normal" behavior for a considerable period of time. Nevertheless, though it is impossible to make a sharp distinction between normal and pathological sexual behavior, some of the deviations are far enough removed from the usual to justify the pathological label. Extreme sexual behavior that is fixed and exclusive is described as *perversion;* similar activities engaged in prior to or as a part of sexual intercourse and to heighten sexual excitement are considered normal. For example, scopophilia is considered normal as a part of sexual relations but not in voyeurism.

Perversion is characterized by particular sexual fantasies, masturbatory practices, sexual props, and/or special requirements for a sexual partner. Typical examples are fetishism, transvestism, voyeurism, exhibitionism, sadomasochism, and pedophilia. Homosexuality is often considered a normal variation, but some types of homosexuality conform to the definition of perversion given here.

It is not uncommon to find a complex variety of perverse behavior in one individual. By providing relief from anxiety related to both prephallic and phallic developmental conflicts, perverse sexuality allows genital orgasm when otherwise it would be inhibited. Perversions may be practiced with or without a partner and may or may not be practiced exclusively. When the perverse activity is not exclusive and obligatory, it is experienced either as more gratifying than heterosexual genital intercourse or as a necessary precondition for it. By contrast, normal forepleasure employs token amounts of infantile sexuality to enhance the desired goal of heterosexual genitality.

Freud (1905) recognized the precursors of perversion in the fantasies and preoccupations of children. He also discovered that perverse wishes and fantasies were unconscious in neurotic individuals—the neurotic symptoms are, in part, reactions to the perverse ideas. He hypothesized that sexual perversion results when childish libidinal investments were directly carried into adult life—the infantile sexuality failed to succumb to repressive forces that would convert it into neurotic symptoms. Subsequently theorists recognized the defensive nature of perversions—they are complex compromise formations. The unconscious fantasy central in perversions denies the anatomical distinctions between the sexes, the reciprocal attraction inherent in these distinctions, and the prerogatives of sexual maturity. The functions of the perversion are complex and multidetermined. In addition to its role as a compromise formation between drive derivatives and the superego, it has important ego-sustaining functions, including relief from separation and castration anxieties, control of aggression, propping up of the body image, expression of feminine identification and triumph over it, dehumanization and neutralization of objects experienced as threatening and frightening, bridging of gaps in the sense of reality, and relief from such painful affects as depression.

Because the term *perversion* has attained a pejorative connotation, it is sometimes replaced with *sexual deviation* or *paraphilia. Paraphilia* emphasizes the unusual quality or nature of the object of erotic interest, while *sexual deviation* refers to sexual activity that is not statistically or culturally normative.

These terms suggest an isolated entity, but perversion is rarely a single clinical pathological manifestation. Rather, it occurs together with a spectrum of disorders including psychoses and gender identity disorders at one end and neuroses, in which the perversity gradually becomes more and more repressed, at the other. The difference between perverse and gender-dysphoric patients seems to depend upon the degree to which castration fantasies can be dealt with by symbolization. Perversion allows restitution for incestuous libidinal and aggressive strivings through symbolic castration; in gender identity disorder the individual's symbolic capacities appear to be inadequate and the male seeks actual castration.

While the ramifications of perverse fantasies pervade psychic life, perversion does not always preclude relations with consensual partners. Stable object relationships are known to occur among persons with all varieties of perversions.

See CASTRATION ANXIETY; COMPROMISE FORMATION; GENDER IDENTITY; OEDIPUS COMPLEX; PSYCHOSEXUAL DEVELOPMENT; SCOPOPHILIA; VOYEURISM.

References

Bak, R. C. (1968). The phallic woman. *PSOC*, 23:15–36.

______ & Stewart, W. A. (1974). Fetishism, transvestitism, and voyeurism. In *American Handbook of Psychiatry*, ed. S. Arieti. New York: Basic Books, vol. 3, pp. 352–363.

Freud, S. (1905). Three essays on the theory of sexuality. *SE*, 7:135–172.

______ (1927). Fetishism. *SE*, 21:152–157.

Gillespie, W. (1956). The general theory of sexual perversion. *IJP*, 37:396–403.

Glover, E. (1933). The relation of perversion-formation to the development of reality sense. *IJP*, 14:486–504.

Greenacre, P. (1968). Perversions. *PSOC*, 23:47–62.

Meyer, J. (1985). Paraphilia. In *Comprehensive Textbook of Psychiatry*, ed. H. Kaplan & B. Sadock. Baltimore: Williams & Wilkins, 4th ed., pp. 1065–1077.

Ostow, M. (1974). *Sexual Deviation*. New York: Quadrangle.

■ PHALLUS

The Latin word, derived from the Greek, for penis; also, since ancient times, used as a metaphor for the generative forces in nature. In psychoanalysis it has both anatomical and symbolic meanings. Anatomically, it refers to the penis in the male and the clitoris in the female, both derived from the genital eminence in the embryo. Symbolically, the adjective *phallic* describes such personality traits as strength, assertiveness, aggression, and potency (figuratively)—these are usually associated with masculinity as contrasted to femininity. Conversely, a great variety of symbols represent the phallus. The term is commonly used in psychoanalysis in the following contexts:

Phallic phase refers to that period of psychosexual development during which the phallus is the primary erogenous zone for both sexes; it has its onset at about two years of age and extends into the oedipal phase, which immediately follows it. It is during this phase that boys' and girls' developmental courses diverge.

Phallic narcissism designates a satisfaction with the self based on an overestimation of the penis. The discovery of the differences between the sexes leads to *phallic pride* in boys—an almost hypomanic self-confidence and self infatuation including a preoccupation with such toys as guns, knives, airplanes, and racing cars and an interest in games and fantasies that symbolically celebrate the phallus. In such play aggression predominates over eroticism, but its goal is self aggrandizement rather than discharge. These attitudes and activities also defend against, and overcompensate for, castration anxiety. Boys fear and demean girls because they lack the penis. While the move into the overlapping oedipal phase is accompanied by a shift from narcissistic overvaluation to a more object-directed expression of libido, phallic narcissism frequently persists into adult life in the structure of a phallic character.

The *phallic character* or *phallic-narcissistic character* is a regressive defense against oedipal-phase anxieties. The individual unconsciously perceives his or her body as a phallus, and phallic qualities are often attributed to and expected of it. For example, he or she may unconsciously equate vomiting with ejaculation, or coming and going may take on the significance of the in-and-out motion of the penis in sexual intercourse. The syndrome is more common in men than in women; it is characterized by a constellation of traits including exaggerated and exhibitionistic self-confidence, often to the point of arrogance; haughty reserve; easily injured vanity resulting in depression; contempt for and fear of women; a prevalence of narcissistic over object libido; a relative absence of reaction formation; a view of the penis as an instrument of aggression rather than of love; and recklessness. Underlying these traits is an overcompensated oral dependency; erectile potency obscures inability to reach orgasm.

Castration anxiety, penis envy directed toward other males, and latent homosexuality are strong.

Phallic mother refers to a fairly universal unconscious fantasy during the phallic phase that one's mother possesses a penis. Early in the phallic phase this idea is based on the naïve belief that all people possess a penis. When the anatomical difference between the sexes is discovered, this fantasy is used as a defense against acknowledging the mother's lack of a penis with its implication of castration. During the oedipal phase the fantasy may change, so that the child believes that the penis mother is supposed to possess is in fact the father's. The girl's wish for this penis becomes an expression of rivalry with mother. In later life the fantasy of the phallic mother is displaced to other women. Such a *phallic woman* is perceived as masculine and aggressive; she is an object of fear who also serves as a defense against wishes that stir up castration anxiety.

Phallocentric implies a viewpoint biased by an exaggerated belief in the importance of the phallus in influencing human sexual attitudes and behavior, in particular masculinity and femininity. The term is usually applied disparagingly to theoretical views, in particular to Freud's statement (1932) that "for both sexes, only one genital, namely the male one, comes into account. What is present, therefore, is not primacy of the genitals, but a primacy of the phallus" (p. 142). This early conclusion of Freud's is contradicted by increasing evidence of a primary femininity for girls.

See CASTRATION; CHARACTER; FEMALE PSYCHOLOGY; NARCISSISM; PSYCHOSEXUAL DEVELOPMENT.

References

Edgcumbe, R. & Burgner, M. (1975). The phallic-narcissistic phase. *PSOC*, 30:161–180.

Freud, S. (1923). The infantile genital organization. *SE*, 19:139–145.

Jones, E. (1933). The phallic phase. *IJP*, 14:1–33.

Lewin, B. D. (1933). The body as phallus. *PQ*, 2:24–47.

Reich, W. (1933). Some circumscribed character forms. In *Character Analysis*. New York: Orgone Institute Press, pp. 200–207.

■ PHANTASY

See KLEINIAN THEORY: Fantasy.

■ PHOBIA

A psychological symptom characterized by the obligatory avoidance of specific situations or objects which, though not objectively dangerous, cause severe anxiety. Literally translated from the Greek, the term means morbid "fear" or "dread." A prefix is often added to indicate the object, condition, or circumstance dreaded. Among the more common terms are zoophobia (fear of animals), acrophobia (fear of heights), claustrophobia (fear of enclosed, especially small places), and agoraphobia (fear of the street or open places). Recently there has been a trend to use a simple description of the phobia instead of the combination of Greek derivatives.

For Freud (1909), *phobic neurosis* was a phase of anxiety hysteria in which usually diffuse, nonspecific anxiety, often in the form of attacks, became bound to specific external objects or situations, the avoidance of which became the central symptom of the illness. These *phobic objects* and *situations* represent, unconsciously and usually symbolically, the underlying psychic conflict and the infantile dangers involved. Though *phobia* and *anxiety hysteria* are sometimes used interchangeably, *phobic neurosis* now seems to be the preferred term.

The phobia, like any other psychoneurotic symptom, is a compromise between unacceptable, threatening, sexual and aggressive derivatives and the defending forces of the personality, whose conflict has resulted in signal anxiety. In addition to the invariable basic repressions, specific defense mechanisms determine the form of the neurosis. These are displacement (from one object to another, for example, from a feared father to a feared animal) and projection or externalization (for example, from frightening sexual excitement to frightening vehicular motion). Thus the phobia serves to transform and disguise the unconscious psychological danger. The advantages are evident: conscious awareness of aggression toward a parental figure, for example, is eliminated, permitting continued closeness, while the animal or situation to which the fear becomes related can be avoided.

Virtually any sexual and aggressive drive derivative unconsciously experienced as dangerous may be the occasion for the formation of a phobia. The symptom is therefore seen in connection with a wide range of psychopathologic states, from the mildest to the most severe. Certain phobic reactions (for example, fear of animals, the dark, and thunder) are so common between the ages of two and five that they are considered normal. Phobias related to disease are frequently associated with hypochondriasis (excessive concern over bodily symptoms and illness) in naricissistic neuroses, borderline states, depression, and schizophrenia.

In a *phobic neurosis* the etiological unconscious conflicts are usually oedipal, and the anxiety involved is typically related to the danger of castration—but often regressively expressed in preoedipal terms. When stable phobic avoidances are well rationalized and constitute a predominant, habitual means of dealing with anxiety, the person is said to have a *phobic character*. If anxiety becomes too intense to be contained by existing phobic symptomatology, the area of irrational fear and avoidance can expand, sometimes leading to a *phobic state* in which activity is drastically curtailed over an extended period of time.

Counterphobia refers to the unconscious effort to deny or overcome a phobic tendency by seeking contact with the dreaded object or situation. For example, a person might take up mountain climbing in order to deal with an underlying fear of heights. Realistically regulated counterphobic mechanisms may be quite adaptive, as when the choice to become a physician originates as an effort to master a fear of disease.

See ANXIETY; ANXIETY DISORDER; COMPROMISE FORMATION; DEFENSE; EXTERNALIZATION; SYMPTOM.

References

Bornstein, B. (1935). Phobia in a 2½-year-old child. *PQ,* 4:93–119.
Fenichel, O. (1945). *The Psychoanalytic Theory of Neurosis*. New York: Norton.
Freud, S. (1909). Analysis of a phobia in a five-year-old. *SE,* 10:135–152.
——— (1926). Inhibitions, symptoms, and anxiety. *SE,* 20:87–174.

■ PLASTIC REPRESENTATION

See DREAMING, DREAMS.

■ PLAYING

See WINNICOTT'S THEORY.

■ PLEASURE EGO

See REALITY.

■ PLEASURE/UNPLEASURE PRINCIPLE

In constructing his model of the mind and how it works, Freud postulated that certain basic principles regulate all mental functioning. One of these was the *pleasure/unpleasure principle*. Freud at first used the term *unpleasure principle,* then—for many years—*pleasure/unpleasure principle,* finally he adopted, probably for reasons of simplicity, the term *pleasure principle*. Each of these terms refers to the basic idea that the aim of all psychic activity is to seek pleasure and avoid unpleasure. This idea rests on another set of conceptions: that there are quantities of energy operating within the mind and that an increase in energy levels or drive tension is unpleasant while elimination of drive tension is pleasant. The pleasure principle regulates the need to recreate by action, or by fantasy, any situation which has afforded satisfaction through the elimination of drive tension. Its regulatory role in mental functioning is also seen in conjunction with the ego's response to signal anxiety, which is a warning of perceived danger. Since anxiety is unpleasant, the pleasure/unpleasure principle is set into motion and the various functions of the mind needed to deal with the perceived danger are activated.

This principle has both biological and psychological connotations. The biological model for Freud's use of the term *pleasure principle* was the *constancy principle,* a term coined by the father of experimental psychology, Fechner. The constancy principle, and the pleasure/unpleasure principle as well, assume that the organism seeks to avoid or eliminate undue tension and to keep tension at as low a constant as possible. The psychological concept similarly assumes that human beings strive to gratify various needs equated with pleasure and to eliminate excessive tension, which is usually accompanied by unpleasure. As Freud gained more experience, however he noted that certain situations, such as sexual foreplay, involved pleasurable buildup of drive tension. He concluded that the relationship between drive tension and pleasure/unpleasure was not as simple as he had originally thought, and he speculated that the rhythm and rate of accumulation and discharge may help determine the subjective experience of pleasure or unpleasure.

The pleasure/unpleasure principle also needs to be viewed in a developmental context. The behavior of infants and small children is chiefly regulated by the pleasure principle. As he or she grows older, the child learns that wishes sometimes clash with reality (for instance, one cannot touch a hot stove without harm), or fail to meet the requirements of the environment. The child therefore learns, often through parental precept, warnings, and examples, of the existence and importance of the *reality principle*.

See PSYCHIC ENERGY, REALITY.

References

Freud, S. (1911). Formulations on the two principles of mental functioning. *SE,* 12:215–226.
——— (1915). Instincts and their vicissitudes. *SE,* 14:111–140.

——— (1924). The economic problem of masochism. *SE,* 19:157–170.
——— (1926). Inhibitions, symptoms, and anxiety. *SE,* 20:77–174.

■ POLYMORPHOUS PERVERSITY
See COMPONENT INSTINCTS.

■ POST-TRAUMATIC STRESS DISORDER
See ANXIETY DISORDER; TRAUMATIC NEUROSIS.

■ POTENTIAL SPACE
See WINNICOTT'S THEORY.

■ PRACTICING SUBPHASE
See SEPARATION-INDIVIDUATION.

■ PREADOLESCENCE
The final part of the latency years, during which a subjective sense of physiological and hormonal shifts antedates the obvious physical changes of adolescence. This period is marked by an increase in drive intensity and by anal and oral regressive defenses against oedipal urges and the impact of the inexorable alterations of the self. Clinically this may be expressed in coprophilic language and eating problems. Defensive ego regression may also involve difficulties with verbal expression and poor school performance. *Preadolescence* is different from *prepuberty,* which designates the physical and physiological changes during the several years preceding the onset of puberty.

See DEVELOPMENT.

References

Blos, P. (1962). *On Adolescence*. New York: Free Press.
Blum, G. S. (1963). Prepuberty and adolescence. In *Studies in Adolescence,* ed. R. E. Grinder. New York: MacMillan.
Wieder, H. (1978). The psychoanalytic treatment of preadolescents. In *Child Analysis and Therapy,* ed. J. Glenn. New York: Aronson.

■ PRECONCEPTION/CONCEPTION
See BION'S THEORY.

■ PRECONSCIOUS
As a noun, refers to one of the systems of the psychic apparatus described in Freud's (1915) topographic theory. The other two systems were the conscious and the unconscious. Both the preconscious and unconscious systems may be considered unconscious in a descriptive sense, but the contents of the preconscious are readily accessible to consciousness; they are only temporarily unconscious. The adjective *preconscious* denotes this distinguishing characteristic. There are other significant differences between the systems. While the preconscious has access to consciousness and motility, the contents of the unconscious may not flow freely to the preconscious because its contents are censored and an anticathectic energy is used to maintain repression. In contrast to the mobile energy of the unconscious, the energy of the preconscious is said to be "bound." And although the preconscious may be influenced by the primary process, it tends to operate, as does the conscious, with secondary-process and logical thought formulated in verbal language.

Freud postulated a second censorship between the preconscious and conscious, stating that something's becoming conscious was no mere act of perception, but probably involved a hypercathexis as well. He assigned various functions to the preconscious that are now associated with the system *ego:* conscious memory, the inhibition of discharge of cathected ideas, the intrapsychic communication of different ideational contents, giving such contents a temporal aspect, reality testing, and the reality principle. The superego was also said to have some preconscious attributes.

See CATHEXIS; CONSCIOUS; PRIMARY PROCESS; TOPOGRAPHIC POINT OF VIEW; UNCONSCIOUS.

References

Freud, S. (1900). The interpretation of dreams. *SE,* 5:508–621.
——— (1915). The unconscious. *SE,* 14:166–204.
——— (1923). The ego and the id. *SE,* 19:12–59.
——— (1933). New introductory lectures on psychoanalysis. *SE,* 22:5–182.

■ PRECURSOR OBJECT
See WINNICOTT'S THEORY.

■ PREGENITAL MASTURBATORY EQUIVALENT
See MASTURBATION.

■ PREMATURE EJACULATION
See IMPOTENCE.

■ PRIMAL CAVITY
The oral cavity, including cheeks, lips, the interior of the mouth, the oral and nasal pharynx. René Spitz (1955), who introduced the term, observed

that in the newborn perceptions of the outside and the inside of the body meet and fuse in the primal cavity. In Spitz's words, it bridges the chasm between inside and outside, between activity and passivity; it is the matrix of both introjection and projection and is the place of transition for the development of intentional activity, for the emergence of volition from passivity. In this primal (oral) cavity, multiple contact-type modalities of sensation are simultaneously available—smell and taste, touch, pain and temperature, and deep muscle sensations accompanying the swallowing reflex. With its perceptual endowment, the primal cavity is the first conglomerate sensing organ the newborn employs to explore the environment. Its use for this purpose antedates the development of distance vision.

The hand, the acoustic labyrinth (both vestibular and auditory subdivisions) and the outer skin surface also participate in the infant's perceptions of the nursing experience.

See FACE–BREAST EQUATION, ORALITY.

References

Isakower, O. (1938). A contribution to the pathopsychology of phenomena associated with falling asleep. *IJP,* 19:331–345.

Lewin, B. K. (1946). Sleep, mouth and the dream screen. *PQ,* 15:419–434.

Spitz, R. A. (1955). The primal cavity. *PSOC,* 10:215–240.

■ PRIMAL FANTASY

A term used by Freud to denote some common sexual fantasies of children which may assume special importance in the pathogenesis of neurosis, especially fantasies of observing intercourse between one's parents, of seduction by an adult, and of castration. Such fantasies may be constructed, even in the absence of any actual experience, with the help of all the hints that reality may offer the child (that is, observation of animal intercourse, prohibition of masturbation, discovery of the female genitals). Freud also believed that a phylogenetic factor, arising out of the repetition of such experiences in the history of humankind, participated in the formation of these fantasies, either by predisposing to their arousal by suitable situations or by transmitting memory traces of the experiences of past generations. This phylogenetic view, born out of Freud's strong Lamarckian convictions, is no longer considered acceptable today.

See FANTASY; PRIMAL SCENE.

References

Freud, S. (1917). Introductory lectures on psychoanalysis. *SE,* 16:358–377.

——— (1918). From the history of an infantile neurosis. *SE,* 17:3–123.

——— (1939). Moses and monotheism. *SE,* 23:7–137.

Jones, E. (1957). *The Life and Work of Sigmund Freud,* vol. 3. New York: Basic Books.

■ PRIMAL HORDE

A type of primitive social organization hypothesized by Darwin (1874), in which human beings lived in small, more or less organized groups ruled over despotically by a powerful, violent, jealous man (the *primal father*) who appropriated all the women and kept them from his sons and other younger men. This, according to J. J. Atkinson, led to a rebellion in which the primal father was slain and cannibalized (Atkinson & Birch, 1970). In *Totem and Taboo,* Freud noted striking parallels between his clinical findings, especially in cases of obsessional neurosis, and the studies by Darwin, Atkinson, and W. Robertson-Smith (1894), who viewed the killing of the revered totem animal, the ritual, communal eating of it, and the subsequent mourning over it as the very essence of totemic religions.

Freud concluded that this primal deed, the memory of which he felt may have been phylogenetically transmitted to the present day, led to a new type of social organization. To prevent the recurrence of the murder and of the guilty feeling attached to it, the totem animal was substituted for the father, incest was forbidden, and exogamy (the taking of wives only from the outside of the clan) was instituted. Thus the development of totemism as a practical solution to the oedipal problem marked the beginning of ethical restrictions, religion, and social organization. Robertson-Smith's work and various aspects of the primal horde theory, including the possible phylogenetic transmission of the memories and the remorse connected to the murder of the primal father, have been widely criticized. Freud was fully aware of the hypothetical nature of this reconstruction, yet the points of contact between his clinical findings and the studies of Darwin, Atkinson, and Robertson-Smith studies were so close and convincing that he never lost confidence in its basic correctness.

See AMBIVALENCE; OEDIPUS COMPLEX; OBSESSION.

References

Atkinson, J. W. & Birch, D. (1970). *The Dynamics of Action.* New York: Wiley.

Darwin, C. (1874). *The Descent of Man*. New York: Hurst.
Freud, S. (1913). Totem and taboo. *SE*, 13:1–161.
——— (1939). Moses and monotheism. *SE*, 23:7–137.
Smith, W. R. (1894). *The Religion of the Semites*. New York: Meridian Library, 1956.
Wallace, E. R. (1983). *Freud and Anthropology*. New York: Int. Univ. Press.

■ PRIMAL SCENE

A universal childhood recollection or fantasy of a couple, usually father and mother, engaging in sexual intercourse. Whether the developing child has actually observed or only imagined this scene, it may be the focus of his or her subsequent curiosity and may shape his fantasies regarding the physical nature of the intimate relationship between his parents. As the majority of the world's families probably inhabit one-room dwellings, actual observation of intercourse cannot be rare, and it is reflected in universal myths and customs.

In the course of psychoanalytic therapy, the patient usually focuses attention at some point on associations related to the primal scene. The nature of the patient's fantasies or recollections and the extent of their traumatic significance appear largely to be determined by the circumstances surrounding the childhood experience, for example, the degree to which it was associated with violence between the parents or toward the child; and the cognitive capacities of the child at the time of the event or the emergence of the fantasy. A universally sadomasochistic concept of parental intercourse, or the inevitability of traumatic and pathogenic consequences from the experience, are not borne out by recent clinical and cross-cultural data. If primal scene experiences were traumatic, however, the child may develop fantasies that parental intercourse is sadomasochistic, damaging, or even castrating. In such instances the fantasies may be associated (though not necessarily causally) with a wide variety of clinical disturbances in childhood and adult life.

References

Edelheit, H. (1971). Mythopoiesis and the primal scene. *Psychoanal. Study Society*, 5:212–233.
Esman, A. (1973). The primal scene. *PSOC*, 28:49–81.
Freud, S. (1918). From the history of an infantile neurosis. *SE*, 17:3–23.
Greenacre, P. (1973). The primal scene and the sense of reality. *PQ*, 42:10–41.

■ PRIMARY CREATIVITY

See WINNICOTT'S THEORY.

■ PRIMARY IDENTIFICATION

See INTERNALIZATION.

■ PRIMARY MATERNAL PREOCCUPATION

See WINNICOTT'S THEORY.

■ PRIMARY PROCESS
□ Secondary Process

Two fundamentally different modes of psychic functioning that Freud originally conceived of in neuronal terms in "Project for a Scientific Psychology" (1895). He returned to them, most notably in his discussions of dreams, symptoms, and jokes, as a way of providing a uniform explanation for the bewildering array of seemingly irrational or meaningless phenomena.

In Freud's view (expressed primarily in economic and topographic terms), the *primary process* is the earliest, most primitive form of mentation; it seeks immediate and complete discharge by recathecting the iconic memory trace of the need-satisfying object in accordance with the pleasure principle (this is called hallucinatory wish fulfillment). The freely mobile cathexis in the Unconscious allows one idea within the wish-related associative network to symbolize another idea (a process known as displacement); one idea can also symbolically express several others (condensation); thus unacceptable ideas can evade the censorship of the Preconscious-Conscious system. On a more descriptive level, the concept of primary process embraces such characteristics of unconscious mentation as the disregard of logical connections, the coexistence of contradictions, the absence of a temporal dimension and of negatives, and the use of indirect representation and concretization (imagery).

From a developmental perspective, the primary process is gradually (albeit never completely) inhibited in the normal waking state by the *secondary process*. The latter operates with bound cathexis and verbal, denotative symbols. Governed by the reality principle, it accounts for reality-attuned, logical thought, exemplified by delayed, modulated drive gratification through problem-solving (the internal activity of trial and error).

In contemporary psychoanalytic theory, the primary and secondary process modes of thought lie on a continuum; all thought products (dreams, symptoms, slips, fantasies, daydreams, directed problem-solving) show varying degrees of organizational structure and admixtures of primitive, regressive, defensive, and mature mechanisms. The concept of "regression in the service of the ego," introduced by Ernst Kris (1952), is an example of a nonpathological admixture described in the context of artistic creation and art appreciation.

See CATHEXIS; CONSCIOUS; METAPSYCHOLOGY; PRECONSCIOUS; TOPOGRAPHIC POINT OF VIEW; UNCONSCIOUS.

References

Arlow, J. A. & Brenner, C. (1964). *Psychoanalytic Concepts and the Structural Theory*. New York: Int. Univ. Press.

Freud, S. (1895). Project for a scientific psychology. *SE*, 1:295–387.

——— (1900). The interpretation of dreams. *SE*, 4–5.

——— (1905). Jokes and their relation to the unconscious. *SE*, 8.

Gill, M. M. (1967). The primary process in motives and thought. In *Motives and Thought*, ed. R. R. Holt. New York: Int. Univ. Press, pp. 259–298.

Kris, E. (1952). *Psychoanalytic Explorations in Art*. New York: Int. Univ. Press.

■ PRIMORDIAL IMAGES

See ANALYTICAL PSYCHOLOGY TERMS: Archetype.

■ PRINCIPLE OF CONSTANCY

See PSYCHIC ENERGY.

■ PRINCIPLE OF MULTIPLE APPEAL

See MULTIDETERMINISM.

■ PRINCIPLE OF MULTIPLE DETERMINISM

See MULTIDETERMINISM.

■ PRINCIPLE OF MULTIPLE FUNCTION

See MULTIDETERMINISM.

■ PRIVACY

The state of being apart from the company or observation of others; seclusion; hence, the opposite of being "public." In the technical legal sense: a broad term regarding the "right to be let alone" (Justice Brandeis); a profound constitutional right inherent to a democracy and prerequisite to optimal creativity; the right of a person to be free from unwarranted publicity, to withhold him- or herself and his or her property from public scrutiny if he or she so chooses.

This right, strongly felt by most individuals, is the basis for the requirement of confidentiality in the analytic situation.

See CONFIDENTIALITY, PRIVILEGE.

■ PRIVILEGE

A legal term referring to the protection afforded by statute or common law against the disclosure while giving testimony during a deposition or trial of communications obtained in a confidential professional relationship. Hence, a *privileged* or *confidential communication* is one that the recipient of the confidence cannot be compelled legally to disclose. Examples are lawyer–client, physician–patient, priest–penitent, and husband–wife relationships. The derivation of privilege reveals the basis for inclusion of the husband–wife relationship. It comes from the Latin *privilegium*, derived from *privus* (private, peculiar), and from *lex, lege* (law); thus it means a private law providing special prerogative or exemption, originally obtained as the result of position or power.

Privilege applies to psychoanalytic communications to the same degree that common law and local statutes protect communications between psychiatrist and patient or psychotherapist and patient. If a patient waives privilege, he or she thereby waives privilege for all communications unless there is a prearrangement with the judge and/or adversary lawyer. In most jurisdictions the privilege belongs only to the patient. At times a patient may not remember the content or realize the significance of his or her communications and therefore must be carefully counseled before privilege is waived.

See CONFIDENTIALITY; PRIVACY.

■ PROJECTION

A mental process whereby a personally unacceptable impulse or idea is attributed to the external world. As a result of this defensive process, one's own interests and desires are perceived as if they belong to others, or one's own mental experience may be mistaken for consensual reality.

The ideas or feelings that a person cannot tolerate may unconsciously undergo a transformation before they are projected, as is often the case in paranoid projections. Freud (1911) elaborated and clarified this process in describing a paranoid patient who denied his own sexual and aggressive feelings while experiencing himself as sexually persecuted by a lecherous and cruel god. Frightened by his homosexual wishes, the patient unconsciously transformed his feelings of love into hatred and then at-

havior includes an examination of the energic cathexes and countercathexes involved. It also requires identification of the kinds of energies used, whether libidinal, aggressive, or neutralized, and how these energies are deployed.

See INSTINCTUAL DRIVE; METAPSYCHOLOGY; PLEASURE/UNPLEASURE PRINCIPLE; PRIMARY PROCESS.

References

Freud, S. (1894). The neuropsychoses of defence. *SE,* 3:45–61.
——— (1920). Beyond the pleasure principle. *SE,* 18:7–64.
——— (1923). The ego and the id. *SE,* 9:12–66.
Holt, R. R. (1967). Beyond vitalism and mechanism. In *Science and Psychoanalysis,* ed. J. H. Masserman. New York: Grune & Stratton, vol. 2, pp. 1–41.
Kubie, L. S. (1947). The fallacious use of quantitative concepts in dynamic psychology. *PQ,* 16:507–18.
Rosenblatt, A. D. & Thickstun, J. T. (1970). A study of the concept of psychic energy. *IJP,* 51:265–278.

■ PSYCHIC IMPOTENCE

See IMPOTENCE.

■ PSYCHOANALYSIS

A branch of science developed by Sigmund Freud and his followers, devoted to the study of human psychology. It is usually considered to have three areas of application: (1) a method of investigating the mind; (2) a systematized body of knowledge about human behavior (*psychoanalytic theory*); and (3) a modality of therapy for emotional illness (*psychoanalytic treatment*).

The method of investigation involves the use of free association and the analysis of dreams, fantasies, thought processes, and behavior in relation to affects. *Psychoanalytic methodology* usually refers to the systematic study of the psychoanalytic method itself.

Psychoanalytic theory comprises the factual data derived from clinical psychoanalytic observation, organized according to a gradually evolved system of hypotheses (for example, libido theory, metapsychology, structural theory). The data and hypotheses are applied to normal mental development and functioning as well as to abnormal mental processes and disorders.

As a therapeutic method, psychoanalysis is most effective for patients with symptom and character neuroses (but it is increasingly applied to more severe disturbances). Its principles are also widely applied to the understanding of other mental conditions.

See ANALYSIS; ANALYTIC TECHNIQUE.

References

Brenner, C. (1973). *An Elementary Textbook of Psychoanalysis,* rev. ed. New York: Int. Univ. Press.
——— (1979). *The Mind in Conflict.* New York: Int. Univ. Press.
Freud, S. (1915–17). Introductory lectures on psychoanalysis. *SE,* 15–16.
Hendrick, I. (1958). *Facts and Theories of Psychoanalysis,* 3d ed. New York: Alfred Knopf.
Valenstein, A. F. (1979). The concept of "classical" psychoanalysis. *JAPA,* 27(suppl.):113–136.

■ PSYCHOANALYTIC PSYCHOTHERAPY

See ANALYTIC THERAPY; PSYCHOTHERAPY.

■ PSYCHODYNAMICS

The aspect of psychoanalytic theory that explains mental phenomena, such as thoughts, feelings, and behavior, as the results of interacting and opposing goal-directed or motivational forces. The theory focuses on the interplay of such forces, illuminating processes, developments, progressions, regressions, and fixations. The concept of the psychic apparatus as a tripartite structure of the mind aids in understanding the dynamics postulated. The id represents the instinctual drives, the ego the executive and inhibiting agency, and the superego the influence of conscience and ideals; all are manifest in any psychic phenomenon. Id tensions force the person to seek satisfaction, that is, the discharge of tension. The ego judges the safety or danger of gratification and exerts restraining forces to frustrate, delay, or detour such discharge so that its ultimate expression is in keeping with the demands of reality and the superego. The opposition between these agencies gives rise to intrapsychic conflict, and the result of unconscious mental arbitration may emerge into conscious awareness as a neurotic symptom. Innate and environmental factors operate at all levels of development and in all mental structures. Genetic and developmental contributions to behavior also come into play in a psychodynamic explanation; they include fixation or regression to earlier libidinal or ego stages of development. The extent of the regression determines the nature of the conflict and its resolution in respect to the specific dangers involved in gratifying instinctual demands at a given phase. If difficulty did not occur at the particular stage of development suggested by a symptom, the symptom may indicate regression from a later stage at which the problem arose.

See CONFLICT; FIXATION; METAPSYCHOLOGY; REALITY; REGRESSION; STRUCTURAL THEORY.

References

Gill, M. M. (1963). *Topography and Systems in Psychoanalytic Theory. Psychol. Issues,* monogr. 10, New York: Int. Univ. Press.

Meissner, W. (1981). Metapsychology: who needs it? *JAPA,* 29:921–938.

Rapaport, D. (1960). *The Structure of Psychoanalytic Theory. Psychol. Issues,* monogr. 6, New York: Int. Univ. Press.

Schafer, R. (1975). Psychoanalysis without psychodynamics. *IJP,* 56:41–55.

■ PSYCHOGENESIS

The psychological origin of normal and pathological mental phenomena. Attempts to understand psychogenesis are based on the premise that what happens in the mind in the present is influenced or even determined by events and processes that happened in the past (i.e., psychic determinism). Discontinuities and phenomena that appear random and unexplainable can be understood by following a chain of causation in the sequential relationship of psychic events arising from a complex interplay of conscious and unconscious forces. The methodology of psychoanalysis sets up conditions in which it is possible to view the vicissitudes of infantile conflicts as they are expressed in the current life situation and in respect to the analyst (transference). In his 1920 paper "The Psychogenesis of a Case of Homosexuality in a Woman," Freud demonstrates how it is possible to gain an understanding of the origin and development of a patient's mental processes.

See ANALYSIS; CONFLICT; CHARACTER; PSYCHIC DETERMINISM; SYMPTOM FORMATION.

References

Fenichel, O. (1945). *The Psychoanalytic Theory of Neurosis.* New York: Norton.

Freud, S. (1920). The psychogenesis of a case of homosexuality in a woman. *SE,* 18:147–172.

Gero, G. (1943). The idea of psychogenesis in modern psychiatry and in psychoanalysis. *Psychoanal. Rev.,* 30:187–211.

■ PSYCHOLINGUISTICS

An interdisciplinary science combining the knowledge and skill of linguists and psychologists and representing the hybrid concerns of these two disciplines. Linguistics is the study of language, its manifestations and formal characteristics. Modern linguistics began with Saussure (1911) and Bloomfield during the first half of the twentieth century. It underwent a revolution under the leadership of Noam Chomsky during the late 1950s. Interest in the molecular structure of language gave way to study of its formal characteristics, grammar, and innateness. Theoretical revisions followed based on the semantic model of language. Pragmatics and sociolinguistics have recently become more significant in the field. Chomsky suggested that linguistics should deal with ideal speakers in a homogeneous speech community. Thus, his approach to language is contextless, while sociolinguists like Labov (1972) favor dealing with language as it is used in the context of the life situation of the speaker.

Psychology usually involves the study of mental and behavioral aspects of animals and human beings. However, the branch of psychology dealing with cognition and development has become significantly concerned with linguistic questions: When is there evidence that varying language structures are understood or produced? What are the mechanisms by which the emergent forms come about? Is there psychological reality to the formal models of transformational grammar? What is the relationship of the patterns of thought, cognition, and logic to the formal grammatical patterns of language? Brown (1970) claims that psycholinguistics was "born" at a 1952 meeting of the Social Science Council, when three linguists and three psychologists met for an interdisciplinary conference. It is true that the term achieved some popularity at that time. Psycholinguistics became a burgeoning intellectual force in the late 1960s as workers in both linguistics and psychology found an overlapping area of inquiry. In addition, the more theoretical areas of linguistics mixed with philosophy, creating a similar amalgam known as the philosophy of language.

Psychoanalysts have long been interested in words and meanings, beginning with Freud's interest in the early philologists and the study of aphasia. Freud wrote a number of papers addressing linguistic themes that intertwine with psychology. "The Antithetical Meaning of Primal Words" (1910), "The Uncanny" (1919), "On Negation" (1925), and his early book *On the Interpretation of the Aphasias* (1891) all attest to Freud's concern with language and to the application of language theory to the complex psychological processes studied by analysts. Recent work within psychoanalysis has further developed the hybrid field of clinical psycholinguistics as explicitly defined by Shapiro (1979); others have applied linguistic models to psychoanalytic data.

References
Brown, R. (1970). *Psycholinguistics.* New York: Free Press.
Chomsky, N. (1978). Language and unconscious knowledge. In *Psychoanalysis and Language,* ed. J. H. Smith. New Haven: Yale Univ. Press, vol. 3, pp. 3–44.
Freud, S. (1891). On the interpretation of the aphasias. *SE,* 3:240–241.
——— (1910). The antithetical meaning of primal words. *SE,* 11:155.
——— (1919). The uncanny. *SE,* 17:219.
——— (1925). On negation. *SE,* 19:235.
Labov, W. (1972). *Language in the Inner City.* Philadelphia: Univ. Penn. Press.
Saussure de, F. (1911). *Course in General Linguistics.* New York: McGraw Hill.
Shapiro, T. (1979). *Clinical Psycholinguistics.* New York: Plenum Press.

■ PSYCHONEUROSIS

A major category in psychoanalytic and psychiatric nomenclature characterized by symptoms expressing a variety of disturbances in thought, feelings, attitudes, and behavior. These symptoms originate in mental conflict, the contending elements of which are largely unconscious. As Freud first pointed out, psychoanalytic therapy reveals psychological connections, often symbolically expressed between the conflict and the symptoms. The term applies to a number of psychopathological entities consisting of specific symptom complexes. These include involuntary movements, changes in bodily functions, or painful or disagreeable sensations, as in hysteria; episodic dysphoric affects or moods, as in anxiety attacks or neurotic depressions; uncontrollable and repetitive thoughts and actions, as in obsessive-compulsive neuroses; or restriction of adaptive behavior due to consciously irrational fears, as in phobias. The patient experiences these symptoms as strange and unintelligible (ego-alien), outside the realm of conscious will, and disturbing to usual patterns of adaptive functioning. Their ego-alien quality distinguishes symptomatic psychoneurotic disturbances from character disorders. In the psychoneuroses, reality testing tends to be maintained, whereas in the psychoses it is considerably impaired; drive inhibitions that are lost in perversions and impulse disorders are also maintained in psychoneuroses. Character disorder, paraphilia, impulse disorders, and psychotic disturbance may coexist with psychoneurosis, however, as may borderline conditions and pathological narcissism. Typically, those exhibiting psychoneurotic symptoms have backgrounds of character disorder. Overly dependent traits and/or histrionic personality disorder are characteristic in the interpersonal relationships of those who suffer hysterical psychoneurosis; compulsive and/or passive-aggressive traits are often evident in those who develop obsessional psychoneuroses. Mixed characterological problems of interacting and relating may have been conspicuous features of other histories. Character disorder, comprising consolidated ego-syntonic defenses, is psychodynamically related to the absence of psychoneurotic symptoms, but when these character defenses partially fail symptoms occur.

Psychoneuroses result from heightened conflict between sexual and aggressive drives or their derivatives; they are attempts to control and limit the expression of such drives. This struggle is not based upon a realistic appraisal of the current situation with its opportunities for gratification under the reasonable restraint imposed by the normal superego. Rather, the inhibiting tendency is based on frightening unconscious fantasies and memory traces relating to infantile experiences involving danger situations typical for successive phases of psychosexual development and an unduly harsh archaic superego. The psychoneurosis may be precipitated when the adult finds him- or herself in a situation that reactivates memory traces of an earlier traumatic experience. The new experience becomes a repetition of the original conflict, evoking unconscious fantasies usually related to the oedipus complex. In the new conflict the ego reacts to the emergence of the drive-organized fantasies with signals of anxiety, which stimulate repression and other defensive mechanisms. Because of the continuing energic charge of ungratified wishes, however, the defense against them eventually becomes inadequate and there is a *return of the repressed* in the form of symptoms. Analysis shows these symptoms to be compromise formations, composed of disguised substitutive expressions of the forbidden sexual and aggressive drives, the defenses against them, and punitive representations of the superego. In addition, symptoms often express a wish for sympathy and thus function to attract attention. The ego strives to integrate the opposing claims of the id, superego, and social reality in such symptomatic compromise formations; this illustrates the principle of multiple function described by Waelder (1936), a principle that also holds for adaptive ego functioning.

The different psychoneuroses reflect fixations

at different libidinal levels of early development to which there is regression following frustration and conflict. Correlative regressive repetoires of ego defenses (against infantile libidinal strivings and the increment of hostility associated with thwarted gratification) are likewise involved in the "choice of psychoneurosis." At first Freud stressed the regression of libido. Later it was recognized that vulnerability to psychoneurosis also depends on the vicissitudes of the aggressive drive and how mature the ego was when traumatic situations gave rise to conflict. Biological as well as experiential determinants are also of importance in determining the strength of the sadomasochistic components of infantile sexuality.

Psychoneurotic symptoms may break out in response to increases in the warded-off drives, as during puberty or the climacteric, or when the individual is exposed to a particularly arousing temptation. A decrease in the strength of defenses may bring on anxiety and guilt before other definitive symptoms occur.

The first neuroses Freud described were the *actual neuroses,* which he thought were due to the transformation of dammed up libido into anxiety as a result of improper or unsatisfactory sexual practices. Freud separated the psychoneuroses from the actual neuroses on the basis that the former came from intrapsychic conflict based on early childhood fantasies and trauma, but he thought that the conditions often coexisted and were sometimes indistinguishable.

Whatever distinctions once existed between the terms *neurosis* and *psychoneurosis* have now become blurred; the terms are now often used interchangeably. Freud grouped hysteria, phobia, and obsessive compulsive neurosis in the category *transference neuroses:* these patients readily repeat the childhood neurotic pattern within the transference during psychoanalytic treatment. Patients afflicted with melancholia and schizophrenia are less capable of mature object relationships; this obscures adequate elucidation during the analysis of such childhood patterns of relationship. Freud termed these entities *narcissistic neuroses.*

In many traditionally oriented cultures or subcultures, psychoneurotic disturbances are interpreted in terms of a religious idiom, such as demonic possession, and ritual healing may be sought with the help of a shaman or priest and the religious community.

See ACTUAL NEUROSIS; ANXIETY; BORDERLINE PERSONALITY DISORDER; CHARACTER; CONFLICT; DEPRESSION; EGO-DYSTONIC; HYSTERIA; NARCISSISM; OBSESSION; PERVERSION; PHOBIA; PSYCHOSIS; SYMPTOM.

References

Abse, D. W. (1985). *Hysteria and Related Mental Disorders.* Bristol: John Wright.

Freud, A. (1936). *The Ego and the Mechanisms of Defense. WAF,* 2.

Freud, S. (1916). Introductory lectures on psychoanalysis. *SE,* 16:243–448.

Fenichel, O. (1945). *The Psychoanalytic Theory of Neurosis.* New York: Norton.

Waelder, R. (1936). The principle of multiple function. *PQ,* 5:45–62.

■ PSYCHOPATHIC PERSONALITY

See PERSONALITY.

■ PSYCHOSEXUAL DEVELOPMENT

Freud's (1905) frame of reference for conceptualizing development based on his examination of the origin and dynamics of neurotic symptoms and character traits in relation to successive phases of the libidinal drives. He had observed that the early phases of what he called *infantile sexuality* were organized around the libidinal investment of the oral, anal, and phallic erotogenic bodily zones, each achieving in turn a relative dominance over the preceding phases. The sensuous features of the libidinal zones consist of pleasurable activities and sensations; predominantly sucking, mouthing, and biting during the *oral period;* expelling and retaining feces during the *anal period;* and finally manipulating ("infantile" masturbating) the external genitals—penis and testicles in boys, clitoris and labia in girls—during the *phallic phase. Urethral erotism* overlaps the late oral, the anal, and the early phallic stages.

Bodily activities and sensations connected with each libidinal zone are accompanied by phase-related fantasies and conflicts with the parents or other important persons in the child's environment. In the phallic period the anatomical differences between the sexes become highlighted. Recent investigations have shown that the child becomes aware of the distinction between male and female genitals at the age of fifteen to nineteen months. Castration anxiety and penis envy thus appear even prior to the phallic phase. Pregenital sexuality therefore plays an important role in the formation of neurotic symptoms, character traits, and deviant sexuality. During the *phallic phase,* age two and a half to five years, the child's instinctual drives, object relations, conflicts, and fantasies become centered on the parents or their substitutes. In the latter part of this phase (called the *phallic-oedipal*), the oedipus complex comes to its full expression and eventually is resolved. The formation of the superego and a prevalent identification with the parent of the same sex is the usual outcome of this resolution. The type of object choice, hetero- vs. homosexual, depends on the positive or negative nature of the oedipus complex, but other factors, pregenital as well as postoedipal, play a role in determining the eventual choice of love objects.

Freud assumed that there was little difference in the early psychosexual development of boys and girls until the resolution of the oedipus complex, but recent investigations make it necessary to revise this global assumption. Biological factors and parents' subtly different expectations and reinforcements, as well as their unconscious fantasies, influence the child's sexual and gender identity in addition to identificatory processes. The phallic phase, however, highlights the significant differences between the sexes. Interest in the naked body, curiosity about the opposite sex, and a wish to look at (scopophilia) and to have the genitals seen (exhibitionism) originate during this phase. The girl's feelings of inadequacy about her genital organs, penis envy, and competitive attitudes toward boys can be observed. In boys, castration fears become more clearly evident.

Beginning about the age of six, following the Oedipus complex, a period of relative sexual quiescence ensues. This period of *latency* lasts about six to seven years, during which hormonal changes activate the somatic changes of puberty, initiating the developmental stage of *adolescence*. After genital dominance is reached following puberty, the sensuality characteristic of earlier infantile periods may manifest itself in the sexual act as forepleasure. If elements of the earlier stages of sexuality remain the prevalent aim of adult sexual strivings, genital sexuality is considered either inhibited or deviant. Psychic derivatives of earlier psychosexual stages often contribute to the formation of symptoms and character traits. Through sublimation they may also give rise to social, professional, or creative achievements.

See ADOLESCENCE; ANALITY; GENDER IDENTITY; GENITALITY; INFANTILE SEXUALITY; OEDIPUS COMPLEX; ORALITY; PHALLUS; SUBLIMATION.

References

Bornstein, B. (1951). On latency. *PSOC*, 6:279–285.

Freud, S. (1905). Three essays on the theory of sexuality. *SE*, 7:130–243.

Galenson, E. & Roiphe, H. (1976). Some suggested revisions concerning early female development. *JAPA*, 24 (suppl.):29–57.

——— (1980). The preoedipal development of the boy. *JAPA*, 28:805–827.

Greenacre, P. (1968). Perversions. *PSOC*, 23:48–62.

Tyson, P. (1982). A developmental line of gender identity, gender role, and choice of love object. *JAPA*, 30:61–86.

■ PSYCHOSIS

A form of mental disorder characterized by marked ego and libidinal regression with consequent severe personality disorganization. Psychoses fall into two groups, the *organic* and the *functional*. Those in the first category are secondary to physical disease (for example, syphilitic general paresis, brain tumor, arteriosclerosis); the latter are primarily related to psychosocial factors, though there may be biological predispositions as well. The major functional psychoses are the *affective disorders* (manic-depressive psychosis) and the *thought disorders* (schizophrenia and true paranoia).

In regard to the psychoses, especially schizophrenia, considerable controversy exists about the relative importance of genetic or constitutional neuroendocrine, somatic, and metabolic patterns versus developmental and environmental determinants operating psychologically. There is abundant evidence, however, that individual experiences and psychological reactions do play a major role in the etiology and development of the psychotic process and symptom formation.

The phenomenological characteristics of the psychoses are, to a greater or lesser degree, bizarre behavior, delusional ideas, inappropriately labile and intense affective reactions, withdrawal, and a significant disturbance in the sense of reality and reality testing. Perceptual disorders, especially hallucinatory experiences, difficulty in communication (loose associations and blocking of thought), and hypochondriasis are often prominent.

Freud's conceptualization of the psychopathology of the psychoses emphasized a fundamental unity between the mental processes in psychoses and neuroses. However, he also pointed out certain significant differences. One is that the psychotic individual is unconsciously fixated to an earlier level of libidinal development, the narcissistic phase. This leads, through regression, to the most important feature in the development of psychosis—the change in the patient's relationship with the persons and objects of his or her environment. The patient may see others as withdrawn and detached or even strongly hostile. This is usually related to the idea that the world and the people in it have somehow changed, which sometimes expands into a fantasy that the world is destroyed and everybody is unreal. Freud believed that these symptoms represented the patient's break with reality and the most characteristic single feature of the psychoses.

The narcissistic regression described above may be considered the first of a two-stage process. In this first stage the mental representations of external persons and objects are decathected, and the libido is freed to cathect the person's self, a basis for some of the hypochondriacal symptoms common in psychoses. In the second or restitutive stage the patient attempts (frequently through delusions and hallucinations) to recathect the object representations in order to reestablish contact—often pathological—with the outer world. Successful restitution sometimes leads to partial recovery.

On the basis of considerable clinical and theoretical evidence, analytic observers have recently suggested that the later concepts of Freud's structural theory, in particular regression of ego functions, explain the clinical phenomena of the psychosis better than do his earlier concepts of libidinal decathexis and recathexis. They believe that most of the changes in the ego and superego functions associated with psychosis are defenses against the emergence of anxiety; but the alterations are so extensive that the disruption of the patient's object relationships can be considered a break with reality.

Freud differentiated the psychoses from the neuroses on the basis of certain characteristic differences. Neurosis involves the repression of the prohibited demand of the id and its return in a distorted form (symptom formation). In psychosis there is a decathexis of object representations (the break with reality) and, second, the attempts to regain the lost reality. The return of the repressed is the significant feature in neurosis; the loss of reality is of major importance in psychosis. In neurosis the struggle is predominantly between the instinctual drives of the id and the defensive processes of the ego; in psychosis the id (and in part the superego) overwhelm the ego defenses but come into conflict with a frustrating reality, which can be dealt with only by its fantasied destruction and distorted restitution.

Along with other clinical observations, the investigation of the psychoses led Freud and others to reevaluate the libido and topographic theories. A better understanding of narcissism, the aggressive drive, and the concept of the self contributed to the development of the structural theory and the dual instinct theory, resulting finally in ego psychology's gaining a more significant place in psychoanalysis. Treatment of psychoses and borderline states also facilitated the study of early ego states and development because of their significance in psychotic regression.

Generally, psychoanalytic therapy has focused on the neuroses, and later the character neuroses and perversions. As part of a "widening scope of psychoanalysis," however, psychoanalytic technique has been applied to selected cases of psychoses, in particular by members of the Kleinian school. Various degrees of success have been reported; usually certain parameters (alterations of the classical method) are necessary.

In the early years psychoanalysts thought that no transference relationship could develop with psychotic patients because of the degree of narcissism present in such patients. It now seems that quite intense and distorted transferences (sometimes described as *transference psychoses*) develop. They have to be handled and resolved with great care since they represent the patient's initial, very tenuous efforts to reestablish a genuine object relationship with another human being.

See ANXIETY; BORDERLINE PERSONALITY DISORDER; CHARACTER; PSYCHONEUROSIS; PSYCHOTIC CHARACTER; PSYCHOTIC PROCESS; REGRESSION.

■ PSYCHOSOMATIC CONDITIONS

Medical entities in which psychological factors are thought to play a special role in the etiology, development, course, and outcome of the disease. Alexander regarded the following seven disorders as classically "psychosomatic": peptic ulcer, bronchial asthma, ulcerative colitis, rheumatoid arthritis, hypertension, neurodermatitis, and hyperthyroidism. Other diseases can be added to this list. A specific psychic conflict was considered characteristic of each disorder; this formed the basis for the concept of specificity.

The term, though in common use, is broad and somewhat inaccurate. More accurately, all disease should be considered both *psychosomatic* and *somatopsychic,* in that psychological and somatic factors are always present, active, and intertwined at many levels through complexly reverberating systems. Engel's *biopsychosocial model* stresses the role of social as well as purely somatic or psychological factors in disease.

See ORGAN NEUROSIS.

References

Alexander, F. (1950). *Psychosomatic Medicine.* New York: Norton.

Engel, G. L. (1962). *Psychological Development in Health and Disease.* New York: Saunders.

——— (1967). Psychoanalytic theory of somatic disorder. *JAPA,* 15:344–365.

■ PSYCHOTHERAPY

Literally, psychological treatment. It refers to any method utilized by a professionally trained therapist regardless of the origin of the disorder being treated. The term is applied to a wide variety of mental illnesses of varying severity, to somatic disorders thought to be of psychological origin, and to behavioral maladaptions for which the patient seeks treatment.

Involuntary treatment is a violation of human rights. Essentially, psychotherapy utilizes the relationship and communication (verbal and nonverbal) between a patient and the therapist for the purpose of removing, modifying, retarding, or suppressing pathological processes that interfere with personality function and development. Historically, such treatment has employed such means as advice, encouragement, guidance, re-education, reassurance, suggestion, hypnosis, and more recently behavior modification. In this broad context, psychoanalysis may be regarded as a form of psychotherapy, though there are important reasons for differentiating the two.

In psychoanalysis such factors as the frequency and intensity of treatment, systematic and explicit consideration of the evolving transference as expressed in the therapeutic process, and possibilities for understanding and explicitly defining underlying pathological and pathogenic factors offer the most benefit for suitable patients. *Psychoanalytic psychotherapy* (sometimes called *insight therapy*) refers to a more limited form of psychotherapy based on the principles of psychoanalytic theory and technique. However, depending on the case, it fulfills only some of the technical or therapeutic requirements of psychoanalysis. *Supportive therapy* is a term applied to procedures involving either directly supportive measures (such as encouragement or exhortation) or more sophisticated measures involving attempts to support the patient's personality strengths. *Expressive therapy* facilitates the conscious recognition and verbalization of hitherto repressed or suppressed ideation and affects; *suppressive therapy,* in contrast, is intended to help a patient contain such phenomena when they are judged to be too disturbing or disruptive. *Relationship therapy* attempts to utilize the interaction between therapist and patient in its own right, usually without examining or understanding transference factors. It may be compared in its efficacy to the benefits conferred in an everyday, psychologically naïve way by a good friend or family member.

See ANALYSIS; ANALYTIC THERAPY; PSYCHOANALYSIS; TRANSFERENCE.

References

Bibring, E. (1954). Psychoanalysis and the dynamic psychotherapies. *JAPA,* 2:745–770.

Kernberg, O. F. (1986). *Severe Personality Disorders.* New Haven: Yale Univ. Press.

Sachs, D. M. (1979). On the relationship between psychoanalysis and psychoanalytic psychotherapy. *Bull. Phila. Assn. Psychoanal.,* 6:119–145.

Wallerstein, R. (1975). *Psychotherapy and Psychoanalysis.* New York: Int. Univ. Press.

■ PSYCHOTIC CHARACTER

A disturbance in character structure viewed as a specific and recognizable clinical entity, the counterpart of the *neurotic character.* It is roughly synonymous with *borderline personality.* As in the neurotic character, elements of intrapsychic conflict are crystallized in the character structure, bringing about predictable modes of adaptation and response to stress. Though the individual is not psychotic, these modes of responding are frequently governed by the same features that underlie psychotic reactions. Under stress, therefore, the individual develops anxieties, reactive patterns, and impairment of functions similar to those of the psychotic. Indeed, psychotic symptoms do sometimes occur, but in contrast to those of the psychotic, they are reversible; and many identifiable psychotic characters go through life without showing psychotic symptomatology.

The psychotic character shows a proclivity for marked regression and loss of differentiation between self and nonself (all the external world, including objects); he or she is also usually capable of reversing these processes. Object relations are established, but on a more infantile level than those of healthy and neurotic individuals. The relationship to reality, the sense of reality, and the ability to test reality are severely impaired but generally preserved in contrast to the situation of the psychotic.

The term *psychotic character* should not be used for a transitional phase on the way to or from psychosis; it should be reserved for individuals who have such identifiable features as an integral part of their character structure.

See BORDERLINE PERSONALITY DISORDER; CHARACTER; EGO FUNCTION; PSYCHOSIS.

■ PSYCHOTIC PROCESS

A formulation of the dynamic forces that invariably contribute to the clinical manifestations of psychosis, but that may exist as well in severe character disorders, which have some of the characteristic features of psychosis but retain intact reality testing (Frosch, 1983). Three frames of reference help delineate the salient features of the psychotic process: the nature of the conflict and anxiety; the nature of the defenses; and impaired ego functioning together with the presence of ego states reflecting such impairment.

The basic danger most feared in psychosis is dissolution and disintegration of the self. This danger of loss of identity gives rise to an amorphous, pervasive, nonspecific anxiety, termed *basic anxiety*. At first it is present on a biological, nonideational level, but it ultimately relates to the idea of survival. It recapitulates the sense of helplessness in the earliest stages of psychic development when the child is unable to cope with overwhelming accumulating tensions. For the psychotic the threat of dedifferentiation and eventual self-disintegration is very real and especially frightening because reversing the process seems impossible. In dealing with basic anxiety the defective ego may resort to various regressive defenses, including introjective-projective reactions, projective identification, fragmentation, splitting, and massive denial. While severe ego disturbances (for example, loss of reality testing) may help preserve the object by creating a substitute, such radical defenses increase the danger of loss of self through regressive dedifferentiation.

The third feature of the psychotic process is the existence of impaired ego functions and states. Normally, the ego mediates the demands of reality, the id, and the superego. But in psychoses, id-derived fantasies and impulses may invade the ego. The result can be disturbances in the relationship with love objects and reality, including the feeling of that a stable reality exists and the capacity to test it. The nature and level of object relations has a direct bearing on psychic reality. Primitivization of object relations or regression to archaic object relations is an underlying potential in the psychoses. In extreme cases the patient may regress to pre-object levels of undifferentiated psychic development—that is, primary narcissism, most clearly seen in schizophrenia. Diffuse ego boundaries make it difficult at times for the psychotic individual to distinguish between self and nonself, human and nonhuman objects. This adds to his or her anxiety. Interference with the development of object constancy also affects reality constancy and the internalization of reality testing. Earlier modes of testing reality, significantly influenced by parental images and the superego, persist. Such patients do not learn to trust their own perceptions and need constant external affirmation.

Many authors believe that dedifferentiation of the psychic structures is responsible for psychotic symptomatology. Libidinal and aggressive id derivatives continually invade ego functions and dominate the ego's adaptation in all areas. The influence of the primary process is evident in many spheres of ego functioning—thinking, feeling, and behavior. Such regressive phenomena can be seen in the primitive, pregenital manifestations of the instinctual drives, which are frequently reflected in a markedly ambivalent attitude toward objects. A lack of differentiation also affects the superego functioning. Some patients' superegos appear not to have attained a degree of depersonification characteristic of mature development. Archaic and regressive superego precursors have an alien quality and tend toward externalization and projection. Impulsive breakthroughs are accompanied by hypercritical and harsh reactions, disproportionate guilt, and depression.

A variety of regressed ego states characterize psychoses—such disordered states of consciousness as oceanic feelings, a sense of cosmic identity, and feelings of unreality, depersonalization, estrangement, and dissolution. These reflect the diffusion and blurring of ego boundaries. The psychotic is unable to see him or herself appropriately in reality; he or she tends to hold bizarre attitudes about social responsibilities and to depart from social amenities. Psychic and material reality is denied and alloplastically modified, replaced by a "new reality" built out of autistic productions. The outcome is an ego-syntonic adaptation, but it does not allow adequate functioning in the external environment. Disturbances in the ego's relationship with reality may also show up in such perceptual distortions as hallucinations and illusions. The individual may also experience unreality or depersonalization, marked body-image distortions, and feelings of estrangement.

See ANXIETY; DEFENSE; DIFFERENTIATION; EGO

DEFECT; REALITY; RESTITUTION; STRUCTURAL THEORY.

References
Arlow, J. (1970). The psychopathology of the psychoses. *IJP*, 51:159–160.
Beres, D. (1956). Ego deviation and the concept of schizophrenia. *PSOC*, 11:164–235.
Frosch, J. (1967). Delusional fixity, sense of conviction and the psychotic conflict. *IJP*, 48:475–495.
——— (1980). Neurosis and psychosis. In *The Course of Life*, ed. S. J. Greenspan & G. H. Pollock. Washington, D.C.: National Institute of Health, vol. 3, pp. 381–407.
——— (1983). *The Psychotic Process*. New York: Int. Univ. Press.
Hartmann, H. (1953). The metapsychology of schizophrenia. *PSOC*, 8:177–198.
Jacobson, E. (1954). Contribution to the metapsychology of psychotic identifications. *JAPA*, 2:239–262.
——— (1967). *Psychotic Conflict and Reality*. New York: Int. Univ. Press.

■ QUASI-INDEPENDENCE
See FAIRBAIRN'S THEORY.

■ RAPPORT
The state of conscious, harmonious accord, sympathy, and mutual responsiveness between two or more persons. Mesmer (1965) borrowed the word from the contemporary physics of his day. In his experiments people formed chains by touching each other, thus transmitting to one another the electrical current emanating from a machine. Mesmer used the term to describe "tuning in" to a patient with his "animal magnetism."

Janet (1924) extended the meaning to refer to the hypnotized patient, who became permanently suggestible to the influence of one person, the hypnotist. Freud (1905) called rapport the state in which the hypnotized patient excluded everything in the world save the hypnotist (p. 295). Sexual undercurrents were noted between hypnotist and patient. Freud (1914) thus described rapport as the prototype of transference (p. 12). He advised that a therapist wait to begin making communications to the patient "until an effective transference has been established . . . a proper rapport" (1913, p. 139). Knight (1972) described rapport as the optimal transference level at which productive work can be done.

See COUNTERTRANSFERENCE; TRANSFERENCE.

References
Ellenberg, H. F. (1970). *The Discovery of the Unconscious*. New York: Basic Books.
Freud, S. (1905). Psychical (or mental) treatment. *SE*, 7:283–302.
——— (1913). On beginning the treatment. *SE*, 12:123–144.
——— (1914). On the history of the psychoanalytic movement. *SE*, 14:7–66.
——— (1921). Group psychology and the analysis of the ego. *SE*, 18:69–143.
Janet, Dr. Pierre. (1924). *Principles of Psychotherapy*. New York: Macmillan.
Knight, Robert P. (1972). *Clinician and Therapist: Selected Papers of Robert P. Knight*, ed. Stuart C. Miller. New York: Basic Books.
Lowinger, J. (1976). *Ego Development*. San Francisco: Jossey-Bass.
Mesmer, Franz Anton. (1965). *The Nature of Hypnosis*, ed. Ronald E. Shor and Martin T. Orne. New York: Holt, Rinehart and Winston.

■ RAPPROCHEMENT SUBPHASE
See SEPARATION-INDIVIDUATION.

■ RATIONALIZATION
A process by which an individual employs subjectively "reasonable," conscious explanations to justify certain actions or attitudes, while unconsciously concealing other unacceptable motivations. Rationalization is always considered defensive, though it does not specifically refer to any of the mechanisms of defense. Several different types have been described, all of which have the same result: other possible causal factors—such as underlying instinctual drive gratifications and superego or ego ideal strivings—are ruled out as noncontributory or inappropriate and consciously dismissed. The conscious explanation is not questioned; indeed, it is often regarded as unquestionable. Rationalization reinforces repression. It differs from intellectualization, a form of isolation of affect in which potentially objectionable ideational content is permitted conscious awareness, albeit without emotional impact.

See DEFENSE; INTELLECTUALIZATION.

References
Fenichel, O. (1965). *The Psychoanalytic Theory of Neurosis*. New York: Norton.
Jones, E. (1908). Rationalisation in everyday life. *J. Abnorm. Psychol.*, 3:161–169.

■ REACTION FORMATION

See DEFENSE.

■ REACTIVE DEPRESSION

See DEPRESSIVE NEUROSES.

■ REALITY

A basic premise about the existence, essence, and human experience of the world. Psychoanalysts do not always agree about the nature of that premise. One viewpoint emphasizes the existence and the essential nature of the world; and reality is an absolute, fixed, and objective description of the external, material world and its events. It is a self-evident, given set of facts, and there is only one correct version. Another viewpoint emphasizes the human experience of that world and its events; reality is seen as a relative, mutable, and subjective description of that experience. It is an interpretation of perceptions, and multiple versions are possible. Most psychoanalytic theories encompass some aspects of both viewpoints. The resultant understandings of reality are intimately involved in psychoanalytic conceptualizing about human development, mental functioning, psychopathology, and psychoanalytic treatment.

Presumably, in the newly developing human organism, the concept of reality first enters the picture in the primitive distinctions between me and not-me, and between inside and outside. As development proceeds and moves through stages of greater self-differentiation and ego development, the awareness of reality as "outside" develops as the external component of this differentiating process. *Reality constancy* develops concomitantly with self and object constancy, evolving from the internalization and stabilization of environmental images. These include, but are not limited to, experiences with love objects. The resulting structure provides a stabilized internal representation of the outer world; it helps preserve the identity of the self and its orientation amidst alterations and changes in the environment without appreciable psychic disruption or adaptational dysfunction. Anticipation, predictability, perception, reality testing, and other ego functions are facilitated by reality constancy. Defects in reality constancy contribute to feelings of unreality, difficulty in experiencing new and experimental situations, and problems in preserving contact with reality. Object constancy both combats and facilitates regression according to the circumstances, thus contributing to ego autonomy and strength.
In this context, reality could be considered as the preexisting, natural world of concrete objects functioning in ways that can be objectively verified by scientific observations. From this viewpoint, *external reality* would correspond to the related terms *factual (material) reality* and *objective reality*.

Freud (1911) postulated two regulatory principles of mental functioning essential to understanding reality concepts. Earlier and more basic is the pleasure principle, under which all human behavior is aimed at the most immediate experience of pleasure and the avoidance of unpleasure through the uninhibited satisfaction of needs and wishes. Out of the frustrating failure to achieve immediate and constant pleasure and out of the growing knowledge of the cause-and-effect conditions of real life (as opposed to fantasied wish fulfillment), the pleasure principle is gradually modified so that the individual delays immediate, but uncertain, gratification in favor of long-range gratification and self-preservation. This is the *reality principle*. Although modes of acting in accord with the demands of outside reality gain hegemony as mental functioning matures, the motivating force of pleasure is not replaced—it is safeguarded, albeit in a delayed or dimished form. When a child postpones going out to play in order to do his or her homework first, or when a new father decides to give up his exciting but dangerous hobby of sky-diving and to forego the pleasure of an extramarital affair in order to preserve a good marriage and family life, these behaviors are governed by the reality principle. This is *reality-syntonic* behavior—these actions correspond to an understanding of cause and effect in the outside world of reality, including the world of human relationships. However, one may at any time disregard this view of reality in favor of immediate pleasure; this behavior may be a temporary regression or a conscious choice. Related to pleasure principle and reality principle are the corresponding terms *pleasure-ego* and *reality-ego*. Seldom used today, these terms have been used in different and contradictory ways to describe the relation of the ego and the ego instincts to the outside world.

Reality testing is that function of the ego which, at the most basic level, distinguishes thought from perception, thus allowing for the separation of inner and outer experience. That is, the individual is capable of knowing when a mental representation arises from an internal event, such as memory or fantasy, and when it arises from an event in the external world as perceived through the sense organs. Modern research, however, has shown that no such simple dichotomy exists. Sensory input may be influenced by inhibitions and distortions even before reaching the level of conscious perception. And memories and fantasies may be induced by external stimuli. Nevertheless, one can still think of reality testing as having to do with distinguishing inner experience from experience of the outer world. It functions to define ego boundaries and to clarify self and object differentiation.

A more complex function of reality testing is the constant attempt to reconcile discrepancies between inner and outer experience. When there are discrepancies, at times the inner representations (derived from memories, learned patterns, beliefs, and fantasies) will be altered by the new perceptions. For example, new experiences may alter the belief that all furry animals are friendly. At other times, the mental representations will prevail, and the individual will conclude that the perception is false, as, for example, when one corrects for an optical illusion. In the realm of human interactions, this function becomes infinitely complex, especially where beliefs and fantasies play a large part in forming the inner experience.

Reality testing has a developmental line of its own, beginning with the simple inner/outer, self/object distinctions and evolving into a complex process for evaluating experience. These higher levels of reality testing, sometimes called *reality processing,* include the capacity to perceive and evaluate one's own affects, motivations, and internal object representations; the ability to distinguish between past and present; and a more complex and subtle apprehension of the outer world of experience. It might include, for example, awareness of the effects that one's prejudices, character traits, and transference distortions have on relationships with other people. Psychoanalytic treatment can improve one's reality testing at this level.

Whereas the term reality testing implies a searching and comparing function that occurs mostly automatically and unconsciously, the related terms *sense of reality* and *feeling of reality* refer to the subjective awareness that what seems to be happening, both within and without, is real, not imaginary, and that it is consistent with what one knows of oneself and of the world.

Adaptation to reality refers to the individual's behavioral adjustments to and psychological acceptance of the changing demands of the external world, including those of human relationships.

The functions of reality testing, the sense or feeling of reality, and adaptation to reality together constitute the *relationship to reality,* which implies the capacity to apprehend both internal and external worlds of experience, to differentiate the two, and to maintain appropriate boundaries and reactions. Any or all three of these functions may become impaired, either regressing to more primitive levels or disappearing entirely, as the result of psychopathology, severe stress, sensory deprivation, or organic brain dysfunction due to drugs, toxicity, or disease.

Impairment in the adaptation to reality ranges from the minor lack of flexibility caused by a compulsive character structure to total lack of regard for the surroundings, found in the regressed psychotic or organic brain syndrome patients. Severe loss of reality-testing capacity, with resulting delusions, hallucinations, and loss of self-differentiation, occurs in the psychoses. In organic brain dysfunctions, disorientation is usually the prominent symptom of disordered reality testing; some hallucinatory and delusional symptoms also occur. Impairment at the higher levels of reality processing, along with less severe problems with adaptation to reality, are characteristic of the psychoneuroses and character pathologies. Disturbances in the feeling of reality and identity diffusion, without major loss of reality testing, occur occasionally in borderline patients. In contrast, schizophrenic patients experience protracted depersonalization, feelings of strangeness and doom, and body-image distortions.

Thus far, aspects of reality have been defined from the oversimplified viewpoint that reality is more or less synonymous with the external world. When we look at reality from the viewpoint of human experience, then we must take into account the reality of the inner world of subjective experience, as well as the possibility that more than one interpretation of the external world exists. The complexity of this viewpoint becomes evident in confronting such questions as, "Is an idea less real than a table, a poem less true than a scientific measurement?" and "Which has greater reality value—your memory of your sixth-year birthday party, or what can be observed by viewing movies made of that same birthday party?"

In common usage, *psychic reality* designates the individual's total subjective experiential world, including thoughts, feelings, and fantasies as well as perceptions of the external world, regardless of whether they accurately reflect the external world as viewed by another observer. Thus defined psychic reality is synonymous with the terms *inner reality* and *subjective reality*. These terms reflect the important psychoanalytic view that subjective experience is another kind of reality alongside the world of physical objects. Psychic reality is seen as one version of reality, personally constructed out of the interplay of perceptions, which originate from the outer world, and fantasies, which originate from the inner world. The resultant integration is the individual's subjective experiential world, his or her psychic reality. For example, it is the child's subjective experience of a traumatic event that is preserved in his or her memory of the event. This subjective experience and the resulting fantasies about the event, in this case, constitute a true memory, reflecting what the child actually experienced—even though the memory may be grossly distorted when compared to the "objective" facts as seen by a disinterested observer. Psychic reality, then, is not a fantasy that distorts an actual event but a true recollection of an experienced event that was, at the time, a mixture of perception and fantasy.

Some more exacting theorists, however, make a distinction between psychic reality and inner reality. In their view, psychic reality is equated with the inner source of subjective experience, that is, the unconscious fantasies, just as the sensations perceived from the external world are the outer source of subjective experience. These theorists retain the term *inner reality* for the total subjective experience, derived from the integration of fantasies and perceptions.

Just as inner reality is not a pure product of fantasy, *external reality* has its own complexities. One may postulate two kinds of external reality: one is made up of preexisting, scientifically verifiable objective facts; the other is an artificial reality of consensually validated or simply intersubjectively accepted values, institutions, myths, world views, and traditions of interpersonal and group behavior. Some theorists would extend this subjective component of external reality further and regard even the laws of science as a reality created by human beings, as a particularly useful way of organizing the data to give meaning to natural observations. This line of thinking is opposed by others, who regard it as a philosophical world view with no relevance to the psychoanalytic enterprise.

A few words about reality with regard to psychoanalytic treatment are in order. Behavior modification and some forms of supportive therapy focus primarily on improving the patient's adaptation to reality with no consideration of unconscious processes. Drug therapy and structured environments are aimed at restoring disrupted capacities for reality testing and feelings of reality. In contrast, psychoanalytic treatment takes as its field the higher levels of reality processing and psychic reality. It is a process that attempts to understand the analysand's subjective experiential world and how it came to be through the mutual contributions from perceived external reality and from unconscious wishes; to clarify the ways past inner realities persist and help distort present experience; and to expand the analysand's knowledge of and freedom within his or her own experiential world. Psychoanalysis does not attempt to impose a particular view of reality or a preconceived, "correct" adjustment to reality.

See EGO DEVELOPMENT; EGO FUNCTION; FANTASY; INDIVIDUATION; PLEASURE/UNPLEASURE PRINCIPLE.

References

Freud, S. (1911). Formulations on the two principles of mental functioning. *SE,* 12:218–226.

Frosch, J. (1966). A note on reality constancy. In *Psychoanalysis—A General Psychology,* ed. R. M. Loewenstein, L. M. Newman, M. Schur & A. J. Solnit. New York: Int. Univ. Press, pp. 349–372.

Hurvich, M. (1970). On the concept of reality testing. *IJP,* 51:299–312.

Panel (1985). Perspectives on the nature of psychic reality. R. Roughton, reporter. *JAPA,* 33:645–659.

Robbins, F. & Sadow, L. (1974). A developmental hypothesis of reality processing. *JAPA,* 22:344–363.

Wallerstein, R. Reality. *PMC.* Forthcoming.

(See also the classic writings on reality by Arlow, Freud, Frosch, Hartmann, and Loewald listed in the bibliography of this paper).

■ RECONSTRUCTION

□ Construction

A formulation about important early experiences in the life of the patient that have been forgotten (repressed). It represents an attempt to recover and correlate evidence of such experiences in order to deepen understanding of the genetic factors and dynamic forces that have contributed to character formation and psychopathology. It is based on memory traces of significant forgotten events gradually revealed in the patient's free associations, dreams, actions, and transference. The transference in particular provides convincing truth for such formulations.

Patients sometimes initiate reconstructive attempts by advancing hypotheses about the influence of events in their past, but more often the analyst selects an appropriate time to sum up his or her impressions about what happened and its effect on the patient. Reconstruction is a gradual process that often leads to the patient's further recall of repressed memories or other associations, supplying new data for understanding and interpretation. Freud noted that a sense of conviction about the truth of the reconstruction may have a therapeutic effect even when the patient fails to recall confirmatory memories. The attempt to formulate an important segment of the patient's past deepens both the patient's and the analyst's understanding of the analytic experience.

The work of reconstruction has been compared to the archaeologist's painstaking efforts to learn about earlier civilizations from fragments and traces found in the present. It is necessary to keep in mind, however, that psychoanalytic formulations are complex hypotheses that most likely do not exactly replicate earlier events. Theoretically, that would be impossible, and so the formulations are *constructions* (Freud's term) rather than reconstructions. This designation has gained popular usage in the United States.

In the early years of psychoanalytic treatment great emphasis was placed on the curative effect of the recovery of repressed memories. Psychoanalysis has since developed into a more complex process. Nevertheless, constructions are still an important part of psychoanalytic therapy, because repressed early experiences are often highly charged with emotional conflict. They exert a strong influence on the character and play a major role in the origin and perpetuation of psychopathology. Constructions, or reconstructions, thus lead to important new insights into the historical background of current behavior.

See ANALYSIS; CHARACTER; DEVELOPMENT; METAPSYCHOLOGY; INTERPRETATION; SCREEN MEMORY; SYMPTOM; REPRESSION.

References

Blum, H. P. (1980). The value of reconstruction in adult psychoanalysis. *IJP*, 61:39–52.

Davidoff-Hirsch, H. (1985). Oedipal and preoedipal phenomena. *JAPA*, 33:821–840.

Freud, S. (1937). Constructions in analysis. *SE*, 23:255–269.

Greenacre, P. (1975). On reconstruction. *JAPA*, 21:693–712.

Jacobs, T. J. (1986). Transference relationships, the relationships between transferences and reconstruction. In *Psychoanalysis, the Science of Mental Conflict*, ed. A. D. Richards & M. S. Willick. Hillsdale, N.J.: Analytic Press, pp. 301–320.

■ REGRESSION

A return to a more developmentally immature level of mental functioning. It usually occurs when a phase-appropriate mental organization is substantially disrupted. Regression is regarded as one of the mechanisms of defense. The concept is intimately related to the hypothesis that in the course of psychological development an individual passes through a series of phases, each with specific instinctual, ego, ego-ideal, and superego characteristics. These phases are inferred from (1) the nature of instinctual drive discharge, (2) the way ego functions operate, and (3) the manifest ideals and indications of conscience.

Regression is usually considered under two headings. *Libidinal regression* is a retreat to an earlier phase of instinctual organization that can occur in the course of normal development if the individual is unable to meet the challenge of a biologically determined maturational step. Unresolved conflicts and anxieties from earlier developmental phases may have left the mental apparatus with "areas of weakness" (fixations). These often determine the level to which the mental functioning regresses. Or the regression may occur in response to new events within a developmental phase that are experienced as psychologically traumatic. In childhood, when the development of the sexual drives is still fluid, such libidinal regressions are common. For example, a five-year-old under stress in connection with rivalry toward a younger sibling may resume thumb-sucking, a self-comforting activity he or she had previously relinquished. If heterosexual genital sexuality confronts an adult with anxiety and guilt feelings that cannot be mastered, he or she may defensively replace genital sexuality with some prephallic form in a perversion.

Ego regression is the return to modes of mental functioning typical of an earlier period from a more highly developed stage of mental organization. Ego regression often occurs together with libidinal regression and usually affects only the ego functions involved in conflict. It is expressed in the formal qualities of the fantasies accompanying the conflicted drive derivatives. Common examples from childhood include loss of bladder control or speech in response to stress—for example, when the child is called upon to recite and exhibitionistic fantasies are aroused. Superego regression may occur in a masochistic patient when internalized parental authorities are reexternalized and projected onto the analyst, who is perceived as sadistic in the transference.

The causes of regression are manifold. Some forms are normal in both childhood and adult life, occurring in response to a variety of needs that arise from internal and external pressures. As part of the forward and backward movement of development, regression permits reworking and subsequent reintegration at a higher level. In adults certain conditions may trigger a recurrence of archaic patterns of instinctual expression and behavior—these conditions include states of sleep and dreaming, religious and aesthetic experiences, love, and war. Regression is also an essential element of the psychoanalytic process, permitting the analysand to return to the developmentally immature phases of mental organization to rework unresolved conflicts within the transference. Regression may be precipitated by such unpleasant feelings as anxiety, guilt, depression, shame, frustration, or narcissistic mortification; or by physical illnesses, drug intoxication, fatigue, and so on. Pathological manifestations are to be found in the neuroses, psychoses, and perversions. The most common dynamic factor is probably the unresolved oedipus complex, with its associated castration anxiety, and guilt-provoking unconscious sexual and aggressive impulses.

See DEFENSE; DEVELOPMENT; TRAUMA.

References

Arlow, J. A. (1963). Conflict, regression and symptom formation. *IJP*, 44:12–22.

Freud, S. (1909). Notes upon a case of obsessional neurosis. *SE*, 10:153–318.

——— (1916). Introductory lectures on psychoanalysis. *SE*, 16:339–377.

——— (1917). On transformations of instinct as exemplified in anal erotism. *SE*, 17:125–133.

——— (1926). Inhibitions, symptoms, and anxiety. *SE*, 20:77–178.

Joseph, E. D. (1965). *Regressive Ego Phenomena in Psychoanalysis*. Monograph 1, Kris Study Group. New York: Int. Univ. Press, pp. 68–103.

Panel (1958). Technical aspects of regression during psychoanalysis. K. T. Calder, reporter. *JAPA*, 6:552–559.

■ REGULATORY PRINCIPLES

See PSYCHIC ENERGY.

■ REJECTED OBJECT

See FAIRBAIRN'S THEORY.

■ RELATIONSHIP THERAPY

See PSYCHOTHERAPY.

■ REPARATION

See KLEINIAN THEORY.

■ REPETITION COMPULSION

Clinically, the compulsion of certain individuals to repeat distressing, even painful, situations during the course of their lives without recognizing their own participation in bringing about such incidents or the relationship of current situations to past experiences. Patients tend to attribute the stressful episodes—which may develop unexpectedly and seem unrelated to the individual's personality or general behavior—to the operation of bad luck or destiny. Persons with such recurrent but usually similar life tragedies are said to be suffering from *fate neurosis* or from the operation of the repetition compulsion.

The repetition compulsion, in contrast to other psychological phenomena, including masochism, is relatively uninfluenced by the pleasure-unpleasure principle. This observation struck Sigmund Freud (1920) so forcibly that he gave his first published study of the repetition compulsion the title "Beyond the Pleasure Principle"; and he used this characteristic as a means of differentiating mental operations that are more primitive in a biological, evolutionary sense from those operations that are regulated by the pleasure-unpleasure principle.

Freud also used the repetition compulsion to develop his theory of the life and death instincts. He regarded the repetition compulsion as operating to promote the dominating function of the mental apparatus, that is, to bind tension and eliminate excitation. He viewed it as an expression of the nirvana principle, and thus as a derivative of the ultimate aim of the aggressive (death) instinct, the return to an inorganic state.

In Freud's first mention of the compulsion to repeat in a paper on technique (1914), he drew attention to the patient's repetition, in the relationship to the doctor, of behavior and attitudes characteristic of earlier experiences. Freud recognized that repetition in action is a way of remembering, substituting for verbal recollection of forgotten memories. He also saw that the transference itself is a repetition.

The repetition compulsion, however, is not confined to the treatment situation; it occurs in normal activities and relationships as well as in the neurotic situations described above. Among its other varied manifestations are the repetitions in children's play that serve to master the experience of loss—they are often also devoted to the active repetition of various passively experienced traumatic events. This issue is also of significance in the recurrent nightmares which follow traumatic events. Further manifestations include reenactment of childhood conflicts during psychoanalytic treatment and certain character disorders with a persistent need for self-defeating behavior.

Other psychoanalytic authors have added a broader perspective to the repetition compulsion phenomenon, relating it to the ego's function of mastery and regulation (restitutional and recreative repetition), redefining it as a variant of masochism, or identifying it as one manifestation of the biological drives responsible for the maturation of mental structure and functioning (drives that press for discharge despite the operation of the pleasure-unpleasure principle).

Repetition is characteristic of many phenomena and processes of life, biological and psychological, not all of which are determined by the repetition compulsion. It occurs in the motor and mental development of the child as part of the learning process, in attempts to avoid the new, in responses to the same stimuli when the result is pleasurable, and when intended actions have not been completed. In the psychological sphere Loewald (1971) distinguishes between relatively passive or automatic repetitions and active repeating. Infantile unconscious prototypical experiences are passively reproduced in neuroses, while revival of the infantile neurosis in analysis is an active recreation on a higher organizing level which makes resolution of conflict possible.

See ACTING OUT, INSTINCTUAL DRIVE, MASOCHISM, PLEASURE/UNPLEASURE PRINCIPLE, TRAUMATIC NEUROSIS.

References

Bibring, E. (1941). The conception of the repetition compulsion. *PQ,* 12:486–519.

Freud, S. (1914). Remembering, repeating and working-through. *SE,* 12:147–156.

——— (1920). Beyond the pleasure principle. *SE,* 18:7–64.

Loewald, H. W. (1971). Some considerations on repetition and repetition compulsion. *IJP* 52:59–65.

■ REPRESENTATION

A likeness or image that gives an impression of the original. A *psychic representation* is a more or less consistent reproduction within the mind of a perception of a meaningful thing or object. It may be subject to an increase or decrease in cathexis depending on the ebb and flow of dynamic forces. As such, it constitutes a substructure of the ego and is regarded as one of the ego's contents.

Presumably there are no psychic representations at birth, but with experience an awareness of differences between inner and outer, self and nonself begin to register. Memory traces of perceptions differentiating the self from the nonself are laid down, and with maturation and development, nuclei of these self and object representations are elaborated and may become available to consciousness. At first they are not stable, and the differentiation between self and object vanishes as satiation and sleep set in. When the baby awakens hungry and cries in distress, the early forms of self and object representation once more appear distinct and separate. Accordingly, the stage of the need-satisfying object designates the developmental period when differentiation of self and object representations takes place in relation to need. With further maturation, psychic representations become more complex and unique and are eventually continually cathected without regard to the state of need—the stage of object constancy. All aspects of the psychophysiological self find representation in the psychic representation of the self. Similarly, all aspects of objects, animate and inanimate, that are important to the individual find psychic representation as part of that person's *representational world,* an inner world of objects.

Ideational representation is the psychic representation providing the basis for thoughts or ideas. It is virtually synonymous with psychic representation. *Instinctual representation* refers to the presence in the self representation of aspects of the individual's drives (id); the ego itself and superego are also represented. Just as a person has an image in his or her mind of his or her talents, abilities, weaknesses, inhibitions, constraints, anxieties, moral and ethical standards, he or she also has an image of the nature of the drives, their intensity, pliability, displaceability, and readiness for taming or sublimatory transformation.

See BODY EGO; EGO; OBJECT; SELF.

References

Jacobson, E. (1964). *The Self and the Object World.* New York: Int. Univ. Press.

Sandler, J. & Rosenblatt, B. (1962). The concept of the representational world. *PSOC,* 17:128–145.

■ REPRESSION
□ Primal Repression
□ Repression Barrier
□ Repression Proper

A defensive process by which an idea is excluded from consciousness. The ideational content repressed carries potentially troublesome instinctual drive derivatives and their impulses. These threaten overexcitation, anxiety, or conflict, which bring painful affects. Originally, Freud postulated that repression was the unique pathological consequence of forgotten memories of actual childhood sexual experiences being reawakened by distressing adult sexual events. He soon expanded the concept, recognizing it as a ubiquitous psychological phenomenon. Early in the history of psychoanalysis *repression* was used as a generic designation equivalent to *defense*. Though repression still occupies an especially important place among the defenses, the earlier usage must be distinguished from the later limited meaning Freud gave it in 1926.

Primal (or *primary*) *repression* is that phase of the repressive phenomenon originating in childhood. (Repression occurring in adult traumatic neurosis may also be included.) Such primal repressions are attributed to the immaturity of the childhood mental apparatus. Primal repression is thought to be largely responsible for the "normal" amnesia of childhood.

Although associated with the earliest outbreaks of anxiety, primal repression is not a defense present in the first days or weeks of life. Freud explicitly stated that before the mental apparatus reaches the state of organization requisite to primal repression, instinctual impulses are fended off in other ways, such as reversal into the opposite or turning round upon the subject's own self. At first he thought the end of primal repression coincided with the acquisition of speech, but in 1926 he claimed it ended with the formation of the superego, an end point more consistent with the theory as a whole, clinical experience, and a variety of observable phenomena including the usual range of childhood amnesia.

In the topographic model a *repression barrier* was posited at the junction of the system Unconscious and system Preconscious, and in the structural model at the intersection of id and ego.

Freud described two processes as explaining primal repression. Certain early impressions and the force of the wishes they engender are "primarily repressed" because development of the secondary processes is deferred in childhood. He characterized this as a "passive lagging behind" subject to "fixation." The forces involved continue to exert an indirect, and at times profound, effect on mental life, but their ideational representatives, because of a lack of preconscious representation, are inaccessible to consciousness. The later fulfillment of these wishful impulses is unpleasant because of the discrepancies between the primary and secondary processes and, inferentially, because of the standards and prohibitions associated with the latter. Later, associatively related impulses are subject to the same repressive forces; hence primal repression is a necessary precondition for the defense known as *repression proper* (also called *secondary repression* or *subsequential repression*), which occurs in late childhood, adolescence, or adulthood.

In his 1926 reformulation of theories related to anxiety and defense, Freud explicitly defined a motive for primal repression—avoidance of the specific stimulus that would produce unpleasure. He added the new proposition that it was a response to painful overstimulation of the immature mental apparatus. Evidently Freud considered both the earlier and later formulations valid, and clinical experience confirms this assumption. In each, primal repression is thought to be maintained by countercathexes. Repression proper, however, is assumed also to involve eliminating the energy of involved preconscious ideation (that is decathexis), functionally removing the ideation.

Primal repression makes related emotionally charged ideas during late childhood, adolescence, and adulthood vulnerable to *repression proper*. This phenomenon occurs as the result of either later intrapsychic or environmental stimulation. Originally it was postulated that the earlier primal repressions attract later associated ideas, which are then subject to the childhood repressive forces. They also attract ideas resulting from the disharmony in adult mentation produced by conflict between drives and standards or prohibitions (a "push-pull" theory). According to his first anxiety theory, Freud assumed that the instincts associated with repressed ideation might later manifest themselves as anxiety. His subsequent theory conceived of repression proper as one possible defensive reaction against instinctual impulses that evoke signals of anxiety generated by a series of developmental threats.

The dynamic balance maintained in repression may be altered by changes in the drive force (for example, during puberty or aging), external stimuli corresponding to previously repressed ideas, or changes of the repressing organization, (the ego) caused by, for example, illness, sleep, or maturation. If the repressing forces give way, the *return of the repressed* may cause neurotic symptoms, parapraxes, and related dream content.

Successful repression means that the cathected idea persists outside of consciousness. A continual expenditure of countercathexis energy is required to maintain it there. Or the idea's energy might be diverted into another channel. Finally, repression may cause the mental organization to shift to earlier or more primitive phases of needs or organization (regression).

Repression was the first defense associated with the neuroses Freud (1895; 1896) described in the 1890s. It is still considered to apply in cases of hysteria. Repression is an important psychoanalytic concept outside the theory of defense as well, because of its intimate association with such issues as the theory and characterization of the unconscious, developmental theory, major and minor psychopathology, and increasingly sophisticated models of treatment which implicated removal of repressions as essential.

See ANXIETY; DEFENSE; FAIRBAIRN'S THEORY; HYSTERIA; PSYCHIC APPARATUS; REGRESSION; STRUCTURAL THEORY; TOPOGRAPHIC POINT OF VIEW.

References

Brenner, C. (1957). The nature and development of the concept of repression in Freud's writings. *PSOC,* 12:19–46.

Frank, A. & Muslin, H. (1967). The development of Freud's concept of primal repression. *PSOC,* 22:55–76.

Freud, S. (1895). Project for a scientific psychology, Appendix A: Freud's use of the concept of regression. *SE,* 1:350–51.

——— (1896). Draft K, January 1, 1896, Neuroses of defense (A Christmas fairytale). In Extracts from the Fliess papers (1892–99).

——— (1915). Repression. *SE,* 14:141–146.

——— (1926). Inhibitions, symptoms, and anxiety. *SE,* 20:77–178.

——— (1933). New introductory lectures on psychoanalysis. *SE,* 22:5–157.

Willick, M. Defense. *PMC.* Forthcoming.

■ RESISTANCE

A paradoxical phenomenon regularly encountered in the course of insight-oriented psychotherapy, particularly psychoanalysis. The patient, who has sought professional help to uncover neurotic problems, opposes the process in a variety of ways that would serve to defeat the objective of change. Resistance may take the form of attitudes, verbalizations, and actions that prevent awareness of a perception, idea, memory, feeling, or a complex of such elements that might establish a connection with earlier experiences or contribute insight into the nature of unconscious conflicts. Though often evidenced by an avoidance of free association, resistance in a broader sense encompasses all of a patient's defensive efforts to avoid self-knowledge. Usually unconscious at first, it may persist long after it is consciously recognized. It varies from large complex actions to the most circumscribed forms, "from falling asleep to brilliant argument" (Stone, 1973).

Resistance is pervasive in every analysis. It varies in form and intensity from patient to patient and in the same patient at different stages in the analysis. Resistance is a special instance of the ego's defensive efforts. Analysis threatens to bring into awareness (through free association) unacceptable childhood wishes, fantasies, and impulses that would produce painful affect; the ego defends against this possibility by opposing the analysis itself.

Resistance has played a central role in the development of psychoanalytic technique and theory. Initially, Freud considered resistance as simply an obstacle to be overcome by authority and persuasion. He thought of it as an automatic defense against remembering the dynamically forgotten (repressed) memories of traumatic events that had led to the formation of symptoms. When he discovered that resistance operated unconsciously, he recognized that its appearance, recognition, and interpretation are essential to the work of analysis. Analysis of the resistance and the transference then became the hallmark of psychoanalytic treatment. Further, Freud's recognition that resistances (defenses) operated unconsciously and could not be located in the systems Conscious or Preconscious made the topographic hypothesis untenable and led to his introduction of the tripartite structural model. He thought then that resistance stemmed primarily from the defensive efforts of the ego, but he also believed that the id provides its own resistance by continuing the operation of the repetition compulsion beyond when insight is first achieved. The superego too contributes its share of resistance, which emanates from a sense of guilt or need for punishment. This element of punishment serves to prevent the patient from achieving the success of recovery through analysis; it thus is the basis for a potential negative therapeutic reaction.

Of particular importance in the course of every analysis are the resistances that emerge in the sphere of the transference, that is, *transference resistance.* They may take the form of defenses against awareness of transference wishes, fantasies, and thoughts. Or, once in awareness, transference wishes and attitudes may become so intense as to interfere with the progress of the analysis. One set of transference wishes and attitudes may operate as a profound resistance against awareness of another, more threatening set. The transference itself may be thought of as a resistance, since the patient endeavors thereby to gratify his or her narcissistic, erotic, or aggressive wishes in the present rather than to remember their origins in past object relationships. Hence, acting out may be a major and very serious resistance.

Resistance in the analytic situation does not emanate exclusively from the patient; it may also reflect the state of the analytic dyad, which is profoundly affected by the analyst's style, personality, and countertransference problems. Technical misjudgments, such as inappropriate timing of transference interpretations, have been observed to contribute to resistance, particularly in the form of acting out.

Once the patient's unconscious conflicts have been uncovered and some insight obtained, resistance may lead to delay or even failure to progress, reflecting an unconsciously determined reluctance to give up inappropriate childhood wishes and their maladaptive, defensively distorted expressions in symptoms, character, or behavior. Moreover, the relief or mental equilibrium that the neurotic symptoms achieved for the individual is hard to give up. These many factors contributing to resistance make the process of working through an essential part of analytic work.

See CONFLICT; COUNTERTRANSFERENCE; DEFENSE; NEGATIVE THERAPEUTIC REACTION; STRUCTURAL THEORY; TOPOGRAPHIC POINT OF VIEW; WORKING THROUGH.

References

Dewald, P. (1982). Psychoanalytic perspectives on resistance. In *Resistance, Psychodynamics, and Behavioral Approaches*, ed. P. Wachtel. New York: Plenum Press, pp. 25–68.

Freud, S. (1926). Inhibitions, symptoms, and anxiety. *SE*, 20:77–175.

Laplanche, J. and Pontalis, J.-B. (1983). *The Language of Psychoanalysis*. London: Hogarth Press, pp. 394–397.

Rangell, L. (1983). Defense and resistance in psychoanalysis and life. *JAPA*, 31(suppl.):147–171.

Stone, L. (1973). On resistance to the psychoanalytic process. In *Psychoanalysis and Contemporary Science*, ed. B. B. Rubinstein. New York: Macmillan, vol. 2, pp. 42–73.

■ RESOMATIZATION

See SOMATIZATION

■ RESTITUTION

Refers to a hypothetical psychic process by which psychotic patients attempt to recapture reality after they have severed themselves from it. Restitution is indicated by such symptoms as delusions, hallucinations, language peculiarities, and catatonic mannerisms. It is the third of three major events Freud (1911) described in schizophrenia. He saw these events as results of the redeployment of object libido. The first is a break with reality as object libido is defensively decathected. The world and its objects no longer seem real. Second, hypochondriasis and delusions of grandeur occur as object libido is transformed into narcissistic libido. The third phase, restitution, is marked by a miscarried recathexis of object representations commensurate with the extent of the regression. It represents a desperate attempt to regain contact with the world. Currently, restitutive symptoms are viewed not only as a consequence of a defensive redeployment of libido but also as compromise formations expressing intersystemic conflicts. They are caused by a major disruption in ego functions, involving reality testing in particular as well as primitive defensive maneuvers.

See PSYCHOSIS; REALITY; SCHIZOPHRENIA.

References

Arlow, J. A. & Brenner, C. (1969). The psychopathology of the psychoses. *IJP*, 50:5–14.

Freud, S. (1911). Psychoanalytic notes on an autobiographical account of a case of paranoia. *SE*, 12:9–82.

______ (1915). The unconscious. *SE*, 14:166–215.

■ RETURN OF THE REPRESSED

See PSYCHONEUROSIS; REPRESSION.

■ REVERIE

See BION'S THEORY.

■ RITUAL

In psychoanalytic usage, a symptomatic, stereotyped, compulsive repetition of a behavior pattern. Each element in a ritual represents a compromise formation that expresses, in a disguised, distorted way, both unconscious sexual and aggressive drive derivatives and defensive forces. The various elements of a ritual symbolize one or more aspects of the unconscious conflict, often involving magical thinking. Rituals are frequently symptoms of the obsessive-compulsive neurosis; the defense mechanisms typical of that neurosis—reaction formation, undoing, isolation of affect, and intellectualization—are evident in the rituals. The underlying sexual and aggressive drive derivatives defended against by the use of rituals are usually related to anal and masturbatory conflicts. The ritual may symbolically undo a forbidden wish—for example, a handwashing ritual might undo a wish to smear feces.

Transient rituals are common and often developmentally appropriate, as exemplified by the repetitive games of childhood. They may become connected with almost any activity. In adults, repetitive behavior ranges from adaptive daily routines and prescribed religious ceremonies through neurotic obsessive-compulsive rituals to the magical rituals of psychotics. The psychoanalytic term *ritual* is usually used to refer to such behavior only when it is self-imposed as a defense. Rituals may or may not be ego-syntonic, but if they are interrupted, the anxiety and guilt break through, often requiring that the ritual be repeated again from the beginning. Rituals may also serve functions other than intrapsychic defense. For example, one may attempt to control other people by imposing the ritual on them. This both expresses aggression and defends against anxiety, guilt, and helplessness.

See COMPROMISE FORMATION; DEFENSE; OBSESSION.

References

Freud, S. (1909). Notes upon a case of obsessional neurosis. *SE*, 10:153–319.

Reik, T. (1919). *Ritual*. New York: Int. Univ. Press.

■ RIVALRY

The act or state of striving to gain an object in opposition to someone, and thereby to equal or excel that person. The competition is usually for access to or the love of the primary object or possession of the things or traits of another. The rivalry may be conscious or unconscious. Associated affects usually include antagonism toward the rival, affection and yearning for the object vied for, and anxiety regarding the outcome of the rivalry. Sometimes affection for the rival is evident as a reaction formation.

Rivalry in triadic relationships is part of the preoedipal experience. Typically, it emerges as *sibling rivalry,* in which one competes with a brother, sister, or sibling surrogate for the love of one or both parents. It also emerges in connection with mother's relationship to father. Transformed by oedipal conflict, rivalry becomes linked to jealousy. In *oedipal rivalry,* the child vies with one parent for the love of the other. Rivalry continues throughout development during latency, adolescence, and adulthood, and shows itself in familial and extrafamilial relationships side by side with the capacity to recognize and share the rights of others. Rivalry in adulthood can be intensified by the continuing influence of displaced childhood rivalry.

See ENVY; JEALOUSY.

References

Neubauer, P. B. (1982). Rivalry, envy, and jealousy. *PSOC,* 37:121–142.

■ SADISM

A perversion in which one individual derives sexual pleasure from inflicting pain and humiliation upon another. Freud (1905) recognized early that sadism and masochism are universal components of the sexual instinct and that both exist in all individuals; he related them to activity and passivity and the "instinct to mastery." Mild manifestations of both sadism and masochism are considered within normal limits in sexual foreplay. In the masochistic character both tendencies are present, though unconscious. Consciously tolerated violent physical abuse, torture, and rape, however, are characteristic only of perversions, usually in individuals with borderline or psychotic personalities. *Sadism* is sometimes confused with *aggression* and applied in circumstances where the sexual element is apparently absent or at least unconscious, as in the work of Melanie Klein and her followers.

At first Freud (1915) thought that sadism antedated masochism, which he viewed as sadism turned back on the self. When he advanced the hypothesis of a "death instinct" in 1920, however, Freud was able to assume a self-directed, destructive impulse (a primary masochism) that operated independently from birth, even in contradiction to the pleasure principle. This made sadism, rather than masochism, secondary. Freud attributed sadism to the deflection to outside objects of the destructive instinctual drive initially directed toward the self.

See AGGRESSION; COMPONENT INSTINCTS; MASOCHISM; SADOMASOCHISM (including references).

■ SADOMASOCHISM

The coexistence in the psyche of sadistic and masochistic wishes, fantasies, and drive derivatives. They may show themselves in character traits or in sexual behavior ranging from the relatively normal to the perverse. When physical pain is a requisite for the sexual relationship, sadism and masochism are considered perversions.

Freud expanded the concept beyond the sexual perversions. Conscious and unconscious sadomasochistic gratifications are involved in many different kinds of behavior: teasing, sarcasm, clowning, slander, and passive aggression of all kinds. *Moral masochism* refers to the need some people have to suffer or be punished out of an unconscious sense of guilt.

Sadism (and masochism) initially become evident between the sixth month and the end of the second year of life, during what has been called the *oral-sadistic stage* of psychosexual development. The painful pleasure of teething, combined with the new experience of discharging frustration and anger through biting, seems to inaugurate a lifelong oral association with certain modes of sadistic discharges. This oral sadism is expressed in actual biting in some regressed states or in sexual foreplay, and in verbal teasing and sarcasm. The quality and intensity of oral-sadistic residues depend on such constitutional factors as the time of teething, bone structure, and pain thresholds, combined with the nature and quality of the object relations and the adaptive defenses the infant employed to deal with psychic conflicts.

The *anal-sadistic stage,* which follows the oral stage, is the dominant organizer of sadomasochism. Anal erotism grows intense as sphincter control is achieved, and the fusion of aggressive and erotic satisfactions in the act of defecation becomes the paradigm for the discharge of sadistic wishes. Retention of the fecal mass to create a pleasurable and controllable internal pain represents a new masochistic choice. Again, constitutional factors combine with environmental inputs to determine the quality and intensity of fixations that will influence character development. The timing and nature of toilet training, the use of cathartics and enemas, and the administration of punishments all play determining roles; again, the defenses employed to deal with intrapsychic conflicts are the most decisive determinants.

Neither sadism nor masochism exists without the other, at least unconsciously. The sadist gains sadistic pleasure from hurting the object and vicarious masochistic pleasure from simultaneously identifying with the object. The sadist may also anticipate and provoke punishment for his or her sadistic pleasures. Similarly, the masochist punishes his or her tormentor by evoking guilt feelings. In sadomasochistic perversions the partners often take turns being sadist and masochist.

Both sadism and masochism are blends of pleasure and pain, of erotic and aggressive drive elements. The difference is that sadism is directed toward an object outside the self and masochism is directed at the self. In psychoanalytic theory sadism and masochism represent fusions of the libidinal and the aggressive drives. Freud postulated a primary masochism projected outside the self (becoming sadism) by an intrinsic propensity to project. Whatever the primary state, later manifestations of sadism and masochism result from such a complex series of internalizations and externalizations that the phenomena are inseparable.

See SADISM; MASOCHISM; PERVERSION; PSYCHOSEXUAL DEVELOPMENT.

References

Brenner, C. (1959). The masochistic character. *JAPA,* 7:197–226.

Chasseguet-Smirgel, J. (1978). Reflections on the connection between perversion and sadism. *IJP,* 59:27–35.

Freud, S. (1905). Three essays on the theory of sexuality. *SE,* 7:125–243.

——— (1915). Instincts and their vicissitudes. *SE,* 14:109–140.

——— (1919). "A child is being beaten." *SE,* 17:179–204.

——— (1920). Beyond the pleasure principle. *SE,* 18:3–64.

——— (1924). The economic problem of masochism. *SE,* 19:159–170.

■ SCHIZOID CHARACTER

A nosological designation for a broad group of shy, timid people who construct their lives and vocations so as to avoid social contacts. Their perception of others is contaminated by fantastic internal object representations that lead them to withdraw in fright under the threat of annihilation. The psychopathology appears to be due to the persistence of early infantile defenses against overwhelming frustration, which impedes interpersonal learning throughout development. The adjective *schizoid* refers to this defensive tendency to retreat from the complexity of interpersonal reality to the familiarity of a simplified inner world of objects.

The term *schizoid character* (or *schizoid personality*) was coined by Eugen Bleuler to describe the premorbid personality style of patients who ultimately developed schizophrenia. Melanie Klein elucidated some of the schizoid mechanisms: according to her theory, a split between good and bad internal objects (during what she called the schizoid paranoid position, which occurred in the first few months of life) serves to externalize the child's innate aggression while preserving good object experience. This is followed in the second half of the first year by the depressive position, in which objects are experienced as whole, with less ambivalence, and the former internal objects are integrated into the superego structure. Klein believed that schizoid mechanisms persist in the personality if the child fails to enter or to resolve the depressive position.

Fairbairn's view was that extreme frustration during early development leads to a psychic structure ill equipped to meet complex adult interactions. Patients so affected intensely long for loving objects, but their inner worlds are dominated by fierce attacks from split-off, hating objects, and actual interpersonal experience with others remains impoverished. Winnicott focused on the importance of the maternal "holding environment," which helps the child manage frustration and develop a safe inner world that can be relied on in human interactions. More recently, Kernberg included the schizoid personality in a larger group of patients who have problems with structuralized internal object relations. He termed these problems of borderline personality organization.

See BORDERLINE PERSONALITY DISORDER; FAIRBAIRN'S THEORY; KLEINIAN THEORY; WINNICOTT'S THEORY.

References

Fairbairn, W. R. D. (1954). *An Object Relations Theory of the Personality.* New York: Basic Books.

Guntrip, H. (1968). *Schizoid Phenomena, Object Relations, and the Self.* London: Hogarth Press.

Klein, M. (1952). Notes on some schizoid mechanisms. In *Developments in Psycho-Analysis,* ed. Joan Riviere. London: Hogarth Press, pp. 292–320.

Winnicott, D. W. (1960). Ego distortions in terms of true and false self. In *The Maturational Processes and the Facilitating Environment.* New York: Int. Univ. Press, 1965, pp. 140–152.

■ SCHIZOPARANOID POSITION

See KLEINIAN THEORY: Paranoid-Schizoid Position.

■ SCHIZOPHRENIA

A disorder (or group of related disorders) beginning before age forty-five, lasting at least six months, and characterized during acute phases of the illness by psychotic symptoms not due to organic mental disorder or affective disorder. These symptoms include delusions, hallucinations, and other disturbances of thought and perception involving serious distortions of reality.

During acute phases of the illness, schizophrenic patients regress to very primitive levels of intrapsychic and interpersonal functioning. Their conscious experience is dominated by primary process thought characterized by condensations, displacements, extensive use of symbols, and perceptual distortions. These phenomena result in the hallucinations, delusions, uncontrolled instinctual discharge, and other bizarre behavior typical of acute schizophrenia. Intrapsychically, self and object representations profoundly deteriorate, instinctual urges are no longer inhibited (primitive aggressive derivatives predominate), superego functioning regresses to frighteningly primitive and grossly unreliable levels, and there are major disturbances as well in most other intrapsychic functions, especially reality testing.

Between psychotic periods, the schizophrenic individual devotes mental resources to warding off primitive thoughts and instinctual derivatives and to dealing with fears associated with the threat of their reemergence. In general, such individuals avoid intimate relationships, where this threat is greatest, although certain intensely disturbed family relationships are often maintained. The patient often returns to considerably more mature and integrated functioning, although some primitive mental mechanisms remain active. Such defensive operations as primitive denial, projection, isolation, and splitting are characteristic of schizophrenic individuals' attempts to maintain inner controls and supportive social relationships while avoiding psychotic regression under stressful circumstances.

Psychoanalysts usually attribute schizophrenia to early development in families where parents suffer from profound psychopathology. However, there is no consensus about the cause of schizophrenia. Genetic as well as environmental factors are likely involved. Most analysts feel that schizophrenic patients benefit from psychotherapy based on psychoanalytic principles but containing elements of support and limitations on the regression that is expected to occur in psychoanalysis proper. Such psychotherapy is usually provided in conjunction with psychopharmacological treatment.

See PRIMARY PROCESS; PSYCHOSIS; REALITY.

References

American Psychiatric Association (1987). *DSM-III.* Washington, D.C.

Arlow, J. A. & Brenner, C. (1969). The psychopathology of the psychoses. *IJP,* 50:5–14.

Hartmann, H. (1953). Contribution to the metapsychology of schizophrenia. *PSOC,* 8:177–198.

Lidz, T., Fleck, S., & Cornelison, A. R. (1965). *Schizophrenia and the Family.* New York: Int. Univ. Press.

■ SCOPOPHILIA

An inherent drive to look and to derive pleasure from looking. The prefix is derived from the Greek root *scop,* "to look" (also in *telescope, microscope, otoscope*). *Scopophilia* is a translation of the German *Schaulust*. *Scoptophilia* is sometimes erroneously used instead of scopophilia. *Scopt* is the Greek root for jeering or ridiculing, and *scoptophilia* would refer to pleasure in derision, a meaning never intended.

Scopophilia is one of the paired component or partial instincts described by Freud (1905). It is considered the active component, the passive being exhibitionism, the wish to be looked at. In normative development, scopophilia and exhibitionism are thought to contribute to such sublimated personality traits as curiosity, learning ability, and creativity, but anxieties about such impulses can cause neurotic conflict and inhibitions. Fixations to component instincts, including the active and passive forms of cruelty, play a prominent part in psychoneuroses; the adult perversions of voyeurism and exhibitionism are based on them.

Pleasure is greatest in looking at the naked body, at genitals, or at sexual acts. *Voyeurism* most commonly refers to the perversion of sexual looking; in this perversion the desire to look at sexually stimulating scenes leads most often to masturbation rather than to participation in the sexual act with a partner.

Since active and passive wishes usually coexist, scopophilia may also include pleasure in being looked at. For this reason, Allen (1974) has proposed that *scopophobia*, a seldom used term meaning the fear of being looked at or of exhibiting, be applied to fear of looking in both the active and passive senses.

See COMPONENT INSTINCTS; EXHIBITIONISM; VOYEURISM.

References

Allen, D. W. (1974). *The Fear of Looking*. Charlottesville, Va.: Univ. Press of Virginia.

Freud, S. (1905). Three essays on the theory of sexuality. *SE*, 7:191–192.

Strachey, J. (1963). Obituary (Joan Riviere). *IJP*, 44:229.

■ SCREEN MEMORY

A purported recollection that conceals other memories and their associated affects or drives. The screening memory is often a rigidly fixed, seemingly innocuous recollection of an affectively charged, traumatic early childhood experience. It represents a compromise between denial and memory—a painful experience is screened or covered by the benign recall of something less significant.

Such memories can be "retrogressive" or "retroactive" (that is, what is recollected consciously preceded the hidden memory); "pushed ahead" or "displaced forward" (the concealed memory precedes the event recollected); or "contemporary" or "contiguous" with the concealed memory. Originally, screen memories were thought to be fragments of memory traces; subsequent experience has determined that they may be important elements of the "personal myth," a more integrated and comprehensive self-historical construction. Even as it conceals, however, the screen memory betrays the underlying secrets. It is an analyzable compromise in which the revealed content condenses or displaces the latent ideation, affects, or drives in a manner comparable to dreams or neurotic symptoms. At times a feeling-laden underlying content is represented by seemingly indifferent recollections. Or one explicitly traumatic memory may conceal another. Neither the subject's conviction that the memory is real nor external confirmation of its historical validity preclude a memory's screening function.

The difficulty in reconstructing the memory screened, and the intensity of its repression, may be related to the trauma's occurrence at an early, often preverbal stage of development. Sensory traumas at this stage are principally in the auditory and visual spheres, a fact hypothetically reflected in the visual intensity and luminosity of such memories (Greenacre, 1949).

The screening of memories should not be confused with their "telescoping." Telescoping refers to the representation of many similar, repeated, traumatic events as one equivalent traumatic happening. Such telescoping is the product of a mnemic rather than a defensive process.

See AMNESIA; DEFENSE; DENIAL; MEMORY.

References

Arlow, J. A. (1979). Metaphor and the psychoanalytic situation. *PQ*, 48:363–385.

Boesky, D. (1973). *Déjà raconté* as a screen defense. *PQ*, 42:491–525.

Freud, A. (1951). Observations on child development. *PSOC*, 6:18–30.

Freud, S. (1899). Screen memories. *SE*, 3:301–323.

——— (1901). Childhood memories and screen memories. *SE*, 6:43–52.

——— (1914). Remembering, repeating, and working-through. *SE*, 7:145–156.

Glover, E. (1929). The "screening" function of traumatic memories. *IJP*, 4:653–681.

Greenacre, P. (1949). A contribution to the study of screen memories. *PSOC*, 3/4:73.

■ SECTORS OF THE SELF

See SELF PSYCHOLOGY.

■ SELF

The total person of an individual in reality, including one's body and psychic organization; one's "own person" as contrasted with "other persons" or objects outside one's self. *Self* is a commonsense term used for the everyday concept; its usage in that sense embraces and overlaps more technical aspects included in the terms self-concept, self-image, self schemata, and identity. *Self schemata* are enduring cognitive structures that actively organize mental processes and code how one consciously and unconsciously perceives oneself; they range from realistic to distorted self views which the individual has had at different times. They are based on *self representations,* mental contents in the system ego that unconsciously, preconsciously, or consciously represent aspects of the bodily or mental self, including the drives and affects perceived in reaction to the person's own self and to the outer world. Together with object schemata, self schemata provide the organizing base and reference material for all adaptive and defensive functions. Various self schemata are hierarchically arranged into supraordinate forms and then into an overall self organization during maturation. The encoding of the self in a sensory mode of thinking is referred to as a *self-image,* which may be visual, auditory, or tactile; while the view one has of oneself at a particular time in a specific situation is called a *self-concept.* It consists complexly of one's body concept and the representation of one's inner state at the time. The mind constructs the self-concept from the direct experiences of sensations, emotions, and thoughts, and from indirect perceptions of the bodily and mental self as an object. A self-concept may be conscious or unconscious, realistic or unrealistic. It may mirror all the physical, emotional, and mental features of an individual in a relatively realistic way, or it may be unrealistic because of distortions resulting from the repression or displacement of unacceptable features and their substitution by fantasied ones in accordance with the individual's wishes and defensive needs.

Self-esteem is the end result of a process in which current self-appraisals are related to ideal self-concepts, ambitions for the self, and one's values, as well as to concepts of important others in personal or social hierarchies. This process of comparison is usually not fully conscious. Self-esteem is also usually not clearly conscious; it is noticed more when it is absent. When the value judgment is positive, the affective response is characterized by heightened confidence and expansiveness. Deflated self-esteem may be more keenly experienced as humiliation, but it may also operate unconsciously, influencing decision-making and mood.

The term *self* has been used in various ways in psychoanalysis. Freud often used *ego* to mean *self,* particularly before the structural hypothesis. In such concepts as an instinct turned against the self, *self* (or *ego*) was the opposite of *object.* Hartmann clarified the problem by separating ego as a group of functions from self. Narcissism then came to be regarded as the libidinal cathexis of the self rather than the ego. Jacobson used *self* to refer to the whole person, while conceiving of self representations as slowly built up intrapsychic structures. Schafer clarified three usages of *self:* the self as agent, the self as place, and the self as object. Kohut has defined *self* as an independent center of initiative. Others (Meissner, Lichtenberg, Stern) have used *the self* as a way to refer to experience, either as a sense of self or as the development of self in a world of subjectivity and interrelatedness. Whether regarded as a psychic structure or a subjective point of reference, *self* is a term more closely related to experience than id, ego, and superego.

See ANALYTICAL PSYCHOLOGY TERMS; IDENTITY; INTERNALIZATION; OBJECT; SELF PSYCHOLOGY.

References

Horowitz, M. J. (1979). *States of Mind,* 2d ed. New York: Plenum, 1987, chap. 3.

Kamyer, M. (1985). Identification and its vicissitudes. *IJP,* 66:19–30.

Lichtenberg, J. D. & Kaplan, S. (1983). *Reflections on Self Psychology.* Hillsdale, N.J.: Analytic Press.

Rangell, L. (1985). The object in psychoanalytic theory. *JAPA,* 33:301–335.

Spruiell, V. The self. *PMC.* Forthcoming.

■ SELF PSYCHOLOGY

An elaboration of the psychoanalytic concepts of narcissism and the self, developed by Heinz Kohut and his colleagues. Self psychology is characterized by emphasis on the vicissitudes of the structure of the self; the associated subjective, conscious, preconscious, and unconscious experience of selfhood; and the self in relation to its sustaining selfobjects. Self psychology recognizes as the most fundamental essence of human psychology the individual's needs to organize his or her psyche into a cohesive configuration, the self; and to establish self-sustaining relationships between this self and its surroundings, relationships that evoke, maintain, and strengthen structural coherence, energic vigor, and balanced harmony among the constituents of the self.

While the self is a superordinate concept in self psychology, organizing all of the individual's experience, the field of study of self psychology is coextensive with that of psychoanalysis. Vicarious introspection—that is, a sustained, empathic-introspective immersion into the patient's subjective world as reflected in the transference—is the primary means of data collection. A central tenet is the achievement of conceptual contiguity of self psychological constructs with other related sciences.

For the most part, self psychology employs the vocabulary of classical psychoanalysis, but some terms have been modified and others have been added. Terms related specifically to self psychology are presented in this section; some of them are also defined from the viewpoint of classical psychoanalysis elsewhere in this book.

In the course of the development of self psychology, libido and aggression came to be viewed in a significantly different way from that based on Freud's second dual instinct theory. Kohut originally employed the term *libido* in a classical fashion, using the economic metapsychological point of view. He defined libido as a positive investment of psychic energy and used qualifying adjectives to indicate the nature of the investment. Thus, *idealizing libido* invests a selfobject so that it becomes an *idealized selfobject,* and *grandiose-exhibitionistic libido* invests the self, which becomes the *grandiose self.* After publication of his book *Analysis of the Self* (1971), Kohut gradually discontinued use of metapsychology. Cathexis with *object libido* then became perception of the other as an independent center of initiative; and cathexis with *narcissistic libido* became perception of the other as part of the self or as someone serving the needs of the self.

In *Analysis of the Self* Kohut used libido to explain exhibitionism, narcissism, idealization, and object instinctual desires. When he subsequently discarded much of metapsychology and dropped the economic point of view, he presented the phenomena traditionally described in libidinal terms in what he regarded as more "experience near," descriptive language. He subsumed libidinal development as a whole under the umbrella of healthy self development, referring to it as the child's affectionate manifestations, requiring an experience of empathic reception from selfobjects preoedipally, during the oedipal period, and postoedipally. He believed children who manifested healthy affects or emotions had had such experiences of empathic reception from important selfobjects, and he claimed that optimal development involves persistence of sustaining selfobjects throughout adolescence and adult life. This is contrasted with the "gross sexuality" that result from experiences of less than optimal frustration by important selfobjects during the preoedipal and oedipal periods. Kohut thus saw blatant sexual drive expressions as the breakdown products of a fragmenting or endangered self, in reaction to unempathic responses; the drive manifestation is a sexualized search for self-repair. Kohut conceptualized perverse, addictive, and compulsive sexuality in adolescence and adulthood as resulting from "fragmentation" of the self or fragmentation anxiety secondary to selfobject failures.

In contrast to most classical analysts, Kohut discarded the primary drive nature of *aggression.* In his theory, nondestructive aggression is subsumed under the umbrella of a healthy self, and destructive aggression is viewed as reactive, but it is also a constituent of the healthy personality unless greatly exaggerated. These two types of aggression follow separate developmental lines. Normal aggression, alloyed with assertiveness, develops from experiences of optimal frustration, which teach one to do for oneself what had been done by others and gain initiative thereby. Hostile, destructive aggression, which results from experiences of less than optimal frustration that engender anger and the intent to harm the other, has a second developmental line. As development proceeds, the quality of this anger changes in a phase-appropriate manner, so that aggressive physical assault is replaced by verbal assault, and aggression subsides when the goal is reached. Inherent in this concept is Kohut's expectation that all development includes experiences of both optimal and less than optimal frustration. When the latter is excessive, however, the self is endangered, and episodes of gross and isolated anger emerge. Kohut characterized these episodes as breakdown products of the endangered or fragmenting self. The prototype for this "drive-as-breakdown product" is *narcissistic rage,* a reaction to narcissistic injury that suffuses the individual with unforgiving hatred, cruelty, and the need to hurt—in contrast to ordinary aggression, which is mobilized to eliminate an obstacle to a goal.

Following Hartmann, Kohut at first viewed *narcissism* as the cathectic investment of the self with libido. As he discovered major manifestations of archaic narcissism in selfobject types of transference, however, he came to view narcissism nonpejoratively. His theory postulates a line of development for narcissism distinct from that of object love, thus differing from Freud's developmental progression from archaic narcissism to mature object love. This distinction enabled Kohut to delineate mature forms or *transformations of narcissism,* such as wisdom, humor, and creativity.

Kohut reserves the term *oedipus complex* for the pathological configuration that results when a child who was developing normally experiences unempathic selfobject responses during the oedipal period. This situation is posited to occur when the parents are either sexually stimulated by the child's intensified affection or feel endangered by the child's increased assertiveness. In contrast, the *oedipal stage* is presumed to be a healthy, joyfully undertaken developmental step dominated by affectionate and prideful responses from the parental selfobjects. The *oedipal period* (or *oedipal phase*) merely refers to a neutral time-limited phase in the life of the child; it implies neither normal nor pathological development.

Guilty man and *tragic man* are terms Kohut uses to designate the directions human beings' aims may take; the terms epitomize the conflict formulations of classical psychoanalysis and the defect conceptualization of self psychology. The aims of guilty man are directed toward satisfying pleasure-seeking drives. His psyche is conceptualized in terms of the structural model of the mind; Kohut describes as a classic example superego conflict in regard to incestuous wishes. Tragic man, on the other hand, conforms to the conceptualizations of the psychology of the self; in expressing the pattern of his nuclear self, he aims toward fulfillment with endeavors that lie beyond the pleasure principle. As humanity's failures overshadow its successes, Kohut refers to this aspect of human endeavor as "tragic" rather than "self-expressive" or "creative."

An individual's failures are thought to be due to defects in the self, brought about not by conflict but by selfobject figures' nonempathic responses during childhood. To deal with such defects certain structures are built up in early life. *Defensive structures* function to cover over these defects so as to preserve, however damaged it may be, the core structure of the nuclear self. Some of these defensive structures, through developmental progression, may become assets in the mature personality. *Compensatory structures* more than merely cover the defect; undergoing their own development, they remedy the defects and functionally rehabilitate the self. A weakness in one sector of the self is often made up for by strengthening the other sectors, preserving hope that adequate selfobjects in the future may consolidate the weakened self. Compensatory structures and defensive structures lie at opposite ends of a spectrum; a variety of intermediate forms are usually assignable to one or the other category.

Another defensive process of importance in self psychology is *splitting*. Kohut identifies two types, horizontal and vertical. In the *vertical split,* percepts of internal or external reality are disavowed or denied. Grandiose fantasies may be conscious but disavowed to protect against the humiliation associated with the holding of what appear to the self as unacceptable, childish ambitions. The *horizontal split* is comparable to the repression barrier; it protects the self from conscious awareness of unacceptable selfobject needs and strivings. Painful fantasies and other unacceptable ideational material originating within the psyche are kept out of consciousness. Often a vertical split is recognized, interpreted, and worked through during the first phase of analysis, permitting work on the horizontal split during a second, later phase.

In analytic treatment, *empathy* is considered by the self psychology school to be the cardinal means of data collection and a primary therapeutic instrument. Empathy involves gaining access to another's psychological state by feeling oneself into the other's experience (compare Freud's use of *Einfühlung*). The analyst totally immerses him- or herself in the subjective world of the analysand, thereby more fully understanding that world. The analyst explains his or her insights at an appropriate time. Empathy is not to be confused with sympathy or kindness. It does not designate an affective attitude. Rather, it is a form of vicarious introspection. Though the concept as used in self psychology is similar to psychoanalytic understanding of the term, Kohut and his colleagues place a greater emphasis on its centrality to the analytic process. The reliability of empathy in obtaining psychoanalytic data depends on the analyst's training and experience in its controlled use, as well as on careful self-monitoring of potential countertransferential distortions.

Another vital occurrence in analyses of self disorders, according to Kohut, is the phenomenon of *transmuting internalization.* This is described as a process of effective internalization, initiated by the analyst's optimal, nontraumatic frustration of the patient. It leads to structure formation whereby the self is able to execute vital selfobject functions in the absence of experiences with the selfobject. The process effects a translocation of the function from the person of the selfobject to the subject alone. Kohut stresses four attributes that differentiate his concept from Hartmann's concept of internalization: (1) the internalization is effective; (2) the patient is ready for the internalization; (3) it is the result of an optimal, rather than a sudden or overwhelming, frustration of selfobject needs; and (4) its connection with the selfobject is depersonalized. Alternatively, the selfobject had not been fully personalized to begin with, since it is often experienced as part of the self rather than as a separate center of intentionality or initiative. Hence, the selfobject functions internalized are not linked to an identifiable object or given a definitive object tag as happens in introjection and identification. Instead, the function becomes a "seamless" addition to the self structure.

□ The Self

A depth-psychological concept referring to the nuclear core of the personality. It is thought to be made up of various constituents that emerge into a coherent and enduring configuration through the interplay of inherited factors and environmental influences. The effects of such interaction are processed within the individual in the course of experiences with his or her early selfobjects, and the enduring unity of the self develops in the lawful, gradual manner of a psychological structure. The self is the center of initiative, the recipient of impressions, and the depository of the individual's constellation of nuclear ambitions, ideals, talents, and skills. These motivate and permit the self to function as a self-propelling, self-directed, self-aware, and self-sustaining unit, providing a central purpose to the personality and yielding a sense of meaning to the person's life. The patterns of ambitions, skills, and standards, the tension among them, the program of action they create, and the resultant activities that shape the individual's life are all experienced as continuous in space and time, and they give the person a sense of selfhood—a sense that he or she is an independent center of initiative and of impressions.

Constituents or *sectors of the self* are: (1) the pole from which emanate basic strivings for power and recognition (*the pole of goals and ambitions*); (2) the pole that maintains the guiding ideals (*the pole of ideals and standards*); and (3) the *arc of tension* between the two poles that activates the basic talents and skills. The healthy self has a sectorial functional continuum from one pole to the other. Kohut used the term *bipolar self* to emphasize the structure derived from the two poles and to distinguish this concept from other descriptions of the self in the literature.

Since the self has different attributes depending on its level of development and/or its structural state, various *self types* have been described:

The *virtual self* refers to the image of the neonate's self as it resides in the parent's mind. Parents shape the self-to-be of the infant, since the virtual self determines how a particular parent addresses the neonate's as yet unformed self potential.

The *nuclear self* may be defined as the nascent organization first emerging as a cohesive structure during the second year of life.

The *cohesive self* is the relatively coherent structure of the normally and healthily functioning self.

The *grandiose self* describes the normal, early infantile, exhibitionistic self, which is dominated by the blissful experience of being the omnipotent center of all existence.

In addition, several pathological conditions of the self, or *self states,* have been described:

The *archaic self* is a pathological condition said to exist when the nuclear self configuration of early childhood, normal at that stage, exists in an adult.

The *fragmenting self* designates a chronic or recurrent state of the self characterized by diminished coherence. The fragmenting results from faulty selfobject responses or other regression-promoting conditions. Fragmentation anxiety ranges from mild nervousness (a signal) to overwhelming panic, which heralds a near total loss of self structure.

The *empty self* describes the loss of vigor and general experience of depletion depression. It results from failure of the selfobject to respond joyfully to the self's existence and assertiveness.

The *overburdened self* is deficient in its capacity to soothe itself because it has no opportunity to merge with a calm omnipotent selfobject.

The *overstimulated self* is prone to recurrent experiences of excessive emotionality or excitement as a result of unempathically excessive or phase-inappropriate early selfobject responses.

The *imbalanced self* maintains its precarious cohesion by overemphasizing one of the major constituents of the self at the expense of the other two. If the self lacks appropriate guidance from a weak pole of values, it suffers psychopathically heightened ambition. Another self is guilt-ridden and overly constrained due to an excessively strong pole of values. A third imbalance is characterized by two relatively weak poles and an excessive emphasis on the tension arc between them. This self is estranged from both restraining ideals and personal goals, leaving the individual vulnerable to environmental pressures. An example is the technical specialist who is dedicated to the perfection of competence without normal regard for issues of personal ambition or ethical values. Severity of this imbalance varies from the more or less normal "organization man" to the near-psychotic Adolf Eichmann.

Both normal and pathological structures of the self are related to the internalization of interactions between the self and selfobjects. The *selfobject* is one's subjective experience of another person who provides a sustaining function to the self within a relationship, evoking and maintaining the self and the experience of selfhood by his or her presence or activity. Though the term is loosely applied to the participating persons (objects), it is primarily useful in describing the intrapsychic experience of various types of relationships between the self and other objects. It also refers to one's experience of imagos needed for the sustenance of the self. Selfobject relationships are described in terms of the self-sustaining function performed by the other or the period during which the function was meaningful.

Infantile selfobject experiences normally sustain the self during early infancy. They are merging experiences involving cognitive indistinctness between self and selfobject. The selfobject is not experienced as having a separate center of initiative or intentionality.

Archaic selfobjects pertain to a pathological need for functions normally provided by selfobjects in infancy. This need is pathological if it persists into or is revived during adulthood.

Mirroring selfobjects sustain the self of wishful fantasies by accepting and confirming the grandness, goodness, and wholeness of the self.

Idealizable (or *idealized*) *selfobjects* provide the experience of merger with the calm, power, wisdom, and goodness of idealized persons.

Alter-ego selfobjects offer the sustaining experience of perceiving another as similar to oneself in some essential aspect.

Adversarial selfobjects provide the experience of being a center of initiative by permitting nondestructive, oppositional self-assertiveness.

□ Self Disorders

Also called selfobject disorders, these occur when the self has failed to achieve cohesion, vigor, or harmony, or when these qualities are lost after they had become established tentatively. The major diagnostic categories listed below always imply impairment of the self's structural integrity and strength secondary to the experience of faulty selfobject responsiveness.

Psychosis is characterized by serious, permanent or protracted damage to the self. No effective defensive structures cover the defect. An inherent etiological defect is generally postulated as underlying serious selfobject failures. The condition is not ordinarily considered analyzable.

Borderline states also involve serious, permanent or protracted damage to the self, but complex defenses protect the self from decompensation or fragmentation. Borderline states are usually not analyzable except under special circumstances, for example, when iatrogenic factors can be eliminated, or when an unusually facilitative selfobject transference is present.

Narcissistic behavior disorders demonstrate temporary damage to the self that is remediable through appropriate psychoanalytic treatment. Symptoms express an alloplastic attempt to force the environment to yield soothing or idealized perceptions of restored functioning. They include addiction, perversion, and delinquency.

Narcissistic personality disorders also exhibit temporary damage to the self that is responsive to appropriate psychoanalytic treatment. Symptoms express tensions associated with the damage to the self or related to autoplastic attempts to restore selfobject functioning. They include hypochondria, depression, and hypersensitivity.

Depression is subdivided into three types by Kohut. (1) *Preverbal depression* is related to primordial trauma and is characterized by apathy, a sense of deadness, and diffuse rage. (2) *Empty depression* is accompanied by depletion of self-esteem and vitality as a consequence of inadequate mirroring and lack of idealized selfobject responses. (3) *Guilty depression* is marked by unrealistically heightened self-blame and self-rejection related to lack of selfobject experiences with a calming, idealizable person. Persons with this type of depression did not have sufficient merger experiences with an idealizable selfobject.

□ Selfobject Transference

The displacement onto the analyst of the analysand's need for a responsive selfobject matrix. This term has replaced the term *narcissistic transference*. The displacement is derived in part from remobilized and regressively altered editions of archaic selfobject needs; in part from current age- and phase-appropriate selfobject needs; and in part from selfobject needs mobilized in response to the analyst and the analytic situation. Selfobject transferences become apparent in the patient's demands on the analyst, whether direct or implied, or through defenses against the expression of these demands. In this respect they are similar to the classical transferences and should likewise be handled by interpretation (or explanation). They differ from the classical transferences in the timing of interpretations and in the fact that the self-psychological definitions include current age- and phase-appropriate strivings. Currently, three major selfobject transferences, with one subclass (the merger type), are delineated. Each expresses different needs and connotes a separate line of selfobject development:

Mirror transference was originally a generic term that included the merger transference, alter-ego transference, and mirror transference proper—in contradistinction to the idealizing transference. The generic grouping is now outdated, and what was once called the *mirror transference proper* is now meant when the term *mirror transference* is used. Mirror transference refers to the reestablishment within the analysis of an early need for acceptance, approval, and confirmation of the self by the selfobject matrix to strengthen the damaged pole of ambitions. It is manifested by demands on the analyst (or defenses against such demands) for recognition, admiration, affirmation, or praise.

Idealizing transference exists when the need for idealization, or merger with a calm, strong, wise, and good selfobject, is reestablished in an effort to strengthen the damaged pole of ideals. It may show up as more or less disguised admiration for the analyst and his or her character and values, or as defenses against this tendency, for example, prolonged and hostile criticism of the analyst. Until Kohut made an effort to discard metapsychology in his theorizing, he described this transference as a manifestation of idealizing libido.

Alter-ego or *twinship transference* occurs when an early, reassuring latency or prelatency experience is reestablished. It represents the need to see and understand, as well as to be seen and understood by, someone like oneself. It is expressed in analysis by the patient's manifest wish to be like the analyst in appearance, manner, outlook, and opinion. The essential alikeness and sense of empathic connectedness augment and strengthen the damaged intermediate area of skills and talents and provide a strong feeling of hope for the future. The alter-ego relationship may be associated with the fantasy of an imaginary playmate in early development and may play an important role in the acquisition of skills and competence. Kohut initially classified the alter-ego transference as a subcategory of mirror transference, but later he established it as a separate type.

Merger transference, a subcategory, represents the reestablishment of an archaic identity with the selfobject of childhood through an extension of the self to include the analyst. The analyst is not perceived as having a separate center of initiative; he or she functions under the patient's control—that is, as an integral part of the self. The patient expects the analyst to be completely attuned to his or her needs and thoughts—to know them without being told. A merger transference may be an aspect of any of the three major selfobject transferences; thus, a patient may experience a twinship merger transference, an idealizing merger transference, or a mirroring merger transference.

Transference of creativity is a special category Kohut used to describe the transient need of certain creative personalities for merger with a selfobject while engaged in a taxing creative effort. An example might be Freud's need for Fliess during the writing of *The Interpretation of Dreams.*

See AGGRESSION; EMPATHY; INSTINCTUAL DRIVE; INTERNALIZATION; LIBIDO; NARCISSISM; OBJECT; SELF; TRANSFERENCE.

References

Basch, M. F. (1976). The concept of affect. *JAPA,* 24:759–777.

——— (1981). Selfobject disorders and psychoanalytic theory. *JAPA,* 29:337–351.

——— (1983). Empathic understanding. *JAPA,* 31:101–126.

Goldberg, A., ed. (1978). *The Psychology of the Self.* New York: Int. Univ. Press.

——— (1983). Self psychology and alternate perspectives on internalization. In *Reflections on Self Psychology,* ed. J. Lichtenberg & S. Kaplan. Hillsdale, N.J.: Analytic Press, pp. 297–312.

Kohut, H. (1971). *The Analysis of the Self.* New York: Int. Univ. Press.

——— (1977). *The Restoration of the Self.* New York: Int. Univ. Press.

——— (1978). *The Search for the Self,* ed. P. Ornstein. New York: Int. Univ. Press.

——— (1984). *How Does Analysis Cure?* ed. A. Goldberg & P. Stepansky. Chicago: Univ. Chicago Press.

Kohut, H. & Wolf, E. S. (1978). The disorders of the self and their treatment. *IJP,* 59:413–425.

Shane, M. & Shane, E. (1982). Psychoanalytic theories of aggression. *Psychoanal. Inquiry,* 2:264–281.

——— (1985). Change and integration in psychoanalytic developmental theory. In *New Ideas in Psychoanalysis,* ed. C. F. Settlage & R. Brockbank. Hillsdale, N.J.: Analytic Press, pp. 69–82.

Stolorow, R. (1984). Self psychology—a structural psychology. In *Reflections on Self Psychology,* ed. J. Lichtenberg & S. Kaplan. Hillsdale, N.J.: Analytic Press, pp. 287–296.
Tolpin, M. & Kohut, H. (1980). The disorders of the self. In *The Course of Life,* ed. S. Greenspan & G. Pollock. Washington, D.C.: U.S. Dept. Health and Human Services, pp. 425–442.
Wolf, E. S. (1976). Ambience and abstinence. *Annu. Psychoanal.* 4:101–115.
——— (1980). On the developmental line of selfobject relations. In *Advances in Self Psychology,* ed. A. Goldberg. New York: Int. Univ. Press, pp. 117–130.
——— (1983). Empathy and countertransference. In *The Future of Psychoanalysis,* ed. A. Goldberg. New York: Int. Univ. Press, pp. 309–326.
——— (1984a). Disruptions in the psychoanalytic treatment of disorders of the self. In *Kohut's Legacy,* ed. P. Stepansky & A. Goldberg. Hillsdale, N.J.: Analytic Press, 1984, pp. 143–156.
——— (1984b). Selfobject relations disorders. In *Character Pathology,* ed. M. Zales. New York: Bruner/Mazel.

■ SELF STATES
See SELF PSYCHOLOGY.

■ SELF TYPES
See SELF PSYCHOLOGY.

■ SELFOBJECT
See SELF PSYCHOLOGY.

■ SELFOBJECT DISORDERS
See SELF PSYCHOLOGY.

■ SELFOBJECT TRANSFERENCE
See SELF PSYCHOLOGY.

■ SEPARATION
The physical act of withdrawing from or parting company with an object. In psychoanalytic usage, separation also refers to one of the intrapsychic processes involved in separation-individuation, specifically those whereby the individual gains a sense of the self as a distinct entity functioning separately from the object. This ability is an essential part of human growth and development. The capacity to tolerate separation is one indicator of that developmental achievement. Untimely, sudden, or abrupt separation of the developing child from the nurturing object can be traumatic and can contribute to deviant development and undesirable adaptations, such as prolonged mourning, and future psychopathology. Such traumatic ruptures can be due to either physical or emotional unavailability of the object.

See DEPRESSION; MOURNING; OBJECT; SEPARATION-INDIVIDUATION.

References
Bowlby, J. (1980). *Attachment and Loss,* vol. 3. New York: Basic Books.
Freud, S. (1917). Mourning and melancholia. *SE,* 14:243–258.
Mahler, M. S. & Furer, M. (1968). *On Human Symbiosis and the Vicissitudes of Individuation.* New York: Int. Univ. Press.

■ SEPARATION-INDIVIDUATION
Mahler's term referring to two complementary processes in the slowly unfolding intrapsychic stages and the psychological birth of the human infant. The term applies to a developmental theory, to a process, and to a complex stage of development. Before the separation-individuation phase are its important "forerunners.": In the *normal autistic phase,* from birth to ten or twelve weeks, in comparison to later phases the neonate is relatively unresponsive to external stimuli. The *normal symbiotic phase,* from about six weeks to the end of the first year, emphasizes the establishment of a specific affective attachment between infant and mother.

The name *mother–infant symbiosis* arose from an inference based on the infant's behavior that suggests he or she experiences the mother and him- or herself as a "dual unity" (Mahler & Gosliner, 1955). There is little affective differentiation between self and object; the mother is perceived as a need-satisfying quasi-extension of his or her own self. As frustration and gratification alternate, the infant gradually becomes aware of "something out there" (outside of the symbiotic dual unit) and develops an increasingly stable image of the mother. The symbiotic relationship with her is manifested by the specific smiling response to the mother. Her conscious and especially her unconscious attitudes toward the child form an important basis for the child's concepts of him- or herself and of the object world.

The onset of the *separation-individuation* phase (which lasts until about twenty-four months) occurs at the height of the symbiosis at about five to six months. *Separation* refers to those intrapsychic processes through which the child emerges from the symbiotic dual unity with the mother. It includes the development of object relationships, with the formation of a mental representation of the mother separate from the self. *Individuation* refers to those processes by which the child distinguishes his or her own individual characteristics, so that the self becomes differentiated from the object and is represented intrapsychically as a series of self representations. Mahler divided separation-individuation into four subphases:

1. *Differentiation,* from five to six months to about ten months, wherein the infant progressively shows greater interest in and awareness of the world and behaves as if he or she is "hatching" out of the symbiotic unity.

2. *Practicing,* from about ten to fifteen months, during which the infant tests and practices emergent cognitive and motor skills and becomes accustomed to the experience of physical separation and its psychological consequences; however, he or she needs the availability of the mother for *emotional refueling,* especially when he or she is tired. The mood of this subphase is elation. The toddler is at the height of belief in his or her own omnipotence, which is to a considerable degree accompanied by a belief in maternal omnipotence.

3. *Rapprochement,* from about sixteen to twenty-four months, is the process and phase during which the child must resolve the intrapsychic crisis between the wish to remain with the mother (in symbiotic union) and the wish for autonomy that accompanies the awareness of the self as a separate individual. Cognitive progress makes the toddler painfully aware of his or her separateness from the mother, and the fact that he or she cannot control her. The child now takes active steps to seek out the mother and uses coercive behavior in efforts to control her. Separation anxiety surfaces again, and the toddler, now aware that he or she is not omnipotent, loses self-esteem and the belief in the shared omnipotence characteristic of the practicing subphases. Conflicts derived from anal and early oedipal psychosexual phases compound the difficulties between mother and child during this subphase. Pervasive ambivalence and ambitendency only slowly give way to calm as the child develops a more realistic sense of self and belief in his or her own autonomy.

4. *On the way to object constancy,* twenty-four to thirty-six months, the child is concerned with the quality and function of the mental representation of the mother. Libidinal object constancy implies that the loving quality of the mental representation of the mother produces in the child nearly the same sense of security and comfort as does the mother's actual presence. The intrapsychic representation of the mother receives positive cathexis even when the child is angry at the mother or separated from her for a reasonable time.

As no memory or mental representation can fully substitute for the reality of the love of the object, "on the way to object constancy" is an open-ended, lifelong process which may never be fully completed.

See OBJECT CONSTANCY; SEPARATION; SYMBIOSIS.

References

Mahler, M. S. (1968). *On Human Symbiosis and the Vicissitudes of Individuation,* New York: Int. Univ. Press.

Mahler, M. S. and Gosliner, B. J. (1955). On symbiotic child psychosis. *PSOC,* 10:195–212.

Mahler, M. S., Pine, F. & Bergman, A. (1975). *The Psychological Birth of the Human Infant.* New York: Basic Books.

■ SEXUAL DEVIATION

See PERVERSION.

■ SEXUAL IDENTITY

See GENDER IDENTITY.

■ SHADOW

See ANALYTICAL PSYCHOLOGY TERMS.

■ SHAME

Refers to a broad spectrum of painful affects—embarrassment, humiliation, mortification, and disgrace—that accompany the feeling of being rejected, ridiculed, exposed, or of losing the respect of others. Early experiences of being seen, looked at, exposed, and scorned are significant in producing shame.

Shame resembles anxiety in that it is an affective signal, warning of exhibitionistic wishes and anticipating rejection by the external world or by the superego if the wishes are gratified. Shame also represents a defense against exhibitionistic wishes, based on the anticipation of rejection for improper behavior. It may then become a character trait that protects against any disgraceful exposure in order to maintain self-respect. It encompasses discretion, tact, and sexual modesty. In this sense shame preserves ideals and values that are specific not only for the individual but also for the culture.

One may experience shame for exposing something in particular or for the *act* of exposing. One may fear being rejected or may fear being seen as flawed, failing, weak, dirty, defective, ridiculous, or disgraceful. Or one may become generally afraid of all *actions* of looking and being looked at, listening or being heard. All such means of exposure, even curiosity itself, then become shame-laden and have to be warded off.

One way of understanding shame (Wurmser, 1981) is to conceptualize an outer or object pole, in front of whom one feels ashamed, and an inner or self-related pole, about which one feels ashamed. During development, both poles become internalized and form a part of the ego ideal. The tension between them is then felt as a sharp discrepancy between what one expects oneself to be and how one perceives oneself.

Important ways of defending against shame affects include turning the feelings against others—showing up others as contemptible and ridiculous instead of oneself—and using such affects as defiance, rage, and scorn. Attitudes of haughtiness, arrogance, and withdrawal are reaction formations against shame. The inner sense of shame may be externalized, mostly by inviting degradation from the outside instead of suffering shame from within. Or shame may be projected, as in ideas of reference—delusions of being watched, spied upon, or controlled. *Shamelessness* is a defense against shame rather than its absence. Unconscious shame may show up in a negative therapeutic reaction in which every success has to be "paid for" by preemptive self-disparagement, provoked humiliation, and failure.

The affect of shame apparently does not require vision for its development; other forms of perception and expression suffice for its presence in persons born blind. It has been postulated that precursors of shame anxiety are the early patterns of gaze aversion and later stranger anxiety. Shame emerges during the rapprochement phase. Its basic implications of weakness, dirtiness, and defectiveness relate to the child's conflicts at that stage in regard to breaking free from the symbiotic bond, submitting to or defying toilet training, and fantasies that the penis is missing or may be taken away.

See AFFECTS; DEFENSE; EGO IDEAL; NEGATIVE THERAPEUTIC REACTION; SUPEREGO.

References

Anthony, E. J. (1981). Shame, guilt, and the feminine self in psychoanalysis. In *Object and Self,* ed. S. Tuttman, C. Kaye & M. Zimmerman. New York: Int. Univ. Press, pp. 191–234.

Lewis, H. B. (1971). *Shame and Guilt in Neurosis.* New York: Int. Univ. Press.

Lynd, H. M. (1961). *On Shame and the Search for Identity.* New York: Science Editions.

Piers, G. & Singer, M. B. (1953). *Shame and Guilt.* New York: Norton.

Wurmser, L. (1981). *The Mask of Shame.* Baltimore: Johns Hopkins Univ. Press.

■ SIGN

See SYMBOL; SYMPTOM.

■ SIGNAL ANXIETY

See ANXIETY.

■ SMILING RESPONSE

A specific affective response of the infant which emerges between two and three months. Spitz (1959) used it to denote the first stage in object relations and ego development. In contrast to endogenous smiling, present from birth, the smiling response, or social smile, is a response to external stimulation. It represents a shift toward exogenous functioning, social interaction, and active intentional behavior. In the beginning, this affective response is evoked by the perception of any human face—specifically, a Gestalt with the configuration of two eyes, nose, and forehead in motion (Spitz and Wolf, 1946).

Spitz emphasizes that in the beginning the smiling response is not indicative of an object relationship; rather, it is a time-limited step on the way to recognizing an individual human face and relating to a true libidinal object. The smiling response indicated to Spitz that ego organization had begun and that the infant was now capable of some internal regulation.

The mother quickly becomes the most reliable elicitor of the smiling response if mother and infant are affectively "in tune" (Stern, 1984). The infant quickly learns to expect, anticipate, and to a limited extent regulate interaction (Stern, 1974; Brazelton, Koslowski & Main, 1974). The expansion in social interaction as a consequence of the affective smiling response helps form true object relations. Hence Spitz thought that the smiling response marks a turning point in the infant's psychological development.

References

Brazelton, T. B., Koslowski, B. & Main, M. (1974). The early mother–infant interaction. In *The Effect of the Infant on Its Caregiver,* ed. M. Lewis & L. Rosenblum. New York: Wiley, pp. 49–77.

Emde, R. & Harmon, R. J. (1972). Endogenous

and exogenous smiling systems in early infancy. *J. Amer. Acad. Child Psychiat.* 11:177–200.
Spitz, R. A. (1959). *A Genetic Field Theory of Ego Formation.* New York: Int. Univ. Press.
Spitz, R. A. & Wolf, K. M. (1946). The smiling response. *Genet. Psychol. Monogr.*, 34:57–125.
Stern, D. N. (1974). The goal and structure of mother–infant play. *J. Amer. Acad. Child Psychiat.* 13:402–421.
______ (1984). Affect attunement. In *Frontiers of Infant Psychiatry.* New York: Basic Books, vol. 2, pp. 3–14.

■ SOMATIC COMPLIANCE

The capacity and readiness of a particular body part or organ system to participate in the neurotic process by providing a regressive somatic avenue for discharge of a drive–defense conflict. The somatic compliance of affected organs can derive from a constitutional or an acquired weakness. Somatic compliance is thought to influence the locus of the symptomatology and the manifestations of the pathological process; it plays a role in the "choice of neurosis."

Freud introduced this concept with reference to hysteria in his report on the Dora case and it appears in a few of his early papers. Although the concept has relevance also for organ-neurotic (psychophysiological) disorders, the term has not been widely used in more recent psychoanalytic literature.

References

Fenichel, O. (1945). *The Psychoanalytic Theory of Neurosis.* New York: Norton.
Freud, S. (1905). Fragment of an analysis of a case of hysteria. *SE*, 7:3–122.
______ (1910). The psychoanalytic view of psychogenic disturbance of vision. *SE*, 11:209–218.
______ (1912). Contribution to a discussion on masturbation. *SE*, 12:239–245.

■ SOMATIZATION

The tendency to react to stimuli (including drives, defenses, and conflict between them) physically rather than psychically. Also termed (by Flanders Dunbar) the *somatic short circuit*, somatization describes the shift of psychic energy toward expression in somatic symptoms.

Somatization includes both conversion reactions and organ-neurotic (psychophysiological) disorders, but rather than dwelling on their differences, the term emphasizes what they have in common.

As used by Max Schur, somatization links symptom formation to the regression that may occur in response to acute or chronic conflict. As part of normal maturation, a child's somatic responses to painful stimuli increasingly are replaced by action and/or by thought processes (*desomatization*). In the neurotic individual, however, psychic conflict often provokes regressive phenomena that may include somatic manifestations characteristic of an earlier developmental phase. Schur calls this *resomatization.* Desomatization presupposes the ego's faculty to use secondary processes and to neutralize energy; resomatization, by contrast, is associated with the prevalence of primary processes and with the simultaneous failure of neutralization.

See CONVERSION; ORGAN NEUROSIS; PSYCHOSOMATIC CONDITIONS; PRIMARY PROCESS.

References

Dunbar, F. (1954). *Emotions and Bodily Functions.* New York: Columbia Univ. Press.
Engel, G. L. (1967). Psychoanalytic theory of somatic disorder. *JAPA*, 15:344–365.
Rangell, L. (1959). The nature of conversion. *JAPA*, 7:632–662.
Schur, M. (1955). Comments on the metapsychology of somatization. *PSOC*, 10:119–164.

■ SPLIT INTERNALIZED BAD OBJECT

See FAIRBAIRN'S THEORY.

■ SPLITTING

The separation of psychological representations according to their opposing qualities. The experiential representations that constitute self and object are primarily involved. This hypothetical process is ascribed to the ego and is encountered developmentally, adaptively, and pathologically.

Splitting is thought to play a major role in the normative unfolding of mental life, contributing to psychic organization. It is postulated that during earliest infancy, when psychological experience consists of little more than undifferentiated and unstable tension states, splitting (itself then little more than an inborn pattern of reactions) facilitates the separation of these states according to differences in levels of tension. At this stage splitting serves primitive regulatory functions, helping to stabilize equilibrium and establish stimulus barriers. Later, when tension states result from frustration with others over needs, splitting (now a more active process but still automatically deployed) aids in separating these experiences according to how the infant's needs were satisfied. As a result, representational boundaries are consolidated and self and object are elaborated as representational categories. Finally, when the unities of self and of objects transcend need satisfaction, splitting serves purposes of defense. As a fully active and selectively deployed process, splitting then separates experiences along previously existing lines of difference, thereby avoiding anxieties that accompany their synthesis.

With development the splitting activity that earlier facilitated organization takes on an executive quality, and its defensive functions are assumed by more advanced processes like repression. Splitting then occurs only under conditions of adaptive stress or psychopathology.

When the developmental sequence summarized above fails or is interrupted and reversed (in pathological regression), the defense of splitting assumes prominence. It has been described in a number of conditions, including psychosis, borderline and narcissistic personality organization, perversion, fetishism, and fugue. The multiple meanings emphasized by different authors use various definitions of splitting in describing these types of psychopathology; a lack of clarity about the concept has resulted. See review by Abend, Porder & Willick (1983).

The term *vertical splitting* refers to experiences which, when separated, remain simultaneously within awareness; *horizontal splitting* refers to experiences which, when separated, are placed alternatively or permanently outside awareness through additional repression.

As an adaptive process occurring within specific contexts, splitting helps to maintain psychic organization, and promotes growth and change. For example, during periods of self-reflection in analysis, the experiencing and observing functions of the ego may be temporarily split.

See ADAPTATION; DEFENSE; DEVELOPMENT; EGO; EGO FUNCTION; KLEINIAN THEORY: Splitting.

References

Abend, S. M., Porder, M. S. & Willick, M. S. (1983). Borderline patients. *Kris Study Group Monograph* VII. New York: Int. Univ. Press, pp. 159–165.

Freud, S. (1938). Splitting of the ego in the process of defence. *SE,* 23:271–278.

Kernberg, O. F. (1966). Structural derivatives of object relationships. *IJP,* 47:236–253.

Lichtenberg, J. D. & Slap, J. W. (1973). Notes on the concept of splitting and defense mechanism of splitting of representations. *JAPA,* 21:722–787.

Lustman, J. (1977). On splitting. *PSOC,* 32:119–154.

■ SQUIGGLE GAME

See WINNICOTT'S THEORY.

■ STAGES OF THE LIFE CYCLE

See DEVELOPMENT.

■ STIMULUS BARRIER

Freud's (1920) concept of a "protective shield against stimuli" (*Reizschutz*) that safeguards the infant's psychic apparatus against particularly intense external stimuli. He postulated that a traumatic neurosis might result from excitations powerful enough to break through the protective shield. Later (1938) he suggested that this shield was a special development of the id that acted as an intermediary between the id and the external world—that is, a precursor of the ego.

Freud's statements about the protective shield are ambiguous. In some passages it seems to serve a screening function, diminishing the original intensity of stimuli instead of totally excluding them. It is unclear whether he saw the shield as a passive or an active agency.

Infant observation studies indicate that the normal neonate actively seeks stimulation and is able to perceive, discriminate among, and respond selectively and adaptively to a variety of external stimuli without evidence of traumatic effect. The infant is now viewed as having not a stimulus barrier but "an innate, selective, maturing screening mechanism that admits stimuli of certain types and intensities under certain conditions, but excludes others on the basis of either quantitative or qualitative considerations." The brain and mental apparatus may be regarded as "information-processing systems . . . [with] an inherent tendency to seek and respond to stimuli that will activate and promote this function" and also promote object attachment (Esman, 1983, p. 204).

See PSYCHIC APPARATUS; TRAUMA; TRAUMATIC NEUROSIS.

References

Esman, A. H. (1983). The "stimulus barrier": A review and reconsideration. *PSOC,* 38:193–207.

Freud, S. (1920). Beyond the pleasure principle. *SE,* 18:3–64.

——— (1938). An outline of psycho-analysis. *SE,* 23:141–207.

Furst, S. (1978). The stimulus barrier and the pathogenecity of trauma. *IJP,* 59:345–352.
Gediman, H. K. (1971). The concept of the stimulus barrier. *IJP,* 52:243–257.

■ STRANGER ANXIETY

An affective, behavioral manifestation that Spitz used as an indication that the second shift in ego organization has taken place. It is also called *eight-month anxiety.* Spitz observed that between six and eight months of age an infant begins to react to the unfamiliar in a new way. Whereas the infant earlier had responded with a smile and pleasure to the approach of any human being, he or she now reacts with distress to a stranger. The response varies from apprehension, avoidance of eye contact, and hiding to crying, screaming, and a refusal to make contact.

Spitz labeled this response *anxiety,* but it is now generally recognized that anxiety is a complex emotion integrating physiological, cognitive, and affective components and that the ego of the eight-month-old infant cannot experience anxiety. Therefore, the response observed by Spitz is more properly referred to as *distress* (Katan, 1972; Brenner, 1982).

Although Spitz's contemporaries in experimental psychology believed that this dramatic response to a stranger indicated the capacity to distinguish familiar from unfamiliar (a developmental achievement now demonstrated to emerge by three to four months), this response has more far-reaching implications for psychoanalytic theory. It indicates the establishment of a true object relationship—the mother has become the libidinal object. She remains the most important object regardless of whether wished-for gratification has been satisfied. In addition, the response indicates advances in ego development as judgment (Spitz, 1957) and a wider range of affects becomes available (Emde, Gaensbauer & Harmon, 1976). Cognitive functioning advances and prohibitions and commands begin to have meaning, an indication of superego precursors. Social interaction becomes more complex, and precursors of defenses can also be observed. In other words, the ego has become a more complex organization with a series of interacting systems.

See OBJECT CONSTANCY; PSYCHIC APPARATUS; SMILING RESPONSE.

References

Brenner, C. (1982). *The Mind in Conflict.* New York: Int. Univ. Press.
Emde, R. N., Gaensbauer, T. J. & Harmon, R. J. (1976). Emotional expression in infancy. *Psychol. Issues,* monogr. 37. New York: Int. Univ. Press.
Katan, A. (1972). The infant's first reaction to strangers. *IJP,* 53:501–503.
Spitz, R. A. (1957). *No and Yes.* New York: Int. Univ. Press.
______ (1959). *A Genetic Field Theory of Ego Formation.* New York: Int. Univ. Press.
Tyson, P. Development. *PMC.* Forthcoming.

■ STRUCTURAL CHANGE

The generally accepted goal of psychoanalysis. Symptomatic change may be rewarding to the patient and to others and therefore an acceptable goal for psychotherapy; however, symptoms may change as a result of resistance to treatment (a defensive flight into health to avoid exploration of painful conflicts), transference cure (a desire to please the therapist), or a change in life circumstances (a new love object or promotion that enhances self-esteem). Such change represents another compromise formation, replacing symptoms, and may be only temporary unless structural changes have taken place.

Structural changes are modifications within each of the major agencies of the psychic apparatus that reduce the conflicts among those agencies. Though the ego, which mediates the forces of all the mental systems as well as the influences of the external world, is the principal focus of analysis, major changes are also sought in the id and superego. With regard to the id, loosening fixations, diminishing regressions, and reducing the force of the repetition compulsion are principal objectives. In the superego, unduly harsh and punitive trends need to be attenuated, ideals regarded more realistically, lacunae filled in, and inconsistencies reconciled. Ego functions that have been impaired by conflict, such as perception, memory, and the regulation of action, should gain a larger degree of autonomy as a result of analysis. In addition, the mosaic of defense mechanisms and other defensive processes is modified to allow the sexual and aggressive drives to be recognized, regulated, and discharged without inappropriate inhibition, anxiety, or guilt. The synthesis or integration of various drives, tendencies, and functions is facilitated.

Conflicts among the diverse functions of id, ego, and superego are reduced, so that relations among them become more harmonious. The goal of analysis is to make these alterations far-reaching and enduring.

This analytic goal is consonant with the *outcome goals of psychoanalytic treatment.* The latter include the elimination of symptoms and inhibitions, modifications in character structure, improvement in capability to initiate and sustain fruitful object relationships, increased ability to work productively and creatively. Further goals are increased self-knowledge and self-acceptance, including the realization that perfection is illusory and unattainable.

Although some other forms of therapy strive for many of the same goals, they differ from psychoanalysis in respect to the intermediary aims; that is, they place less emphasis on structural change and attempt to modify symptoms and behavior more directly. In psychoanalysis the immediate objective is structural change, from which other benefits are expected to flow.

See CONFLICT; PSYCHIC APPARATUS; STRUCTURAL THEORY; THERAPEUTIC AIM.

References

Bibring, E. (1937). On the theory of the therapeutic results of psychoanalysis. *IJP,* 18:170–189.

Brenner, C. (1976). *Psychoanalytic Technique and Psychic Conflict.* New York: Int. Univ. Press.

Wallerstein, R. S. (1965). The goals of psychoanalysis. *JAPA,* 13:748–770.

■ STRUCTURAL THEORY

An attempt to explain by means of models the enduring, organized, and interrelated aspects of mental functioning—that is, those that operate in particular ways and are slow to change. The *tripartite model* advanced by Freud in 1923 is most commonly referred to as the structural theory, though his earlier *topographic theory* and subsequent models by other authors may also be considered structural.

Freud's tripartite theory was developed because of inconsistencies and inadequacies in the topographic model that limited its usefulness in explaining certain observable data. Prior to 1923, intrapsychic conflict was understood to occur between the conscious mind, containing the repressing forces and moral prohibitions, and the unconscious, which contained the warded-off instinctual drives. Observing that the mind's defenses against the drives also act unconsciously, and that an unconscious sense of guilt manifests itself in various clinical conditions (negative therapeutic reactions, melancholia, obsessional neurosis, and certain criminal behavior), Freud introduced a new theory to explain how the mind functions in situations of conflict over instinctual drives. According to this second structural theory, now largely accepted as the most heuristic, the mind (psychic apparatus) is divided into three groups (agencies, systems, or structures) of relatively constant and enduring motivational configurations. They are called *ego, id,* and *superego.* It should be noted that the structural theory does not reify or personify these structures, which have no material form or location.

The *id* is comprised of the psychic representations of both instinctual drives, libido and aggression, and represents the basic, pleasure-seeking motives of human psychic life. The *ego,* which Freud conceived of as developing out of the id, is more coherent and organized; it regulates or opposes the drives, mediates between them and the demands of the external world and effects compromise formations in symptoms, fantasies, dreams, actions, and character development. The ego's functions may be used to facilitate gratification of id wishes or may be used defensively when the wishes are unacceptable to the superego or dangerous to the ego. Signal anxiety is another ego function that serves to initiate defenses (Freud, 1926).

Freud theorized that with the resolution of the oedipus complex, the third agency, which he called the *superego,* formed as a part of the ego, an internalization of parental attitudes and values, a conscience, in order to control the sexual and aggressive instincts of the oedipal phase. Though there are preoedipal and postoedipal elements in superego formation, the greatest contribution occurs during the oedipal period. The structural theory therefore describes conditions in the mind after the resolution of the oedipus complex.

Some theorists have argued that the structural theory should be equated with the structures of the tripartite model. In their view, earlier developmental conditions in the mind are transformed by the experiences of the oedipal phase and are therefore not available, in any simple derivative form, in the experiences of the adult personality. Analyzability, in such a view, rests essentially on psychopathology centering in the oedipal phase. An alternative view emphasizes the need to attend to patterns of interaction and tension-regulatory mechanisms that persist as preneurotic symptomatic behavioral residues of early childhood experiences and as arrests, distortions, and primitive preserves in the complexities of character formation. The widened scope of psychoanalysis has brought intense clinical interest in narcissistic states and in the phenomena associated with separation-individuation and has resulted in the elaboration of other models of the mind to account for such analytic experiences. For the majority of contemporary psychoanalysts, however, the tripartite structural theory remains the most useful paradigm for formulating and applying psychoanalytic theory because it explains intrapsychic conflict well and is compatible with expansion and assimilation of new observations and perspectives.

See CONFLICT; EGO; ID; INSTINCTUAL DRIVE; METAPSYCHOLOGY; PSYCHIC APPARATUS; SUPEREGO; TOPOGRAPHIC POINT OF VIEW.

References

Arlow, J. A. (1975). The structural hypothesis. *PQ,* 44:509–525.

Arlow, J. A. & Brenner, C. (1964). *Psychoanalytic Concepts and Structural Theory*. New York: Int. Univ. Press.

Beres, D. (1965). Structure and function in psychoanalysis. *IJP,* 46:53–63.

Boesky, D. Structural theory. *PMC*. Forthcoming.

Freud, S. (1923). The ego and the id. *SE,* 19:3–66.

______ (1926). Inhibitions, symptoms, and anxiety. *SE,* 20:77–178.

Gedo, J. E. & Goldberg, A. (1973). *Models of the Mind*. Chicago: Univ. Chicago Press.

Rothstein, A. (1983). *The Structural Hypothesis*. New York: Int. Univ. Press.

Schlessinger, N. & Robbins, F. (1983). *A Developmental View of the Psychoanalytic Process*. New York: Int. Univ. Press.

■ STRUCTURAL VIEWPOINT

See METAPSYCHOLOGY.

■ STRUCTURE

Enduring patterns and configurations in the mind, (motivational, defensive, and controlling) that may be abstracted from behavior and the analysis of intrapsychic content. They are derived from the interaction of maturing constitutional givens and environmental influences in the various phases of development. They take shape through identification in early relationships, through learning, and through the resolution of adaptive conflicts.

To account for the complexity of these determiners of behavior, theorists have variously defined structure as modes of organization in contrast to functions, as stable functions, as a number of functions in a coherent unit, as the ordering of patterns of stimuli in the service of adaptation, as organizations of aims and motives, as the interrelation of elements rather than elements themselves, and as supraordinate regulators of behavior.

Such definitions are at varying levels of complexity and and are themselves dependent on specific theories of behavior. In a discharge model, structure refers to the channels for and limitations of discharge; in a a drive-defense model, structure is defense; in the tripartite model, structures are enduring motivations; in an adaptational model, structures are enduring functions; in an object relations model, structures are a product of identification; and in a learning theory model, structures are learned behavior patterns.

As a broad concept, psychic structure should be differentiated from the narrow definition of the structural theory, which attempts to describe conditions existing in the psyche after the resolution of the oedipus complex. Developmental theorists have introduced separation-individuation as an earlier nodal point at which significant enduring internalizations occur that shape behavior throughout the life cycle.

See STRUCTURAL THEORY.

References

Hartmann, H., Kris, E. & Loewenstein, R. M. (1946). Comments on the formation of psychic structure. *PSOC,* 2:11–38.

Levey, M. (1985). The concept of structure in psychoanalysis. *Annu. Psychoanal.* 12–13:137–154.

Nagera, H. (1967). The concepts of structure and structuralization. *PSOC,* 22:77–102.

Rapaport, D. (1959). The structure of psychoanalytic theory. *Psychol. Issues,* monogr. 6. New York: Int. Univ. Press.

■ SUBLIMATION

A psychic process that Freud defined in two ways. As first conceptualized (1905), sublimation involved instinctual drives' being somehow deflected from their original aims and/or objects to more socially valuable ones, thus obviating the need for continuing repression. Freud originally proposed that all behavior originated from and was powered by the libidinal drives, whose aims were often in conflict with cultural and social directives. This hypothetical process was his attempt to explain the existence of socially valuable, apparently nonsexual and nonconflicted activities—artistic creation, work, wit, and so on.

The term *sublimation* appears to have been derived from two sources: (1) the chemical process whereby a solid is vaporized by heating and the vapor is cooled and allowed to recondense, yielding a purified form of the original substance; and (2) the poetic metaphor of the sublime as opposed to the ridiculous or base. Thus, socially valuable behavior represents a "purified" and more "sublime" version of the original "base" drive. Freud originally considered sublimation to be a vicissitude of the instinctual drive; later he viewed it as a function of the ego, a special form of defense.

The concept as originally formulated provoked a number of criticisms (Bernfeld, 1931; Glover, 1931; Jones, 1941; Kubie, 1962). The definition rests upon a value judgment of the social desirability of the behavior in question, a dubious approach to defining a mental process. Even if *ego-syntonic* is substituted for socially valuable aims (as suggested by Bernfeld), the amended definition still does not distinguish between sublimation and an ego function that has become "sexualized" and used as a character defense. Nor does the definition take into account the degree of secondary autonomy (Hartmann's term) that the behavior has achieved from its original, presumably instinctual, source. Finally, the definition makes no provision for sublimation of aggressive drives.

Freud's second definition was far more abstract, involving a theoretically inferred (not clinically observable) desexualization of psychic energy. So defined, sublimation became the pathway for the formation of character traits and later became an indispensable conceptual tool to account for what Freud considered to be crucially important developmental alterations of libido. In this second sense, sublimation was central in Freud's views about the desexualization of libido, and he saw it in his later writings as the energic basis for identification. Thus, his second definition, very different from the first, expressed Freud's commitment to the idea that psychic energy is fundamentally important to the theoretical views expressed in his metapsychology.

Hartmann also attempted to redefine sublimation in purely energic terms. Sublimation, for him, "refers to a psychological process, this process being a change in the mode of energy, away from an instinctual and toward a noninstinctual mode" (1955, p. 223). Thus, sublimation is equated with either neutralization of libidinal or aggressive instinctual energy, or with the use of noninstinctual, innately neutral energy available to the ego. Since the presumed mode of the hypothetical energy can be inferred only from clinical observation, some regard as tautological the use of such an energic definition to explain the selfsame clinical observations. Moreover, emphasis on transformations of psychic energy (a concept that is itself under attack) detracts from consideration of the interactive participation of drive derivatives, ideational content, defenses, aspects of conscience (superego), and considerations of reality.

When he postulated inborn ego apparatuses with primary autonomy, Hartmann implicitly recognized that one need not assume all behavior originally has sexual or aggressive aims. Consequently, it is unnecessary to invoke the idea of some transformation such as sublimation to explain all nonsexual or nonaggressive behavior. There is no need, for example, to assume that using visual perception to acquire useful information must constitute a sublimation of voyeurism or some scopophilic instinctual drive.

From a clinical standpoint, the phenomena to be accounted for are those behaviors that once had sexual or aggressive goals and later became altered, so that their goals are neither explicitly sexual nor explicitly aggressive, but are socially appropriate (if not useful), consciously satisfying, and adaptive and flexible (rather than compulsive. The term *sublimation,* without energic or drive implications, may be applied descriptively to such changes in behavior, leaving open the possibility of other explanations for the underlying mechanisms of change, such as learning, maturation, and interpenetration of motivational systems.

See CHANGE OF FUNCTION; CHARACTER; EGO; INSTINCTUAL DRIVE; INTERNALIZATION; METAPSYCHOLOGY; PSYCHIC ENERGY; SUPEREGO.

References

Bernfeld, S. (1931). Zur Sublimierungslehre. *Imago,* 17:399–403.

Boesky, D. (1986). Questions about Sublimation. In *Psychoanalysis the Science of Mental Conflict,* ed. A. D. Richards & M. S. Willick. Hillsdale, N.J.: Analytic Press, pp. 153–176.

Freud, S. (1905). Three essays on the theory of sexuality. *SE,* 7:156.

——— (1908). Character and anal erotism. *SE,* 9:167–175.

——— (1923). The ego and the id. *SE,* 19:30.

——— (1924). The dissolution of the oedipus complex. *SE,* 19:173–179.

Glover, E. (1931). Sublimation, substitution, and social anxiety. *IJP,* 12:263–297.

Hartmann, H. (1955). Notes on the theory of sublimation. *PSOC,* 10:9–29.

Jones, E. (1941). Evolution and revolution. *IJP,* 22:193–208.

Kubie, L. S. (1962). The fallacious misuse of the concept of sublimation. *PQ,* 31:73–79.

■ SUBSIDIARY EGOS

See FAIRBAIRN'S THEORY.

■ SUBSIDIARY OBJECTS

See FAIRBAIRN'S THEORY.

■ SUBSTITUTION

See DREAMING, DREAMS.

■ SUCCESS NEUROSIS

A term originated by Sandor Lorand to designate patients whom Freud had described as "those wrecked by success." The patients appear to have been symptom-free prior to their successes. Typical is a male patient from a family background of modest circumstances who has achieved considerably more than his father, sometimes even great financial success. The achievement, however, is ruined for the patient by conflict based on the significance of success as an oedipal victory, and the individual is overwhelmed by guilt and self-torture. Freud (1914–16) gave examples from literature, examining Shakespeare's Macbeth and Ibsen's Rebecca in *Rosmersholm* to show how these characters' sense of guilt ruined what would otherwise have been oedipal victories.

For some patients success gives rise to homosexual anxiety, since it offers the prospect of being loved by father. Conflict and anxiety may, therefore, derive from both the positive and negative oedipal connotations of success. Comparable phenomena are found in fate neuroses and in the negative therapeutic reaction.

More recently, some authors have used the term in a less specific sense to signify a variety of difficulties in relation to achievement, including characterological problems and preoedipal difficulties. Among the phenomena included are academic or other underachievement and the problems women have in striving for success. These problems may be viewed as part of a masochistic continuum or may be related to narcissistic pathology. Separation individuation and, in particular, rapprochement phase pathology may play a role in prohibiting gratification through the attainment of success apart from the mother. In general, however, these phenomena do not conform to the specific circumstances described by Freud, Lorand, and Szekely, and referred to by Bressler as well, in which specific neurotic symptoms begin following the achievement of a longed-for success. For clarity and consistency, the term should be reserved for neuroses in which symptoms begin in the circumstances described by these authors.

See NEGATIVE THERAPEUTIC REACTION.

References

Bressler, B. (1965). The concept of the self. *Psychoanalytic Review*, 52:425–445.

Frank, H. (1977). Dynamic patterns for failure in college students. *Can. Psychiat. Assn. J.*, 22:295–299.

Freud, S. (1914–16). Some character types met with in psychoanalysis: (II) Those wrecked by success. *SE*, 14:316–331.

——— (1936). A disturbance of memory on the Acropolis. *SE*, 22:239–248.

Lorand, S. (1950). *Clinical Studies in Psychoanalysis*. New York: Int. Univ. Press, pp. 245ff.

Szekely, L., (1960). Success, success neurosis and the self. *Brit. J. Med. Psychol.*, 33:45–51.

■ SUPEREGO

One of three hypothetical systems of the tripartite (structural) model, the superego sets up and maintains an intricate system of ideals and values, prohibitions and commands (the conscience); it observes and evaluates the self, compares it with the ideal, and either criticizes, reproaches, and punishes, leading to a variety of painful affects, or praises and rewards, thereby raising self esteem. Freud introduced the term *Über-Ich* (superego) in 1923, used it synonymously with his earlier term *Ich Ideal* (ego ideal), and described it as a step (*Stufe*) or differentiation within the ego. He viewed it as largely unconscious, reflecting the clinical observation that in many patients self-criticism and conscience were as much outside of awareness as the drives: "not only what is lowest but also what is highest in the ego can be unconscious."

While the superego is considered a high-level abstraction comprising a number of relatively stable functions in a more or less coherent configuration (or structure), its derivatives are readily observable in phenomena metaphorically described as an *inner voice*, an *inner authority*, or *inner judge*. These personlike inner configurations have given rise to the familiar terms *inner objects, inner object relations*, and *introjects*. Such designations are largely due to the separation felt to exist between the superego and the rest of the personality. This separation is apparent because of conflict between the ego and superego, conflict manifested by painful feelings of inferiority or by shame and guilt.

Freud believed the superego is derived partly from early parental identifications maintained after the parents had been given up as objects of sexual love, that is at the time of the "dissolution of the oedipus complex." He described the superego or ego ideal as the heir of the oedipus complex, hence as a representative of the most powerful love relationships of early childhood. He added, however, that it is not simply a residue or precipitate of a love object that had been given up—it also entails strong reaction formations against such identification. It contains two messages: "you ought to be like this" and "you may not be like this." Moreover, the child's superego may be modeled more on the parents' superegos than on the perceived image of the parent. Freud was also aware that the severity of the superego was not in proportion to the parents' severity or the child's experiences with the parent, but rather in proportion to the individual's aggressive wishes. Thus he noted (p. 54), "the more a human being controls his aggressiveness, the more intense becomes his ideal's inclination to aggressiveness against the ego" (dynamically: the aggression is turned against the self).

Freud (1923) maintained that the superego emerges in the course of efforts to resolve oedipal conflicts. The boy, fearing castration, gives up oedipal incestuous wishes and identifies with the father/ideal and with the father's moral wishes. Earlier dangers—loss of object, loss of love, and castration—become internalized as specific superego threats. Freud understood the female superego less, but today many distinguish between a male and female superego on the basis of its contents (what is held to be ideal or prohibited), not on the basis of the inferiority or superiority of the structure.

Many have studied the more archaic preoedipal steps in superego development (Jacobson, 1964; Reich, 1954; Sandler, 1960; Tyson and Tyson, 1984). Work with young children suggests that they internalize parental expectations long before the oedipal phase. While at first these are directed against others, in the form of blaming and accusing (A. Freud, 1936), they are soon transformed to self-expectations, and self-criticism follows infraction of ideal standards. However, the oedipus complex provides an impetus for integration of early stages of superego formation. The child begins to fear loss of the superego's love more than he or she fears loss of the parents' love. Punishment is experienced as a loss of self-esteem and as guilt, the "hallmark" of the superego (Beres, 1958).

After the oedipal phase the various superego functions gradually become more impersonal and attain greater autonomy from external objects. While the superego becomes a relatively stable system, functioning with considerable consistency, defects or lacunae appear due to inconsistent functioning or defenses (such as denial, turning passive into active, and reexternalization) against important parts of the superego. Thus the superego remains "by no means a uniform, coherent, integrated, harmonious structure . . . but a mass of contradictions" (Arlow, 1982).

See EGO IDEAL; FAIRBAIRN'S THEORY; GUILT; IDEALIZATION; INTERNALIZATION; SHAME.

References

Arlow, J. A. (1982). Problems of the superego concept. *PSOC*, 37:229–244.
Beres, C. (1958). Vicissitudes of superego functions and superego precursors in childhood. *PSOC*, 13:325–351.
Jacobson, E. (1964). *The Self and the Object World.* New York: Int. Univ. Press.
Freud, A. (1936). *The Ego and the Mechanisms of Defense.* New York: Int. Univ. Press.
Freud, S. (1923). The ego and the id. *SE*, 19:3–66.
——— (1930). Civilization and its discontents. *SE*, 21:59–145.
Furer, M. (1972). The history of the superego concept in psychoanalysis. In *Moral Value and the Superego Concept in Psychoanalysis,* ed. S. C. Post. New York: Int. Univ. Press, pp. 11–62.
Holder, A. (1982). Preoedipal contributions to the formation of the superego. *PSOC*, 37:245–272.
Reich, A. (1954). Early identifications as archaic elements in the superego. *JAPA*, 2:218–238.
Sandler, J. (1960). On the concept of the superego. *PSOC*, 15:128–162.
Tyson, P. & Tyson, R. L. (1984). Narcissism and superego development. *JAPA*, 34:75–98.

■ SUPPORTIVE THERAPY

See PSYCHOTHERAPY.

■ SUPPRESSIVE THERAPY

See PSYCHOTHERAPY.

■ SYMBIOSIS

The interdependent condition of the human infant and its mother. The term was introduced to psychoanalysis by Alice Balint (1949) and further developed by Therese Benedek (1949). It draws attention to the need each has for the other and the different gratifications each gives to and gets from the other.

Mahler (1952; Mahler & Gosliner, 1955; Mahler & Furer, 1968) separately and autonomously introduced the same term with a different meaning—the infant's inferred experience and intrapsychic registration (with representation) of a state of oneness with the mother. Mahler's term, used as a metaphor, did not reflect the mother's experience of her baby, but the concept, as she explained in 1968, "dovetails, from the infant's standpoint, with the concept of [symbiosis, of] the mother-child dual unity which Therese Benedek has described . . . from the standpoint of both partners of the primary unit" (p. 8). And "the term 'symbiosis' does not describe, as the biological concept of symbiosis does, what actually happens between two separate individuals. It was chosen to describe that state of . . . fusion with mother, in which the 'I' is not yet differentiated from the 'Not-I' and in which inside and outside are only gradually coming to be sensed as different" (p. 9).

In 1975 Mahler, Pine, and Bergman seemed to expand her definition to include that of Benedek: "Symbiosis refers to a stage of sociobiological interdependence between the 1 to 5-month-old infant and his mother . . . in which self and maternal intrapsychic representations have not yet been differentiated. From the second month on, the infant behaves and functions as though he and his mother were an omnipotent dual unity within one common boundary (the 'symbiotic membrane')" (pp. 290–291).

See SEPARATION-INDIVIDUATION.

References

Balint, A. (1949). Love for mother and mother-love. *IJP*, 30:251–259.

Benedek, T. (1949). The psychosomatic implications of the primary unit. *Amer. J. Orthopsychiat.*, 19:642–654.

Mahler, M. S. (1952). On child psychosis and schizophrenia. *PSOC*, 7:286–305.

Mahler, M. S. & Furer, M. (1968). *On Human Symbiosis and the Vicissitudes of Individuation.* New York: Int. Univ. Press.

Mahler, M. S. & Gosliner, B. J. (1955). On symbiotic child psychosis. *PSOC*, 10:195–212.

Mahler, M. S., Pine, F. & Bergman, A. (1975). *The Psychological Birth of the Human Infant.* New York: Basic Books.

■ SYMBIOTIC PHASE

See SEPARATION-INDIVIDUATION; SYMBIOSIS.

■ SYMBOL
□ Symbolism
□ Symbolization

Symbolism is a form of indirect representation, and *symbolization* is a uniquely human psychic process in which one mental representation stands for another, denoting its meaning not by exact resemblance but by vague suggestion, or by some accidental or conventional relation. In a broad sense, therefore, symbols encompass all substitutes for words representing an idea, quality, or totality; they are used in mathematics, physics, chemistry, music, phonetics, and language. In psychoanalysis, however, two types of such indirect representation are distinguished. In the case of the conscious *sign* or token, the relationship between signifier (sound-image) and what is signified (a concept) is arbitrary and dictated by conventional agreement (as is the case with most words). The *symbol,* on the other hand, has a conscious manifest form but also latently represents unconscious mental content, and the relationship between the symbol and its referent is not arbitrary but is based on, for example, some perceived similarity or analogy: a house might represent the human body or a tower represent the penis. The linguist Saussure (1966) called the nonarbitrary elements in this narrower definition of symbol *motivated.* Similarly, what Freud labeled *symbolic* are peculiarly motivated, and the meanings are often not discernible in the patient's associations.

Signs "aim at communication with delay of discharge . . . [Symbols] achieve immediate discharge by repression and distortion of the unconscious content. Communication . . . may be a secondary result . . . effected unconsciously" (Beres, 1960, p. 330). The distinctions between signs and symbols, and conscious and unconscious symbolic processes, are dealt with differently in the writings of Piaget (1962) and Werner and Kaplan (1984).

The symbolic may be thought of as subsidiary either to language (a purely conventional system) or to the conscious and unconscious organization of thought revealed by a patient's free associations. Conversely, language, sign systems, and organized thought may be subsets of an innate capacity for representation (symbolization in the wide sense) by means of which they are all realized and sustained.

Psychoanalytic interest in symbols has a long history, originating in Freud's observations about the parallels between forms of representation found in primitive cultures and those characterizing neurotic symptoms and dream symbols. Freud understood all symbols to result from unconscious, primary process mental activity, the goal of which was reducing anxiety by repressing unacceptable wishes and ideas. Symbol formation delays the discharge of tension produced by a stimulus by interposing mental indicators between the stimulus and response. It also displaces wishes from forbidden objects onto substitutes, permitting immediate gratification. The compromise of partial expression through symbolic forms serves both the individual and the culture.

Freud noted that subjects which tend to be symbolically represented are body parts and their functions, family members and relationships, and birth, sexuality, and death. The reductionistic nature of symbols may be attributable to the fact that the conflicts, inhibitions, and symptoms that bring people to treatment arise from such sources. Or it may be that the human child is born into a culture or symbolic order generated over the millenia by the basic questions related to such matters. The latter hypothesis might account for how symbols can "involve a development of the self that opens up to what the symbols disclose" (Ricoeur, 1970, p. 478). Specific symbols and symbolic enactments evoked in disorders of thought, mood, and character could be understood as efforts to restore an absent object or a lost order—an order that has arisen by virtue of the human capacity for symbolization in the broad sense.

Freud's early belief that symbols and primal fantasies are universal and inherited has now been largely replaced by the assumption that symbols' recurrence across cultures has to do with the similarity of human beings' experiences and interests from infancy onward and of the cognitive processes involved in symbol formation. These processes may, however, follow schemata (Freud, 1918) not related to the individual's life experience. If so, symbols may represent not only what is absent from the past but also what is as yet missing; that is, the schemata are not determined by the past, but rather shape both past and future (Smith, 1976).

Although, as Freud observed, symbols in dreams usually do not give rise to associations, knowledge of the common unconscious meanings of symbols, cautiously applied, is useful in understanding the patient's conflicts. Symbolism produces ambiguity, and the symbol may have one of several meanings indicated only by its place in the total context. It may serve either defensive or adaptive purposes. From developmental and theoretical points of view some of the questions for interdisciplinary exploration of symbolism involve the origins and early development of symbolization, the relationship among symbolic forms produced in various states of consciousness, and the degree to which conflict must be involved in various processes of symbolization.

See DREAMING, DREAMS; PRIMARY PROCESS; REPRESENTATION.

References

Beres, D. (1960). Perception, imagination and reality. *IJP*, 41:327–334.

Blum, H. Symbolism. *PMC*. Forthcoming.

Freud, S. (1900). The interpretation of dreams. *SE*, 4–5.

——— (1915–16). Introductory lectures on psychoanalysis. *SE*, 16:243–481.

——— (1918). From the history of an infantile neurosis. *SE*, 17:7–104.

——— (1939). Moses and monotheism. *SE*, 23:7–132.

Piaget, J. (1962). *Play, Dreams and Imitation in Childhood*. New York: Norton.

Ricoeur, P. (1970). *Freud and Philosophy*. New Haven: Yale Univ. Press.

——— (1976). *Interpretation Theory*. Forth Worth: Texas Christian Univ. Press.

Saussure, F. de (1966). *Course in General Linguistics*, ed. C. Bally and A. Riedlinger; tr. W. Baskin. New York: McGraw-Hill.

Smith, J. (1976). Language and the genealogy of the absent object. In *Psychiatry and the Humanities*, vol. 1, ed. J. H. Smith. New Haven: Yale Univ. Press.

Sperber, D. (1974). *Rethinking Symbolism*. Cambridge: Cambridge Univ. Press.

Waldhorn, H. F. & Fine, B. (1971). Trauma and symbolism. *Kris Study Group monogr*. V. New York: Int. Univ. Press.

Werner, H. & Kaplan, B. (1984). *Symbol Formation*. Hillsdale, N.J.: Lawrence Erlbaum.

■ SYMBOLIC EQUATION

See KLEINIAN THEORY.

■ SYMBOLIC REPRESENTATION

See DREAMING, DREAMS.

■ SYMPTOM

□ Symptom Formation

A *symptom* may be defined in a narrow sense as a manifestation (of an illness) of which a patient complains, while a *sign* is an observable indication of abnormality. The difference is one of subjectivity versus objectivity. Nevertheless, according to the *Oxford English Dictionary*, the word *symptom* is also defined more broadly to include "any [bodily or mental] phenomenon, circumstance, or change of condition arising from or accompanying a disease or affection and constituting an indication or evidence of it" (p. 2111). This definition eliminates the distinction between signs and symptoms.

Symptoms are usually more transient and more ego-dystonic or even dysphoric than are character traits. An inhibition—behavior characterized by a restriction of an area of ego function—may be either a symptom or a character trait. But since both inhibitions and some character traits fit the broader definition of *symptom,* these distinctions in terms cannot be very precise, and clinical usage reflects this fact.

Psychoneurotic symptoms are caused by unconscious psychic conflict arising from contending forces within the individual. These forces consist of repressed derivatives (unconscious fantasies, impulses, wishes) of childhood instinctual drives (both sexual and aggressive)—especially those closely associated with the oedipal stage of development—and also of psychic structures (ego, superego) that oppose the entrance of such derivatives into conscious thought or behavior for moral or reality-adaptive reasons.

Such unconscious conflict is universal and unavoidable, and childhood instinctual conflicts do not always cause symptoms. They may, for example, give rise to stable defensive patterns that play a major role in character formation; or they may be sufficiently resolved to permit either a degree of acceptable direct gratification of instinctual drives or their highly modified expression in useful sublimations.

When the equilibrium between the instinctual and the repressive forces is disturbed (either when the former are strengthened, as in puberty, or the the latter weakened, as in physical illness), the repressed drive derivatives threaten to emerge into consciousness, giving rise to anxiety or guilt. If the affective responses are so intense as to go beyond the signal function, symptoms usually develop. Such symptoms are compromise formations simultaneously containing a partial, substitute gratification of drive derivatives and the unconscious fantasy wishes associated with them; and the opposition of repressing and adaptive psychic agencies. The compromise formation is thus a highly disguised, incomplete, and consciously unrecognizable form of drive expression.

The suffering associated with most neurotic symptoms is also important to this complex compromise. The suffering satisfies the superego's unconscious demand for punishment, made necessary because conflictual drive derivatives achieve substitute gratification in the symptom. At the same time, psychoneurotic symptoms permit the sufferer to avoid some of the guilt and anxiety that a full, undisguised breakthrough of instinctual derivatives would produce.

Psychotic symptoms, though formed in a manner similar to neurotic ones, are derived from conflicts associated with an earlier level of libidinal and ego development. They often reflect a change in the patient's relationship with persons and environment, leading to a disturbance in the sense of reality.

The particular symptoms that arise and the nosological syndromes characterized by them are based on both constitutional predisposition and early life experiences that lead to complex variations in the nature of the neurotic conflict, the particular instinctual forces and defenses employed, the strengths and weaknesses of the psychic apparatus and its component parts, including the character structure, and the nature of the response and the intensity of later external stresses and traumas. The particular form a psychological illness takes has been called the *choice of neurosis.*

See ANXIETY; CHARACTER; COMPROMISE FORMATION; CONFLICT; INHIBITION; PSYCHONEUROSIS; PSYCHOSIS; STRUCTURAL THEORY.

References

Arlow, J. A. (1953). Masturbation and symptom formation. *JAPA,* 1:45–58.

Arlow, J. A. & Brenner, C. (1964). *Psychoanalytic Concepts and the Structural Theory.* New York: Int. Univ. Press.

Freud, S. (1913). Editor's note. The disposition to obsessional neurosis. *SE,* 12:313–326.

Pulver, S. E. Symptomatology. *PMC.* Forthcoming.

■ SYMPTOMATIC ACT

An action, such as a slip of the tongue or pen, forgetting, or some limited aspect of behavior, that is the result of the interaction of psychic forces. When equilibrium is disturbed due to fatigue or added tension, one or another force gains ascendancy and is discharged suddenly in a seemingly innocuous fashion; this represents the breakthrough of an impulse or an intensified defense or compromise formation. The discharge sometimes takes the form of a somatic response such as a muscle spasm. These short-lived symptomatic actions have motives and intentions; they are not random occurrences but rather are indicative of underlying unconscious mental processes. They may signify serious psychic disorder or they may be ego-syntonic expressions without psychopathological significance. Other more complicated results of the interaction of psychic forces include dreams, fantasies, and ideas or actions that may satisfactorily resolve the conflict or may led to adaptive or maladaptive behavior.

References
Freud, S. (1905). Fragment of an analysis of a case of hysteria. *SE*, 7:76–9.

■ TERMINATION PHASE

Both the end phase of treatment, as set apart from the beginning and middle phases, and a process that encompasses the end phase. Therapeutic-analytic goals (as contrasted to life goals) should have been met before the termination process is initiated. Therapeutic-analytic goals must embody the analyst's theoretical and practical concepts of mental health, but they should be free of countertransferential interference and idiosyncratic perfectionist ideals. Some indicators that it is time to begin the termination process include: meliorative structural change, optimal access to and satisfactory modulation of affects, alteration of defenses in the direction of mature and healthy balance and adaptation, symptom reduction, phase-appropriate object relationships, reconstruction of an adequate life narrative, and perhaps most significant, movement toward resolution of an adequately delineated transference neurosis.

A satisfactory resolution of the transference is the cardinal goal of analysis, but its status cannot be adequately assessed without what Glover (1955) has called "the touchstone" of the termination decision and experience. The extent and permanence of the beneficial changes resulting from the analytic work, especially as manifested in the transference, can best be evaluated through the termination process, during which the analysand's reactions to both the initiation and process of termination are assessed and fully analyzed.

The patient should more or less agree with the analyst that the analysis can be brought to a close. This agreement marks the beginning of the termination phase; a specific date for ending is established later. The process of termination is usually characterized by the full range of affects associated with separation; it may be complicated by a regression that brings back symptoms; and it may take the form of a recapitulation of an adolescent individuation experience.

The transference neurosis is being resolved before and during the termination phase, but it almost never permanently dissolves—even after the analysis has ended. Follow-up studies reveal a ready, though elastic, regression to neurotic transference reactions in successfully analyzed patients, but such individuals also demonstrate a relatively autonomous capacity to analyze such reactions in themselves.

The post-termination phase is of considerable significance to the analytic result. The analysand should achieve an asymptomatic resolution and integration of the experiences and insights of the analysis.

Termination is different from other ways that psychoanalysis may end—interruption imposed by extraneous factors (relocation, illness), "flight into health," transference cure, or agreement between patient and analyst that the analysis has reached a stalemate and should be discontinued.

References
Firestein, S. K. (1978). A review of the literature. In *Termination in Psychoanalysis*. New York: Int. Univ. Press, pp. 223–257.
Glover, E. (1955). The terminal phase. In *The Technique of Psychoanalysis*. New York: Int. Univ. Press, pp. 138–164.
Rangell, L. (1966). An overview of the ending of an analysis. In *Psychoanalysis in the Americas*, ed. R. E. Litman. New York: Int. Univ. Press, pp. 141–165.
Shane, M. & Shane, E. (1984). The end phase of analysis. *JAPA*, 32:739–772.
Ticho, E. (1972). Termination of psychoanalysis. *PQ*, 41:315–333.

■ THANATOS

See INSTINCTUAL DRIVE.

■ THERAPEUTIC AIM

Psychoanalytic treatment aims to effect intrapsychic change: to remove the stigmata of childhood events and eliminate their painful repetition; to alter unreasonable and maladaptive defensive structures; and to allow psychological development to resume.

In the 1890s, when Freud was beginning the treatment which developed into psychoanalysis, the therapeutic aim was implemented through efforts to reunite affects and their originally associated ideation, which had been dissociated from each other as a result of trauma. The objective was to elicit a healthy "abreaction" through which the underlying affects could be appropriately discharged; once this had happened, they would not continue to manifest themselves as symptoms. Beginning around 1900, psychoanalysis undertook the more challenging task of making unconscious phenomena available to consciousness. The rationale was that unconscious processes had not, or could not, become conscious because of the immaturity of the mental apparatus at the time of their inception, and that this situation predisposed to later symptomatology. Freud anticipated that the more mature adult mind, exposed to a translation of the unconscious contents, could view the situation from a more realistic perspective and make more reasonable judgments. Implicit in this belief was the hope that instinctual investments might be applied to purposes more appropriate to an adult after childhood fixations were removed and regressions reversed.

After 1923 this aim was replaced by Freud's pithy expression that where there had been id there should ego be. Treatment was now intended to strengthen the executive organization of the mental apparatus by exposing and resolving unconscious instinctual manifestation of childhood. A related approach was based on the assumption that the conscience (superego) could be modified through interpretations that would allow harsh parental figures to be replaced by more benevolent and realistic representations of the analyst in the patient's mind. Further efforts were directed toward strengthening the ego by interpreting conflicts and defenses, leading the patient to understand the influence of the ego's own properties.

Each subsequent theory of psychopathology led to new approaches to implementing therapeutic aims. For example, Melanie Klein and her followers attempted in analysis to interpret very early pathological structures that patients destructively attributed to themselves or to others. Object relations theorists attempted systematically to identify and interpret a variety of primitive self nuclei. Their efforts were intended to help integrate these pathological, infantile nuclei into a single, cohesive, superordinate adult personality organization. In the model of the *bipolar self*, deficits in structuralization (dating from childhood experiences with pathologically disappointing or unempathic parental figures) were thought to offer therapeutic opportunities for "transmuting internalizations" of the optimally stable and empathic analyst.

It was originally believed that the therapeutic aim of analysis was achieved through explicit interpretation leading to insight. This is still the prevailing view, but some analysts have proposed that change may also be achieved through something inherent in the analytic experience itself.

See ABREACTION; DEFENSE; EGO; FAIRBAIRN'S THEORY; KLEINIAN THEORY; SELF PSYCHOLOGY; STRUCTURAL CHANGE; TOPOGRAPHIC POINT OF VIEW.

References

Freud, S. (1893–95). Studies on hysteria. *SE*, 2.
______ (1916–17). Introductory lectures on psychoanalysis. *SE*, 15–16.
______ (1933). New introductory lectures on psychoanalysis. *SE*, 22:3–182.
Greenberg, J. & Mitchell, S. (1983). *Object Relations in Psychoanalytic Therapy*. Cambridge: Harvard Univ. Press.
Hartmann, H. (1951). Technical implications of ego psychology. *PQ*, 20:31–43.
Kohut, H. (1977). *The Restoration of the Self*. New York: Int. Univ. Press.
Segal, H. (1973). *Introduction to the Work of Melanie Klein*. New York: Basic Books.
Strachey, J. (1934). The nature of the therapeutic action of psychoanalysis. *IJP*, 15:127–159.

■ THERAPEUTIC ALLIANCE

□ Working Alliance

Therapeutic alliance and *working alliance* are roughly equivalent terms characterizing realistic cooperation and collaboration in the therapeutic process. The concepts are both ambiguous and controversial. It is assumed that the analyst is capable of such an effort, but the patient's ability and willingness to respond similarly is in question.

Freud stated that a patient's positive transference was all that was needed for a therapeutic alliance to develop. Others also emphasize elements of the transference, that is, the analytic repetition of childhood attitudes of trust, reliance, and cooperativeness, as exclusively involved in the analytic collaboration. The implication is that such actions and attitudes, although considered to be of positive value, are no more exempt from analytic understanding of their origins and pathological misapplications than are any other transference phenomena.

The alleged "real relationship" implies that the analyst can be perceived as and reacted to in part as a "real person," a dynamism free of transference contaminations. Similarly, some contend that qualities derived from interaction during childhood are regularly translated into socially valuable character traits, capacities, and areas of functioning relatively autonomous from their infantile or conflictual origin. The proponents of these views consider major aspects of the patient's collaboration and involvement in the joint enterprise as reasonable and realistic and the analysis of their origins as often inappropriate and disruptive.

See TRANSFERENCE.

References
Brenner, C. (1979). Working alliance, therapeutic alliance and transference. *JAPA,* 27:137–157.
Dickes, R. (1967). Severe regressive disruption of the therapeutic alliance. *JAPA,* 15:508–533.
Greenson, R. R. (1965). The working alliance and the transference neurosis. *PQ,* 34:155–181.
Zetzel, E. R. (1956). Current concepts of transference. *IJP,* 37:369–376.

■ THERAPEUTIC SPLIT

See TRANSFERENCE.

■ THOSE WRECKED BY SUCCESS

See CHARACTER; SUCCESS NEUROSIS.

■ TOPOGRAPHIC POINT OF VIEW

One of three viewpoints proposed by Freud (1915) as constituting a metapsychological approach to understanding psychic phenomena. The other two were the *dynamic* and the *economic.* The term *topographic,* derived from Greek, refers to the description of the relative positions and elevations of a place or region. Using the topographic point of view, Freud characterized mental phenomena according to their relationship to consciousness. He postulated three regions, neither anatomical nor spatial, but metaphorically arranged in the "psychic apparatus" on a vertical axis from the surface to the depths. Mental content—memories, ideas, wishes, fantasies, or feelings—within conscious awareness are said to be on the surface of the mind. Content below the surface that can be brought to consciousness by focusing attention is said to be preconscious, while that which cannot be brought to consciousness by an act of attention is said to occur in the deepest region of the mind, the unconscious.

Freud stressed that these terms refer to an attribute that is the point of departure for investigation. They convey only one feature of what he conceptualized as *systems* of the mind. The *system unconscious* (or Ucs.) was characterized by primary process thinking, and the preconscious and conscious systems (Pcs. and Cs.) by secondary process thought, which employed language and logic. Freud also postulated a censorship barrier between the unconscious and preconscious and between the preconscious and conscious.

The terms *conscious* and *preconscious* are now used mainly in their descriptive sense, while *unconscious* has both a descriptive and dynamic meaning. The topographic viewpoint was a means for organizing psychological data, but it was also associated with the early aim of analysis—to make the unconscious conscious. It has been supplemented and largely overshadowed by a second topography, the tripartite model (id, ego, superego) of Freud's 1923 structural theory, which has as an analytic correlate the goals of bringing the id under the mastery of the ego and analyzing psychic conflict. The topographic viewpoint continues to influence thought and technique in that most of the conflict analyzed is related to unconscious ideas, and interpretation proceeds from the surface to the depths.

See CONSCIOUS; DEPTH PSYCHOLOGY; METAPSYCHOLOGY; PRECONSCIOUS; STRUCTURAL THEORY; UNCONSCIOUS.

References
Arlow, J. A. & Brenner, C. (1964). *Psychoanalytic Concepts and the Structural Theory.* New York: Int. Univ. Press.
Freud, S. (1900). The interpretation of dreams. *SE,* 5:508–621.
——— (1915). The unconscious. *SE,* 14:166–215.
——— (1923). The ego and the id. *SE,* 19:12–66.

■ TRAGIC MAN

See SELF PSYCHOLOGY.

■ TRANSFERENCE

The displacement of patterns of feelings, thoughts, and behavior, originally experienced in relation to significant figures during childhood, onto a person involved in a current interpersonal relationship. Since the process involved is largely unconscious, the patient does not perceive the various sources of transference attitudes, fantasies, and feelings (such as love, hate, and anger). The phenomenon appears unbidden from the point of view of the subject and is at times distressing. Parents are usually the original figures from whom such emotional patterns are displaced, but siblings, grandparents, teachers, physicians, and childhood heroes are also frequent sources.

Transference is a type of object relationship, and insofar as every object relationship is a reediting of the first childhood attachments, transference is ubiquitous. Extra-analytic transferences occur in a wide range of circumstances: in other types of psychotherapy, in medical relationships, and in school, office, and social interactions. But in the psychoanalytic situation transference is apt to appear with particular clarity and intensity. The reason may be that as analysis proceeds, the patient begins to tolerate the derivatives of childhood compromise formations that underlie transference. Moreover, the conditions of abstinence and frustration intrinsic in analysis promote regression to a more infantile personality structure, which enhances the unfolding of the transference. The relative anonymity of the analyst facilitates the patient's transfer of revived early images onto his or her person. In the absence of information about the analyst's attributes and personal life, the patient generates fantasies relatively uncontaminated by perception of the present. The patient concentrates on the figure of the analyst with such intensity that a *transference neurosis* develops, which replicates the childhood neurosis. The transference is dynamic; it oscillates within the analytic situation, so that the analyst may represent several figures from the patient's past.

Not all the patient's reactions to the analyst are transference. Some are based on the analyst's attitudes or actual behavior.

Transference can fuel the strongest resistance to analysis, but it can also be a powerful ally. For it is through interpretation of the transference that the patient becomes convinced that the connections and reconstructions made during analytic treatment are valid.

Transference invariably reflects love and hate intertwined, and so its manifestations are often ambivalent. However, it is useful to distinguish *negative* and *positive transferences*. The terms refer to the quality (aggressive and hostile or friendly and affectionate) of the manifestations dominating at a particular moment in the analysis. In actual practice the whole range of human affect can be experienced within the context of transference. What has been termed the "unobjectionable" part of transference refers to that which is benign or even helpful to the analytic outcome—that which allows the patient to begin work and to cooperate in the process. Experience teaches, however, that such manifestations may change their significance and may become allied with resistance during the course of the analysis.

Analysis and interpretation of the content of transference is central to the therapeutic process. Indeed, some analytic authors have stated that only transference interpretations are mutative. The transference may be appreciably modified in the course of treatment, but it is doubtful that it is completely resolved, or that such resolution is necessary for successful analysis.

Transference—an automatic, unconscious repetition—is different from the *therapeutic* or *working alliance,* which is a conscious aspect of the relationship between the analyst and patient. In such an alliance, the patient identifies with the aims and method of analytic treatment and understands the need for genetic insight. The patient's desire to cooperate is complemented by the analyst's wish to help him or her achieve insight, understanding, and conscious control (conceptualized as the *working ego* of the analyst). The alliance is predicated on a *therapeutic split* in the patient's ego: one area of ego functioning splits off and observes a part that experiences. A strong therapeutic alliance is often essential to the continuation of the analysis during periods of strong negative transference.

See COMPROMISE FORMATION; COUNTERTRANSFERENCE; PSYCHONEUROSIS; REPETITION COMPULSION; THERAPEUTIC ALLIANCE; WORK EGO.

References

Bird, B. (1972). Notes on transference. *JAPA,* 20:267–302.

Freud, S. (1912). The dynamics of transference. *SE,* 12:97–108.

——— (1915). Observations on transference-love. *SE,* 12:159–171.

Hill, M. (1982). Analysis of transference. In *Theory and Technique,* vol. 1. New York: Int. Univ. Press.

Stone, L. (1961). *The Psychoanalytic Situation.* New York: Int. Univ. Press.

——— Transference. *PMC.* Forthcoming.

Zetzel, E. R. (1956). Current concepts of transference. *IJP,* 37:369–376.

■ TRANSFERENCE NEUROSIS

See PSYCHONEUROSIS; TRANSFERENCE.

■ TRANSFERENCE OF CREATIVITY

See SELF PSYCHOLOGY.

■ TRANSFERENCE RESISTANCE

See RESISTANCE.

■ TRANSFORMATIONS OF NARCISSISM

See SELF PSYCHOLOGY.

■ TRANSITIONAL OBJECT

See WINNICOTT'S THEORY.

■ TRANSITIONAL PHENOMENA

See WINNICOTT'S THEORY.

■ TRANSITIONAL STAGE TECHNIQUES

See FAIRBAIRN'S THEORY.

■ TRANSMUTING INTERNALIZATION

See SELF PSYCHOLOGY.

■ TRANSSEXUALISM

A clinical syndrome produced by a group of disorders characterized by aberrations in both gender and sexual identities. The term is often applied loosely. Though there is sufficient overlap in the manifestations of this group of disorders to justify the designation of a clinical syndrome, *gender identity disorder* is a preferable designation since the term *transsexualism* suggests a more clearcut entity. Individuals presenting the syndrome are called *transsexuals*.

The syndrome is found in both sexes, although the ratio of males to females is 10 to 1. It is distinguished by a wish for sex reassignment. The individual actively contemplates or pursues two primary goals: the surgical modification of primary sexual organs to the fullest extent possible, and the acquisition of opposite-sex facsimiles as close as possible to ideal anatomy and function. While transsexuals do not deny their physical sex, they deny the psychological significance of their maleness or femaleness. Associated with the wish for physical modification is the wish to assume the gender role of the opposite sex both socially and sexually and to be socially assimilated into that role.

Clinically, transsexuals are anywhere from relatively normal to psychotic. The majority are not psychotic unless their denial of the meaning and significance of their genital anatomy approaches delusional proportions. As in the perversions, transsexualism is characterized by marked aggression, anxiety, and depression. These affects are more related to the sexual body image than they are in other patients, including those usually classified as borderline character disorders. Perversion and transsexualism may be distinguished from one another by the degree to which conflicts surrounding annihilation and castration are manifested and defended against symbolically. In perversions, sexual fantasies and rituals represent at the symbolic level conflicts about the physical distinctions between the sexes, body image, and castration. These symbolic fantasies and acts protect physical integrity from the threat of castration and protect the ego from paralysis. Transsexuals' capacity to represent these conflicts symbolically seems periodically or chronically deficient, so that their body image is fluid and they identify with the opposite sex. What are ordinarily castration fears become wishes that can be gratified only through physical changes to the genitals.

The rare transsexuals who are relatively free from conflict are designated *true* or *primary;* those exhibiting more conflict are termed *secondary*. The etiology of transsexualism or gender identity disorder is controversial. Hypotheses include a biological etiology, a nonconflictual symbiotic phase abnormality (in some primary transsexual males only), and the more usual psychic processes of conflict, regression, and fixation.

See BORDERLINE PERSONALITY DISORDER; FIXATION; GENDER IDENTITY; PERVERSION; PSYCHOSIS; REGRESSION.

References

Limentani, A. (1979). The significance of transsexualism in relation to some basic psychoanalytic concepts. *Int. Rev. Psycho-Anal.*, 6:139–153.
Meyer, J. (1982). The theory of gender identity disorders. *JAPA*, 30:381–418.
Person, E. & Ovesey, L. (1974). The transsexual syndrome in males. *Amer. J. Psychother.*, 28:4–20.
Socarides, C. (1970). A psychoanalytic study of the desire for sexual transformation ("transsexualism"). *IJP*, 51:341–349.
Stoller, R. (1982). Near miss. In *Eating, Sleeping, and Sexuality*, ed. M. Zales. New York: Brunner/Mazel, pp. 258–283.

■ TRANSVESTISM

A perversion, usually considered to occur only in males, characterized by fantasized or actual dressing in female clothes for purposes of psychological security and arousal. Cross-dressing often serves as an adjunct to masturbation or coitus. Usually more than one article of clothing is involved—not infrequently, the individual collects an entire wardrobe, including wigs. Cross-dressing ranges from solitary, guilt-ridden behavior to ego-syntonic, sociable membership in a transvestite subculture. The cross-dressing in transvestism has multiple functions, but at a simple level it is a compromise formation expressing feminine identification, punishment for incestuous oedipal wishes, and the fantasy of the phallic woman. Masturbation to ejaculation allows triumph over feminine identification and castration, particularly at the moment of orgasm.

Although superficially similar to the cross-dressing in homosexuality and transsexualism, the cross-dressing in transvestism has a fetishistic quality; heterosexual object choice is maintained, and male gender identity is relatively intact. Homosexual cross-dressing functions primarily to caricature the female and to express a feminine sexual identity. Transsexual cross-dressing functions primarily to reflect a skewed gender identity.

While boys are known to begin cross-dressing

as early as the second year of life, longterm follow-up indicates that most of these children become homosexual rather than transvestite. Transvestite cross-dressing (with its typical qualities of secrecy and risk-taking, its incestuous overtones, and its fantasies of guilt, duress, and danger and escape from castration) usually begins in latency or early adolescence. The dressing and related fantasies then become a fundamental element of the transvestite's erotism, although there are fluctuations in the degree to which the activities are endorsed by the ego or have access to the ego's executive apparatus.

The clinical distinctions between transvestism and transsexualism are sometimes blurred. While most transvestites are not transsexual, almost all nourish some fantasies of becoming women. As the individual ages, the sexual aspects of the transvestite cross-dressing usually become less important and the comfort derived from feminine identification increases. A subgroup of aging transvestite men, particularly those who have sustained losses or who have low self-esteem, may suffer an acute collapse of the defensive function of their transvestism. These men may increasingly identify as transsexual and may pursue sex reassignment. They are at risk for suicide, autocastration, and autopenectomy and their condition should be treated as a medical emergency.

References
Bak, R. (1968). The phallic woman. *PSOC*, 23:15–36.
Gillespie, W. (1956). The general theory of sexual perversion. *IJP*, 37:396–403.
Meyer, J. (1985). Paraphilia. In *Comprehensive Textbook of Psychiatry*, ed. H. Kaplan & B. Sadock. Baltimore: Williams & Wilkins, 4th ed., pp. 1065–1077.
Stoller, R. (1971). The term "transvestism." *Arch. Gen. Psychiat.*, 24:230–235.
Stoller, R. (1974). Hostility and mystery in perversion. *IJP*, 55:425–434.

■ TRAUMA

The disruption or breakdown that occurs when the psychic apparatus is suddenly presented with stimuli, either from within or from without, that are too powerful to be dealt with or assimilated in the usual way. A postulated stimulus barrier or protective shield is breached, and the ego is overwhelmed and loses its mediating capacity. A state of helplessness results, ranging from total apathy and withdrawal to an emotional storm accompanied by disorganized behavior bordering on panic. Signs of autonomic dysfunction are frequently present. The *traumatic state* varies both in intensity and duration from one individual to another. Its consequences can be negligible or can include an incapacitating *traumatic neurosis*.

The concept of trauma played an integral part in Freud's early theory of neurosis. Although he first thought of affective reactions (such as fright, anxiety, shame, or physical pain) as determining a trauma, later studies delineated factors that constitute the preconditions for trauma or determine its outcome. In traumatic neuroses the intensity of the stimulus in relation to the preparedness of the stimulus barrier seemed paramount, but in these neuroses as well as those derived from intrapsychic conflict, constitution and past experience determined how well the ego dealt with the traumatic stimulus. Trauma is ubiquitous in development, but some trauma experiences affect development adversely and increase the ego's vulnerability to trauma. Constitutional factors and fixations and regressions in ego and superego development, growing from problems in the early relation to the mother, affect the ego's vulnerability. Repeated minor failure to meet the infant's needs may add up to a cumulative trauma that seriously affects the child's structural development and adaptation and predisposes him or her to further trauma. Correlation between a traumatic stimulus and the libidinal phase in which it occurs (known as *phase specificity*) determines whether a trauma will occur and what its effect will be. The environmental and psychic circumstances prevailing at the time of the trauma, the individual's reaction to the event rather than the event itself, the archaic pathological attempts to master it, and the support given by self-esteem and by objects all help determine the outcome. Well-defined, acute trauma symptoms are sometimes followed by strengthening of the ego, improved adaptation, and accelerated development.

See EGO; PSYCHIC APPARATUS; STIMULUS BARRIER; TRAUMATIC NEUROSIS.

References
Freud, A. (1962). Comments on psychic trauma. In Furst (1967), pp. 235–245.
Freud, S. (1939). Moses and monotheism. *SE*, 23:3–137.
Furst, S. S. (1967). Psychic trauma. In *Psychic Trauma*, ed. S. S. Furst. New York: Basic Books, pp. 3–50.
______ Trauma. *PMC*. Forthcoming.
Kris, E. (1956). The recovery of childhood memories in psychoanalysis. *PSOC*, 11:54–88.

Krystal, H. (1978). Trauma and affects. *PSOC,* 33:81–116.
Waelder, R. (1967). Trauma and the variety of extraordinary challenges. In Furst (1967), pp. 221–234.

■ TRAUMATIC NEUROSIS

A specific form of neurosis resulting from exposure to the threat or actual experience of severe physical or psychic trauma (that is, intense and sudden "stress"). Though recognized for centuries under various names, traumatic neurosis has received the most attention in connection with psychological casualties of war. It also frequently occurs following criminal assault, accidents, and catastrophic events, especially those outside the usual range of human experience. Traumatic neurosis is a "stress-related disorder" of the anxiety type, often severe enough to justify the term panic. It may be acute, delayed, or chronic. The anxiety may be dealt with using various neurotic mechanisms—hysterical (somatic symptoms or fugue states—called traumatic hysteria), phobic, or obsessional.

The symptomatology of traumatic neurosis has been clearly delineated. It involves repetitive reexperiencing of the traumatic event, numbing of responsiveness, reduced involvement with the external world, and a variety of autonomic, dysphoric, and cognitive manifestations. An absolute prerequisite to the diagnosis is the presence of repetitive dreams in which the traumatic event is repeated with minimal alteration. The dream is always associated with anxiety, agitated restlessness, and fear that the dream will occur again, which leads to insomnia. Irritability, social estrangement, alienation, and a distrust of others also occur, resulting in deterioration of interpersonal relationships and diminished social interaction. An attitude of withdrawal and indifference has been called blunting of affect, but close observation of the individual in a therapeutic relationship reveals that he or she experiences intense, painful, and at times overwhelming affect.

Persistent obsessive ruminations and episodic flashbacks to the precipitating circumstances are common. Such flashbacks are sudden, unpredictable, and all-consuming. The person feels as if he or she is reliving a very painful experience. Various stimuli, usually highly personal, can trigger the event. At such times the person is often irritable, highly fractious, socially withdrawn and isolated, and sometimes violently destructive—often toward those closest to him or her and those trying to be of help.

Following the traumatic event, the individual feels changed; he or she loses a sense of self as previously experienced. He or she feels uncertain and insecure and functions with difficulty. He or she feels altered but has difficulty understanding how the change occurred. The person feels no longer able to trust him- or herself and believes others cannot protect him or her. The patient may struggle for years to reconcile the existing self functions with the remembered self.

The recurrent dreams represent an effort to cope with the original trauma by means of denial. So real are the dreams that the dreamer cannot immediately determine their true nature—hence he or she can feel that the actual event was no more than a dream. Flashbacks may serve the same purpose or conversely may help establish the facts of the traumatic event. Patients are often uncertain on this point and may be helped by the therapist's assurance that the event actually happened.

While intensely disturbing and even disruptive, the neurosis resulting from severe psychic trauma is responsive to psychotherapy embodying a basic understanding of the disorder.

See PSYCHONEUROSIS; TRAUMA; WAR NEUROSIS.

References

Geerts, A. E. & Rechardt, E., reporters (1978). Colloquium on 'trauma.' *IJP,* 59:365–375.
Krupuick, J. L. & Horowitz, M. J. (1981). Stress response syndromes. *Arch. Gen. Psychiat.,* 38:428–435.
Moses, R. (1978). Adult psychic trauma. *IJP,* 59:353–363.
Rappaport, E. A. (1968). Beyond traumatic neurosis. *IJP,* 49:719–731.

■ TRAUMATIC STATE

See ANXIETY.

■ TRIEB

The German word Freud used to refer to endogenously derived motivational forces. It was translated as "instinct" in the *Standard Edition.* Hartmann and Schur proposed the term *instinctual drive* to emphasize the psychic representation of such forces and to distinguish them from the biological patterns of behavior implied by the word *instincts.*

See INSTINCTUAL DRIVE.

■ TRIPARTITE MODEL

See STRUCTURAL THEORY.

■ TRUE SELF, FALSE SELF

See WINNICOTT'S THEORY.

■ TURNING AGAINST THE SELF

See DEFENSE.

■ TWINSHIP TRANSFERENCE

See SELF PSYCHOLOGY.

■ TYPOLOGY

See ANALYTICAL PSYCHOLOGY TERMS.

■ ULCERATIVE COLITIS

The most common inflammatory disease of the colon. It was one of seven so-called psychosomatic disorders studied by Alexander (1950). All of the entities in this colon group seem to be precipitated and exacerbated by emotional conflicts.

Murray (1930) was the first psychoanalytic author to note the psychopathology involved in ulcerative colitis. Many observers—medical, psychological, psychiatric, and psychoanalytic—have confirmed and elaborated on his findings. Characterologically, many patients who suffer from ulcerative colitis appear superficial, their fantasy life, dreams, and introspection are poor and they often lack awareness of their own feelings. These characteristics were labeled *alexithymic* by Sifneos (1967), but psychoanalytic investigation reveals extensive denial in cases of ulcerative colitis. These patients use pregenital defenses against intense primitive sadistic impulses directed at both the perceived contemporary object and the internalized primary object. If the patient recognizes and mobilizes such impulses, with their accompanying fantasies (drive derivatives), he or she is frequently able to give up the colonic symptoms, but acting out and depression often follow. Occasionally, transient psychotic symptoms may intervene.

In the early stages of treatment it is frequently necessary to apply some modification of classical psychoanalytic technique. An authoritative, but not reassuring, interpretive stance is often useful. After pregenital problems have been analyzed and symptoms resolved, a more classical analytic approach is sometimes possible.

After a review of sixty-eight cases, Weinstock (1962) concluded that with the exception of surgery, psychoanalysis or psychoanalytic therapy offered the greatest possibility of cure or long-term remission in such cases. But despite the many reports of remissions following psychoanalytic treatment in patients who have been studied for decades, the role of psychopathology and analytic therapy in the treatment of such conditions remains controversial. In recent decades psychoanalysis has moved away from the treatment of psychosomatic conditions. One reason may be that the treatment of such patients is incompatible with usual psychoanalytic practice; too many parameters and supportive interventions are necessary.

See ALEXITHYMIA; PSYCHOSOMATIC CONDITIONS.

References

Alexander, F. (1950). *Psychosomatic Medicine*. New York: Norton.

Karush, A., Daniels, C. E., Flood, C. & O'Connor, J.F. (1977). *Psychotherapy in Chronic Ulcerative Colitis*. Philadelphia: Saunders.

Murray, C. D. (1930). Psychogenic factors in the etiology of ulcerative colitis and bloody diarrhea. *Amer. J. Med. Sci.*, 180:239–248.

Weinstock, H. J. (1962). Successful treatment of ulcerative colitis by psychoanalysis. *Brit. J. Psychoanal. Res.*, 6:243–249.

■ UNCANNY

Used most commonly to describe the feeling of fear and unease experienced when something happens that seems to confirm an early belief in the omnipotence of thought (which has been surmounted more than rectified or repressed) and to reactivate an animistic mode of thinking. Classic examples of such occurrences are seeing one's "double," experiencing déjà vu, and feeling that someone who is dead has returned to life. Repressed complexes such as the castration complex and womb fantasies may give rise to an uncanny feeling; they are more often brought to consciousness via fiction than in actual life.

See DÉJÀ VU.

References

Arlow, J. A. (1959). The structure of the *déjà vu* experience. *JAPA*, 7:611–631.

Freud, S. (1913). Totem and taboo. *SE*, 13:1–161.

——— (1919). The uncanny. *SE*, 17:217–252.

Wolf, E. S. & Trosman, H. (1974). Freud and Popper-Lynkeus. *JAPA*, 22:123–141.

■ UNCONSCIOUS

As an adjective refers to mental content not available to conscious awareness at a given time, as demonstrated by parapraxes, dreams, and disconnected thoughts and conclusions. The mind is always active, performing many functions during both the waking state and sleep, but only a small amount of this mental activity is conscious at any one time. Affective dispositions related to instinctual drives give rise to wishes and motivatations that strive for conscious expression but are opposed by other forces (now conceptualized as the ego and superego). Freud's idea that such forces operated in conflict was a dynamic view of mental processes far removed from the psychology of his day.

What is excluded from awareness, even though some (the preconscious, or Pcs.) may be evoked by focusing attention, belongs to what has been designated the *descriptive unconscious* (abbreviated Ucs.).

As a noun, the unconscious (Ucs.) relates to one of the dynamic systems described by Freud (1915) in his early topographic theory of the psychic apparatus. He believed that a portion of the mental contents and activities representative of the instincts had never been conscious. They had been denied access to consciousness by a rigorous censorship imposed on the Ucs. by the Pcs. (*primal repression*). Other contents did eventually gain consciousness but were then repressed (*repression proper*). The repression was maintained by means of a special energy, an *anticathexis*. This concept of the distribution and interplay of psychic energies constituted the third, *economic* viewpoint of Freud's metapsychology.

Although Freud thought that some affective structures in the Ucs. might become conscious, he believed that there were no unconscious affects comparable to unconscious ideas. Unconscious affects are those that have been avoided because the ideas to which they are attached are repressed. Such affects may be displaced onto other ideas having some relationship to the repressed but sufficiently different to be acceptable to consciousness. While some of these *unconscious derivatives* may attain consciousness as substitute formations or symptoms, others are turned back to the unconscious at the second censorship barrier, between the preconscious and the conscious.

In the unconscious, Freud said, instinctual impulses can exist side by side without influencing or contradicting each other. There is no negation, doubt, or degree of certainty. Cathexes are mobile, easily subject to displacement or condensation; they conform to what Freud called the *primary process*. Unconscious processes are subject to the pleasure principle, regardless of reality, and are timeless. Childhood wishes in particular are represented in the unconscious; they persistently provide strong motivation for seeking gratification without regard for reality or logical thought.

The contents of the unconscious may be roughly equated with the id of the structural theory, but some aspects of the ego (defense mechanisms, affects, etc.) and superego (moral standards) are also unconscious. Freud's discovery of this led him to develop his second topography, now known as the tripartite model or *structural theory*.

See CATHEXIS; CONSCIOUSNESS; ID; PLEASURE/UNPLEASURE PRINCIPLE; PRECONSCIOUS; PRIMARY PROCESS; REPRESSION; STRUCTURAL THEORY; TOPOGRAPHIC POINT OF VIEW.

References

Arlow, J. A. & Brenner, C. (1964). *Psychoanalytic Concepts and the Structural Theory*. New York: Int. Univ. Press.

Freud, S. (1915). The unconscious. *SE*, 14:166–215.

Winson, J. (1985). *Brain and Psyche*. New York: Anchor Press.

■ UNDIFFERENTIATED ENERGIES

See PSYCHIC ENERGY.

■ UNDIVIDED EGO

See FAIRBAIRN'S THEORY.

■ UNDIVIDED OBJECT

See FAIRBAIRN'S THEORY.

■ UNDOING

See DEFENSE.

■ VAGINA DENTATA

A Latin term for the idea that the vagina has teeth that may bite and injure the penis during sexual intercourse. The vagina dentata legend, conveying dread of sexual intercourse, has been reported by anthropologists in various parts of the world. Originally described by Otto Rank (1924) and elaborated by Sandor F. Ferenczi (1925), it is found with some regularity in men with neurotic and sexual problems. The fantasy is linked with the dread of castration; in displacement from the mouth, the vagina is viewed in oral terms as a devouring organ. The fantasied teeth in the vagina often symbolize the father's penis. Occasionally vagina dentata symbols include rats and snakes with big, biting jaws. Women may also have unconscious fantasies of having a vagina dentata as a means of retaliation toward men.

Penis dentata, the counterpart to vagina dentata, refers to the idea that the penis has teeth that will injure the vagina. Such legends coexist with those of the vagina dentata. Women more often have fantasies about the penis dentata, but men may also have this fantasy, accompanied by hostile and sadistic wishes toward women.

References

Ferenczi, S. (1925). Psychoanalysis of sexual habits. In *The Theory and Technique of Psychoanalysis*. New York: Basic Books, pp. 278–281.
Rank, O. (1924). *The Trauma of Birth*. New York: Robert Brunner, 1952, pp. 48–49.
Schuster, D. B. (1969). Bisexuality and body as phallus. *PQ*, 38:72–80.
Shengold, L. (1967). The effects of overstimulation. *IJP*, 48:403–415.
Wilson, C. P. (1967). Stone as a symbol of teeth. *PQ*, 36:418–427.

■ VERTICAL SPLIT

See SELF PSYCHOLOGY.

■ VOYEURISM

The act of looking at the intimate, mostly sexual, activities of other people. It has a compulsive but pleasurable quality. The term encompasses a broad spectrum of clinical conditions, some of which are considered normal, others, perverse. According to Freud, a voyeuristic tendency (scopophilia) derives from the scopophilic component instinct; it plays an important part in normal sexuality. Voyeurism also occurs in various clinical constellations involving an admixture of normal and perverse sexuality. The basic common element is the compulsive need to look, directly or indirectly (as in reading pornographic material or in perverse telephoning), at sexual objects and sexual activities. Perverse voyeurism involves an obligatory, insatiable need; it may result in intense anxiety, feelings of guilt, and masochistic behavior. The act of looking itself often carries a sadistic significance. It may also serve a defensive function by protecting the looker against acting. The fantasy of incorporating through the eye is a common feature of voyeurism, as is the presence of exhibitionistic impulses—the wish to look at another person's genitals is transformed into the wish to have one's own genitals seen.

The sublimation of scopophilic impulses may lead to scientific curiosity, artistic creativity, and a generally inquisitive propensity. Their repression may bring about character inhibitions, shyness, and suppression of normal curiosity.

Three sets of factors contribute to the genesis of voyeurism:

(1) A congenital, primary, general hypercathexis of the visual function, little understood, is apparently a predisposing factor to voyeurism in some cases. This hypercathexis is often evident in artists, chess players, creative thinkers, and mathematicians. The facility for eidetic, autosymbolic, or hypnagogic phenomena and general visual-mindedness are much more common in voyeurism than is generally suspected.

(2) Also predisposing to voyeurism are postnatal experiences that powerfully affect the development of object relationships and sexuality. These experiences begin during the nursing period when the infant sees the mother's face and breast and an all-important visual interchange takes place between mother and child. Fear of object loss is also involved. Early sexual experiences, such as exposure to the primal scene and to adult genitals, also predispose to voyeurism. Castration anxiety connected with seeing the female genitals may lead to the need to reenact the traumatic visualization in the voyeuristic act in order to gain reassurance and achieve belated mastery.

(3) Voyeuristic perversion appears to be conditioned by a particularly strong trauma at a very early age (around the first and second years of life) accompanied by severe disruption of the mother–child relationship. Such traumas result in severe pregenital fixations, sexual identity problems, impairment of ego and superego functioning, difficulty in achieving sublimation, and inadequate defense formation—all factors contributing to perverse voyeurism. Simple scopophilia involves less serious, later traumas; the psychological results are correspondingly much less severe.

See COMPONENT INSTINCTS; FACE–BREAST EQUATION; PERVERSION; SCOPOPHILIA.

References

Almansi, R. J. (1960). The face–breast equation. *JAPA*, 6:43–70.
______ (1979). Scopophilia and object loss. *PQ*, 47:601–619.
Freud, S. (1918). From the history of an infantile neurosis. *SE*, 17:3–122.
Peto, A. (1976). The etiological significance of the primal scene in perversions. *PQ*, 44:177–190.

■ WAR NEUROSIS

A traumatic neurosis occurring in connection with experiences during wartime. The symptomatology is the same as that of the traumatic neurosis—an alienation of the self, social withdrawal, irritability, recurrent dreams and flashbacks repeating the details of the experience, and severe anxiety. The precipitating event (or *stressor*) is usually overwhelmingly life threatening. Such experiences are common in combat when the individual finds him or herself in a situation from which escape or survival seems unlikely. Others witness the sudden, unexpected death of comrades and the violent destruction of their surroundings, from which they extrapolate their own imminent death.

Often overlooked in dealing with post-traumatic symptoms is the "high" (the elation of denial) experienced in the heat of battle. It is analogous to and even more intense than the "highs" associated with use of drugs. Patients may crave the "high" and may have flashbacks in order to reexperience it.

Patients exposed to such severe and intense psychic trauma frequently have great difficulty in interpersonal relationships. They often provoke fights and other disturbances, re-creating in miniature the battles in which they participated. In doing so they often reexperience the "high" but also feel overwhelming guilt and shame. Such occurrences contribute to the feeling of an altered self.

The basic manifestations of the disorder were noted by Cagle after World War I and further refined by Grinker (1945), Kardiner (1941), and others during and following World War II. Efforts to relate the disorder to personality structure and functions and to explain the symptomatology in terms of defenses, gains, and somatizations have not been entirely satisfactory, though Grinker pointed out that "the reaction of the man himself under stress carries with it the colouring of his previous personality " (p. 729), but "no matter how strong or normal or stable a man might be, if he had to endure stress sufficient to reach his personal threshold, he would succumb to a war neurosis" (p. 731).

See TRAUMATIC NEUROSIS.

References

Cavenar, J. O., Jr. & Nash, J. L. (1976). The effects of combat on the normal personality. *Comprehensive Psychiat.*, 17:647–653.

Grinker, R. R. (1945). Psychiatric disorders in combat crews overseas and in returnees. *Med. Clin. North Amer.*, 29:729–739.

Kardiner, A. (1941). *The Traumatic Neuroses of War*. New York: Hoeber.

Swank, R. L. (1949). Combat exhaustion. *J. Nerv. Ment. Dis.*, 109:475–508.

■ WINNICOTT'S THEORY

Donald Woods Winnicott was born in 1896 in Plymouth, England, a stronghold of the tradition of religious nonconformism. His father was knighted for civic work, and community-mindedness was always a part of the son's concerns as well. An interest in Darwin led Winnicott to study biology at Cambridge, after which he studied medicine and then pediatrics. Forty years conducting a pediatric clinic at Paddington Green hospital gave him continuous access to the practical concerns of mothers and babies. This acted as both a stimulus and a counterweight to his extraordinary imagination. Winnicott had his first analysis, which lasted ten years, with James Strachey; then he undertook another, shorter one with Joan Rivierc. In the 1930s he had an extensive supervisory experience with Melanie Klein, whom he considered to be his greatest teacher and the most productive psychoanalytic mind after Freud.

In the war years, however, during the crisis in the British Psychoanalytic Society between the followers of Klein and those of Anna Freud, Winnicott proved to be one of the independent group. The struggle with Klein concerned his objection to the use of idiosyncratically Kleinian terms such as projective identification and envy, which he felt excluded non-Kleinians from useful discussion. Winnicott's belief in the importance of the environment in child development also clashed with Klein's absorption with the innate.

Simultaneous with his pediatric work and child analysis, Winnicott treated rather disturbed adult patients. This work often entailed what he called a "phase of management" of a disturbed patient who had "regressed to dependency" (a meaning of regression not found in Freud.) These patients required a period of steady "holding" (in the emotional sense), rather than interpretive work before analytic work could begin (though on rare occasions he actually held a patient's hand.) Through this work Winnicott came to see the importance of his own behavior apart from his function as an interpreter of conflict. This reinforced his convictions about the importance of the actual mother in early child development. Through a wide variety of studies, he developed an internally cohesive and powerful theory of early infant development, beginning with the state of mind of the mother of a newborn (*primary maternal preoccupation*) and emphasizing the child's illusion of omnipotence, reinforced in the beginning by perfect maternal attunement and then gradually reduced through manageable failures in mother's adaptation.

There is little mention of the importance of the father in Winnicott's work—he wrote primarily about patients whose problems stemmed from the early relationship to mother.

Winnicott earned fame for his concept of the *transitional object,* with its attendant ideas. He saw the baby's use of the favorite, soothing toy as a moment in which the sense of omnipotence intersects with the environmental provision. The child needs to "create" the perfect object at the very moment the object is provided by someone in the environment. This meeting point of the internal and the external is a "place" of comfort and of paradox. The child is never to be asked whether he or she created or found such an object. In the world of creative living, which includes play and all human cultural experience, the same paradox obtains. Winnicott believed that although human beings must progress in the direction of accepting the indifference of the universe, the "not-me" world, they also require moments of rest, in which the strain of differentiating inner and outer reality need not be maintained.

Winnicott's work with delinquents in World War II enlarged his awareness of what he called "the antisocial tendency." He saw value in the first antisocial acts as evidence of the child's feeling of having been cheated of what was rightfully his or hers, that is, a reliable pair of parents. Winnicott was able to trace the origins of the tendency among children whose normal early upbringing had been interrupted in the second or third year of life.

Winnicott's ideas of the true and false self issue from his observation of the effect of early environmental deprivation on child development. The true self develops in an atmosphere of acceptance and care by the *good enough mother,* who can find value in the child's spontaneous gestures. Interference with this process may result in the child's withdrawal from authenticity and spontaneity. He or she responds to a hostile world with a false self that passes for real. Numerous gradations in such personality derangements are evident in clinical work.

Ideas embodied in one of Winnicott's final papers, "The Use of an Object," have been only gradually appreciated. His lifelong concern was with the nature of reality, and in this paper he theorizes that the aggressive drive, a feature of all relationships, is constantly creating reality. By surviving its continuous destruction, the object becomes "of use." This word does not designate a relation to a part object. Quite the contrary, it represents the farthest development of object relations.

The range and relevance of Winnicott's theories are most persuasively demonstrated in his collection *Therapeutic Consultations in Child Psychiatry* (1971b). In brief interactions with children, often using the *squiggle game,* in which he and the patient alternately contribute to a drawing, Winnicott shows how it is possible to detect the relevance of passing communications and to make out of them interventions that can facilitate the resumption of development. His book-length study of a little girl, *The Piggle* (1977), shows how he could think and act effectively through an abbreviated version of an analysis done "on demand."

Winnicott wrote for many different audiences. A number of his books for the lay public are still widely read. He did not offer advice to parents, always encouraging the actual parent to choose a course of action based upon understanding. Winnicott's influence has gained steadily since his death in 1971. His imaginative contributions to the theory and practice of psychoanalysis stand against the background of a long career in which he remained an exponent of psychoanalysis as a rigorous undertaking, the main instrument of which was interpretation within a context of silent and careful observation.

□ Good Enough Mother

A designation used to indicate a mother who offers a holding environment providing an optimal amount of constancy and comfort for the infant who is wholly dependent on her. Such a mother meets the baby's symbiotic needs, thereby helping to form its "gestural" bodily self and supplying the bases for loving an object in a hearty, active manner. She offers at the "right time" instead of imposing her own timing and needs. Then, when the infant must face frustration, aggression, and loss, she also provides support within a setting of ongoing basic empathy and holding. Those attributes enable her to meet the infant's omnipotent needs without having to challenge them overtly, so that the infant has a gratifying human context for a subjective sense of his or her own being, expression, and creativity.

A mother is "good enough" according to her own private and natural sense of mothering, and Winnicott stresses that this spontaneous process cannot be learned in guidebooks on good mothering. Soon, however, the mother's adaptation to the infant decreases. Her failures gradually teach the child that he or she is not omnipotent—as does the infant's psychomotor development, which separates him or her from mother and the inability to cope. While the infant loses the experience of omnipotence, he or she gains a sense of adventure and differentiated aggressive use of the object world.

See AVERAGE EXPECTABLE ENVIRONMENT; WINNICOTT'S THEORY: Holding; True and False Self. Refer to Winnicott, 1958, 1965, at the end of this section.

□ Holding

A maternal provision that organizes a facilitative environment that the dependent infant needs. Holding refers to the natural skill and constancy of care of the *good enough mother*. Through this holding the infant experiences an omnipotence that Winnicott regards as an essential and ordinary feature of a healthy child's development. It provides sufficient security that after a while the infant is able to tolerate the inevitable failures of empathy that result in rage and terror when the holding is lost. The holding or *environmental mother* is different from Winnicott's *object mother,* who provides both parties' object-directed id satisfactions when the infant's object relations and ego organization are sufficiently developed. The holding environment should prepare the infant for these later phases and the disjunctive experiences they inevitably involve.

The concept of the holding environment has also been used by Winnicott, Modell, and others to conceptualize the nonspecific, supportive continuity provided by the analyst and the analytic situation. The regularity of visits, rituals of coming and going, the underlying empathy, the steadiness of voice, and the very continuity of the objects, spaces, and textures of the analytic room all contribute to a metaphorical holding that can help contain the disruptions that occur during meaningful treatment.

See Good Enough Mother. Refer to Modell, 1968; Winnicott, 1965, at the end of this section.

□ Playing

Winnicott places himself in the tradition of those who relate play to the creative process, for example, Schiller, Groos, Rank, Hutzinga, Callois, and Bruner. Free play (and games that are not rule-dominated) extends the dialogue between the feeding infant and the mother through the use of toys or playthings, the derivatives of transitional objects and phenomena being created and played with in a metaphorical, potential space. Winnicott therefore uses the term *playing* in its progressive, creative, developmental sense. As the true self (the inherited disposition of the infant) evolves through spontaneous gestures, playing becomes a medium for the expression and elaboration of this true self.

Play is the "work" of childhood, and for some it becomes the work of psychotherapy. Optimally, it is an ego activity only minimally invested with libidinal or aggressive energy. Playing takes place not only in the potential space between baby and mother, but also between therapist and patient. If psychotherapy occurs in the overlap of two areas of playing, that of the patient and that of the therapist, then free association and analytic interpretation constitute a play of two subjectivities, to facilitate the articulation of the patient's true self. There is a close relationship between ludic (play) symbols and oneiric (dream) symbols. This concept of play is easily extended to language development and the field of speech play.

See Potential Space. Refer to Bruner, Jolly & Sylva, 1976; Winnicott, 1971a, at the end of this section.

□ Potential Space

A hypothetical area of mutual creativity that occurs between an infant and the mother. For example, the mother may introduce an object to the infant at the right time, so that the infant both uses the object to express his or her subjective idiom and also enhances his or her grasp of the independent qualities of objects. The space between infant and mother is only a potential area, as its availability depends on good enough maternal care. Once established and used, this space becomes a generative, intersubjective accomplishment internalized by the infant as a psychic attribute so that he or she can create this potential area between him- or herself and other objects. "Within" potential space, an interplay between "inner" and "outer" occurs; at first transitional objects emerge and, after further development and internalization, the capacity for symbolic play and creative and aesthetic experience materializes.

Other disciplines, such as aesthetics, anthropology, literature, and drama, have found the concept of potential space useful, both as a model and for its developmental significance. Concepts such as virtual space, theatrical illusion, liminality, the suspension of disbelief, negative capability, and the objective correlative have all been compared to certain aspects of Winnicott's potential space.

See Transitional Objects. Refer to Bergman, 1978; Schechner and Schuman, 1976; Winnicott, 1971a, at the end of this section.

□ Precursor Object

Inanimate objects offered by the mother, or parts of the child's or the mother's body, that the child mouths and uses for consolation. A term originally suggested by Winnicott but described in the literature by Renata Gaddini (1978). The child may use his or her tongue, hair, fingers, hand, pacifier, or bottle in this way. Renata Gaddini distinguished the early "into-the-mouth precursor object" (for example, a pacifier) from the later "skin contact and tactile sensation precursor object" (for example, a teddy bear). The latter serves as a functional progenitor of the transitional object. In the course of healthy development, the into-the-mouth object is gradually given up in favor of the tactile object, which becomes the transitional object. Disturbances of development that concern the precursor object may include very early psychosomatic difficulties, such as infantile colic, infantile asthma, and rumination. This suggests that the presymbolic, sensorimotor, somatopsychic stage during which these objects are used determines the level of pathology surrounding a specific developmental difficulty involving these objects.

See Transitional Object. Refer to Gaddini, 1978, at the end of this section.

□ Primary Creativity

The earliest manifestations and primal origins of the child's creative capacity. Primary creativity refers to the crucial capacity to see the world in a creative way and to play. The term concerns the creativity of everyday life rather than the creative processes of a genius or an artist.

The basic model for the capacity to experience creatively is the infant's experience within the object world presented by a good enough mother. The infant can entertain the sense that the object was not placed there but that he or she created it. This unchallenged primitive illusion precedes the later, more complex self states that involve true play and the use of subjective modes of experiencing, that is the capacity for the suspension of disbelief. With the concept of primary creativity, Winnicott is describing the beginnings of a developmental line.

See Good Enough Mother; Holding; Transitional Object. Refer to Winnicott, 1958, 1971a, at the end of this section.

□ Primary Maternal Preoccupation

A maternal state of mind, beginning before the baby is born and continuing for several weeks after delivery, in which the mother is deeply preoccupied with the infant. The mother ignores the external world to a degree that would be considered pathological withdrawal if no baby were present. But maternal preoccupation is an adaptive withdrawal, a "healthy illness" that is necessary to provide for the infant's easy transition from the prenatal state into the external world. The mother becomes a "holding" or "environmental" mother who offers stability, constancy, and a primordial sense of "going on being." She satisfies not drives but needs, as, according to Winnicott, the drives are not yet an organized entity at this stage of infant development.

See Good Enough Mother; Holding. Refer to Winnicott, 1958, at the end of this section.

□ Squiggle Game

A short, evaluative, therapeutic contact with children devised by Winnicott. The therapist draws a simple linear form and the child continues the drawing. The game combines aspects of free play and association and enables the child to freely establish him- or herself in relation to the therapist. The sense of the interaction is one that is mutually constructive. The squiggle game can serve as a model of the interpretive use of images in both child and adult analysis and psychotherapy. This is in keeping with a constructivist, developmental point of view of the psychoanalytic process.

See Potential Space; Transitional Object. Refer to Green, 1978; Winnicott, 1971b, at the end of this section.

□ Transitional Object, Transitional Phenomenon

The transitional object is the infant's first "not-me" possession, something inanimate but treasured (usually a small soft blanket or toy), which the child uses in the course of emotional separation from the primary love object at times of stress, often on going to sleep (Winnicott, 1953). The transitional object often must have a characteristic odor and feeling thought to be reminiscent of the mother. It preserves the illusion of the comforting and soothing mother at times when the mother is unavailable; it promotes autonomy in the toddler, for the transitional object is under his or her control, whereas the mother is not. The original object is relinquished by age two to four, but later toys may continue to comfort.

Winnicott defined *transitional phenomena* more broadly. They include sounds—the infant's babbling or singing as he or she settles down to sleep or material objects not fully recognized as belonging to external reality. By displacement from the original love objects these sounds or objects function in later life as transient, hypercathected, and hypersymbolized maternal substitutes. They provide feelings of self-sufficiency and counteract feelings of object loss and abandonment. They indicate the ego's attempt to resolve an object-relations dilemma, the need to preserve the illusion of a loving, comforting, and soothing mother. When previously established object constancy and love are called into question, qualities and functions of the ego and specific items and activities may emerge as generalizations of ego phenomena that in toddlerhood were centered on exclusive possession of a blanket or similarly hypercathected object. Derivatives of the original transitional object may be seen in early adolescence (Downey, 1978). The teenager's style of play, interest in music, clothing, movies, and immersion in a variety of rapidly shifting "important" creative activities may constitute *transitional object phenomena*.

These objects or experiences evoke the illusion of symbiosis with the mother at a period of development in which self and object representations are only partially separated and differentiated. Transitional objects and phenomena are seen as both "me" and "not me," or from the opposite standpoint, both "not me" and "not not me." They are crystallizations of what could be termed a *transitional process* (Rose, 1978), which is a way of indicating the dynamic equilibrium between a relative, fluid self and a shifting reality. This process can also be seen as the interplay between the inner and outer world (Winnicott's "intermediate area") and between the primary and secondary processes. Transitional objects and phenomena are the external manifestations of this process. They can serve as psychic organizers (Metcalf and Spitz, 1978) for the process of separation-individuation; they can facilitate adjustment to the ambivalently experienced mother; they can help delineate a boundary between the self and the world; and they can aid the support of a body image that is more fragile and more easily regressed during periods of stress and sleep.

When transitional objects are obligatory, often as a result of not-good-enough mothering, they take on a fetishistic quality. No longer healthy, developmental facilitators, they become "patches" (Greenacre, 1969, 1970) on the ego, the self, or the body image. There is controversy, however, as to when a transitional object or phenomenon becomes pathological. Some restrict their conceptual use to the period after Mahler's last phase of separation-individuation, on the way to self and object constancy. If transitional objects and phenomena persist after that time, they should, in this view, be designated as fetishistic. Winnicott's conception is broader, however; it is difficult to evaluate. Certainly many children retain these objects and phenomena well into their early teen years. But the concept should not apply so generally that even symbolic objects are called transitional.

See Good Enough Mothering; Potential Space; Precursor Objects; Symbols. Refer to Winnicott, 1953, at the end of this section.

References

Bergman, A. (1978). From mother to the world outside. In Grolnick et al. (1978), pp. 145–165.

Bruner, J., Jolly, A., & Sylva, K. (1976). *Play*. New York: Basic Books.

Davis, M. & Wallbridge, D. (1981). *Boundary and Space*. New York: Brunner-Mazel.

Deutsch, H. (1942). Some forms of emotional disturbance and their relationship to schizophrenia. *PQ*, 11:301–321.

Downey, T. W. (1978). Transitional phenomena in the analysis of early adolescent males. *PSOC*, 33:19–46.

Gaddini, R. (1978). Transitional objects and the psychosomatic symptom. In Grolnick et al. (1978), pp. 109–131.

Green, A. (1978). Potential space in psychoanalysis. In Grolnick et al. (1978), pp. 167–189.

Greenacre, P. (1969). The fetish and the transitional object, part 1. *PSOC*, 24:144–64.

———. (1970). The fetish and the transitional object, part 2. *IJP* 51, vol. 4:447–56.

Grolnick, S., Barkin, L., & Muensterberger, W., eds. (1978). *Between Reality and Fantasy*. New York: Jason Aronson.

Khan, M. (1982). Introduction. In D. W. Winnicott, *Through Paediatrics to Psycho-analysis*. London: Hogarth Press.

Metcalf, D. & Spitz, R. A. (1978). The transitional object. In Grolnick et al. (1978), pp. 97–108.

Modell, A. (1968). *Object Love and Reality*. New York: Int. Univ. Press.

Rodman, F. R. (1987). Introduction. In *The Spontaneous Gesture: Selected Letters of D. W. Winnicott*, ed. F. R. Rodman. Cambridge: Harvard Univ. Press.

Rose, G. (1978). The creativity of everyday life. In Grolnick et al. (1978), pp. 345–362.

Schechner, R. & Schuman, M. (1976). *Ritual, Play and Performance*. New York: Seabury Press.

Winnicott, C. (1978). D. W. W.: A reflection. In *Between Reality and Fantasy*. New York: Jason Aronson.

Winnicott, D. W. (1953). Transitional objects and transitional phenomena. In Winnicott (1958), pp. 229–242.

——— (1956). Primary maternal preoccupation. In Winnicott (1958), pp. 300–305.

——— (1958). *Collected Papers*. New York: Basic Books.

——— (1960a). Ego distortions in terms of true and false self. In Winnicott (1965), pp. 140–152.

——— (1960b). The theory of the parent-infant relationship. In Winnicott (1965), pp. 37–55.

——— (1965). *The Maturational Processes and*

the Facilitating Environment. New York: Int. Univ. Press.

——— (1971a). *Playing and Reality*. New York: Basic Books.

——— (1971b). *Therapeutic Consultations in Child Psychiatry*. New York: Basic Books.

——— (1977). *The Piggle*. New York: Int. Univ. Press.

□ True Self, False Self

Concepts that have special meaning within Winnicott's view of early development. The *true self* is the "inherited potential" that constitutes the "kernel" of the child. Its continuing development and establishment are facilitated by a good enough mother, who provides a healthy environment and a meaningful responsiveness to the very young infant's sensorimotor, postural self. The good enough mother also offers appropriate id satisfaction once the drives are organized as a functioning system. The true self evolves its idiom through a maternal care that supports the child's continuity of being, enabling the child to generate an expressive life from a core self authorized by his or her sense of personal reality. Winnicott viewed the true self as closer to the spontaneous representation of the id, and true self expressions have the same phenomenological ephemerality as instinctual representations.

The false self, like the ego, is a stable and recurring, continuously operative structure. Winnicott understood that some individuals suffer a false self disorder—a particular way of viewing the schizoid character—but he repeatedly asserted that this partition of self into true and false is also normal. True and false thus refer not to a moral order, but to qualities in self–other experiences that support spontaneous expression (true self) or reactive living (false self).

A false self can indicate the absence of a true self or a hidden, secreted true self, usually in a schizoid individual. If the caretaker is unable to meet the sensorimotor, gestural, "id" self of the infant, and imposes herself, reflecting back not what is there but what the self-involved mother feels, then a false self forms in the infant. Apperception wins out over perception.

Every individual has a social self that corresponds to and is constructed from a certain amount of false self structure. At the other end of this spectrum is the person who operates essentially with a false self, corresponding to what Helene Deutsch (1942) described as the "as if" personality. Intellectualization is often associated with the false self.

Refer to Winnicott, 1960a, at the end of this section.

□ Work Ego

The special attributes of the analyst at work (Fliess, 1942). In the seasoned analyst the work ego achieves a relatively stable autonomy, responsive to the vicissitudes of the psychoanalytic situation. Not to be confused with role taking, the work ego may be enhanced and refined by analytic training, provided the candidate has been well selected. The concept has heuristic value in the study of the functioning analyst—his or her psychology, development, motivations, work specifications, and the facilitation or impairment of his or her autonomous analyzing functions. The work ego is similar to but not identical with Isakower's "analyzing instrument" (Malcove, 1975). It does not encompass the skill at analysis developed by the analysand, though certainly this is in part derived from the patient's partial identification with some of the analyst's work ego's operations.

The principal functions of the work ego are: (1) evenly suspended attention, together with structured introspection, observing, and listening in accord with certain psychoanalytic formulas and principles; (2) ability to engage in brief, partial regressions in the service of empathic perceptions, that is, to move between primary and secondary process in a sampling that is parallel with the patient; (3) the integration of empathic and other observational data into a working model of the patient, leading to deeper and broader understanding and permitting tactful and timely interpretations. Finally, the work ego operates within the therapeutic alliance, initiating and reinforcing the recognition and working through of transference and resistance.

See ANALYZING INSTRUMENT; EMPATHY; RESISTANCE; TRANSFERENCE; THERAPEUTIC ALLIANCE; WORKING THROUGH.

References

Fliess, R. (1942). The metapsychology of the analyst. *PQ*, 12:211–227.

Malcove, L. (1975). The analytic situation (and panel discussion). *J. Phila. Assn. Psychoanal.*, 2:1–19.

Olinick, S. (1980). *The Psychotherapeutic Instrument*. New York: Aronson.

■ WORK MODALITY

See BION'S THEORY.

■ WORKING ALLIANCE

See THERAPEUTIC ALLIANCE.

■ WORKING THROUGH

The continuing application of analytic work to overcome resistances persisting after the initial interpretation of repressed conflicts. Freud explained this "id resistance" as a likely occurrence in view of the fact that an instinctual process ongoing for decades is unlikely to immediately take a new path simply because one has just been opened for it. "One must allow the patient time to become more conversant with his resistance with which he has now become acquainted, to work through it, to overcome it, by continuing, in defiance of it, the analytic work according to the fundamental rule of analysis" (Freud, 1914, p. 155).

It is the goal of working through to make insight more effective, that is, to bring about significant and lasting changes in the patient by altering the modes and aims of the instinctual drives. Both the patient and the analyst contribute to the task; it may involve merely repeating and elaborating the usual analytic work, extending and deepening the analysis of the resistances, which need to be overcome repetitively and progressively and in some cases require special intervention. Prior interpretations often require expansion or modification, so that they become more comprehensive or to the point, identifying basic themes or highlighting the countless ways in which the conflictual situations are embedded in character structure. The process leads eventually to the inclusion in the personality of previously warded-off components as resistances are gradually relinquished and the patient is made aware of how insights gained about specific situations (for example, the intent behind an extratherapeutic event) apply to other events, the transference, developmental conflicts, changes in behavior, feelings and attitudes, and continued resistance.

Working through is now considered a crucial part of the analytic process. When traumatic experiences in early childhood are combined with an event in latency that organizes and perpetuates the psychic reaction to the earlier trauma, there may be a special need for working through.

See ANALYSIS; CONFLICT; DEFENSE; INSTINCTUAL DRIVE; INTERPRETATION; RESISTANCE.

References

Fenichel, O. (1945). *The Psychoanalytic Theory of Neurosis*. New York: Norton.

Freud, S. (1914). Remembering, repeating and working-through. *SE,* 12:147–156.

Greenson, R. R. (1967). *The Technique and Practice of Psychoanalysis*. New York: Int. Univ. Press.

Schafer, R. (1983). *The Analytic Attitude*. New York: Basic Books.